American Education
An Introduction to Teaching

Fourth Edition

American Education
An Introduction to Teaching

John H. Johansen
Northern Illinois University

Harold W. Collins

James A. Johnson
Northern Illinois University

wcb
Wm. C. Brown Company Publishers
Dubuque, Iowa

OTT

Book Team

James L. Romig
Senior Editor

Susan J. Soley
Associate Developmental Editor

David A. Welsh
Production Editor

Marilyn A. Phelps
Anthony L. Saizon
Designers

Faye Schilling
Visual Research Editor

Mavis M. Oeth
Permissions Editor

wcb group

Wm. C. Brown *Chairman of the Board*
Mark C. Falb *Corporate Vice President/Operations*

wcb Wm. C. Brown Company Publishers, College Division

Lawrence E. Cremer *President*
Raymond C. Deveaux *Vice President/Product Development*
David Wm. Smith *Vice President/Marketing*
David A. Corona *Assistant Vice President/Production Development and Design*
Janis M. Machala *Director of Marketing Research*
William A. Moss *Production Editorial Manager*
Marilyn A. Phelps *Manager of Design*
Mary M. Heller *Visual Research Manager*

Contents

List of Figures

List of Tables

Preface

American Education: An Introduction to Teaching was written to help individuals decide whether teaching could be a viable and satisfying career for them. Teaching has been a satisfying career for many people, yet others have found teaching to be frustrating and unsatisfying, wishing they were doing something else.

This book has five sections arranged in the following sequence: Becoming A Teacher, The Teaching Profession, The Role of Education in the United States, The Learning Process, and The Organization and Administration of Public Education in the United States. The material presented in the book is relevant to the purpose of the book—helping individuals decide whether teaching could be a satisfying career for them. We started this book with Becoming A Teacher and The Teaching Profession because the material presented in those sections and chapters is likely to be of immediate interest to those considering teaching as a career; they also provide a frame of reference for the sections that follow. The nature and organization of the book, however, is such that content can be presented in differing sequences to accommodate various course structures.

The first seven chapters, sections 1 and 2, are particularly pertinent to teaching as a career choice. Those chapters provide information about what teaching is like, how the public views teaching, why people choose to teach, how to become a teacher, the role of a teacher, educational careers other than classroom teacher, teacher employability, teacher organizations, and the opportunities, rewards, and frustrations of teaching.

Section 3, The Role of Education in the United States, presents an overview of the past and present goals of education in society, and of the expectations of both society and individuals for education, with its problems and its potential. It also addresses the critical social problems in today's schools; the history of educational thought and the persistent issues of education as related to the contemporary scene; and the current attitudes toward schools in respect to both traditional and progressive beliefs about education.

Section 4, The Learning Process, includes information about the nature of learners, the nature of curriculum, and the instructional resources available to teachers today. Section 5, The Organization and Administration of Public Education in the United States, deals with the organization for learning, the control and legal basis of education, and the financing of the educational enterprise.

Pedagogical study aids include: brief quotations that stimulate thinking and reinforce content, and which appear throughout the book; charts, graphs, tables, photos; and examples which help the reader identify with, and better understand the content. The discussion in each chapter closes with a brief, pertinent article selected to stimulate thought. In some instances these articles provide more detailed information about a topic, and in other instances they introduce different perspectives to the topics discussed in their respective chapters. The articles reflect the views of college professors, practicing teachers and other professionals, and school board members. Fourteen of the seventeen articles in the previous edition have been replaced, and the comments from those who reviewed the book supported the retention of three articles. Bibliographic information, discussion questions, and other supplementary learning activities conclude each chapter.

The textbook has a supplementary manual, *Instructor's Manual to Accompany American Education: An Introduction to Teaching*. For each chapter in the book, the manual contains instructional objectives, an outline presenting the major points and topics discussed, test items, media resources, and transparency masters. The suggested teaching aids in the manual provide an additional resource to instructors using this textbook.

This volume represents a revision in which material has been deleted, useful information updated, and new concepts and issues including multicultural education and "mainstreaming" incorporated to reflect current trends in American education. Teaching as a career has been presented in a realistic fashion. The interrelationships among American education, individuals, a pluralistic society with its promises and problems, and the teaching profession have been stressed.

American Education: An Introduction to Teaching has been shaped by the authors' experiences as teachers and administrators at all levels of education. The contributions made by the readers of earlier editions, the opinions of colleagues and students, and the evaluations of many experienced reviewers have been incorporated into the preparation of this edition. Appreciation is expressed to the many authors and publishers who granted us permission to use their materials in this revision. Special recognition is given to Nita Collins for her role in typing the manuscript.

American Education
An Introduction to Teaching

Becoming a Teacher

Teaching has been a satisfying career for many people, while others have found teaching so frustrating and unsatisfying that they left it very shortly after they started. Still others, unhappy and suffering, and wishing they were doing something else, remain in teaching. They feel "locked in." Recently, some teachers with many years of experience have left teaching expressing the sentiment that they just can't take it anymore. This phenomenon is referred to as teacher burnout.

What is teaching like? How can persons determine whether or not teaching would be a desirable and satisfying career for them? What do teacher training programs consist of? What do teachers do as they practice their chosen profession? What opportunities are available for work as an educator outside the traditional classroom setting in public and private schools? This section of the book attempts to provide direct answers to questions like these. It provides suggestions for ways in which prospective teachers can assess their interest in, and qualifications for teaching. It encourages action, thinking, and reflection on teaching as a career.

Like many other careers, teaching requires a minimum of four years of undergraduate work for the earning of an entry level certificate. The earlier individuals can determine whether or not teaching is for them, the easier it is to change career direction without setbacks. Teaching is not for everybody. It requires a commitment to become a teacher, and dedication to remain one. Successful teaching requires enthusiasm, a quality that unhappy persons, for example, have difficulty attaining. It is hoped that this section of the book can help persons of all temperaments determine whether or not teaching is the career for them. If some determine that teaching is for them, and become teachers, and enjoy productive and satisfying careers, then they, their students, and society will all benefit. If others determine that teaching is not for them, they, the students they might have worked with, and society are all probably better off. It is hoped that this section of the book, along with the remainder of the book, will help persons make the correct decision for themselves.

Is Teaching a Career for You?

1

This Chapter
- Provides contemporary perceptions of the desirability of teaching as a career.
- Presents reasons why persons decide to become teachers.
- Identifies personal qualities needed for teaching.
- Discusses suggestions for verifying an individual interest in teaching.
- Points out information on the importance of teaching to society.
- Describes education as an investment in society.
- Includes a glimpse of some of the great teachers of the past.
- Provides a realistic point of view on the importance of the teacher in creating a classroom atmosphere conducive to learning.

Teaching is one of the oldest and largest professions. Students considering teaching as a career can only benefit from gaining more information about teaching and the teaching profession. In examining teaching as a career it seems only logical to consider contemporary viewpoints on how the public perceives teaching, how practicing teachers feel about teaching, and why individuals chose to teach.

Public Viewpoint of Teaching as a Career

Would you like to have a child of yours take up teaching in the public schools as a career? In 1980, when parents were asked that question, only 48 percent responded YES. When the same question was first asked in 1969, 75 percent of the respondents said they would like to have a child of theirs take up teaching. In 1972, 67 percent responded affirmatively.[1] It is clear that the attractiveness of teaching in public schools as a career has declined. Some reasons for the decline undoubtedly include: publicity about the surplus of teachers at many levels, and in many subjects and geographic areas; low teacher salaries which have not kept up with inflation; changes in school-age children, including low motivation; and increases in violence, vandalism, and the use of drugs in school.

Teacher Attitude: Teacher Burnout

"Why did you quit teaching?" "Well, I'll tell you. Among other reasons—low pay, lack of pupil interest, lack of parental support, not getting results, overcrowded classes, expected to solve most of society's problems, mountains of paperwork required for a variety of bureaucratic reports, and just plain constant hassle. I was fed up. I couldn't take it anymore." The previous quote is from a fictitious person, but does represent an attitude becoming increasingly common among teachers.

A recent survey of teachers found that 35 percent of the respondents expressed dissatisfaction with their current job as a teacher, with almost 9 percent responding that they were very dissatisfied. Two-fifths (41 percent) *probably* would not (29 percent), or *certainly* would not (12 percent) become teachers if they could go back and start college over again. Exactly 9 percent will leave teaching as soon as they can, with another 20 percent undecided. Only 43 percent said they will continue until retirement.[2]

It is obvious that there are many people who do not view teaching as a desirable career choice, including an alarmingly high percentage of currently employed teachers. There is also little question that teaching is difficult and demanding. For some it is seen as a thankless, stressful, frustrating, and devastating occupation. Yet, there are others who find it gratifying, satisfying, and intrinsically rewarding. The challenge for those considering teaching as a career is to determine whether or not they are suited for teaching as it is today. It is pertinent to consider why practicing teachers chose to teach.

Why Teachers Became Teachers

Why do individuals choose teaching as a career? A recent survey of practicing teachers indicated three main reasons: a desire to work with young people, an interest in a subject-matter field, and the value or significance of education in society.[3] Of these three, the primary reason by far was a desire to work with young people (71 percent), followed by an interest in a subject-matter field (38 percent), and last, the value or significance of education in society (34 percent). Other reasons, along with their respective percentages, were: influence of a teacher in elementary or secondary school (21 percent), long summer vacation (19 percent), influence of family (18 percent), job security (17 percent), never really considered anything else (17 percent), and opportunity for a lifetime of self-growth (17 percent).

The major difference between the responses from elementary teachers and those from secondary teachers occurred in respect to an interest in a subject-matter field. Only 16 percent of the elementary teachers included this as a main reason for becoming teachers, in contrast with 59 percent of the secondary teachers. It seems clear that if a person feels inclined to want to work with young people, and feels that education is of importance to society, then he or she should *consider* teaching as a potential career. Those with some interest in teaching at the secondary level should also be interested in developing expertise in a subject matter discipline ordinarily offered at that level. Knowing why practicing teachers became teachers, however, is only a part of the information a person speculating about a teaching career needs to consider.

Personal Qualities Needed for Teaching

Most people agree that a teacher's personality is a vital ingredient in successful teaching. Yet, there is very little research evidence that relates specific aspects of personality to successful teaching. One national survey sought to determine the

personal qualities that people today regard as the most important in the ideal teacher. Each person interviewed was asked: "Suppose you could choose your child's teachers. Assuming they all had about the same experience and training, what *personal* qualities would you look for?" The qualities mentioned in order of frequency of response were as follows:

1. The ability to communicate, to understand, to relate.
2. The ability to discipline, be firm and fair.
3. The ability to inspire, motivate the child.
4. High moral character.
5. Love of children, concern for them.
6. Dedication to teaching profession, enthusiasm.
7. Friendly, good personality.
8. Good personal appearance, cleanliness.[4]

While there may be some question as to what the respondents really had in mind for each of the above, the responses do provide some indication of the personality traits many adults (parents and nonparents) believe are important for teachers.

It is apparent that no one person could hope to possess all of these traits to a liberal degree, and exhibit them all consistently day after day under all circumstances; nevertheless, unless one does possess most of these traits, he or she should not consider a career in the teaching profession.

The most frequently mentioned response in the poll dealt with communicating, understanding, and relating. Teaching can be characterized as communicating, understanding, and relating. Successful teachers are those who communicate to students in a personalized way that they respect them, have confidence in them, believe in them, feel that they are important, and that they can and will learn. Successful teachers also know how to organize and communicate the knowledge that the students are expected to learn. Furthermore, they expect success for their students, and communicate that expectation to them. The likelihood of such messages being received by students is enhanced by teachers who do, in fact, believe sincerely that students should be re-

A major reason for choosing teaching as a career is
a desire to work with young people.

spected, are important, and have confidence that
each and every student can and will learn. Communication is further enhanced by understanding
the nature of young persons, and being understanding of them. Relating has its basis in communicating and understanding.

How do teachers communicate? Obviously
they use words. They also send powerful messages nonverbally through facial expressions,
shrugs, and other forms of body language. Nonverbal communication is an effective means of
communication. Oftentimes though, the sender
is unaware of the message being sent and how it
is received. To say, "I believe in you" to a student,
and at the same time have a student perceive
your nonverbal cues and overt actions otherwise,

is in fact very ineffective communication. Effectively communicating with, and relating to colleagues and parents are also vital to being a
successful teacher. Being perceived by them, as
well as by students, as being sincere, interested,
positive, and enthusiastic gives promise of success.

Lastly, if a teacher relates well, but does not
know or communicate the knowledge and skills
for which he or she is responsible, and students
for that reason do not learn, failure of the teacher
is inevitable. The skills to transmit knowledge are
largely technical, and are learned in teacher education programs. How do individuals considering teaching as a career verify their interest in,
and their personal potential for becoming a successful teacher?

A teacher affects eternity; he can never tell where his influence stops.

Henry Adams

He who governs well, leads the ignorant; he who teaches well, trains them to govern themselves in justice, mercy, and peace.

Alexander G. Ruthven

Verifying Interest in Teaching

Teaching is one profession that many people feel they are knowledgeable about and understand. Why? Probably because they spent a number of years in school as a student. They were affected by teachers, remember what they liked or disliked about them, and have ideas about what teaching behaviors they thought were effective or ineffective. Experiences as a student, however, are not the same as experiences as a teacher.

Earlier in this chapter it was pointed out that the major reason reported by practicing teachers for having chosen teaching as a career was that they desired to work with young people. The best way for the would-be teacher to verify such a desire is to work with young people. In effect, prospective teachers need to have encounters with children or adolescents in situations best described as instructional, both formal and informal. Time spent as a teacher aide in a classroom, as a helper to an athletic coach, as a helper in a church nursery or child care center, or as a youth leader in a YWCA or YMCA can be helpful in testing whether or not you truly desire to work with young people. Preferably you should test that desire with young people at varying age levels: preprimary, primary, early adolescent, and late adolescent. As a college student seeking to decide (1) if teaching is an appropriate career choice, and (2) what level or age group might be most satisfying to work with, your images of what tenth graders or first graders are like may or may not be reinforced by reality encounters. Real encounters are undoubtedly the best way to decide

Verifying an interest in teaching can be done in settings other than the traditional classroom.

It is clear then that there should be legislation about education and that it should be conducted on a public system. But consideration must be given to the question, what constitutes education and what is the proper way to be educated? At present there are differences of opinion as to the proper tasks to be set; for all peoples do not agree as to the things that the young ought to learn, either with a view to virtue or with a view to the best life, nor is it clear whether their studies should be regulated more with regard to intellect or with regard to character.

Aristotle

whether or not you have a desire to work with young people. Furthermore, real encounters can help an individual decide whether or not one has the necessary personality attributes to cope and survive as a teacher in today's schools. Many teacher training programs today require such experiences early in the program to assist students in deciding about teaching as a career choice.

Ways to vicariously explore teaching include reading books, such as *Goodbye, Mr. Chips* by James Hilton; *Up the Down Staircase* by Bel Kaufman; James Herndon's *The Way it Spozed to Be;* and *36 Children* by Herbert Kohl. Films related to teaching can also be helpful. The prospective teacher, however, in viewing such films, needs to be aware that productions of this kind tend to overdramatize or heighten the experiences portrayed to a degree greater than that faced by the normal teacher. Prospective teachers should also seek information from former teachers, counselors, placement persons, and professors.

Importance of Teaching to Society

Another main reason practicing teachers reported that they chose teaching as a career was its value or significance to society, for teaching serves an important function in today's society. Educated individuals benefit both themselves and society. Further, education is also viewed as a vehicle for solving societal problems and thus changing the nature of our society. In the United States, public education is a service provided by various governmental levels to serve the nation and its people.

Educated individuals, for example, are less likely to become prison inmates, and less likely to become residents in mental hospitals. Educated individuals are more likely to earn higher incomes, and less likely to be unemployed or suffering in poverty. While it is not possible to document a perfect cause and effect relationship between the incidence of crime and education, mental health and education, and income and education, there is sufficient evidence to strongly suggest that education tends to reduce crime, reduce admissions to mental hospitals, and enhance personal income.

Schools are frequently selected to act directly as agents to improve or change society. One illustration of this function is the provision of monies by the federal government to local school districts to improve the educational experiences of children from low income families (Title I, ESEA). A second illustration is the role the schools are expected to play in fostering an integrated society by desegregating schools. In both instances, schools are clearly viewed as agents of societal change, and teachers are viewed as important persons expected to foster the desired changes.

Lastly, but basic to the traditional purpose of education in America, is the premise that only with an educated citizenry can democracy be expected to survive. The major functions of teaching are to transmit knowledge and culture. The skills necessary to be an informed citizen (such as literacy), and the skills necessary for problem solving are developed and enhanced through education. The values of society, that is, the ways of life that we cherish, are transmitted in part through our educational system. While not particularly dramatic, these functions of teaching are perhaps the most important.

Education as an Investment

Education provides substantial economic returns for both society and individuals. At one time economists used a formula containing the elements of land, labor, and capital to estimate economic development. It soon became evident that another variable was exerting a significant influence. There is now general agreement that education is that significant variable. Using gross national product as an economic index, it can be shown that there is a positive relationship between gross national product and educational development. While this type of analysis is beset with some difficulties, such as comparable data indices and the time lags associated with the contribution of education in terms of when the education was acquired and when its effects were realized, nevertheless the evidence does indicate the importance of education to economic development. Investment in education is an investment in the human resources of our society.

A second economic benefit of education accrued to society is teaching individuals a skill. As the demand for unskilled labor decreases, a proportionate demand for skilled labor increases, thus leaving education to fulfill the need to give the unskilled a skill to meet our society's needs.

Education is an investment in the socioeconomic welfare of our society.

The very spring and root of honesty and virtue lie in good education.

Plutarch

Great Teachers of the Past

One of the reasons that teaching is now a respected profession and that contemporary educators occupy a prestigious place in our society is that there have been many great teachers in the past. All of us can recall teachers that we have had who were influential in the shaping of our lives.

History is replete with educators who have made great contributions to mankind. Only a few of the more notable ones will be mentioned at this time.

Socrates (470–399 B.C.) is often mentioned as one of the world's first truly great teachers. This man, who lived in the Greek city-state of Athens, devoted his life to teaching the students who followed him wherever he went. His main method of teaching consisted of asking leading questions which helped the students to discover the answer for themselves. In fact, this technique has been so closely identified with Socrates that it has come to be known as the "Socratic Method" of teaching. Socrates was eventually put to death for inciting the people against the government in his relentless search for truth. His dedication to teaching, knowledge, and truth inspired many of his students to become renowned educators in their own right. Plato became one of Socrates' most famous students.

Another famous teacher of his day was Quintilian (A.D. 35–95), a Roman educator. Quintilian, also a prolific educational writer, exhibited a perceptive understanding of students far in advance of his time when he wrote:

I am by no means in favor of whipping boys, though I know it to be a general practice. In the first place, whipping is unseemly, and if you suppose the boys to be somewhat grown up, it is an affront in the highest degree. In the next place, if a boy's ability is so poor as to be proof against reproach he will, like a worthless slave, become insensible to blows. Lastly, if a teacher is assiduous and careful, there is no need to use force. I shall observe further that while a boy is under the rod he experiences pain and fear. The shame of this experience dejects and discourages many pupils, makes them shun being seen, and may even weary them of their lives.

One of the most famous teachers of the Dark Ages was an Englishman by the name of Alcuin. Alcuin became Charlemagne's educational advisor and established the Palace School at Frankland which Charlemagne himself frequently attended.

There were many famous educators during the Renaissance and Reformation periods, including Erasmus (1466–1536), Melanchthon (1497–1560), Ignatius of Loyola (1491–1556), Jean Baptiste de la Salle (1651–1719) and Johann Amos Comenius (1592–1670). Comenius authored a great number of textbooks, and his textbooks were some of the very first to contain pictures. Comenius was also among the first to recommend that a series of schools be established. Concerning this point he wrote, "There should be a maternal school in each family; an elementary school in each district; a gymnasium in each city;

Relics of a Roman school from a wall painting now found in a museum at Naples. The left-hand case contains three styli for writing; the upper right is a capsa containing rolls or books. Leaning against it is a book. At the bottom a capsa is open showing the scrolls. Leaning against it on the left is a writing tablet.

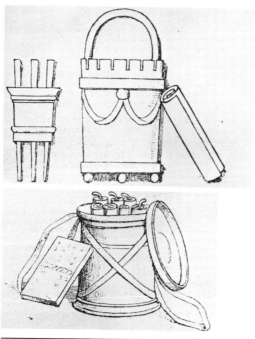

Flaccus Alcuin (735–804) helped Charlemagne establish a school at the royal court and thus revive learning in Western Europe. For these efforts and for his staunch defense of orthodoxy, Alcuin was named abbot of Tours in A.D. 796. His scholastic contributions included metrical annals and instruction manuals for grammar, composition, and logic.

Dipticha, or Roman wax tablet with stylus—found on the Esquiline Hill, Rome, and preserved in the local museum. The tablets were covered with wax and were used for accounting or in schools by writing on the wax with the stylus. The name on the upper end of the left illustration, Galleri Concessi, shows its owner to have been a man of some importance.

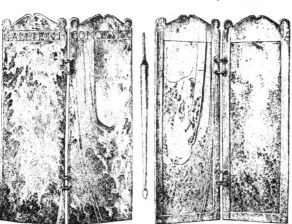

A page from the early edition of one of Comenius's books, *Orbis Pictus,* published in 1657. Comenius's textbooks were among the first to use pictures. On this page, the idea was to have the child learn the sound of each letter in the alphabet through some sound in nature with which he was familiar. Hence, the illustration of the wind, the goose, the cricket, etc.

The direction in which education starts a man will determine his future life.

Plato

The lower schoolroom of Eton College founded in 1440. The wood from which these benches were made, as well as the wainscoting and timbers in the room, was taken from the wrecked vessels of the Spanish Armada. This was one of the means by which patriotic ideals were instilled in the English boys.

The library of the University of Leyden in the sixteenth century. By this time, the library had become an important part of the university. The books are chained to the shelves so they could not be stolen—an indication of their scarcity and value. Leyden was founded in 1575, and for over a century was the center of advanced thought and instruction.

an academy in each kingdom, or even in each considerable province."[5]

There were countless numbers of great educators during the eighteenth and nineteenth centuries. Some of the famous American educators from this period, such as Benjamin Franklin, Horace Mann, Henry Barnard, and Samuel Hall, are discussed in more detail elsewhere in this book. There were also a number of famous European educators during this time whose work greatly influenced American education. These in-

cluded, among others, Jean Jacques Rousseau (1712–1778), Johann Friedrich Herbart (1776–1841), Friedrich Froebel (1782–1852), and Johann Heinrich Pestalozzi (1746–1827). Of these, Pestalozzi, a Swiss educator, stands out as one who gained a great deal of fame as the founder of two schools—one at Burgdorf (1800–1804), and another at Yverdun (1805–1825).

It was at these schools that Pestalozzi put into practice his educational beliefs that children should be treated with love, respect, understanding, and patience (a belief that was in contradic-

Pestalozzi's first teaching experience was at Stans in 1798. There he took charge of a group of children orphaned by one of the massacres of the French Revolution. There were no teaching aids so Pestalozzi taught by using objects. This illustration is from an early nineteenth century woodcut.

Pestalozzi eventually moved to Yverdun where, at this castle, he conducted an experimental school for twenty years. Educators came from all around the world to visit and study the teaching methods and materials he developed here.

tion to the prevailing, religiously inspired view that children were born full of sin and inherently bad). Pestalozzi reflected his beliefs when he wrote:

I was convinced that my heart would change the condition of my children just as promptly as the sun of spring would reanimate the earth benumbed by the winter. . . . It was necessary that my children should observe, from dawn to evening, at every moment of the day, upon my brow and on my lips, that my affections were fixed on them, that their happiness was my happiness, and that their pleasures were my pleasures. . . .

I was everything to my children. I was alone with them from morning till night. . . . Their hands were in my hands. Their eyes were fixed on my eyes.[6]

Pestalozzi also believed that teachers should use objects and games to help students learn. In fact, he developed a series of teaching materials which were very advanced for their time. A number of American educators visited Pestalozzi's schools and brought many of his ideas back to the United States where they were put into practice.

The number of Americans who have earned a reputation as outstanding educators is great indeed. In fact, to list them would be an impossible task. Perhaps it will suffice to say that ed-

Is Teaching a Career for You?   15

Teaching and learning should always involve lighter moments.

ucators such as Horace Mann, Henry Barnard, Samuel Hall, Cyrus Pierce, John Griscom, Noah Webster, Frederick Douglass, Edward Sheldon, David Camp, William Phelps, Catherine Beecher, Charles and Frank McMurry, Francis Parker, John Dewey, George Counts, among many, many others far too numerous to mention, have made very significant contributions to our society through their various educational works. Many contemporary educators are also among our leading statesmen, scientists, artists, civil rights leaders, Nobel prize winners, civic leaders, authors, researchers, and philosophers. In fact, many educators can be found in all of the most important walks of life in our American society.

The purpose of this brief chapter was to help the reader to assess teaching as a viable career choice. Other chapters in Section One and Section Two provide more information about teaching as a career.

A world whose schools are unreformed is an unreformed world.

H. G. Wells

Point of View

Recently, seven Gannett News Service reporters visited a number of schools throughout the United States. They were seeking to learn what was happening in the nation's classrooms as the 1980s began. One of the articles written as a result of their visits is entitled "Teachers: A Kid Takes 'Pot Luck'." In this article they essentially report on the stark contrast among the capability and effectiveness of classroom teachers. The article provides insight into the characteristics of effective teachers. It also provides a realistic description of what teaching is really like, and what it can be like.

Teachers: A Kid Takes 'Pot Luck'

High school sophomores playing "Go to the Head of the Class?"

During the entire 54 minutes of biology class?

It happened recently at a high school in Claymont, Del., but this game was not played on a board with wooden pieces and dice. The "pieces" were the students themselves, and they advanced or regressed from desk to desk based on their ability to correctly answer questions, on the inner workings of a frog, fired by teacher Susan Stetler.

Desk No. 1 was the "head of the class," and it was coveted keenly. As one girl achieved the top spot after a half-hour of trying, she announced, "I'm gonna hold it the rest of the period." She did.

Stetler's class learned a lot about frogs.

Source: "The Endangered Dream," Gannett News Service (Washington, D.C.: 1980). Reprinted by permission.

The game was a simple review for a major test the following day, and similar review periods were taking place in other biology classrooms elsewhere in the country. But in many of them, students were using the time to catch up on sleep, joke with neighbors and read magazines. Teachers were asking questions about ferns or starfish. Getting no responses they offered their own. Only a few students bothered to take notes.

The contrast is stark, but it pervades American education. In public schools from New York to California, Gannett News Service reporters found classrooms in which students were involved enthusiastically in learning across the hall from rooms in which they were putting in time until the bell rang. In almost all cases, the difference was the atmosphere created by the teacher.

As GNS reporter Vic Pollard put it, after two weeks in the schools of Sacramento, Calif., "Skill and dedication can be found in public education," but "a kid takes pot luck."

The luck of the pot varies widely, even for the same student.

At an East Coast high school, a burly 18-year-old, attired in rumpled jeans, a black leather jacket and collar-length hair, showed up for first-period English class as if it were a curse that had to be tolerated to get a diploma.

He sat in a corner with five similarly inspired friends, who cracked jokes and laughed through much of the class. The teacher's questions, when not ignored, were answered in grunts.

The teacher says he has warned them that "they have the right to fail" and he won't deprive them of that right.

Two hours later, the same burly 18-year-old, with the jacket gone, was in a social studies class discussing current events. Now he was responding in coherent, intelligible sentences. As he discussed a local newspaper series, it was obvious he had read it, understood it and was eager to share his opinions. The rest of the class reflected the same enthusiasm.

The English teacher was a baby-sitter. The woman in control of the social studies class was teaching.

"Baby-sit" is a term heard frequently in our public schools, especially from teachers—as in "I'm not going to baby-sit him." It was uttered with great irritation in the teachers' lounge of a California elementary school by a woman who was told one of her students was outside with a problem. She refused to interrupt her break, which is guaranteed by the union contract.

Dave, a full-time substitute at a high school in Tallahassee, Fla., considers himself a full-time baby-sitter. "I sub in everything," he says. "All it is is a baby-sitting job."

"Sometimes teachers leave reading assignments, sometimes they don't. If there's nothing telling me what to have the kids do, they just talk all period."

Then there are teachers like Janice Mazza at a Tallahassee elementary school. On a recent afternoon, she was sitting under a tree with some colleagues watching the kids at recess. Another teacher saw one of Mazza's pupils instigate a shoving match.

"Goodbye," Mazza said to the other teachers, arising and marching to the scene of the action. She called the girl to her, spoke quietly, and the girl sat on the sidelines for the remainder of recess.

A successful classroom does not grow solely from discipline, but discipline is a substantial part. One reporter, after several days in classrooms, concluded that only incompetent teachers display anger at students because anger is a sign that a class is out of control. That conclusion was offered subsequently to students, teachers and principals. None disagreed.

An important factor, many educators say, is the students' perception of the teacher's expectations.

"Most kids will accept your discipline if they feel you care about them," says Philip Read, principal of a Wilmington, Del., elementary school, who begins each day greeting students by their first names as they arrive.

Harold Deal, principal of a junior high in Charlotte, N.C., says test scores plummeted in his city during the first years of desegregation because "most folks did not demand proficiency in the classroom. There were no expectations."

"Now we're saying we expect you to be good in the classroom," Deal says. "The social issues have receded to the background. And studies show kids respond to the expectations of their teachers."

Creating a positive atmosphere, says Wilmington's Read, is "something you have to work at."

And Tallahassee's Ionia Smith, who has been county teacher of the year three times, says she works at it 90 to 100 hours a week.

"That's because I don't grade papers or even take oral attendance in class," Smith says. "I pass around a roll sheet which students must sign. Of course, it takes a lot of time after class for me to go back and transfer that sheet to my gradebook."

It takes only a few minutes to determine whether a classroom contains that combination of discipline, expectations and a caring teacher that produces an enthusiastic class.

If the teacher is ready to go with a lesson when the bell rings, it probably is there. If the teacher kills time fiddling with papers or chatting with a couple of students, he or she probably is trying to reduce the baby-sitting time.

If a teacher asks a question and several answers are volunteered, the rapport exists. If the teacher must answer the question, the class is just waiting for the bell.

Consider two boys named John, one in Florida, and one in Delaware. Each is taking a high school math course in which his interest is less than overwhelming.

In Florida, John is not the only student talking during class. The teacher interrupts the lesson to say, "If you don't want to pay attention, fine, but I'm not going to talk over you." And she tells John: "Do be quiet. There are people sleeping in here."

In Delaware, the class is engaged in a rapid-fire dialogue in which the teacher shoots out a problem, calls a name and gets a quick answer. John is the only one who looks lost when his name is called.

"We'll get back to John when he has the answer," says the teacher, moving quickly to the next question. Five minutes later, John has found the place in the textbook, his hand is in the air and he offers the correct answer.

In many schools visited by GNS, good teachers appeared to be in a majority. But some students, for whom the potluck hasn't been good, face an entire day of classes out of control.

The odds against finding a good teacher in a classroom could be increasing. A survey by W. Timothy Weaver of Boston University shows that the academic quality of people leaving college teaching programs, as measured by four standard achievement tests, has plunged steadily for a decade.

Several educators blamed this on the increasing acceptance of women in other professions, luring away many bright females who in the past would have been teachers.

Oscar Satow, principal of a Sacramento elementary school, listed five qualities that make a good teacher: an interest in the children's welfare, high expectations of them, willingness to give them extra time before and after school, firmness in dealing with them, and "consistency" in discipline.

All five of the qualities Satow lists probably can be lumped together as the difference between the teacher who refuses to interrupt her union-guaranteed break and the teacher who learns that a pupil is causing trouble and tells her colleagues "goodbye."

Questions for Discussion

1. Of the teachers you have had, which do you remember favorably and why? What qualities did they have that made them "good" teachers?

2. What experiences have you had that verify your interest in teaching? Why?

3. Why do you think teaching is important to society?

4. What do you see as the advantages and disadvantages of teaching as a career?

5. At what level, preprimary—elementary—secondary—adult, do you wish to teach? Why? Do you wish to teach handicapped persons? Why?

Supplementary Learning Activities

1. Interview an early childhood, elementary, secondary, adult education, or special education teacher to discuss how he or she feels about teaching as a career.

2. Visit a classroom or other educational setting, and after the visit record your feelings and/or questions about teaching. Share your comments and questions with your peers, professors, or former teachers for their responses.

3. Write to the major teacher organizations requesting information about teaching as a career. (American Federation of Teachers, 11 DuPont Circle, N.W., Washington, D.C. 20036; National Education Association, 1201 Sixteenth St., N.W., Washington, D.C. 20036.)

4. Invite a first year teacher and a veteran teacher to your class to present their views as to why they entered the field of education and to answer questions.

5. Invite a teacher supervisor or hiring official to your class to present her or his views on the personal qualities needed for teaching and to answer questions.

Notes

1. George H. Gallup, "Twelfth Annual Gallup Poll of the Public Attitudes Toward the Public Schools," *Phi Delta Kappan,* September 1980, p. 38.

2. Bernard R. Bartholomew, "Nationwide Teacher Opinion Poll" (Washington, D.C.: National Education Association, 1980), p. 13.

3. Marsha H. Ream, *Status of the American Public School Teacher* (Washington, D.C.: National Education Association, 1977), p. 39.

4. George H. Gallup, "Eighth Annual Gallup Poll of the Public's Attitudes Toward the Public Schools," *Phi Delta Kappan,* October 1976, pp. 187–99.

5. G. Compayre, *History of Pedagogy,* trans. W. H. Payne (Boston: D. C. Heath and Co., 1885), p. 128.

6. Ibid., p. 425.

Selected References

Action in Teacher Education. The Journal of the Association of Teacher Educators, vol. 2, no. 4, Fall 1980. Reston, Virginia: Association of Teacher Educators. (This issue is entitled "Stress in the Teaching Profession.")

Armstrong, David; Henson, Kenneth; and Savage, Tom W. *Education: An Introduction.* Riverside, New Jersey: Macmillan Publishing Company, 1980.

Denham, Carolyn, and Lieberman, Ann. *Time to Learn.* Sacramento, California: Commission for Teacher Preparation and Licensing, 1980. (Beginning Teacher Evaluation Study, funded by the National Institute of Evaluation.)

Foote, Timothy (ed.). "Help! Teacher Can't Teach,"
     Time. Vol. 115, no. 24, June 16, 1980.

Gallup, George C. "The Twelth Gallup Poll of the
     Public's Attitudes Toward Public Schools." *Phi
     Delta Kappan.* Vol. 62, no. 1, September 1980,
     pp. 33–48. (An annual publication, see previous
     and subsequent issues.)

Gudridge, Beatrice M. *Teacher Competency:
     Problems and Solutions.* Arlington, Virginia:
     American Association of School Administrators,
     1980. (Produced by Education News Service,
     Sacramento, California, for AASA.)

Ryan, Kevin et al. *Biting the Apple: Accounts of
     First Year Teachers.* New York: Longman,
     1980.

Ryan, Kevin, and Cooper, James M. *Those Who
     Can, Teach.* Boston, Massachusetts: Houghton
     Mifflin Company, 1980.

Sadker, Myra, and Sadker, David. *Teachers Make
     the Difference: An Introduction to Education.*
     New York: Harper and Row Publishers, 1980.

Smith, B. Othaniel. *A Design for a School of
     Pedagogy.* Washington, D.C.: U.S. Department
     of Education, U.S. Government Printing Office,
     1980.

Teacher
Education Today

2

This Chapter
- Describes the academic preparation one needs for becoming a teacher.
- Presents new trends in teacher education, including prestudent teaching clinical experiences, microteaching, individualization, student teaching centers, multicultural education, and preparation for mainstreaming handicapped children.
- Discusses the certification process.

- Provides information on the accreditation process for teacher education programs.
- Suggests ways for prospective teachers to enhance their employability.
- Explains the need for and nature of continuing professional education.
- Provides a point of view that deals with growing concerns over teacher competency.

Recently, teacher education has come under serious scrutiny. The following quote is indicative of an increasingly common concern.

Quite simply, if test scores on nationally normed college tests are falling as they have been, then is it reasonable to conclude that all of the blame should be borne by the students themselves, their families, or the fabric of society? Isn't it just as reasonable to believe that a share of the blame should be with schools and teachers? And, when we get to teachers, isn't it possible that in this latter group there might be some who are weak or downright incompetent?[1]

It is true that there are some incompetent teachers. A current challenge for teacher educators is to reform programs of teacher education in order to assure teacher competency. The movement for teacher competency will be discussed in this chapter as one of the recent trends in teacher preparation.

Let us first examine the traditionally common components of all teacher preparation programs.

Today most teacher education programs designed for entry level positions are four-year pro-

grams. While there are some similarities in all programs, there are also differences, institution to institution and state to state.

Teacher Education Programs Today

Teacher education programs are offered by many colleges and universities to prepare a variety of types of teachers. There are some elements common to all programs, yet a program designed to prepare a nursery school teacher will be decidedly different from a program designed to prepare a teacher to work with the mentally retarded, the deaf, or the blind.

Colleges and universities have the responsibility for conceptualizing the various training programs. Basic guidelines used in the process include state teacher certification laws, and the guidelines of various national accrediting associations. Further, the process frequently involves not only college and university specialists in education and subject-matter disciplines, but also practicing teachers, administrators, personnel di-

Here an adviser helps a student select courses for his general education component.

rectors, counselors, and other practitioners in related areas such as social work; personnel from state certification agencies, and from national accrediting agencies; and students, both graduate and undergraduate. Programs so designed usually lead to certification in the state where the institution is located. It should be noted, however, that each state has its own certification laws and such laws do differ somewhat from state to state. Within a state there are likely to be slightly different programs, institution-to-institution, leading to the same certificate. More information about certification and accreditation is provided later in this chapter.

Common Components in Teacher Education Programs

All teacher education programs—elementary, secondary, and special education—contain three common components: general education, professional education including student teaching, and a specialization.

General Education Component

General education or liberal education most often makes up approximately one-third (40–44 semester hours) of a total four-year degree program in teacher education and includes study in the social sciences, the natural and physical sciences, and the humanities. Frequently, the general education requirements for a baccalaureate degree

in any program as prescribed by a specific higher education institution will also be required for those pursuing teacher education programs and will meet the general education requirements for teacher certification. The rationale for the inclusion of general education within teacher education is basically to the effect that teachers have the responsibility for the general education of young Americans, therefore, they are expected to have a rich educational background themselves. Teachers are also expected to be effective purveyors of culture. "They should have acquired the characteristics of a scholar, and reflect excitement about learning in many areas. They should be familiar with a broad continuum of ways of knowing. They should have developed skills to a high degree in both oral and written communication."[2] Table 2.1 illustrates how one state has established objectives for the general education component of teacher education.

Men have sought and still seek an elixir of youth. I've found it as a teacher of junior high school science. Teaching has made it possible for me to enjoy the fun, excitement, wonder, humor, intensity, and sensitivity of youth while enjoying the benefits of mature adulthood (whatever these may be).

Christopher R. Vagts

Table 2.1. Objectives of the General Education Component of Teacher Education.

1. Achieving personal fulfillment through
   a) Attaining optimum physical and mental health,
   b) Clarifying moral and aesthetic values,
   c) Developing creative expression.
2. Developing understanding and skills in symbolics of information.
   a) The ability to speak, read and write English fluently, accurately, and critically, and
   b) Additional understanding and/or performance capability in at least one area of symbolics of information, such as mathematics, computer science, logic, linguistics, communications (verbal and nonverbal), or a foreign language.
3. Understanding the natural and social environments.
   a) A basic understanding of how data, hypotheses, and laws are related within the framework of scientific method;
   b) An appreciation of the interrelatedness and complexity of the natural world, and of human dependence of the living and nonliving environment;
   c) A general understanding of the social forces which shape present and future societies; and
   d) An understanding of the social system of the United States and of social systems which differ from your own.

Source: Division of Teacher Education and Certification, Kentucky Department of Education, *Kentucky Teacher Preparation and Certification Handbook*. (Frankfort, Kentucky: Superintendent of Public Instruction, 1976), pp. 37–38.

Professional Education Component

While the general education component of teacher education programs is likely to be almost identical in all programs, the professional education component is likely to be somewhat different. In general, the professional education component includes courses related to the teaching profession, and to teaching and learning. Those courses dealing with the teaching profession include courses in the history and philosophy of education, and the nature of schools. Those dealing with teaching and learning include psychology, human growth and development, learning theory, tests and measurements, methods of teaching, and student teaching. Differences in the professional component are related to the types of students the teacher education candidate is preparing to teach. For example, students preparing to teach at the elementary school level will take child psychology, while those preparing to teach at the secondary level will take adolescent psychology. Candidates preparing to teach handicapped children will take specific courses related to a specific type of handicap, such as mental retardation, learning disabled, or hearing impaired. Methods courses will also differ, with the individual preparing to teach elementary school children usually taking a series of methods courses in reading and language arts, social studies, mathematics, science, music, art, and physical education; while the candidate preparing to teach secondary school students usually takes a methods course in teaching a specific discipline such as English, mathematics, or art. Those planning to teach the handicapped will take methods courses related to the nature of a specific handicap.

In effect, the professional component of programs designed to prepare elementary school teachers prepares candidates to teach children a variety of courses. The professional component of special education programs prepares candidates to teach handicapped persons either a variety of courses or a specific course area. The professional component of secondary school teacher programs prepares candidates to teach adolescent age youngsters a specific body of coursework.

Student Teaching

Student teaching, the capstone of the professional sequence, is designed to gradually introduce prospective teachers into the full responsibilities of teaching. It is done under the guidance of an experienced teacher and a university supervisor. Currently, it is most often done in off-campus school settings. However, student teaching in some instances can be done on-campus in a laboratory school. The trend today is toward a full semester or quarter of full time student teaching.

Specialization Component

The third common component in all teacher education programs is a specialization, usually taken concurrently with general education and the professional education components. The term *specialization* as used here is usually synonymous with *major* as used in college catalogs. Students preparing to teach at the secondary level usually

Student teaching is an important aspect of teacher education programs.

Nor am I less persuaded, that you will agree with me in opinion, that there is nothing which can better deserve your patronage than the promotion of science and literature. Knowledge is in every country the surest basis of public happiness. In one in which the measures of government receive their impression so immediately from the sense of the community, as in ours, it is proportionably essential. To the security of a free constitution it contributes in various ways; by convincing those who are entrusted with the public administration, that every valuable end of government is best answered by the enlightened confidence of the people; and by teaching the people themselves to know, and to value their own rights; to discern and provide against invasions of them; to distinguish between oppression and the necessary exercise of lawful authority, between burthens proceeding from a disregard to their convenience and those resulting from the inevitable exigencies of society; to discriminate the spirit of liberty from that of licentiousness, cherishing the first, avoiding the last, and uniting a speedy but temperate vigilance against encroachments, with an inviolable respect to the laws.

President George Washington

specialize or take a major in a discipline such as art, music, English, mathematics, or physical education. Students preparing to teach at the elementary level specialize or take a major in elementary education, while those preparing to teach handicapped persons major in special education.

New Trends in Teacher Preparation Programs

There are a number of new trends in teacher education which are likely to have an effect on teacher preparation programs in the future. Among them are (1) competency assessment in teacher education, (2) increased clinical experiences prior to student teaching (early clinical experiences or prestudent teaching clinical experiences), (3) use of microteaching, (4) individualization of programs, (5) use of student teaching centers, (6) required multicultural education experiences in all teacher education programs, and (7) required mainstreaming of handicapped children resulting in some necessary training in special education for all teachers. Many teacher education programs today include some of the aforementioned trends, yet these trends are totally absent in some programs, and only partially developed in other programs. It is predicted that within the next decade these trends will be a part of all teacher education programs.

Competency Assessment in Teacher Education

The movement for teacher competency testing is an outgrowth of a nationwide trend requiring students in elementary and secondary schools to demonstrate specified minimal competencies to pass to the next grade or to receive a diploma. It also represents dissatisfaction with the public schools, and therefore with teachers. It is only a short step from requiring students to demonstrate basic skills and requiring those who teach them to demonstrate competency in basic skills and in the art and science of teaching. In 1978, the state of Florida passed one of the most comprehensive laws dealing with teacher competency. Three aspects of the Florida law are particularly relevant to preservice teacher preparation, and therefore to persons considering teaching as a career. They are:

- as a prerequisite for admission into the teacher education program, that a student receive a passing score, to be established by state board rule, on a nationally normed standardized college entrance examination.
- each applicant for initial certification shall demonstrate on a written comprehensive examination and through other procedures as may be specified by the state board, mastery of those minimum generic and specialization competencies and other criteria as shall be adopted into rules by the state board, including but not limited to the following:
  The ability to write in logical and understandable style with appropriate grammar and sentence structure;

The ability to comprehend and interpret a message after listening;

The ability to read, comprehend, and interpret orally and in writing, professional and other written material;

The ability to comprehend and work with fundamental mathematical concepts;

The ability to comprehend patterns of physical, social, and academic development in students, and to counsel students concerning their needs in these areas.

- no individual shall be issued a regular certificate until he has completed one school year of satisfactory teaching pursuant to law and such other criteria as the state board shall require by rule, or a year-long internship approved by the state board. (The provision that one year of successful teaching experience could serve in lieu of the year-long internship has since been changed to three years of successful teaching experience.)

Florida is not the only state that has legislated some form of teacher competency testing. As of October, 1980, twenty-nine states have been identified that have taken some kind of action related to competency assessments of teachers for entry into teacher preparation programs, for certification, or for both.[3] The Georgia Department of Education along with the University of Georgia has taken leadership in developing the *Teaching Performance Assessment Instruments*.[4] One of the measures of performance includes the observation and rating of teacher behavior in the classroom.

The teacher competency movement is not without critics. The National Education Association at its 1979 convention said that tests such as the National Teacher Examination "must not be used as a condition of employment or as a method of educating educators." Another resolution stated that "no test now in existence is satisfactory for use as a criterion for certification and licensing."[5] The American Federation of Teachers at its 1979 convention went on record opposing the use of teacher examinations for making administrative decisions related to retention, salary or tenure. Nevertheless, they supported the use of exams to qualify new teachers as a part of the process to test their level of literacy, knowledge of subject matter, and pedagogy, and urged that teachers have significant involvement in test review and selection.[6] A recent editorial in the *Phi Delta Kappan* stated: "Minimum competency testing is a hollow means of judging the efficacy of teachers." Furthermore, "More and more, research in education is beginning to provide the answers we need to improve the quality of our teachers and our students. . . . It is within our power as a professional community, for example, to redesign teacher training in a way that takes advantage of valuable research findings. It is within our power to change traditional reward systems so as to attract a higher quality of teachers. Rational planning based on solid research and clear goals can effect constructive changes. Hastily conceived tests of minimum competency will only add to existing confusion."[7]

The teacher competency movement is a powerful one. Persons entering the teaching profession in the future can expect more stringent entry requirements and regular assessment of their development throughout the program. They can also expect assessments not only of their knowledge of basic skills, the content of their discipline, but also of their performance as a prospective teacher.

Early Clinical Experiences

Early clinical experiences can be defined as interactions or encounters prior to student teaching with students of the age and/or type that the prospective teacher eventually plans to work with. Two major objectives for such experiences are: to help prospective teachers determine whether or not teaching is in fact a desirable career choice for them; and to facilitate learning, particularly in respect to relating theory to practice. Teacher education candidates are likely to be expected to participate in a prescribed number of clock hours of early experiences planned to occur throughout the preparation period, usually beginning in the sophomore year. The early experiences are sequenced, generally proceeding from observation through various levels of participation (in the classroom) in activities ordinarily carried on in the classroom with students and by the teacher. The experiences are structured in the sense that the prospective teachers are expected to participate in prescribed activities and achieve specific competencies. The prospective teachers are evaluated throughout the experience and given feedback information on their individual level of performance. It is reasoned that such experiences will, in fact, help prospective teachers in making the decision as to whether or not teaching is a desirable career choice for

them. Further, such experiences will provide better preparation for student teaching, enhancing the quality of the student teaching experience, and therefore the eventual quality of the teacher.

Microteaching

Microteaching, in a microteaching laboratory, involves teaching a minilesson for a few minutes to a few students, demonstrating one or more specific teaching skills. The performance is videotaped, played back, and critiqued by the prospective teacher, the instructor, and occasionally the peers of the prospective teacher. Most often microteaching is done concurrently with methods classes. Microteaching laboratories frequently utilize materials that are designed to assist the candidate in achieving specific teaching skills. Candidates are expected to demonstrate competency in these skills as a part of the teacher training program. Videotaping teacher candidates teaching in a regular classroom setting is also used as a technique to refine teaching skills.

Individualization of Programs

Individualized instruction is increasing in all types of education. Basically, individualized instruction involves students in the pursuit of specific objectives independently, as contrasted with group instruction. Teacher education programs are becoming increasingly individualized. The use of educational technology—for example, videotaping—along with performance based

Audiovisual courses familiarize prospective teachers with equipment that they will use during their careers.

teacher education (PBTE), has decidedly increased the amount of independent learning in teacher education programs. PBTE is based upon specific competencies (knowledge, skills, behaviors) to be demonstrated by students preparing to be teachers.

Some competencies can best be attained through independent study or practice. Many institutions have learning centers designed to foster independent study. Learning centers are equipped with various kinds of "hardware" such as audio recorders and videotape recorders, along with a number of "software" learning packages that individual students can use to develop and demonstrate competencies. Frequently audiovisual laboratories, media materials laboratories, and microteaching clinics are included in learning centers.

Student Teacher Centers

Many teacher education institutions today carefully select a school district, or a cluster of school districts in close proximity to one another, and use these districts for student teaching experiences. It was not unusual in the past to scatter student teachers over a large number of school districts. The selection of a few districts is advantageous to student teachers in that districts can be chosen on the basis of exemplary programs; close cooperation between public school personnel can be developed; and supporting environments for exploring new pedagogical methods can be provided. Since there are sufficient numbers of students in one location, related course work can be offered on site for student teachers, and simultaneously, in-service training can be offered for practitioners. Different types of school districts, i.e., urban, suburban, and rural, can be utilized as centers providing different opportunities for student teachers.

Multicultural Education

Many states, and most recently the National Council for Accreditation of Teacher Education (NCATE), a voluntary national teacher education accreditation association, are requiring multicultural education, including sexism, as a component in teacher education programs. As defined by NCATE,

Multicultural education is preparation for the social, political, and economic realities that individuals experience in culturally diverse and complex human encounters. These realities have both national and international dimensions. This preparation provides a process by which an individual develops competencies for perceiving, believing, evaluating, and behaving in different cultural settings. Thus, multicultural education is viewed as an intervention and an ongoing assessment process to help institutions and individuals become more responsive to the human condition, cultural integrity, and cultural pluralism in society.

Provision should be made for instruction in multicultural education in teacher education programs. Multicultural education should receive attention in courses, seminars, directed readings, laboratory and clinical experiences, practicum and other types of field experiences.

Multicultural education should include but not be limited to experiences which (1) Promote analytical and evaluative abilities to confront issues such as participatory democracy, racism and sexism, and the parity of power; (2) Develop skills for values clarification including the study of the manifest and latent transmission of values; (3) Examine the dynamics of diverse cultures and the implications for developing teaching strategies; and (4) Examine linguistic variations and diverse learning styles as a basis for the development of appropriate teaching strategies.[8]

It is anticipated that states that do not already have a requirement similar to the NCATE requirement will soon adopt such a requirement. The NCATE requirement, while adopted in May 1977, becomes effective in January 1979.

Mainstreaming

In essence, mainstreaming means moving handicapped children from their segregated status in special education classes and integrating them with "normal" children in regular classrooms. Mainstreaming is not new, but it has received a new impetus from the passage of PL94–142, Education of the Handicapped Act, federal legislation hailed as a "Bill of Rights for the Handicapped." While the legislation has many provisions, a significant portion of it reads:

Handicapped and nonhandicapped children will be educated together to the maximum extent appropriate, and the former will be placed in special classes or separate schools "only when the nature of the severity of the handicap is such that education in regular classes," even if they are provided supplementary aids and services, "cannot be achieved satisfactorily."

The one-to-one relationship between the teacher and the student is an effective method of recognizing a student's individual nature.

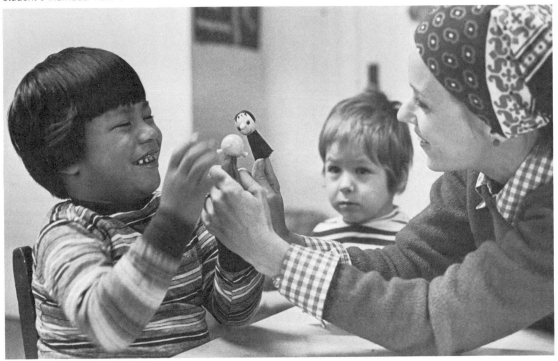

Teacher education programs for the preparation of teachers of "normal" children will need to, if they have not already done so, include some preparation in special education for all teachers to enable them to function in providing effective instruction for all students in mainstreamed classrooms.

Certification

The ultimate goal of individuals pursuing a program of teacher preparation is to achieve certification, which is in effect their license to teach.

Certification is a function of each of the respective states. It has its legal authority in actions of the respective state legislatures, and is most often implemented through a state office of education. Certification is established to protect state interests. Hopkins has provided a rationale for the relationship between state and public interests and a system of certification.

. . . the right and responsibility of the State to certify teachers is a legitimate, moral and rational use of the political power of the State, only to the extent that teacher certification protects and promotes some demonstrably legitimate public interest of the people for whose welfare and benefit State accredited schools are established. Statutes, policies, and procedures which together constitute teacher certification are not authorized to protect private interests, such as the desires of aspiring teachers for some official State acceptance of previous training and experience. Just as the State does not examine and license physicians in order to assist the graduate of a medical school in pursuing his special private interest of setting up a practice and making money, so the proper purpose of State procedures for teacher certification is not to assist the graduate of a school of education in pursuing his legitimate private goal of getting a job.[9]

Teacher education students seeking information in respect to certification requirements in a specific state should write to the state office of education in the state in which they wish to be certified. The state office of education is usually located in the capital city of the state and its specific address can be obtained from a directory in most libraries.

The Certification Process

There are two basic ways in which teachers are certified in the United States today, (1) individual assessment or transcript evaluation, and (2) institutional assessment or program approval. In effect, under transcript evaluation applicants submit their transcript or transcripts to the state agency of education, where they are compared with the state requirements for a specific certificate. If the applicant is judged as meeting the requirements, the appropriate certificate is then issued. Under program approval, the programs of a teacher education institution are evaluated, and either accredited or not accredited by the respective state agency. Students completing accredited programs are granted certification by the state upon recommendation of the institution.

In some states both processes are available, while in other states only one of the two ways is available. Increasing importance and recognition, however, are being placed on program approval. Its major advantages are seen as (1) fixing the responsibility for assessing and recommending individuals on a teacher-preparing institution,

and (2) permitting the development of preparation programs that are not straightjacketed by a set of department and credit hour rules.[10] Its weaknesses are (1) reliance on standards that have no empirically established relationship to the performance of those recommended for certification, (2) reliance on human testimony provided by visitation team members, and (3) reliance on the same institution and ultimately the same personnel both to prepare an individual and to determine whether the same individual should be certified.[11] Nevertheless, it is seen by many as superior to the piecemeal, rule-laden interpretation of transcripts. "In short, even under the best of circumstances, transcript evaluation as a means of certificating is on the one hand too rigid and on the other too abstract to enable one to argue that the resultant certificate is directly related to the promotion or protection of state interests."[12] Increasingly, state reciprocity in certification is based on the completion of a teacher training program approved by a state educational agency.

National Accreditation

The major teacher education accrediting agency at the national level is the National Council for Accreditation of Teacher Education (NCATE). The Council, representing five constituent organizations and open to associate organizations, is a nonprofit voluntary accrediting body devoted exclusively to the evaluation and accreditation of teacher education programs. The constituent organizations holding Council membership include American Association of Colleges for Teacher Education (AACTE), Council of Chief State School Officers (CCSSO), National School Board Association (NSBA), National Education Association, Instructional and Professional Development (NEA), and the National Association of State Directors of Teacher Education and Certification (NASDTEC). Associate organizations include: Association of Teacher Educators (ATE), Council for Exceptional Children (CEC), National Council of Teachers of Mathematics (NCTM), and the Student National Education Association (SNEA). It is important to note that the composition of the Council includes representation from colleges and universities, practicing teachers, state officials and agencies, school boards, and students.

In order for an institution to be eligible *for consideration* for NCATE accreditation, it must have (1) state approval of its teacher education programs, (2) regional accreditation, (3) evidence of a letter of intent to comply with affirmative action guidelines of the United States Office of Education, and (4) graduates from each program presented. Accreditation of the institution results after an evaluation has determined that the programs of the institution have met the standards of the Council.

Students who are graduates of an NCATE accredited institution have an added benefit in certification reciprocity. Currently over thirty states grant reciprocity privileges in teacher certification to graduates of NCATE accredited institutions.

Employability

The eventual goal of most teacher education students is to secure a teaching position. The current supply of teachers in some fields still exceeds the demand, and this situation is likely to continue in the near future. Students, in designing their programs, should remember to make themselves as employable as they possibly can. This is not to say that students should rush to the area of greatest demand irrespective of their aptitude and interests. It is to say though, that while in pursuit of a teacher training program commensurate with their aptitudes and interests, they should, and in most instances can, within the flexibility of their program, include components that will make them more employable.

While there is limited data on the subject, there is some evidence that being able to function in different settings, being able to work with handicapped youngsters in a regular classroom, being qualified to teach in more than one discipline, and being able and willing to work in extracurricular activities are all assets to the individual seeking a teaching position.

Prospective teachers can gain experiences in different settings. Those whose background is suburban can have clinical experiences in city or

Teachers work in many different settings.

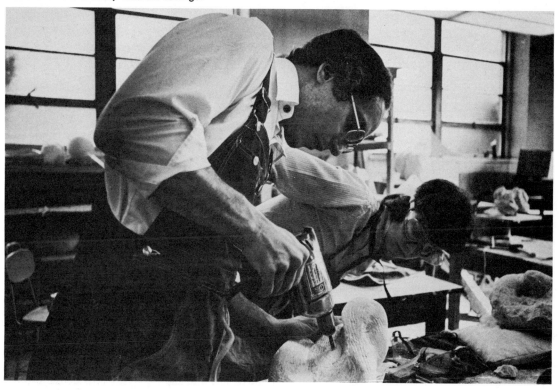

rural settings. Conversely, students with city backgrounds can have experiences in rural or suburban settings, and those with rural backgrounds can have experiences in city or suburban settings. Such experiences broaden the cultural background of the candidate, and along with course work in multicultural education, are likely to enhance employment opportunities.

As was mentioned earlier in this chapter, federal legislation requires that handicapped children be educated in a regular classroom insofar as it is feasible. There are very few teachers prepared to work in such circumstances. For the next few years at least, persons so prepared will have a decided advantage in seeking initial employment.

At the upper grade and secondary levels, persons who are qualified to teach in more than one

discipline such as English and social studies, or science and mathematics, are likely to be more employable, particularly in junior high schools or small high schools. It is also helpful if a candidate is willing and able to serve as a yearbook advisor, a coach of a minor sport or an assistant coach in a major sport, a dramatics coach or an advisor to any number of different clubs. Students should regularly seek information from placement personnel to gain information as to what is being commonly sought in candidates, and to adjust their programs if possible.

Finally, being willing to move to where the positions are located seems to dramatically increase the likelihood of securing a position.

More than any other public institution, schooling has been most dependent on the energies and talents of American women.

Arthur G. Wirth

Continuing Professional Development

The completion of a baccalaureate level teacher preparation program, and the securing of initial certification prepares one to start a teaching career. It does not, however, signal the end of professional development. Practicing professionals, for a variety of reasons, continue to study and improve themselves. Education beyond the initial preparation of teachers is commonly referred to as in-service training.

There are a number of reasons that teachers participate in in-service training. Among them are: (1) upgrading skills because of the changing needs and aspirations of students, (2) developing new skills resulting from new mandates such as multicultural education, mainstreaming of the handicapped, or metric education, (3) responding to dramatic changes in society, and in turn schools, which require changes in role definition, (4) securing a permanent or different credential, and (5) seeking extrinsic rewards such as advancements in salary. There are undoubtedly many other reasons.

A major concern among practicing teachers today centers around who determines or controls in-service teacher education. This is a complicated issue. Obviously in some instances it is the individual self-motivated teacher seeking to improve her or his own performance or advancement. In other instances it is a local board of education that decides that the total staff of teachers or selected teachers need retraining or

additional training. Still in other instances it may be the state or federal government that mandates curricular changes that require in-service education for large numbers of teachers. In instances other than self-motivation teachers feel strongly, and rightfully so, that they should be involved in the decision making. They seek a voice in determining the nature or content of in-service programs whenever possible; mandated programs by state or federal legislation permit only limited choices. Locally determined programs, however, permit many options and choices. Teachers seek a strong voice in how the training will be conducted, and who shall actually provide the training. In some school districts such items have become a part of the negotiated professional agreement between the local board of education and the local teachers' association. There is little question that teachers, through their organizations, local, state, and national, have gained much ground in their quest to control not only the elements of initial certification, but also the nature of in-service training.

Teacher Centers

A giant step forward in the quest for teachers to have more control over in-service training was made with the passage of federal legislation authorizing and funding teacher centers. In essence, the purposes of the centers are to develop and produce curricula to meet the educational needs of the person's community area or state served;

Teacher centers provide an opportunity for continuing professional development.

and to provide training to improve the skills of teachers to enable such teachers to meet better the special educational needs of persons such teachers serve. The teacher centers according to the legislation "shall be operated under the supervision of a teacher center policy board, the majority of which is representative of elementary and secondary classroom teachers to be served by such center fairly reflecting the make-up of all school teachers, including special education and vocational education teachers." The board "shall also include individuals representative of, or designated by, the school board of the local educational agency served by such center, and at least one representative designated by the institutions of higher education with departments or schools of education located in the area."

Teacher centers hold much promise for the improvement of in-service training. They are based on the sound premise that change is most likely to take place in educational practice when practicing teachers, the front-line so to speak of education, take the initiative for their own professional development.

Teacher Preparation Tomorrow

A recent publication presents a design for teacher preparation in the future that is different from the traditional and current programs.[13] Smith proposes a six-year preparation period with a four-year preprofessional curriculum leading to

Student participation and interest can be enhanced by creating an informal classroom atmosphere.

a bachelor's degree. The fifth year of study has as its focus the preparation of prospective teachers for work in the classroom, the school, and the community. It includes classroom clinical observation and experience, and field experiences in the community, along with coursework in exceptionality to provide a framework with which to understand all children, pedagogical psychology, measurement and evaluation, and the school and community. The studies in the second semester of the fifth year are centered around the actual curriculum of schools—not the theory of curriculum development, with a special study concentrated in the pedagogy of a variety of subjects as illustrated in table 2.2. Prospective elementary and secondary teachers are expected to study the entire span of the curriculum from early childhood through high school in order for them to

better understand what occurs at each level so that the entire program can be understood and coordinated.[14] The sixth year is basically a carefully planned internship in teaching. During the second semester of this year the trainee assumes complete responsibility for classwork as nearly as the setting can allow. It is strongly recommended that the trainees work in two different school settings. Trainees are expected to experience the total gamut of a teacher's work, including working with parents and committees of teachers as they plan programs and other essential activities.[15]

The proposed program represents an effort to conceptually design a teacher preparation program from beginning to end based on sound pedagogical principles and research. The time is right for teacher educators to reexamine existing programs which may have been appropriate in

Table 2.2. Program of Studies: Second Semester of the Fifth Year of a Proposed Teacher Preparation Program.

Courses		Semester Hours	Clock Hours Per Week
Curriculum and Instruction		2	2
Curriculum Laboratory (Including Initial Teaching Experience		3	9
	Total	5	11
Concurrent Specialized Courses—Early Childhood Through Middle School			
Pedagogy of Art and Literature		2	2
Pedagogy of Language Arts		2	2
Pedagogy of Mathematics		2	2
Pedogogy of Reading		2	2
Pedogogy of Science		2	2
Pedagogy of Social Science		2	2
	Total	12	12
Concurrent Specialized Courses—Junior and Senior High School			
Pedagogy of Major Subject		2	2
Pedagogy of Minor Subject		2	2
Pedagogy of Secondary Reading		2	2
Electives		6	6
	Total	12	12

Source: Othanel B. Smith, *A Design for a School of Pedagogy*. U.S. Department of Education. Washington, D.C.: U.S. Government Printing Office, 1980.

their time, but now in many instances have become patchwork, give-and-take programs that have drifted away from sound practice. Perhaps the proposed program can help raise teaching to complete professional status accompanied by salaries commensurate with a profession. The consumer public will have to be convinced.

A Look to the Future

Predicting the future of teacher education is a tenuous undertaking at best; nevertheless, some influences can be made based on existing trends. Teacher organizations (AFT and NEA, for example) are likely to continue striving to gain more strength and power at all three levels, local, state, and national. The number of collective bargaining agreements will probably continue to increase, as will the scope of the existing agreements. While in the past many of the benefits gained dealt with teacher welfare, the future is likely to see more agreements giving teachers

more control over the curriculum, in-service training, and teacher evaluation. Teachers' organizations at the state and national levels will continue to support candidates for office and sponsor legislation. The membership of teachers on boards of education has increased fivefold in the last decade. In many states teachers serve on certification boards, having gained that privilege legislatively. They also serve on evaluation teams for the accreditation of teacher education programs. Teachers, in effect, are in control of teacher centers that are federally sponsored. The trend of teachers to gain further control of their profession is likely to continue.

The education of teachers, once almost solely the function of college and university personnel, will be increasingly shared with practicing professionals. Closer relationships between colleges, universities, and public schools will be established. As these relationships strengthen, benefits will accrue to teacher education students,

The use of community resources can enrich and motivate students.

practicing teachers, college and university personnel, and to children and young adults. Teacher education and education in general should benefit as a result.

There is likely to be an increase in teacher-parent contacts and relationships, and perhaps an increasingly important role played by teachers in the community as relationships between schools and communities become more solid.

As the general trend toward individualized instruction intensifies, it is likely that more paraprofessionals, along with more instructional hardware and software, will be used in classrooms. The teacher will become more in the nature of a specialist—managing the learning process, interacting directly with some students and indirectly with others, and also interacting with students' parents in their homes, and in other community facilities.

The level of professionalism will increase. Trends that point toward this include: the increased quality of teacher education in the areas of preservice and in-service, the changing roles of the teacher as mentioned previously, and the increase in teacher/parent interactions.

Point of View

A topic discussed in this chapter was the teacher competency movement, a movement born from basic discontent with the achievement levels of public elementary and secondary schools. As was

Physical activity is an important ingredient in learning.

indicated earlier, the teacher competency movement is controversial; nevertheless, it is upon us and must be dealt with. An article by David S. Seeley offers an approach to the resolution of the issue. In his judgment, teacher accountability is here to stay. "Too many people have awakened to the fact that ignorance is dangerous, and too many of our students are reaching adulthood with dangerously low levels of education. Parents and public will demand—and get—improved pupil performance. The question is not whether there will be more emphasis on pupil accountability in the years to come. The important question is how the issue will be handled."[16] Seeley's essay presents four topics important to the eventual resolution of the teacher accountability issue that are just as relevant, or perhaps more so, than testing for teacher competency.

Reducing the Confrontation Over Teacher Accountability

David S. Seeley

Today thousands of students face denial of diplomas for failure to pass competency examinations. Tomorrow thousands of teachers will be less secure in their jobs because of pressure to make sure that fewer students fail.

This is not a threat but a prediction. The one must follow the other as the night the day. The New York State Board of Regents conducted three hotly debated meetings in a row last spring about its new competency requirements for high school graduation. This fall the

Source: David S. Seeley, "Reducing the Confrontation Over Teacher Accountability," *Phi Delta Kappan,* vol. 61, no. 4, December 1979, pp. 248–251.

Regents took up the issue of teacher competency. There are similar developments across the country.

The link between student accountability and teacher accountability is no doubt what makes many professional educators so fearful about the competency movement. Terry Herndon says that the National Education Association objects to "accountability to standardized tests." Other educators have mounted a campaign against competency testing as if it were a plague. My experience in New York City is that if educators fear that student accountability will lead to staff accountability, their fears are justified. As the public became aware that 7,000 of our high school seniors—15% of the graduating class—had not passed a test of the most basic reading and math skills, questions were bound to be raised. Some asked what these students and their parents have been doing for the past 12 years. But others also ask, and cannot help but ask, What have their *teachers* been doing all this time? What kind of high school courses could these students have been taking with such low academic skills? And finally, why do we have to wait until a student is a senior to find out he cannot read or write? None of these dismal facts is new, but the new diploma requirements are making the public more aware of them. The competency movement may result in pressures for change in our education system more fundamental even than those confronted in the turbulent Sixties. No wonder many in our education establishment are fearful.

But efforts to hold back the movement for improved student performance will not prevail. Too many people have awakened to the fact that ignorance is dangerous, and too many of our students are reaching adulthood with dangerously low levels of education. Parents and public will demand—and get—better pupil performance. They will also demand—and get—improved teacher performance. The question is not whether there will be more emphasis on teacher accountability in the years to come. The important question is how the issue will be handled.

The next few years could bring increasing conflict and recrimination between parents and teachers—and between citizens and professional interests—or we could make up our minds to get the relevant forces together, recognize that we have a problem to solve, and intelligently set about finding ways to improve teacher performance to meet the new demands. I urge that we follow the latter course, for without leadership and foresight both from the profession and from the public, we are headed toward increasing confrontation.

The issue of improved teacher performance is obviously a vast one. I shall discuss briefly four topics that are too often neglected. More important, they are topics that have the potential for creating an alliance between teachers and parents, and between public groups interested in the improvement of education and professional groups interested in protecting professional interests.

The four topics are 1) better recruitment, 2) better school principals, 3) more help for classroom teachers, and 4) sharing the responsibility for education.

Recruitment of teachers into the profession—a factor that may have more to do with the quality of teaching than any other—oddly enough gets almost no attention in the vast literature on improved teaching. We hear much about improved teacher training, both preservice and in-service. We hear about better supervision. We hear about the pros and cons of weeding out those who do not perform well. But how about who gets into the profession to begin with?

We assume that our only job is to pick the best from the pool of candidates who present themselves for appointment. Leaving aside the fact that many school systems do a poor job even on this score, I suggest that the more important question may be whether we are selecting from the right pool. First, we must decide what kind of people we want as teachers. Is a good teacher someone who has taken a certain number of education courses in college? Or someone who gets a certain score on an examination for teachers? I think not. Too many have passed these hurdles who are not good teachers.

We want as teachers people who can help other people learn. Instead, we are getting primarily those who decide to take teacher training courses while they are undergraduates in college. There is discouraging evidence that significant portions of these students are not the most intellectually alive or able. They may not even enjoy teaching; they may be looking for secure civil service careers. Obviously, and mercifully, there are many exceptions. In my home territory of New York City, many marvelous teachers have somehow fought their way through all the Mickey Mouse of education courses, certification, and licensing. They have persisted despite a pathological education bureaucracy interacting with pathogenic social, economic, and political conditions.

But why do we put such barriers in the way? From the first port of entry—the education courses in the colleges—we make public school teaching as uninviting as possible for those with lively and inquiring minds, for those who love ideas and love to share them with others—in short, for those who might make the best teachers.

How can we do a better job of reaching out into our population to find those who are best able to teach? For one thing, we can decide it is an important issue and actively recruit talent into the profession instead of simply reacting to those who present themselves at the end of the teacher training assembly line. Teachers, parents, and the public—all under pressure to produce better results in school—ought to assume a mutual interest in recruiting teaching talent from as broad a pool as possible, both among noneducation majors in college and in the population at large, making clear what kind of people we need as teachers in our school systems and opening paths for them to enter the profession through internships and well-designed college courses, so they can work their way through the licensing hurdles with professional integrity.

More than that, we must provide better working conditions for those who want to make teaching a career. This leads me to my next suggestion for better teachers: namely, better principals.

Some say that good teachers are born, not made. However much that may be true, it is also true that many bad teachers are made, not born. They often come into the profession full of eagerness and capable of becoming good teachers. Within a few years they are cynical, defensive, lazy, and destructive of both education and of children.

Experience tells us that there are some teachers who are so good they'll perform well in any school, and some are so bad they'll bomb no matter where they are. Large numbers of teachers, however, are capable of performing well in schools with a strong sense of their educational mission, high morale, and good supervision; and poorly in schools that are chaotic or poorly led. The difference between the two schools almost invariably lies in the principalship.

Even for those teachers who are bad in any setting, the principal is the key to any remedy, since parents and citizens have little chance of getting rid of such teachers unless the principal is sufficiently committed to the quality of instruction and sufficiently skilled in supervision and personnel management to take remedial action.

Teacher performance and competence is particularly affected by the quality of principals in schools in which teachers get their first experience. Yet these schools often have the worst principals, because they are the schools from which teachers flee as soon as they gain enough seniority, leaving openings behind them to be filled by new recruits.

It is not considered polite to talk about ineffective principals, and it is even less comfortable to talk about what to do about them. But there is no more important topic if our goal is improved teaching. Furthermore, it should be a topic on which parents, teachers, and citizens can unite. Teachers suffer as much as students from ineffective principals. At the very least it should be possible to agree on better ways to select principals and to evaluate their performance during probation so that those who are not effective are not given lifetime tenure.

New York schools Chancellor Frank Macchiarola, during his first month in office, held up the tenure appointments of 79 principals and assistant principals for lack of evidence of adequate performance. This was an unprecedented action for the New York City school system. Yet teachers have said to me (though not in public), "It's about time." Systems such as New York's have been promoting people to principalships for years irrespective of their ability to provide leadership.

Teaching is the heart of education. If a principal cannot help to improve the performance of teaching, there is not much else worth doing. Teachers should have as much interest as students, parents, and citizens in insuring that every school has an effective principal. This becomes increasingly true as the pressure mounts for schools to be educationally effective for all children.

But principals will tell you that their life is not an easy one these days—and they are right. Caught between increasing and conflicting demands of parents, increasing teacher militance, and the insanity of central office bureaucracies, even the most effective principals admit that it is nearly impossible to do a good job—especially in the area we are concerned about: the improvement of teaching. This leads me to my next suggestion.

We must find ways to provide more assistance to classroom teachers. Principals can be expected to improve teaching by setting the right tone in a building, by helping the staff maintain a sense of their educational mission, and by leadership in welding together positive forces and fending off negative ones. But for a variety of reasons principals themselves need help in providing direct assistance to the classroom teachers to improve their instructional performance.

This again is one of the great hidden issues of American education. Talk to principals and superintendents and they will stress how the supervision of teaching is one of their prime functions. Talk to teachers and they will tell you how little help they get.

Teaching is one of the most isolated and unsupported professional functions in our society. Doctors, lawyers, engineers, army officers—almost any profession you can think of provides the opportunity for professional consultation and mutual help in performing professional functions. Teachers, by and large, are left alone in their classrooms to sink or swim—to find professionally effective strategies or to find survival strategies that may kill learning and do untold damage to children.

Teachers need help. But they are afraid to ask for it. And principals are afraid to admit that they cannot provide it.

The National Council for Assistance to Classroom Teachers, a small but dedicated group of educators, has recognized this problem for some years and has been advocating a way to solve it. The council's main suggestion is to provide teachers with professional help that is not part of the official accountability chain. Experienced teaching consultants can apply expertise directly to the problems that a teacher is having, not simply lecture about them. They can help not only with pedagogical technique and curriculum but with relationships between teachers and students, which often turn out to be at the heart of ineffective teaching and learning.

This is particularly useful in urban schools, where many teachers find that a teaching style that might be satisfactory in some schools is ineffective or even destructive in others.

My last suggestion is this: We must accept fully and wholeheartedly that education is a *shared* responsibility between parents, teachers, and students; between home and school; between school systems and communities.

There is an odd thing about this suggestion. On the one hand some people say, "Why, of course, that's what education has always been; that's the way it should be." On the other hand, I have found that some people, both in the profession and among parent and citizen groups, are curiously hostile to the idea.

Regardless of the fact that education "has always been" this way, this does not represent the present state of mind of large numbers of parents, teachers, students, and citizens. Parents and students increasingly blame teachers and schools for poor school performance. Teachers increasingly blame parents and students. Citizens blame teachers, students, or parents—depending on their predisposition. Everyone is blaming everyone else. As long as this attitude prevails, we cannot develop a sense of shared responsibility or loosen the paralysis that immobilizes the forces of school reform.

People have a vested interest in these attitudes. For those in the profession it is comfortable to believe that if students don't learn, the students are to blame.

One of our principals in New York, for instance, in response to the failure of 7,000 seniors to pass a very basic competency test, was quoted as saying, "Some will never learn how to read and write no matter what you do." Another urged the public to abandon its unrealistic expectations that all students can be educated even to levels of minimum competence. Moreover, if one suggests that positive results might be obtained if education were accepted as a shared responsibility, many see this as an invasion of professional turf.

Parents and the public, for their part, have their own reasons for not accepting education as a shared responsibility. It is much easier to think of education as a function that has been delegated to the education bureaucracy, and all that remains to be done if the bureaucracy does not perform is to complain about it.

Parent leaders and school activists fear that if we say education is a shared responsibility we may be letting school systems off the hook. This is the problem that Jesse Jackson's EXCEL program is facing. Because Jackson talks about the importance of student and parent responsibility, people think he is not concerned about teacher and school responsibility. But they are not hearing him. He has said time and again that school systems are not fulfilling their responsibil-ities to students, particularly minority and poor students, but he has also said that they will not fulfill their responsibilities until students and parents become more active in their own education and their children's education. He is not calling for less responsibility from schools but for more responsibility from homes. He surely must be right; yet his critics say that by placing a burden on the home and the student he is undermining efforts to hold schools accountable.

What we have here are some deeply ingrained concepts of education as a service delivery system rather than a shared responsibility of learners and teachers. The professional and parent and community interests all have reasons to preserve these concepts about education. So long as education is something to be delivered by education bureaucracies, the professionals' answer to poor results can be, "Give us more resources and we'll deliver for you." The parents' answer can be, "Those people aren't doing their job."

But education does not work that way. It is not a commodity or a service that can be delivered to people. It is a process of human development—a process that can be helped by professionally skilled practitioners but requires the initiative of those who want to be developed. If learning is what we're looking for, then we must face the fact that students are the prime workers in the enterprise. They must do most of the work to produce learning.

Once we recognize this, we shall realize that students are the most underutilized resource in our schools. The service delivery model has made us think of the teacher as the prime worker. It has made us falsely assume that more work from teachers is the main way to improved productivity in schools. On the contrary, some of the best teachers work less hard than some of the worst, because they have learned how to turn students on and pull them into the enterprise, while ineffective teachers often struggle laboriously to "deliver" education to their students.

We have to change our basic concepts of education so that all participants feel and act upon a more mutually responsible and cooperative philosophy, in which students help each other learn and even help teachers teach, and in which communities and schools work together to accomplish common goals. While there may initially be resistance to adopting such a philosophy, both teachers and parents will find it is far more satisfying to participate in successful schools in which all share in the responsibility for insuring success than in unsuccessful schools in which the only satisfaction the participants have is to blame each other for the failure.

As we now move into a period of increased pressure for schools to perform, we must face the fact that the present concepts do not work, that it will not be possible for schools to produce the levels of successful learning for all students implicit in the minimum competency movement, unless we shift to a more cooperative approach.

The Public Education Association in New York City is advocating such an approach. We announced a "Campaign for Competency" last spring. Its first activity was a tutoring program to help seniors master the basic skills needed to pass the state Basic Competency Test for graduation. Ten major city groups are working with us on this program, including the School Volunteers, the Urban League, the United Parents Association, and NAACP. The school system is cooperating as well. Already 20 of the 100 high schools have requested volunteers, whereas before the campaign only four had done so. We hope to extend the cooperative spirit to the lower grades to insure that, in the future, kids master their basic skills in elementary school as a foundation for greater achievement in high school. This may again sound like one of the tasks that schools were always supposed to do. The fact is, however, that it is so far from what urban schools have actually been doing that achievement of the goal would represent a major change in American education—a "revolution," as Kenneth Clark has called it.

What does all of this effort to develop a sense of shared responsibility for educational achievement have to do with teacher accountability or improved teacher performance? I think it has everything to do with it. As long as we stick with the "service delivery" model, we shall find that the education establishment will close ranks to defend its practices—and will do so successfully in part because its members will be able to convince themselves, if not the public, that failures are the fault of the students, their parents, or the public. If we approach the problem differently, and say first that the job of adequate educational achievement for all *must* be accomplished, and that we *all* have responsibilities for getting it accomplished, then the question of teacher performance becomes one of the factors that we all have to deal with.

I have outlined four areas in which parents, teachers, and communities can work together to improve teacher performance: better teacher recruitment, better principals, assistance to classroom teachers, and a shift to a philosophy of shared responsibility for education.

I offer these suggestions to show that if we put our minds to it we can find areas for constructive action. I also offer them to counter some proposals that are much less likely to be constructive and, indeed, may well be divisive.

One of these is the proposal for state "professional practices boards." This national movement looks like a power grab by teacher organizations under the appealing banner, "Teachers should control their own profession." In view of the growing alienation and disaffection of parents and citizens from public education, in part because they feel that school bureaucracies and unions have already seized too much control, these proposals are misguided. There is hardly a more important and value-laden issue than the question of who will teach our children, and to propose that it should be answered by some organized and unionized professional group is to ask either for trouble or for increased alienation and public apathy.

Another bad idea gaining currency in some states is the proposal to deal with teacher competence through some kind of system for testing teachers. The main problem is that no one has come up with a test that can predict who will make a good teacher—or a good principal, for that matter. No one would be happier than I if one could be found; it would make life much simpler. But at the moment, the most that tests can be expected to do is screen out those whose general educational background is too weak, or those teachers who don't know their subject matter well enough to teach it. Once you get beyond these minimal uses of tests, there is no escape from the need for human judgment followed by very careful monitoring of performance. Since human judgment always risks human error, the greatest care should be taken in selecting those who make the judgments and in providing checks and balances to reduce the risk of favoritism and prejudice. The effort to remove all chance for human error by using mechanical selection systems, however, is doomed only to perpetuate bureaucracy and mediocrity in the public schools.

Proposals such as professional practices boards and teacher selection tests are products of our too-great reliance on the professional establishment to solve its own problems. These are issues of the utmost public concern and interest, and they cannot be left to professional interests alone to decide. Today it may be sufficient in many school systems to staff schools with those who have been labeled "teachers" by some professional certification scheme. Tomorrow it will be necessary to have people who can actually help students—all students—learn. The changeover will require imagination and cooperation among many groups—professional and lay. It is my plea that we get on with this work in as constructive a way as possible—and with some urgency—before confrontations take over as the dominant way of dealing with the issue.

The whole problem will be helped immeasurably if we look at it as one of improving teacher performance rather than emphasizing "teacher accountability" as such. Accountability is but a means to that end,

and by itself, both as a scare word and as a technique, it is often an ineffective means. Accountability as an isolated policy only makes teachers fearful, which is not conducive to good teaching and often increases the least productive bureaucratic controls, since bureaucracies have a tendency to look for uniform measures, while the best teaching does not fit within bureaucratic molds. Improved teacher performance as a goal is more likely to promote constructive change. Teachers as well as parents and the public can agree that it is of benefit to all, and within this more constructive context accountability can be dealt with both more effectively and with less threat.

Questions for Discussion

1. What advantages or disadvantages do you see in prestudent teaching clinical experiences?

2. What advantages or disadvantages do you see in microteaching?

3. Why has training in multicultural education become a requirement for teacher certification in many states?

4. What is the legal basis for teacher certification?

5. What can a prospective teacher include in his or her preparation to enhance employment?

Supplementary Learning Activities

1. Contact the certification officer at your institution or the State Department of Education in your state to learn the certification requirements for various teaching certificates in your state.

2. Visit public school classrooms in different settings, i.e., rural—suburban—urban, to observe similarities and differences.

3. Invite an educational placement official to your class to discuss with you on the subject of teacher employability.

4. Invite a practicing teacher and/or a practicing administrator to your class to present their views on teacher preparation and teacher employability.

5. Study selected college and university catalogs to compare teacher training programs and requirements in different institutions and states.

Notes

1. Robert E. Stoltz, "Teacher Education and Certification: State Actions in the South" (Atlanta, Georgia: Southern Regional Education Board, 1979.), p. 1.

2. Division of Teacher Education and Certification, Kentucky Department of Education, *Kentucky Teacher Preparation and Certification Handbook* (Frankfort, Kentucky: Superintendent of Public Instruction, 1976).

3. J. T. Sandefur, "Competency Assessment in Teacher Education: The State of the Scene of the States." (Unpublished manuscript presented as a speech, November 16, 1980, at a conference in Lexington, Kentucky.)

4. Charles E. Johnson, Chad D. Ellett, and William Capie, *An Introduction to the Teacher Performance Assessment Instruments: Their Uses and Limitations* (Athens, Georgia: College of Education, University of Georgia, 1980).

5. Beatrice M. Gudridge, *Teacher Competency: Problems and Solutions* (Arlington, Virginia: American Association of School Administrators, 1980), pp. 16–17.

6. Ibid.

7. Robert W. Cole, "Minimum Competency Tests for Teachers: Confusion Compounded," *Phi Delta Kappan,* vol. 61, no. 4, December 1979, p. 233.

8. National Council for the Accreditation of Teacher Education, *Standards for Accreditation on Teacher Education* (Washington, D.C.: National Council for the Accreditation of Teacher Education, 1977), p. 4.

9. John Hopkins, *Basic Legal Issues in New York State on Teacher Certification* (Lincoln, Nebraska: Study Commission, 1973), p. 4.

10. Larry Freeman, "State Interest, Certification, and Teacher Education Program Approval," *Legal Issues in Teacher Preparation and Certification* (Washington, D.C.: ERIC Clearinghouse on Teacher Education, Suite 616, One DuPont Circle, N.W. 20036, June 1977), p. 82.

11. Ibid.

12. Ibid.

13. Othanel Smith, *A Design for a School of Pedagogy,* U.S. Department of Education (Washington, D.C.: U.S. Government Printing Office, 1980).

14. Ibid., pp. 31–43.

15. Ibid., pp. 44–45.

16. David S. Seeley, "Reducing the Confrontation Over Teacher Accountability," *Phi Delta Kappan,* vol. 61, no. 4, December 1979, p. 249.

Selected References

Denham, Carolyn, and Lieberman, Ann. *Time to Learn.* U.S. Department of Education. Washington, D.C.: National Institute of Education, 1980.

Gudridge, Beatrice M. *Teacher Competency: Problems and Solutions*. Arlington, Virginia: American Association of School Administrators, 1980.

Howsam, Robert B.; Corrigan, Dean C.; Renemark, George W.; and Nash, Robert J. *Educating a Profession*. Washington, D.C.: American Association of Colleges for Teacher Education, 1976.

Johnson, Charles E.; Ellet, Chad; and Capie, William. *An Introduction to the Teacher Performance Instruments: Their Uses and Limitations*. Athens, Georgia: College of Education, University of Georgia, 1980.

Madaus, George; Airasian, Peter; and Kellaghan, Thomas. *School Effectiveness: A Reassessment of the Evidence*. New York: McGraw-Hill Publishing Company, 1980.

Phi Delta Kappan. Vol. 67, no. 5, January 1981. (An issue devoted to the heritage and future of education.)

Phi Delta Kappan. Vol. 62, no. 2, October 1980. (A special issue devoted to reform in teacher education.)

Rich, John. "A Rationale for the Liberal Education of Educators." *Journal of Teacher Education*. Vol. 31, no. 3, May-June 1980, pp. 27–30.

Robinson, Andrew A., and Morrie, David. "Florida's New Teacher Certification Law." *Phi Delta Kappan*. Vol. 61, no. 4, December 1979, pp. 263–64.

Smith, B. Othanel. *A Design for a School of Pedagogy*. U.S. Department of Education. Washington, D.C.: U.S. Government Printing Office, 1980.

The Teacher's Changing Role

3

This Chapter
- Describes the day-by-day work of the teacher.
- Contrasts the work of the contemporary educator with that of his historical counterpart.
- Illustrates that teachers are better prepared and increasingly competent as professional educators.
- Introduces the concept that the most effective learning takes place when the teacher serves as a "learning facilitator" rather than as a "dispenser of knowledge."

- Articulates the importance of the "planning" that a teacher must do if effective learning is to take place.
- Describes the diagnostic and evaluative functions that an educator must fulfill.
- Discusses the implications of "mainstreaming" for the regular classroom teacher.
- Explores the role of the teacher as a manager of the instructional team.
- Provides a point of view dealing with discipline problems that confront teachers.

A teacher must be willing to make the sacrifice of devoting many long and hard hours of work to the profession. This fact was born out in a recent study completed by the Research Division of the National Education Association in which a large number of teachers were asked how they spend their working week.[1] The average teacher in this study devoted a total of approximately 48 hours per week to her job as a teacher. Of this total time, the teacher spends 29.8 hours actually working with pupils; 6.8 hours performing other duties (such as planning, faculty meetings, clerical work, and preparing teaching materials) during the school day; and 10.8 hours doing school-related work outside of the school day (such as correcting papers, writing reports, scoring tests, preparing lesson plans, and attending professional meetings.) It is obvious that teaching requires many long hours of hard work—and is not a job that would appeal to "clock watchers."

A teacher wears many hats in the course of a school day, a school week, and a school year. For example, each must be a lesson planner, purveyor of knowledge, motivator, disciplinarian, counselor, confidant, mediator, curriculum planner, worker for a professional teacher's organization, human relations expert, and record keeper. Truly, a teacher must have a multitude of talents and be competent in many different roles in order to be successful. In this chapter we will examine some of the more specific tasks included in the role of the teacher.

Attending to Classroom Details

One of the tasks that has historically consumed much of a teacher's time is that traditionally called *keeping school*. School-keeping involves such "chores" as ordering supplies, keeping the classroom tidy and clean (even though most schools now hire competent custodians to do all the major cleaning, a teacher still has a good deal of minor housecleaning chores to perform), keeping attendance records, checking books in and out, collecting lunch money, putting up bulletin boards and displays of various sorts, and filling out forms and reports that the school may require. While school-keeping chores such as these are important and must be done, they have historically consumed too much of a teacher's valuable time—time better spent working with students. Fortunately, in recent years schools have found ways to relieve the teacher of many of these chores. Many schools have developed simplified methods of record keeping that require very little time on the part of the teachers. Also, some schools now employ "paraprofessional" help to do these school-keeping chores, thereby freeing the teacher for spending more time working with students.

Designing Learning Experiences

One of the most important roles that a teacher plays is that of "planner." A teacher is given a great deal of freedom and autonomy in planning what will take place in the classroom. This is as it should be, because today's teacher is a highly trained, competent professional who is the best qualified to determine what each student needs in the classroom. In some instances, a teacher will be given a broad planning document such as a curriculum guide that may originate at the state, county, or school district level. Such documents, however, are only general guidelines, and each individual teacher must still plan the specific day-to-day program. An increasing amount of the planning task is being done cooperatively

Today's teacher devotes many hours to the preparation of teaching materials.

One must learn by doing the thing; for though you think you know it you have no certainty, until you try.

Sophocles

by groups of teachers in conjunction with team teaching, or in summer efforts to prepare various types of units and other curricular materials. More and more, school districts are realizing the value that can accrue from hiring teachers during the summer to do such cooperative planning.

The success of a school program for a given student will be dependent, in large measure, upon the quality of planning that went into that student's program. By the same token, the success of the educational program of an entire school system will be determined by the planning that goes into that program. The same thing is true, incidentally, for the entire American educational system—its success is largely dependent upon the quality of the planning that goes into it.

There are a number of different levels of planning that a teacher must do. These levels are shown in figure 3.1, wherein a teacher begins with a very general long-range yearly lesson plan for each subject taught. This yearly lesson plan must be very flexible so that changes can be made in the plan during the year as the need arises. Figure 3.1 also shows that a teacher must make semester plans as well (or quarter plans, depending upon how the school year may be divided). Like the yearly plan, these semester plans must be very general and very flexible. One of the many values of long-range plans (such as those a teacher makes for an entire school year or for a semester) is that they permit the teacher to gather more and better instructional materials (some of which may be difficult to obtain) by the time they are needed. Long-range planning also permits teach-

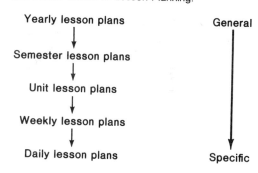

Figure 3.1. Levels of Lesson Planning.

Yearly lesson plans   General

Semester lesson plans

Unit lesson plans

Weekly lesson plans

Daily lesson plans   Specific

ers to think through what they really want the students to learn over a long period of time.

Perhaps the single most important and valuable type of planning that a teacher does is what is commonly known as the unit lesson plan. The unit plan is one that is done for a rather discrete segment of the year's work in a given subject. Units can vary greatly in size; however, most of them range between a week and a month in length. Units can also vary greatly in scope, depending upon the grade level and subject. Examples of typical units are: finger painting in first grade art, the American Indian in third grade social studies, poetry in fifth grade English, the digestive system in seventh grade science, squares and square roots in tenth grade mathematics, forms of mental illness in twelfth grade psychology, or the role of the teacher in a college introduction to teaching course.

The Teacher's Changing Role   53

Instructional planning is done increasingly by teams of teachers.

Libraries and learning centers contain many important resources for learning.

A unit may be defined as an organization of learning activities and experiences around a central theme developed cooperatively by a group of pupils under a teacher's leadership. The essential features implied by this definition are that (1) learning takes place through many types of experiences rather than through a single activity such as reading and reciting; (2) the activities are unified around a central theme, problem, or purpose; (3) the unit provides opportunities for socialization of pupils by means of cooperative group planning; and (4) the role of the teacher is that of leader rather than that of taskmaster.

There are a variety of different approaches that a teacher can take in planning a unit. For instance, a teacher can plan what is essentially a "subject matter unit." A subject matter unit is a selection of subject matter materials, and of educative experiences centering upon subject matter materials, which are arranged around a central core found within the subject matter itself. The core may be a generalization, a concept, a topic, or a theme. The unit is to be studied by pupils for the purpose of achieving learning outcomes derivable from experiences with subject matter.

A teacher may also plan what is essentially an "experience unit." This is a series of educative experiences organized around a pupil purpose, problem, or need, utilizing socially useful subject matter and materials, resulting in the achievement of the purpose, and in the achievement of learning outcomes inherent in the process.

In actuality all units use both experience and subject matter. The difference is primarily one of emphasis. It should be understood that in actual practice the terminology used is not the important consideration. What is important is that the teacher must be concerned with providing rich and varied learning experiences for each student.

Yet a third type of unit plan is that commonly referred to as a "resource unit," which is not ordinarily planned as a single teaching unit. It is usually developed by a committee of teachers with little or no pupil assistance. Hence it becomes a "resource *of* units." Frequently they are not developed with any particular group of children in mind; in fact, the materials may be used in several grades; they cover broad areas of content, and always contain more information and many more suggestions than could be used with any one class. A resource unit on conservation might include materials to be used in teaching several units on recreation, public health, lumbering, fishing, mining, and flood control.

In preparing a unit plan, it is recommended that a teacher:

a. State clearly the purposes (*objectives* or *goals*, as they are often called) of teaching the unit. In other words, what changes does the teacher want to make in the child in terms of knowledge, skills, habits, attitudes, and appreciations? These stated purposes of the unit should be expressed in "behavioral" terms, or, in other words, in terms of student behavior that will be exhibited when the purposes of the unit have been accomplished. When stated this way, a teacher can measure the success of the unit.

b. Look up references on the subject, read them, and write a content outline of the material, listing references.

c. List the materials to be used in the unit. This will include such items as pictures, slides, movies, models, and construction materials.

d. List the ways in which the teacher will lead the children into the unit of work; these are called *possible approaches.*

e. List the activities that will help the children attain the purposes or outcomes of the unit.

f. List the means by which the teacher will evaluate the unit. If a written test is considered, at least a rough draft of the test should be included in the unit.

Many schools ask teachers to make very brief weekly lesson plans so that in the event a regular teacher becomes ill, a substitute teacher would have an idea of what was planned each day for each class. These weekly lesson plans are usually extremely brief—frequently written on special forms prepared for this purpose.

A teacher's most specific planning is that done for a specific lesson on a given day. Daily lesson planning is relatively simple, providing the teacher has already made adequate unit lesson plans. Excellent unit plans will have permitted the teacher to gather all of the necessary learning resources ahead of time and to have clearly thought through the general objectives for the

unit. The final detail and specific objectives necessary in a daily lesson plan flow naturally and quite easily out of a well-done unit lesson plan. The lesson plan is designed simply as a means to good instruction. It has no magic value in and of itself, and cannot be justified as an elaborate masterpiece. The lesson plan is simply a means to an end—a device to help the teacher be well prepared to teach.

Lesson plans may take numerous forms. There is no one best way to prepare lesson plans; however, most teachers find it desirable to follow some structured format and to do much of this planning on paper. One lesson plan format that has been found useful by many educators is that found in table 3.1. This format can serve for all the levels of planning that a teacher must do, whether they be yearly plans, semester plans, unit plans, weekly plans, or daily plans. As the table shows, the first task that a teacher has in planning is to determine the plan's objectives. Objectives become the road map of the lesson—they indicate the purposes of the lesson and the desired learning outcomes for the students. As has already been suggested, educational objectives should always be stated in terms of student behavior that can be measured. This is necessary so that after the lesson is completed, the teacher can determine whether or not each student has achieved the desired outcomes. Objectives thus stated are frequently called *behavioral objectives.*

The table also shows that in planning a lesson, a teacher must determine what materials will be needed for that lesson. As will be indicated in chapter 14, a wealth of instruction materials is now available to educators. A teacher must be familiar with these teaching materials, and must also know which is the most effective material to use in a given situation.

Table 3.1 further indicates that teachers must thoroughly plan the procedure for each lesson. To effectively do this, they must have a thorough understanding of the nature of the learner—a topic discussed in chapter 12. They must also be familiar with a wide variety of teaching techniques.

Lastly, the table shows that a teacher must make provisions for measuring the extent to which the stated objectives for each lesson are achieved. This provides the teacher with a measure of the overall success of the lesson, and also helps in determining which students have learned the contents of the lesson, and which students need additional instruction.

One last important point concerning the planning role of a teacher deals with the need to individualize the learning experiences for each student insofar as it is humanly possible to do so. Unfortunately, since a typical elementary school teacher has between 20 and 30 students, and a typical secondary teacher may have as many as 150 students each day, it is just not possible for a teacher to make a specific lesson plan for each student. At best, a teacher can hope to modify a single lesson plan to fit the individual needs of each specific student. There is an indication that some of the newer innovations in education, such as individually prescribed instruction, modular

Table 3.1. A Suggested Lesson Plan Format.

A. Objectives (Stated in Behavioral Terms That Can Be Measured):
B. Materials Needed:
C. Procedure:
    1. Teacher Activity
    2. Student Activity
D. Provisions for Measuring Extent to Which Stated Objectives Were Achieved:

scheduling, computer-assisted instruction, independent study, team teaching, and a differentiated teaching staff—all of which are discussed in some detail elsewhere in this book—will make it possible for teachers to do a much better job of tailoring an educational program for each individual student.

Helping Students to Learn

Historically, the role of the teacher has been viewed mainly as that of a "dispenser of knowledge." Today's teacher can better be characterized as one who "helps students to learn." This new "helping" role of the contemporary teacher is exemplified by a teacher assisting a group of students as they plan a small group project; circulating in a science laboratory giving help to individual students; listening to an individual student who has a reading problem read aloud; or counseling with a student who has a personal problem. The following factors have helped to bring about this new relationship that the teacher has with the student:

- Whereas colonial school teachers had very few tools to use, except a few poorly written textbooks and their own knowledge of the subject matter they were attempting to teach, contemporary educators have a wealth of teaching aids at their disposal. These instructional devices now make it possible for teachers to help students learn much more efficiently and effectively than was possible when teachers had to "dispense" whatever knowledge the students were to learn.

- An increased understanding of the learning process has also helped educators to assume their present "helping" relationship with students. Since the turn of the century, thanks to the pioneering efforts of the child study movement, and the continued refinement of the discipline of educational psychology, an ever-increasing knowledge of the manner in which learning takes place has been made available to teachers. One of the tasks of teachers is to mold this knowledge of the learning act into excellent learning experiences for each of their students. The colonial schoolteachers had very little knowledge of the learning act at their disposal, and consequently cannot be blamed for their ignorance of the fact that students tend to quickly forget rotely-memorized facts, learn best from firsthand experiences rather than being lectured to, and learn more quickly and

permanently that which they are highly motivated to learn—all of which are examples of important principles of learning that have grown from an increased understanding of those learning processes that guide the work of contemporary educators.

- Another factor that has contributed to the view that teachers should help students learn rather than dispense knowledge has been the changes that have taken place in educational philosophy down through the ages. There was a time, for instance, when children were viewed by the church, most parents, and most teachers to be basically bad and full of original sin which somehow must be beaten from them. And "beat," literally, many schoolteachers did, in their misguided efforts to teach and discipline their students. Fortunately, most contemporary educators agree with Jean Jacques Rousseau (1712–78)—the great French philosopher who deserves at least part of the credit for bringing about this change in the way the young are viewed—that children are born basically good and become bad only in the hands of man. This change in the philosophical view of the nature of a child has had a profound influence on the relationship between teacher and student.

- Another change that has contributed to the idea that teachers should help children learn rather than dispense knowledge has been the gradual infusion and acceptance of the concept of democracy into many education philosophies. Most American educators strongly believe that the relationship between a teacher and students should be a democratic one; that is, one in

Not all learning experiences are provided by books. Various activities used in conjunction with traditional teaching methods make for well-rounded students.

Historically, students have generally been treated badly in schools. A variety of frightening and ingenious punishments have been devised by teachers in the past. This illustration of a German school during the late nineteenth century shows examples of punishment then employed. These included the hanging of various marks of disapproval around the offender's neck, wearing of a dunce cap, hanging of a boy in a basket to the ceiling, tying a boy to a stationary ring, and frequent whippings.

Many excellent learning aids are available for teacher and student use.

which students have a voice and are respected as individuals. Students who participate in such a classroom are likely to enjoy school more, learn more, and become better citizens in our democratic society.

Working with the Mainstreamed Student

As was pointed out early in this book, there has been a recent movement to put the special education student back into the regular classroom. This concept has become known as *mainstream-ing*. This movement has placed another set of demands on the regular classroom teacher. The teacher must now be able to work effectively with students who have a wide range of physical, mental, and emotional handicaps. For instance, it is now quite possible for a teacher to have a class that not only includes the usual range of individual differences found among so-called "normal" students, but also a blind or partially sighted child, a deaf or hard-of-hearing child, a physically handicapped child, a mentally retarded child, an emotionally disturbed child and/or a child with some type of learning disability. Teachers must develop new diagnostic skills so

A contemporary teacher's role can best be described as helping students to learn.

they can identify the particular learning problems these students have. Teachers must also develop a wider range of teaching skills and strategies to provide for the unique needs of the mainstreamed exceptional student. In fact, given the recent advances in the field of special education, it is a considerable challenge for the classroom teacher to simply become familiar with the terminology now used in special education circles. Terms such as Public Law 94–142, dyslexia, orthopedically handicapped, psychomotor dysfunction, neurological impairment, hyperkinetic behavior—to name a few—become important to teachers who have mainstreamed children in their classrooms.

Much controversy surrounds the mainstreaming movement. A growing number of overburdened teachers feel that it is simply impossible to do a good job with handicapped students who are mainstreamed in their classes. This viewpoint is typified by Jeanne Latcham, a counselor in the Detroit School System, who says:

Mainstreaming is ludicrous. We have children whose needs are complicated: a child in the third grade who has already been in 16 schools, children who need love and attention and disrupt the classroom to get it. Ten percent of the students in Detroit's classrooms can't conform and can't learn. These children need a disproportionate amount of the teacher's time. It's a teacher's nightmare—she can't help them, but she never forgets them.[2]

Providing Multicultural Education

Teachers have recently been given yet another
responsibility by society; that of providing multicultural education. As our society has become
more complex, and as the concept of cultural
pluralism has gained in popularity, our schools
have been asked to add this area to an already
crowded curriculum. The goal of this movement
is to help children become aware and more accepting of cultural differences in the United
States and, in fact, throughout the world. Surely,
one cannot disagree with the desirability of this
goal; however, many educators feel that given
their present class size and work load, they are
not able to do justice to this assignment.

Assessing Learning Outcomes

In addition to school keeping, planning, and helping students to learn, a teacher must also be an
evaluator. For it is through a well-planned program of evaluation that a teacher is able to determine the abilities and achievements of each
student. This knowledge is essential for the
teacher to plan an appropriate program for each
student. In his role as an "evaluator" the teacher
is continually assessing each student's abilities,
interests, accomplishments, and needs. To help
him gather data to accomplish evaluation, an educator employs standardized tests, teacher-made
tests, and subjective observations.

Students learn best from firsthand experiences.

Audiovisual aids serve as a means of heightening student interest in each other, as well as the subject matter under study.

A standardized test is one that has been constructed with the employment of carefully prescribed techniques; and one for which norms have been established. There are literally hundreds of commercially prepared standardized tests available for teacher use to measure different dimensions of student aptitude, achievement, and interest. Most school districts now have rather well developed standardized testing programs that supply teachers with a wide variety of data to use in their role as evaluator.

Recently, the use of standardized tests has received a good deal of attention and debate. Millions of dollars are spent each year on these tests, and many increasingly question not only their value, but also their validity. Some of the specific questions now being debated are:

1. Should standardized tests be used to measure student achievement?
2. Would a moratorium on standardized testing serve a useful purpose?
3. Are standardized tests inherently "racist" in design?

4. How can tests be used to promote learning?
5. What kind of tests should be used to guide college admissions?
6. Do criticisms of mental tests reflect flaws or abuses?
7. Can standardized test scores contribute to the individualization of instruction?
8. To what extent are tests themselves responsible for the lower scores that minorities tend to make on them?[3]

Teacher-made tests, as the name implies, are those which teachers themselves construct. These tests are usually designed to measure student achievement in the various subjects. Constructing good teacher-made tests is a time-consuming task, and requires a thorough knowledge of the principles of test construction on the part of the teacher.

In addition to the data obtained from standardized tests and teacher-made tests, a teacher can obtain useful evaluation information by simply observing students. The skilled educator can

Figure 3.2. A Sample Cumulative Record.

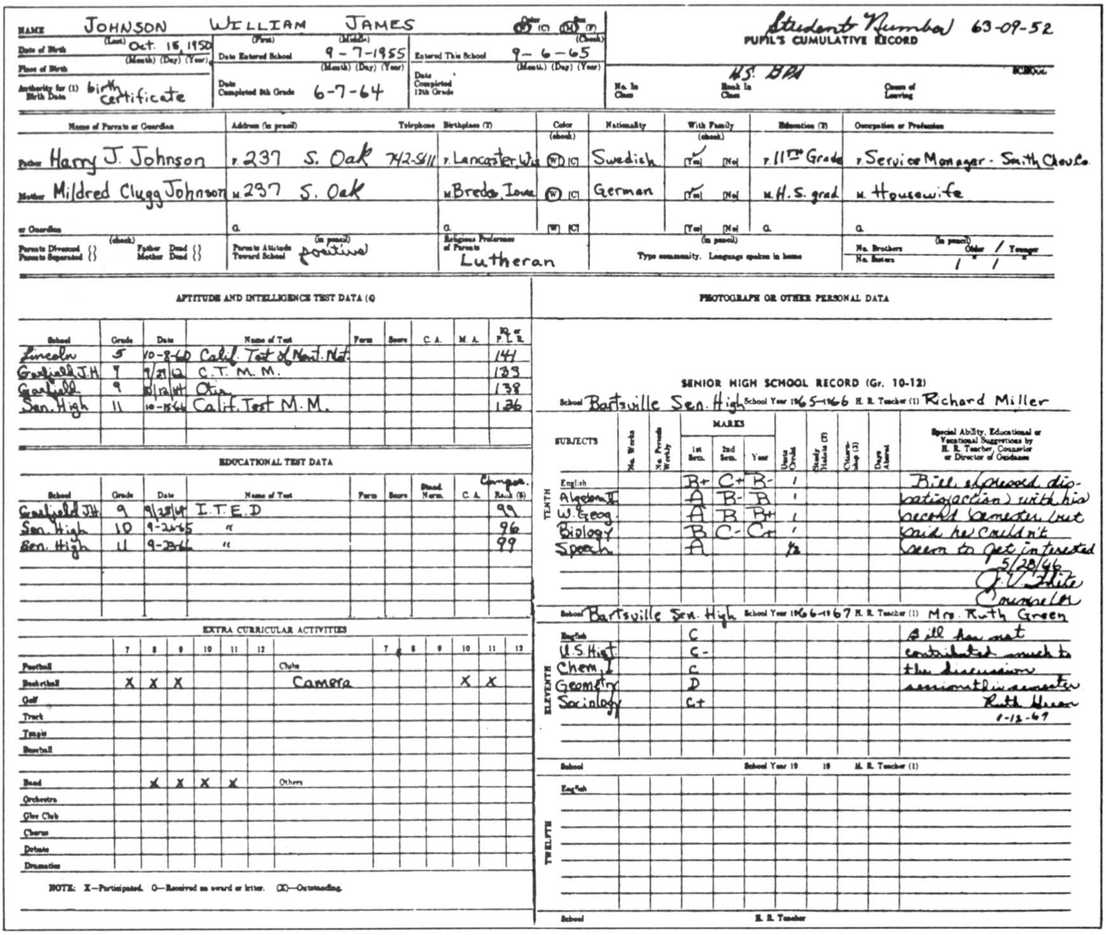

learn a good deal about a student's abilities, achievements, interests, and needs through careful observation.

A record of the evaluative data accumulated on each student is usually kept by a school district. It becomes part of a so-called *cumulative record,* and contains standardized test scores, grades, health information, and other background information about the student. A sample cumulative record card for a pupil is shown in figure 3.2.

Providing Feedback to Pupils and Parents

A role of the teacher that is closely connected with evaluating is that of "reporting," which basically involves making known to the parents their child's progress in school. This is usually accomplished in two ways: in writing, on one of the many different forms that have been created by schools for this purpose, and in person, during a conference.

There is a large variety of forms used by various schools in their efforts to report to parents. In fact, most schools create their own report card forms. An example of such a form is shown in figure 3.3.

Figure 3.3. A Sample Report Card.

STUDENT *Sue Stone*   ENGLISH *III*

ADVISOR *Mrs. Anderson*   TEACHER *Mrs. Anderson*

EVALUATION

	Quarters	Superior	Above average	School average	Below average	Decidedly below average
EFFORT	1				✓	
	2				✓	
	3					✓
	4					✓
ACHIEVEMENT	1	✓				
	2	✓				
	3			✓		
	4			✓		

ANALYSIS OF EVALUATION

		Strength				Weakness			
QUARTERS		1	2	3	4	1	2	3	4
Conduct						✓	✓	✓	✓
Work habits in class						✓	✓	✓	✓
Homework						✓	✓	✓	✓
Skills						✓	✓	✓	✓
Oral activities									
Reading		✓	✓						
Written work		✓	✓						
Content		✓	✓						
Mechanics		✓	✓						
Punctuation		✓	✓	✓					
Grammar		✓	✓						
Spelling		✓	✓						
Penmanship		✓	✓	✓	✓				

The role of "reporter" requires that a teacher possess not only a thorough knowledge of the progress of each student, but also the communication and human relations skills necessary to effectively pass this information along to parents.

Managing the Instructional Team

A relatively new teacher role emergent in many schools has to do with the managing of a larger group of people who, in one way or another, contribute to the instruction program, and may be thought of as members of the "instructional team." Such people include peer student aides, parent volunteer workers, a range of different types of paid paraprofessionals, teacher education students engaged in some type of early clinical experience, student teachers, interns, and junior members of team teaching. In fact, in a real sense other professionals in the school, such as learning center directors, reading specialists, librarians, audiovisual specialists, and even guidance counselors and administrators are at times

School administrators and supervisors are important members of the instructional team.

members of the instructional team, and must be "managed" by the classroom teacher.

The extent to which such persons become involved in the instructional team varies considerably from school to school. Unfortunately, in many schools regular classroom teachers work completely by themselves, and so each is the "only" member of the instructional team. Increasingly, however, many schools are effectively adding a variety of people to the instructional team. Some schools have even developed rather elaborate differentiated staffing systems that include a wide variety of people with different roles on the instructional team. This practice seems likely to increase, conceivably to that point at which nearly all teachers will require the skills needed to manage a larger group of individuals who assist with the instructional program.

Understanding and Getting Along with People

One of the most important general tasks common to all teachers is that of understanding and getting along with the many different people with which each must deal. The teacher must possess good human relations skills and, in a sense, must be a public relations expert. The one who is not able to successfully fulfill this role is destined to failure.

There are many different groups of people with whom the teacher must relate. Obviously, the group that the teacher spends the most time with is the students. It may seem redundant to suggest that a teacher must be able to understand and get along with students; however, there are a number of teachers who do have difficulty in these areas. For instance, the teacher who continually has classroom discipline problems quite likely does not understand students and obviously can't get along very well with them.

Parents constitute another group which a teacher must understand and get along with. Most parents are extremely interested in, and in many instances rather emotional about, their child's progress in school. Furthermore, it is difficult for many parents to be objective about their child's success and/or behavior in school. It requires a good deal of understanding and human relations skill on the part of the teacher, for instance, to tell a mother and father that their child has been behaving badly, and/or is not achieving academically.

Lastly, a teacher must understand and get along with fellow teachers, supervisors, and administrators—colleagues all. This is more true today than it has ever been before due to the fact that education is now a very complex undertaking and teachers often work in teams, do joint planning, have the help of specialists and paraprofessionals, and generally work more closely together than has traditionally been the case (the one-room country school teacher had no colleagues). Some teachers understand and get along with students but find it difficult to relate to their colleagues. The teacher in this situation is doomed to failure just as surely as the one who cannot relate to students.

In order to understand people, teachers must develop insight into human motivations, needs, fears, hopes, weaknesses, prejudices, and desires. Teachers' ability to get along with people is largely dependent upon their own personality, attitudes, and values, as well as the extent to which each basically likes and respects people in spite of the fact that they may be different and may possess weaknesses. Individuals who are considering entering the teaching profession should carefully assess their human relations skills and decide whether or not their personality, attitudes, and values are such as to enable them to get along effectively with the many people with whom they will have to deal as teachers.

A teacher must possess good human relations skills in order to develop the type of relationship with students that is essential for creating good learning experiences.

Becoming a Self-renewing Professional

American education, both the task and the teacher, are rapidly changing. Teachers must not only keep pace with these changes, but must actually bring some of them about through devising improved teaching methods, developing educational innovations, and helping to expand the body of knowledge within their disciplines. This means that teachers must keep up to date on all aspects of their work—advances in knowledge in the subject matter, improved teaching techniques (including discovering some of one's own), changes in our social system, changes in our youth, and changes on the national and international political scene. Then too, teachers must keep up on research findings in education and put into practice those findings that are of use in their own particular work. In fact, teachers, in order to be most effective, must become students of teaching, constantly studying and experimenting with learning, and constantly improving their work as educators.

This means that a teacher must spend a good deal of time reading professional literature; must attend professional conventions, conferences, and workshops; take an active part in in-service training programs; go back to a college or university and take graduate courses, and possibly work on an advanced degree; and, in general, seek out ways of keeping up to date. The recent "teacher-center" movement initiated by the federal government and strongly supported by national teacher associations represents one innovative attempt to help teachers become self-renewing professionals.

Teachers must be self-renewing professionals.

The Teacher of the Future

The college student who is currently enrolled in a teacher education program will probably still be teaching in the year 2010. This fact makes it tempting to speculate about what a teacher's job might be like during the early part of the twenty-first century. It seems relatively safe to predict that the teacher's role will become more complex and, in a sense, more demanding. If one believes that society itself will continue to become more complex, and that the rate of change will continue to accelerate in our society, then it seems logical to believe that our schools and the role of the teacher will likewise become more complex.

It also seems likely that the "knowledge explosion" will continue and probably even accelerate into the next century. This will mean that schools and teachers will have even more content to teach than is now the case. Parenthetically, it is interesting to note that contemporary teachers claim they cannot possibly teach all the material that should be taught now.

Contemporary educators have found it necessary to participate in graduate training at colleges and universities throughout the country.

Back to the present: the role of the contemporary teacher is already a many-faceted one. This chapter has mentioned but a few of the major tasks that a successful teacher must be capable of performing. Perhaps the most important concept presented in this chapter is the fact that today's teacher is no longer merely a dispenser of knowledge, but rather helps arrange learning experiences for the student—in a real sense being a co-learner with the students. Students learn—teachers assist them.

The role of the teacher outlined in this chapter is very complex. It has been suggested that the successful teacher must be extremely dedicated, willing to work long and hard hours, and be a bit of a custodian. On top of that, a teacher must be dedicated to helping students, able to wisely plan a learning program for each student, and be able to motivate each student. The teacher must furthermore be capable of assessing student

The Teacher's Changing Role   69

An excellent teacher is the essential ingredient in
excellent education.

progress and designing remedial learning experiences where required. The teacher must be a
"human relations expert" capable of understanding, communicating with, and getting along well
with a wide variety of people—students, parents,
voters, colleagues, administrators, etc. Above all,
teachers must keep up with the knowledge explosion, and constantly improve their teaching
skills, and, in a sense, be continuing "students of
teaching."

Point of View

Discipline continues to be one of the major problems confronting teachers. The following selection by Dean Tjosvold represents an unusual and
intriguing "point of view" on this complex problem.

Control, Conflict, and Collaboration
in the Classroom

Dean Tjosvold

To many observers of schools, educators have appeared
preoccupied, even obsessed, with the control of students.[1] Principals warn and advise beginning teachers
on how to establish discipline in their classrooms. As
teachers gain experience in schools, they are likely to
become more committed to student control.[2] Teachers
who demand more autonomy from principals in the

Source: Dean Tjosvold, "Control, Conflict, and
Collaboration in the Classroom," *Educational Forum*, Vol.
44, No. 2, January 1980, pp. 195–203.

1. C. W. Gordon, *The Social System of the High School* (Glencoe,
Ill.: The Free Press, 1957); W. W. Waller, *The Sociology of
Teaching* (New York: Wiley, 1932); D. J. Willower and R. G.
Jones, "Control in an Educational Organization," in *Studying
Teaching*, ed. J. D. Raths (Englewood Cliffs, N.J.: Prentice Hall,
1967).
2. Wayne K. Hoy, "The Influence of Experience on the Beginning
Teacher," *School Review* 76 (1968):312–23; Wayne K. Hoy,
"Pupil-Control Ideology and Organization Socialization: A Further
Examination of the Influence of Experience on the Beginning
Teacher," *School Review* 77 (1969):257–65.

areas of curriculum and teaching methods may demand more support from them in matters of discipline.[3] Teacher trainees appear to be so concerned with student control, they neglect to observe that teachers understand and inspire students as well as control them.[4]

Educational practitioners have frequently complained that research is largely irrelevant to their concerns about discipline. A few researchers have responded directly to these concerns by trying to isolate effective disciplinary techniques, but these efforts have not been successful. Kouin and his associates,[5] for example, were unable to identify "desist" influence attempts that were reliably associated with maintaining discipline. Even efforts to identify consistently effective teacher management skills have not been fruitful.[6] Teacher skills found to be related to student involvement in learning are: (a) alertness to events in the classroom in order to respond appropriately to misbehavior, (b) ability to attend to and consider two or more events simultaneously, and (c) smooth pacing of activities so that interruptions and confusions are avoided. These findings only confirm what most teachers are already painfully aware of: they must be both skillful and tireless if they are to keep students actively learning.

These unfruitful research efforts raise doubts about the concept of discipline itself. Discipline, though widely used, lacks clear meaning. It can be defined as preventing misbehavior or inappropriate behavior. Yet behavior appropriate for one person is not for another; behavior appropriate in one situation is inappropriate in another. For example, some teachers encourage student discussions; others consider them misconduct. To determine how to establish discipline is also difficult because there are many kinds of influence attempts that can be used to prevent or to stop inappropriate behavior. These methods include praise, reasoning, commands, threats, persuasion, and promises, which can be combined in many ways, conveyed with varying degrees of intensity, and accompanied by different nonverbal messages. The effectiveness of any of these methods in turn depends on other factors: the teacher-student relationship, the teacher's characteristics, and the student's personality. A theory of establishing discipline that is empirically supported and therefore one in which educators can be confident works may be most difficult to construct.

The concept of discipline appears to be too global and imprecise to be used as a basis for useful research. There is, of course, research that is relevant to the broad domain of discipline. Hamachek has suggested that research in classroom social climates, leadership, group cohesion, and norms has implications for classroom management.[7] Johnson and Johnson have argued that appropriate use of cooperation, competition, and individualization can minimize inappropriate behavior and induce students to become involved in learning activities.[8]

The major focus of this article is to explore the concern of educators with discipline and their commitment to the control of students. In particular, this article explores the effects of educators' control orientation toward students on the learning of students

3. D. E. Edgar and R. Warren, "Power and Autonomy in Teachers," *Sociology of Education* 42 (1969):386–99.

4. P. F. Kleine and P. Pereira, "Limits of Perception: What Teacher Trainees See and Don't See in Classrooms," *School Review* 78 (1970):483–97.

5. Jacob S. Kouin, Paul V. Gump, and James J. Ryan, "Explorations in Classroom Management," *Journal of Teacher Education* 12 (1961):235–46.

6. Jacob S. Kouin, *Discipline and Group Management in Classrooms* (New York: Holt, Rinehart & Winston, 1970).

7. Donald Hamachek, *Behavior Dynamics in Teaching, Learning, and Growth* (Boston: Allyn and Bacon, 1975).

8. David W. Johnson and Roger T. Johnson, "Instructional Goal Structures: Cooperative, Competitive, or Individualistic," *Review of Educational Research* 44 (1974):213–40.

and on the social processes of schools. It argues several points:

1. Educators as a group are preoccupied with the control of students, in part because of organizational requirements, professional values, and the predominance of certain personality characteristics among educators.
2. The control orientation of schools limits the learning of students, especially their learning independence and self-direction.
3. The control orientation impairs the social processes of schools, especially the capacity to identify, resolve, and use conflicts constructively.
4. Teachers often are committed to control because they believe a "free" or *laissez faire* orientation is the only alternative. Collaborative orientation in which students and educators share decision making responsibilities and are mutually responsive is a feasible and effective alternative to a control or *laissez faire* approach.

Educational research supplemented by other relevant research is used as a basis for these propositions. While there is empirical support for these positions, future research is needed to examine and modify them.

As defined here, discipline is established when educators control the behavior of students to a desired pattern. A control or discipline orientation sanctions the educators' right and obligation to unilateral control. A collaborative orientation sanctions educators' attempts to influence and to be influenced by the students as the educators and the students join in making many classroom decisions. A *laissez faire* orientation sanctions the refraining of attempts to influence or control students. Influence refers to attempts to induce another person to perform a desired behavior; actual control occurs when the person performs as desired.

Control Orientation

Observers and researchers have concluded that schools place great emphasis on controlling students. Student teachers and beginning teachers appear to relinquish collaborative values acquired during college in favor of control beliefs.[9] Indeed, adopting a control orientation toward students appears to be a major outcome of professional socialization and may be needed to gain the acceptance of colleagues.

The question remains why many educators are control oriented. According to Willower,[10] educators are control oriented as the aftermath of the organizational requirements of schools: the number of students in comparison to educators, the involuntary membership of students and their possible lack of commitment to school goals and procedures, and the pervasiveness of daily routines. Moreover, educators ultimately believe that the behavior of students must be controlled to aid learning. Exerting control over students unilaterally may also be a way of reducing the demands placed on educators and of helping maintain their psychological well-being.

General professional norms may also strengthen the control orientation of educators. Argyris and Schon have found that control is a central governing value of educators and other professionals.[11] Doctors, for example, have traditionally attempted to control (often unsuccessfully) the behavior of their patients.[12] Powerlessness, dogmatism, and a low level of creativity and self-actualization and other personality characteristics

9. Hoy, "Influence of Experience"; Hoy, "Organization Socialization."
10. Donald J. Willower, "Some Comments on Inquiries on Schools and Pupil Control," *Teachers College Record* 77 (1975):219–30.
11. Chris Argyris and Donald A. Schon, *Theory in Practice: Increasing Professional Effectiveness* (San Francisco: Jossey-Bass, 1974).
12. B. M. Korsch and V. F. Negrette, "Doctor-Patient Communication," *Scientific American* 227 (1972):66–74.

are associated with control orientation.[13] Certain personal needs and styles may then increase educators' commitment to the control of students.

Directive Teaching. Teachers have been found to act consistently with their control beliefs.[14] Observation studies have tried to document the consequences of controlled, directive teaching on classroom social processes and student learning.[15] For example, Flanders classified teaching communication into direct (control) and indirect (collaborative) influence attempts.[16] Direct influence (e.g., lectures, commands) is believed to restrict student freedom of action; indirect influence (e.g., accepts feelings, asks questions) increases student freedom of action. These researchers have proposed that control influence attempts convey nonsupport of the learners and in turn generate negative feelings in the classroom and restrict growth. Consistent with this idea, much of this research has found that teachers who are directive have students who do not initiate, achieve poorly, and dislike school, unlike students whose teachers are collaborative.

Methodological shortcomings (e.g., correlational findings, inconsistent results) of this research make supporting experimental evidence for its conclusions important. Experimental research by social psychologists supports the theory of directive teaching. Control influence attempts have been found to generate resentment and deteriorate the relationship between the influencer and the influenced. Reactance[17] and personal causation[18] theories suggest that persons want to be the cause or the origin of their own behavior and resent attempts by others to control them. Consistent with these ideas, research on influence strategies indicate that persons resist control influence attempts. Persons have, for example, been found to defy threats and to counterthreaten if possible, perhaps because they experienced these as restrictions on free choice.[19] Persons refused to comply with a control influence attempt, though resistance was costly, when they believed that the influencer intended to control them.[20] Moreover, they disliked the influence and perceived a competitive relationship.

Attempts to direct and control students may affect the responses of teachers toward the students as well as the students' responses to the teachers. Perhaps in retaliation to students' frustration of their efforts to control them, teachers under pressure to control were found to punish unmotivated students more severely than teachers who were expected to collaborate.[21] Teachers who try to control students may conclude that students are unable to exercise freedom responsibly and, as a consequence, devalue them and maintain social distance.[22] In summary, the use of controlled, directive teaching appears to induce (a) students to resist the influence and resent the teacher, (b) the teacher to undervalue the students, and (c) the teacher and the students to perceive their relationship as competitive.

13. Willower, "Schools and Pupil Control."
14. N. E. Wallen, R. M. W. Travers, I. E. Reid, and K. H. Wadthea, "Relationships Between Teacher Needs and Teacher Behavior in the Classroom," *Journal of Educational Psychology* 54 (1963):23–32.
15. M. J. Dunkin and B. J. Biddle, *The Study of Teaching* (New York: Holt, Rinehart & Winston, 1974).
16. Ned A. Flanders, "Teacher-Pupil Contacts and Mental Hygiene," *Journal of Social Issues* 15 (1959):30–39.
17. Jack W. Brehm, *A Theory of Psychological Reactance* (New York: Academic Press, 1966).
18. Richard de Charms, *Personal Causation* (New York: Academic Press, 1968).
19. Morton Deutsch, *The Resolution of Conflict* (New Haven: London, 1973).
20. Dean Tjosvold, "Control Strategies and Own Group Evaluation in Intergroup Conflict," *Journal of Psychology* 100 (1978):305–14.
21. Dean Tjosvold and Ted Kastelic, "Effects of Student Motivation and the Principal's Values on Teacher Directiveness," *Journal of Educational Psychology* 68 (1976):768–74.
22. David Kipnis, "Does Power Corrupt?," *Journal of Personality and Social Psychology* 24 (1972):33–41.

Dependency. Though control orientation of school has been defended as helping students develop self-discipline, it is unlikely to do so. Rhea has argued that many students accept their dependent position in schools by concluding that they are unable to make effective decisions and should rely on educators to make decisions for them.[23] Students' beliefs that they lack control over their lives can affect their behavior. Individuals who see themselves as powerless have been found to have little resistance to influence: they value luck rather than skill, lack commitment to social change movements, fail to seek and obtain useful information about their situations, and influence other persons ineffectively.[24] Coleman argues that feeling powerless contributes to the failure of students to achieve academically.[25] Students whose school life is controlled may develop more generalized expectations of helplessness and fail to develop the skills of independence.

De Charms has objected to the control exercised by educators over students.[26] In traditionally organized schools, students do not develop a sense that they personally cause and are responsible for their behavior. They learn to do what others expect of them rather than learn to know and to follow their own ideas and interests. They conclude they are Pawns, not Origins, and fail to develop the skills necessary for self-direction.

Conflict Resolution. Control orientation, as already noted, may increase the incidence of conflict. Control teaching may generate hostility toward the teacher. Teachers under pressure to control students may be punitive toward unwilling students. A minority of students have protested in a variety of ways against their dependent position in schools.[27] A control orientation also appears to affect the management and resolution of conflicts.

Although conflict is pervasive, social scientists have difficulty defining it. Conflict has, for example, been defined in terms of aggression and hostility. As defined here, conflict exists when incompatible activities occur.[28] Interpersonal conflict arises when one person is interfering, preventing, blocking, or in other ways making another person's behavior less rewarding or less effective. Since conflict is inevitable in schools and other organizations, the central issue is the management and resolution of conflicts.[29]

A productive resolution of conflict occurs when the participants (a) reach an acceptable agreement, and (b) strengthen or affirm their relationship. Maintaining a strong relationship is important to resolve future conflicts and problems. Researchers have identified several approaches that contribute to the productive resolution of conflict: (a) acceptance of mutual responsibility for the problem rather than blaming the other participant, (b) open discussion of the underlying issues and possible solutions to the problem, and (c) a willingness to compromise.[30] Control orientation

23. Buford Rhea, "Institutional Paternalism in High School," *Urban Review* 2 (1968):13–15, 34.
24. H. M. Lefcourt, "Internal Versus External Control: A Review," *Psychological Bulletin* 65 (1966):206–20; J. B. Rotter, "Generalized Expectancies for Internal Versus External Control of Reinforcement," *Psychological Monographs* 86 (1966).
25. James S. Coleman et al., *Equality of Educational Opportunity* (Washington, D.C.: U.S. Government Printing Office, 1966).
26. Richard de Charms, *Enhancing Motivation in the Classroom* (New York: Irvington Publishers, 1976).

27. M. A. Chesler and J. E. Lohman, "Changing Schools Through Student Advocacy," in *Organization Development in Schools,* ed. R. A. Schmuch and M. B. Miles (Palo Alto: National Press, 1971), pp. 185–212.
28. Deutsch, *Resolution.*
29. See David W. Johnson and Roger T. Johnson, "Conflict in the Classroom: Controversy and Learning," *Review of Educational Research* 49 (1979):51–70, for a discussion of conflict of ideas in the classroom.
30. David W. Johnson and Frank P. Johnson, *Joining Together: Group Theory and Group Skills* (Englewood Cliffs, N.J.: Prentice-Hall, 1975).

appears to interfere with these effective methods of resolving conflicts.

A control oriented teacher may blame students for any conflict because they have not behaved as he or she required. The students are unlikely to accept full responsibility and may even be willing to continue or escalate the conflict rather than accept responsibility. When both persons accept responsibility for the conflict, they are more likely to believe that they need to work together to try to resolve the conflict.

Educators committed to control may freely express their dissatisfaction with students, but refuse to encourage student expression or view them as "discipline" problems; the preferred course of action is to reestablish discipline by silencing the students and regaining control. A control minded teacher is likely, for example, to tell students who complain about an assignment that they should complete it. Under these conditions, students are not likely to identify their conflicts directly or to discuss them openly with the teachers.

Control minded educators may refuse to compromise toward the position of students, and attribute the responsibility for the problem as residing within the students. They may also be reluctant to make concessions in order to avoid losing social face. Teachers intent on appearing strong and in control may easily feel that students have made them lose social face and, as a consequence, be unwilling to compromise their position.[31] To the extent teachers (and their colleagues) define their goal in the conflict as maintaining control, they are unlikely to make concessions.[32] They may seek to "win" the conflict by inducing the student to do as they command.

This analysis suggests that in control oriented schools, conflicts, when they are not suppressed, are ineffectively managed. In contrast to popular notions that conflict itself is bad and to be avoided, conflict researchers emphasize the possible benefits of conflict. The frustrations of working together can be expressed; persons can feel the stimulation of the full use of their resources; they can increase their self-awareness as they define their interests; the participants can reaffirm the importance of their relationship. Getzels and Thelen have noted that when conflict is suppressed, much of the excitement of a classroom is removed.[33]

A critical function of conflict is to provide a medium in which underlying problems are identified and new, creative solutions devised and implemented. At least some students can be expected to be dissatisfied with the status quo and committed to change. In control oriented schools, students are discouraged from expressing their dissatisfaction and from seeking changes. Control oriented educators are then denying that which could be most useful: student pressures, encouragement, and ideas that could establish more effective procedures and create changes that could facilitate learning.

Collaboration

Educators may be committed to the control of students because they believe the only alternative is a *laissez faire* orientation. As research already reviewed suggests, collaboration is a more effective alternative to control than is *laissez faire*. Collaborative orientation recognizes that educators and students should influence students and in turn be influenced by them; it encourages joint decision making among educators and students. Classroom observation research suggests that

31. Dean Tjosvold, "Threat as a Low-Power Person's Strategy in Bargaining: Social Face and Tangible Outcomes," *International Journal of Group Tensions* 4 (1974):494–510.
32. Dean Tjosvold, "Low-Power Person's Strategies in Bargaining: Negotiability of Demand, Maintaining Face, and Race," *International Journal of Group Tensions* 7 (1977):29–41.

33. J. W. Getzels and H. A. Thelen, "The Classroom Group as a Unique Social System," in *The Dynamics of Instructional Groups: Sociopsychological Aspects of Teaching and Learning* (Chicago: University of Chicago Press, 1960), pp. 53–82.

teachers who have a collaborative orientation and use indirect influence are more effective than those with a control orientation.[34] Results of Lewin and his associates' studies on leadership and social climates can be interpreted as providing support for the idea that teachers with a collaborative orientation are more effective than *laissez faire* teachers.[35] Children whose leaders adopted a *laissez faire* technique felt directionless, dissatisfied, and accomplished little.

In a recent study by Richter and Tjosvold involving fourteen classrooms,[36] students who collaboratively made decisions with their teachers were found to have developed more positive attitudes toward school and subject; were more internally motivated to work on classroom activities; interacted more positively with each other; and demonstrated higher levels of learning than did students in the teacher control condition.

De Charms and his associates argued that experience in collaborative classrooms and direct training could increase the origin or self-direction skills of students.[37] Teachers learned to treat students as origins; they did not simply indulge them. The teachers provided opportunities for the students to make and implement decisions as a classroom and as individuals. They also helped the students develop cooperative groups that encouraged self-examination.

Teachers also focused on specific origin skills. Origins know their own values, interests, and needs; they set goals that help them realize their needs; they are able to take necessary risks to accomplish these goals. Origins feel that they are purposefully working toward their goals; they feel committed to reach these goals; they take personal responsibility for the success or failure of their efforts to reach these goals. Teachers helped students increase their self-awareness, set realistic goals, develop concrete plans, and monitor progress. Results of this four year study suggest that experience in collaborative classrooms and training in origin skills can increase feelings of powerfulness; in turn, these feelings improve academic performance and self-direction.

Collaborative educators do not abdicate their special role and responsibility in the classroom, but use their position and resources to help students in a mutual effort to decide the learning goals, activities, and classroom procedures and to develop necessary skills. Moreover, collaborative teachers help students express their dissatisfactions and accept their own position to reach a mutual agreement. I have provided a more detailed description of collaborative schools and classrooms, the conditions under which they may be effective, and the skills and attitudes educators and students need to make them productive.[38]

Concluding Comments

The commitment of educators to the strong, unilateral control of students appears generally to undermine efforts to help students achieve academically, develop important social skills, and establish relationships in which problems are openly discussed and constructively resolved. Organizational programs should redefine teacher competence from one of the control of students to one of effective collaboration with them

34. Dunkin and Biddle, *Study of Teaching.*
35. Kurt Lewin, Ronald Lippitt, and Robert White, "Patterns of Aggressive Behavior in Experimentally Created Social Climates," *Journal of Social Psychology* 10 (1939):271–99; Robert K. White and Ronald Lippitt, *Autocracy and Democracy: An Experimental Inquiry* (New York: Harper, 1960).
36. Fredrick Richter and Dean Tjosvold, "The Effects of Student Participation in Classroom Decision-Making on Attitudes, Motivation, Peer Interaction, and Achievement," *Journal of Applied Psychology,* in press.
37. de Charms, *Motivation.*

38. Dean Tjosvold, "Alternative Organizations in Schools and Classrooms," in *Social Psychology of Education: Theory & Research,* ed. Daniel Bar-Tal and Leonard Saxe (Washington, D.C.: Hemisphere, 1978), Chapter 12, pp. 275–97.

and in other ways reduce the pressure on educators to be control minded. Educators need opportunities to examine the manner in which control orientation affects the quality of teaching.

Collaboration between educators and students, mutual influence and responsiveness, and joint decision making often are a feasible alternative to control; collaboration can contribute to the learning of students and the development of stronger relationships between educators and students. In order for educators and students to be willing to experiment with effective ways of collaborating, they need to believe they have the skills of two-way communication, group decision making and problem solving, and constructive conflict resolution. Indeed, without these skills, educators may believe that control is the only effective action available to them. Training programs[39] as well as experience in collaborative schools should help them develop these skills and attitudes.

Questions for Discussion

1. How did the role of the teacher in colonial America differ from that of contemporary educators?

2. In what ways might "school-keeping" chores be minimized so that teachers might spend more time working with students?

3. What factors have helped to bring about the idea that teachers, rather than dispensing knowledge, should help students to learn?

4. What qualities must a teacher possess in order to have good human relations skills?

Supplementary Learning Activities

1. Plan a hypothetical lesson using the suggestions presented in this chapter.

39. Johnson and Johnson, *Joining Together.*

2. Analyze the pupil's cumulative record presented in figure 3.2. What does this record tell you about William James Johnson?

3. Interview a teacher concerning his or her role as an educator.

4. Study the report card in figure 3.3. What does it tell you about Sue Stone? How could this type of report card form be improved?

5. Role-play several situations in which a teacher displays poor human relations skills. Also role-play some situations in which a teacher exhibits good human relations skills.

Notes

1. National Education Association, Research Division, *The American Public School Teacher,* research report 1967–R4 (Washington, D.C.: National Education Association Publications, 1967), p. 27.

2. "Help! Teacher Can't Teach!" *Time,* June 16, 1980, p. 54.

3. Robert L. Ebel, "Critical Issues in Standardized Testing," *Thresholds in Education,* vol. 6, no. 1, 1980, pp. 9–10.

Selected References

Dembo, Myron H. *Teaching for Learning: Applying Educational Psychology in the Classroom.* Santa Monica, Calif.: Goodyear Publishing, 1977.

Dodson, Fitzhugh. *How to Discipline with Love: From Crib to College.* New York: Rawson Associates, 1977.

Ebel, Robert L. "Critical Issues in Standardized Testing." *Thresholds in Education.* Vol. 6, no. 1, 1980, pp. 9–10.

Glaser, Robert. "The School of the Future: Adaptive Environments for Learning." *The Future of Education: Perspectives on Tomorrow's Schooling.* Philadelphia: Research for Better Schools, 1975.

Gubser, Lyn. "Competency Testing and National Accreditation in Teacher Education." *Action in Teacher Education.* Vol. 1, nos. 3 and 4, Spring-Summer 1979, pp. 21–27.

Heavilin, Barbara Anne. "Confusion Worse Confounded: Incompetence Among Public School Teachers." *The Teacher Educator.* Vol. 16, no. 2, Autumn 1980, pp. 11–20.

"Help! Teacher Can't Teach." *Time.* June 16, 1980, pp. 54–63.

Patterson, Arlene H. "Professional Malpractice: Small Cloud, but Growing Bigger." *Phi Delta Kappan.* Vol. 62, no. 3, November 1980, pp. 193–96.

Ryan, Kevin, and Cooper, James. *Those Who Can, Teach.* New York: Houghton Mifflin, 1975.

Schwartz, William. "Education in the Classroom." *Journal of Higher Education.* Vol. 51, no. 3, May 1980, pp. 235–54.

Shane, Harold G. *Curriculum Change Toward the 21st Century.* Washington, D.C.: National Education Association, 1977.

Spillman, Carolyn V. "Classroom Management: Mystery or Mastery." *Education.* Vol. 101, no. 1, Fall 1980, pp. 41–45.

Swick, Kevin J. *Maintaining Productive Student Behavior.* Washington, D.C.: National Education Association, 1977.

Thompson, Duane G. *Writing Long-Term and Short-Term Objectives. A Painless Approach.* Champaign, Ill.: Research Press Company, 1977.

Van Til, William. *Education: A Beginning.* New York: Houghton Mifflin, 1974.

Wynn, Richard, et al. *American Education.* New York: McGraw-Hill, 1977.

Alternative Careers in Education

4

This Chapter
- Outlines the training requirements for a number of the more common teaching-related jobs.
- Highlights the work of such educational specialists as school counselor, media specialist, school social worker, librarian, supervisor, and administrator.
- Lists and describes a variety of nonteaching, but education-related careers.
- Provides a point of view dealing with the employment of educators by industry.

The previous chapter dealt with various aspects of the training and qualifications of the regular classroom teacher. There are, of course, a number of other important related careers that are available to those who are considering a career in American education. This chapter will explore some of these alternatives.

Librarians and Learning Center Directors

A school librarian is, in one sense, really a teacher whose classroom is the library. Some people erroneously think of a school librarian as one who only takes care of books and periodicals. Much to the contrary, a good librarian can be one of the most effective teachers in an entire school. One of the major goals of American public education is to help each student become capable of learning on his/her own without the help of the classroom teacher. The library contains many of the resources necessary for independent study, and the task of the librarian is to help each student learn how to use these resources. To do this effectively, a librarian must not only be able to order, classify, catalog, and shelve books, but also must be able to work effectively with individuals and groups of students.

Almost all of the junior and senior high schools in this country have libraries, and therefore, librarians. And only recently have elementary schools begun to have libraries. The library has been expanded into "learning resource centers" where a wide range of learning materials such as books, periodicals, learning machines, programmed self-teaching materials, film strips, single concept films, records, audiotapes, and dial access materials are made available for students to use. Schools of the future are destined to put a greater emphasis on learning centers, and with this emphasis will come an increased demand for well-trained librarians and directors of learning centers.

Media Specialists

A later chapter discusses the general topic of instructional resources that are available for use by teachers. More and more school systems are now employing specialists who have been trained in media, and whose sole job it is to help teachers create and utilize different kinds of media in their teaching. These media specialists must, of course,

Learning center directors must be able to operate a wide variety of audiovisual hardware.

be familiar with all of the different kinds of audiovisual equipment available for use in schools. Such equipment includes, for example, movie projectors, film strip projectors, 35-mm slide projectors, opaque projectors, overhead projectors, audiotape recorders, videotape recorders, record players, overhead transparency makers, photocopy machines, cameras—the list gets longer each year as more and more such hardware is developed and made available for use in schools.

The media specialist, in some schools, also does minor repair work on audiovisual equipment; however, the main function of the media specialist so far as media hardware is concerned is to advise the school system on what hardware to buy, and help teachers use such equipment.

A media specialist should have prior teaching experience and a master's degree with a major in educational media.

Counseling

A school counselor works to a great extent in a one-to-one relationship with individual students. These students may need vocational or college information, help in selecting elective courses, someone to talk with concerning a girl or boyfriend, help with peer or parental conflict, or assistance with any one of a variety of emotional and psychological problems. School counselors do not, however, attempt to provide therapy for students with severe problems, but rather refer such cases to appropriate specialists, such as a clinical psychologist or psychiatrist. The long-term goal of counselors is not to solve problems for the students, but rather to help students solve their own problems. To do this counselors must themselves: be well adjusted, have a good understanding of human psychology, be familiar with and proficient in using a wide variety of counseling techniques, respect the dignity and worth of individual students, and possess a sincere desire to understand and help others.

Coaching is yet another way for teachers to influence their students in a non-classroom setting.

In most states, to be certified as a counselor requires that a person have some teaching experience and possess a master's degree with a major in school counseling. There are some states, however, that do not require prior teaching experience to be certified as a school counselor.

School Social Worker

An educational career closely related to the school counselor is that of school social worker, the distinction being that a social worker goes out into the community, and into the home to work with students and parents. For instance, if a school counselor, in working with an individual student, suspects that the student's problem may be caused by conditions in the home, he/she may then refer the case to the school social worker. The social worker will then visit the home and attempt to work closely with members of the family to bring about a solution to the problem.

Of course, not all schools have a school social worker on the staff. In some school systems this function is carried on by a school counselor, and in other schools the teacher does whatever work in the home with parents that needs to be done. An increasing number of school systems, however, are finding it advantageous to have a school social worker on the staff who is specifically trained to do this kind of work.

A school social worker typically possesses a master's degree with a major in school social work.

The school social worker visits the homes of pupils in an effort to help parents tap the learning potential of their children.

Educational Administration and Supervision

There are many different kinds of specific educational administration careers that one may pursue. These include, for example: general superintendent (in charge of an entire school system), assistant superintendent (assisting the general superintendent with the operation of part of the school operation, such as curriculum, personnel, business, elementary education, or secondary education), principal (in charge of a single elementary or secondary school building), and assistant principal (assisting the principal with specific parts of the operation of a single school building). The size and philosophy of each school district determines the number and type of administrative positions that school district will have.

Many school systems also employ a number of different kinds of supervisors. Whereas administrators typically have a certain amount of authority over the area in which each administers,

Graduates of teacher education programs find employment in a wide variety of positions, including day-care centers.

Small boy scowling over report card to Dad: "Naturally I seem stupid to my teacher; she's a college graduate."

Dallas Morning News

a school supervisor frequently does not actually have authority over teachers. Rather, a supervisor plays more of a "consultant" role. For example, an elementary music supervisor would help the regular elementary teachers do a better job of teaching music by occasionally teaching the music class in each of the elementary classrooms, and/or by helping the regular classroom teacher do a better job of teaching music to the class. Common supervisory positions are those in elementary music, elementary art, elementary physical education, elementary reading; and some schools even have supervisors who have broad responsibility supervising one subject, such as science, for instance, in all grades starting at kindergarten and continuing through the twelfth grade. In many of the larger junior and senior high schools, department heads will have supervisory responsibility for their respective departments.

It is difficult to generalize about administrative and supervisory positions in American schools because the number and nature of such positions vary a great deal from school to school. However, there are a considerable number of such positions existing in the American public school system. To pursue a career in educational administration and/or supervision one must obtain a good deal of successful teaching experience, and at least a master's degree related to that kind of work.

Alternative Careers in Education   85

Table 4.1. Employment of Educators Outside the Schools.

1. U.S. Office of Education (administrator, consultant, director, researcher, teacher corps program developer)
2. U.S. Department of State (administrator, Peace Corps)
3. U.S. Department of Defense (military educator, staff development, foreign teacher)
4. U.S. Bureau of Indian Affairs (administrator, staff developer, program developer)
5. Most other U.S. Agencies (staff development, education specialist, program developer, researcher, editor, writer, media specialist, interpreter)
6. Foreign Countries (educator, education specialist, interpreter, tour director, consultant)
7. Professional Organizations (administrator, public relations, researcher, field worker, editor, writer, media specialist)
8. State Education Agencies (administrator, consultant, researcher, editor, writer, field worker, media specialist, staff developer)
9. Local Municipal Agencies (recreation director, playground supervisor, camp instructor or director, community education worker, community planning and development, educator in special community projects)
10. Private Foundations (administrator, researcher, program evaluator, human relations work, editor, writer)
11. Hospitals and Clinics (patient education, staff development, writer)
12. Religious Organizations (religious educator, instructional materials development, media specialist, writer, editor, youth worker)
13. Banking (staff development, writer, consultant, teller, administrator)
14. Retail Sales (customer relations, advertising, staff development)
15. Insurance (staff development, writer, human relations consultant)
16. Wholesaler (customer relations, writer, market research)
17. Manufacturing (educational product development, researcher, writer, marketing consultant)
18. Advertising (education consultant, writer, researcher, human psychology consultant)
19. Television and Radio (education consultant, TV or radio teacher, researcher, script writer)
20. Newspapers (education writer or editor, consultant, researcher)
21. Publishing (education editor, author, education materials sales, consultant)
22. Private Consultant (proposal writer, evaluator, speaker)
23. Museums (educational consultant, program developer, in-service trainer, public relations consultant, speaker)

Education-related Positions Outside the Schools

In recent years many graduates of teacher education programs have found employment in a rather wide range of education-related positions outside the schools. Increasingly employers are finding that those graduates who have been trained as teachers possess unique skills that can be valuable in business, industry, military, government, institution, and agency settings. Examples of specific positions in these settings for which people trained as teachers are particularly well suited are presented in table 4.1. Many employers feel that persons trained as teachers usually have a good understanding of human behavior, enjoy working with people, and possess excellent human relations skills. These qualities are extremely useful in nearly any position which involves working with people.

Beyond this are a number of education dimensions to nearly all business or agency endeavors. For instance, employees must be trained and retrained to properly and efficiently perform their jobs. Educators possess the unique skills and knowledge to design and carry out these training programs.

The increasing demand for educators in private sectors of our economy have caused some colleges and universities to create new training programs especially designed to prepare educators for such nonclassroom education-related careers. Examples of such programs may be found at the University of Wisconsin–Milwaukee, Northwestern University, Northern Illinois University, and Emory University, to name but a

Educators possess many skills that are attractive to a wide variety of employers.

few. While these programs differ considerably, they are usually highly individualized for each student, and include a good deal of fieldwork in the settings in which the student will eventually work.

Some people are predicting that positions for educators outside the schools will increase substantially in the future as more and more employers discover the value of the educators' unique talents.

In conclusion, this chapter has attempted to briefly discuss some of the careers other than classroom teaching that exist in American public education. All of these education-related careers are essential to education, business, and to society in general.

This chapter has also attempted to point out that there are many specializations within teaching as well as a wide variety of nonteaching jobs that are in one way or another closely related to teaching. This chapter has also attempted to briefly highlight the training requirements for some of the more common types of these teaching-related jobs.

Point of View

The following selection by Beverly McQuigg documents a growing demand for educators by the industrial world.

The Role of Education in Industry

Beverly McQuigg

More and more, education and training are becoming an important part of American business and industry. There is a growing tendency to view one's employees as a resource, and money spent in training and development as an investment rather than an expense. Need, not cost, is the primary factor influencing corporate commitment to training and development. In-house training appears to be exempt from normal managerial decision making, which is heavily cost-oriented.

Most training and development takes place on the job and includes the costs of initial training; retraining each time a job function changes, a new piece of equipment is installed, or a new method or product is introduced; more training each time the employee changes jobs; and replacement training for each new employee.

The peak of interest and activity in training occurs when an organization is growing and is concerned about having an adequate pool of well-trained and -educated employees. This is especially pronounced in those organizations committed philosophically (or by union contract) to promotion from within.

Training and development are also important to high-technology corporations. The further toward the "leading edge" the company operates, the more it must educate its own people. It also occurs when an organization's mission or product mix changes and people have to be trained or retrained for new skills and new roles in the new organization.

The need for in-house training and development peaks when the labor market is tight in general or in particular specialties. Academic institutions are seen as having inadequate resources, doing an inadequate job in a specialized area.[1]

Non-business-oriented motives for training—e.g., dedication to the concept of education solely as a means of upgrading a work force—are rare. Corporate motives for training tend to be short-term, functional, and mission-oriented. With only a few exceptions, companies sponsor training and development because they feel they have to—so the work can get done, so that personnel will be ready when needed.

More frequently than ever before, corporate education and training people and their department heads are full-time professionals. Most department heads have direct access to the top executive. The training and development office is becoming increasingly important, providing a career path in its own right. Education staffs are becoming more dispersed. Professionals are more often assigned to field locations.

The primary role of education staffs is program development and administration. Actual teaching is done by the line management. It is also the line management—especially the department head—who has the most to say about who is to be exposed to formal training and development activities and to what extent. Line management generally defines training and development needs.

A new study of engineering/scientist continuing education by John Klus and Judy Jones reports that enrollments for in-house continuing education programs are roughly comparable to out-of-plant enrollments. Of the out-of-plant enrollments, it is reported that universities train 114,688, associations train 71,904, and community colleges train 14,000 persons.[2]

A survey by the Bureau of National Affairs among 141 organizations reveals that, for their non-management employees, 55% had formal in-house

Source: Beverly McQuigg, "The Role of Education in Industry," *Phi Delta Kappan*, January 1980, pp. 324–25.

1. Stanley Peterfreud, "Education in Industry—Today and in the Future," *Training and Development Journal,* May 1976, p. 36.
2. Robert Craig, *National Report for Training and Development* (Washington, D.C.: American Society for Training and Development, February 1979), p. 2.

training; half of these had separate training departments. The types of courses offered by employers
ranged from graduate-level work to basic reading and
math skills. Ninety percent had tuition aid programs.
Employee relations, counseling, and discipline ranked
as the most important topics for first-line supervisor
training; wage and salary administration and performance appraisal were most important for middle-man-
agement training.[3]

Findings from the Bureau of National Affairs
concerning management training and development
programs show that, of 75 large companies (1,000 employees or more) and 39 small companies, 75% had in-
house training programs, as opposed to 6% who participated in university development programs. Over
half of all the companies also provided training
through outside seminars, professional or trade association meetings, and self-training courses. Employers
provide training primarily because they feel job skills
can best be taught in their own training programs and
because they feel that the education and/or training
background of their employees is inadequate if they
train outside their own programs.[4]

Professional and technical societies are playing an
increasing role in meeting the challenge imposed by
technological and organizational change, according to
a new study by the American Society of Mechanical
Engineers. Eighty-six percent of the major professional
and technical societies operate or are in the process of
developing continuing education programs; 49% co-
sponsor programs with local universities and 33% with
proprietary organizations. In 1976 these societies offered 1,100 courses to 30,000 attendees.

The Department of Labor's Bureau of Labor Statistics has been studying training by employers in 14
occupations in four metalworking industries. Over 90%
of these firms reported that they use the production
shop as a training facility. For noncompany facilities,

more than 25% reported the use of adult education
centers, and more than 10% use community colleges.[5]

A study by Gilbert J. Black shows that American
industry invested $1.2 billion in management evalua-
tion and development in 1976. Sixty-two percent of
the money went for in-house salaries and administrative costs, while 11% was spent on outside seminars
and workshops. The balance, 22%, was divided among
consultants, books and instructional materials, equipment and facilities, tuition refunds, and other expenses.
Management development expenditures are expected
to be over $2.2 billion in the year 1982.[6]

Dealing specifically with management training
and development programs, the Bureau of National
Affairs surveyed 75 large companies and 39 small ones
in 1977, as I mentioned earlier. It found that for first-
level supervisors the most common training activities
are on-the-job coaching, tuition aid for college courses,
and in-house training programs. Programs for middle
managers involve more outside programs, such as attendance at professional or trade association meetings
and attendance at outside job-related seminars. In-
house training programs are provided for first-level supervisors in three-fourths of the companies and for
middle managers in two-thirds of the companies. More
than half the companies have a training and development manager to administer the in-house programs.

The use of outside sources for management training programs is more common in nonbusiness organizations than in business organizations. It is done more
frequently in small firms than in large ones, perhaps
because small firms are less likely to have experts in
certain areas on the payroll. University development
programs were attended most by top-level executives
for programs of upper-level management.

3. Ibid., p. 3.
4. Ibid., p. 8.

5. Ibid., p. 12.
6. Gilbert Black, *Report on the Management, Development, and
Education Market, 1977–1982* (White Plains, N.Y.: Knowledge
Industry Publications, 1977), p. 9.

Large industries have several reasons for doing their training in-house. First of all, such training is often more relevant than training done outside. Knowledge acquired in-house can often be put into practice immediately. The training does not become obsolete before it can be used. Persons in charge of designing the training and development programs are close to the managers of the various divisions within the company and know immediately what the needs are. In-house training is done by using in-house staff who either teach the courses themselves or train the line supervisors to administer the training to persons in their charge. If the training cannot be done by the in-house staff, consultants are hired.

Corporations are designing and teaching courses that will enable employees to earn credit toward undergraduate and master's degrees. Some big corporations and their hometown colleges have had cooperative agreements for years. Schenectady's Union College, for instance, has given credits toward an advanced degree in power systems engineering for more than 20 years to General Electric Company employees who take G.E.'s courses. In most cases, the students are supervisory workers without college degrees or with only two-year associate degrees. The primary aim of the course is to upgrade their job skills. But if the college credits they receive motivate the employees to embark on further college study, that decision is a splendid fringe benefit for the company, many executives say.

Companies offering college credit courses include Xerox, AT&T, Lockheed Missiles and Space, Holiday Inn, TWA, Bank of America, IBM, and John Hancock Mutual Life Insurance. This is only a sampling, of course. Professional educators analyze each training program before recommending the granting of college credits. Unions, trade groups, and government agencies have also begun to offer their own college credit courses. The American Council on Education conducts detailed evaluations of courses for corporations seeking college credit for their programs. Some state education groups conduct similar assessments. The companies are proud of their accredited courses and want to prove that their in-house courses are "equivalent" to the education provided in the traditional environment of a college campus.

Employees respond positively to accreditation. Students seem to work harder when they know they can earn college credits, says an executive of TWA, and more workers sign up to take company courses once the courses receive college accreditation. Some students feel that the college-accredited company programs are better for them than college courses. The advantage over the typical university course is that many are conducted in just one week of intensive work, so that one becomes totally immersed in the material. Also, because the students are currently employed, instructors can relate the material covered to situations the students are involved in every day.

Four of the largest corporations in America — IBM, Xerox, G.E., and AT&T — now offer bachelor's degrees. The Arthur D. Little firm has received authorization to give an MBA in management. University graduates are dissatisfied and feel they are ill-equipped for the "real world." They want learning of a more practical nature. Colleges and universities must now compete with educational programs offered by industry. Continuing inability of traditional U.S. educational institutions to respond promptly to changing learning needs may explain better than any other factor the expanding role of corporations and profit-making schools in postsecondary education. New technology is squeezing unskilled workers out of the labor market and putting a premium on ever more advanced training. Thousands of displaced workers must adjust to other industries and occupations to earn their livelihood. Who is going to provide the education needed to cope with such change? Traditionally,

Americans have relied heavily on formal schools to prepare young people to enter the labor force. This reliance is fading fast. There is a growing public perception that the school system is not keeping abreast, that there is a wide chasm between the courses that schools are offering and the training that people need for the world of work. While educators place a high priority on developing a student's mind and turning out a well-rounded human being, the public seems to be more concerned about jobs. There is growing doubt that colleges and universities really fulfill this job-market purpose, and there is growing debate as to whether they should.

The university and the corporation have much in common. Certain of their objectives are similar. Each has a responsibility to enhance the quality of life. Even though the two institutions may use different means to bring about this result, they will succeed best if they move forward together, each learning from the other, each making its appropriate contribution. Above all, each must recognize that cooperation, not competition, is in the best interest of the people they serve.

Questions for Discussion

1. What do you believe the function and the role of a superintendent should be in a public school system today? a principal?

2. What do you believe would be some of the characteristics of a successful school administrator?

3. Discuss the employment prospects for educators outside the classroom.

4. Discuss the advantages and disadvantages of some of the different types of careers in American public education.

5. What are your views concerning the role of counselors in our educational system? What qualities do you believe a counselor should possess?

Supplementary Learning Activities

1. Invite a public school administrator to your class to discuss his or her work.

2. Visit a relatively large school, and interview the various types of educational personnel you find there.

3. Find out what the relative salaries are for different types of educational jobs.

4. Select one of the educational careers discussed in this chapter, and make arrangements to spend one full day following in the footsteps of someone now serving in that career.

5. Make arrangements for a school librarian or learning center director to discuss his or her work with your class.

Notes

1. Wade N. Patterson, "Teacher-Ranking: A Step Toward Professionalism," *Educational Forum,* January 1969, p. 172. Used by permission. Also permission of Kappa Delta Pi, an Honor Society in Education, owners of the copyright.

Selected References

Armstrong, David G.; Hensar, Kenneth T.; and Savage, Tom V. *Education: An Introduction.* New York: Macmillan, 1980.

Careers in Education. Washington, D.C.: National Education Association, 1974.

Castetter, William B. *The Personnel Function in Educational Administration.* New York: Macmillan, 1976.

Gartner, Alan, et al., eds. *Paraprofessionals in Education Today.* New York: Human Sciences Press, 1977.

Lilly, S. "A Training Based Model for Special Education." *Exceptional Children* 37 (1971): 745–49.

Lusterman, Seymour. *Education in Industry.* New York: The Conference Board, 1977.

Opportunities Abroad for Teachers. U.S. Government Printing Office, 1979. Stock no. 017–080–02041–6.

Para-professionals in the Union: A Matter of Pride. American Federation of Teachers, 1980.

Templeton, Ian. *Paraprofessionals.* Arlington, Va.: National Association of Elementary School Principals, 1974.

The Teaching Profession

The chapters of this section have been developed to provide an overview of the nature of the work, problems, rewards, and frustrations of the teaching profession. Chapter five considers the employment prospects for new teachers, chapter six outlines the rewards and frustrations of teaching, and chapter seven presents information relevant to membership in teacher organizations.

The employment prospects for new teachers are improving. Supply and demand of teachers has more overall balance as the 1980s begin as opposed to the early 1970s. Yet, several factors continue to impinge upon the demand for teachers. The supply and demand picture for new teachers has changed drastically over the last two decades, from a shortage of teachers in the 1950s and early 1960s, to an oversupply in the late 1960s and early 1970s. The general oversupply of teachers continued in the late 1970s with signs of modest shortages of teachers in certain academic areas. As a consequence of continued declining birthrates, subsequent enrollment declines, and taxpayer attitudes toward the rising costs of education, the production of new teachers has been greatly curtailed. As new teacher production decreases, and as the numbers of experienced teachers leaving the profession increases through early retirement and attrition for other causes, the teacher oversupply diminishes proportionately. The job market for elementary teachers will begin to improve in the early 1980s, but the job market for secondary teachers, except for certain teaching areas, will remain depressed during the 1980s. This chapter also presents a practical discussion of the process of obtaining a teaching position, and a point of view related to the impact of the teacher shortage on small schools.

It is reasonable to wonder whether the risk of preparing for a career that appears to be within a circumscribed and crowded field so far as employment is concerned is worth taking. Most people give some attention to economic aspects when seeking a career. Considerable salary data from various sectors of the United States is provided in chapter six for examination relative to such economic concerns. Most people also consider rewards other than economic ones, as well as the inherent problems associated with a career choice. Much is now being written about teacher burnout, violence in the classroom, lack of public confidence in the schools, and the like. These negative statements make the typical comments about the fun of working with young learners, gratification of observing academic and social growth among your students, and other kinds of positive comments seem more "Pollyannish" than ever before. While the authors are biased in favor of the positive aspects of the teaching career choice, they are also mindful of certain hindering conditions, frustrations, and negative public attitudes related to the work of teachers. The point of view at the end of chapter six discusses the potential hidden dilemma associated with role conflicts which often face teachers.

Most communities are aware of the relatively recent thrust of teacher militancy upon the schools. Teacher strikes, or threats of them, have aroused emotions within the teaching profession and within the entire educational community. Teacher organizations are commonly viewed as unions by the lay public. In the larger school systems, teachers are pressured to belong to the teacher organization that represents them to the board of education. Chapter seven provides considerable information about membership, organizational structure, and the objectives of both major teacher organizations, the American Federation of Teachers (AFT) and the National Education Association (NEA). In addition, selected activities and merger trends at the national, state, and local levels are reviewed. The chapter point of view centers on Gallup Poll findings regarding teacher strikes and required union membership.

Employment Prospects for New Teachers

5

This Chapter
- **Supplies information relative to the reduction in teacher production in the United States.**
- **Reports on declining birthrates in the United States, 1960–79.**
- **Formulates a picture of enrollment trends in elementary and secondary education.**
- **Comments briefly on taxpayer attitudes regarding support for education.**

- **Notes that the employment prospects for prospective teachers are brighter as the 1980s begin.**
- **Hypothesizes about the causes of the current oversupply of teachers.**
- **Suggests some of the important aspects of seeking and obtaining a teaching position.**
- **Presents a point of view regarding the impact of teacher shortages on small schools.**

During the early 1970s, an oversupply of teachers resulted from enrollment declines, school budget reductions, and a lag in the overall economy of the United States. Large numbers of all college graduates, including teacher preparation majors, began to find the entry level job markets to be more and more restrictive. With the reduction in the number of available teaching positions, enrollments in teacher education programs began to drop. While the current employment prospects for new teachers are less bright than during the 1960s as increasing numbers of college graduates seek employment in fields other than teaching, the employment prospects for those continuing to pursue teaching are improving.

Now it would appear that supply and demand of teachers has become more balanced overall in 1980, as opposed to the early 1970s. It can be expected that the market will be more favorable for teaching candidates in additional areas beyond those perennially in short supply. Other factors could also influence the supply/demand condition of teachers, and thus deserve constant scrutiny and consideration. These include economic conditions such as inflation rate, teacher salary and benefit changes, conditions of

teaching in the classroom, the public perception of the teaching profession, and other variables having an effect on the teacher market.

Teacher Production

During the 1950s and 1960s when there were dramatic increases in the numbers of elementary and secondary schoolchildren, there were also dramatic increases in teacher production. By the mid-1950s the number of education degrees awarded in the United States reached 60,000 per year. By 1970 the number of education degrees awarded had doubled to 120,000. Also by 1970 the elementary school enrollments began to decline sharply bringing about the much discussed teacher oversupply. Data presented in table 5.1 relative to the supply of new teachers prepared by institutions of higher education indicate that supply reached a high point in the 1971–72 academic year and declined at a rapid rate for the subsequent five-year period. Although the decline has continued through the 1979–80 academic year, the rate of decline was found to be less

Table 5.1. Number of Teacher Education Graduates Produced by Select Institutions in the United States for Select Years.

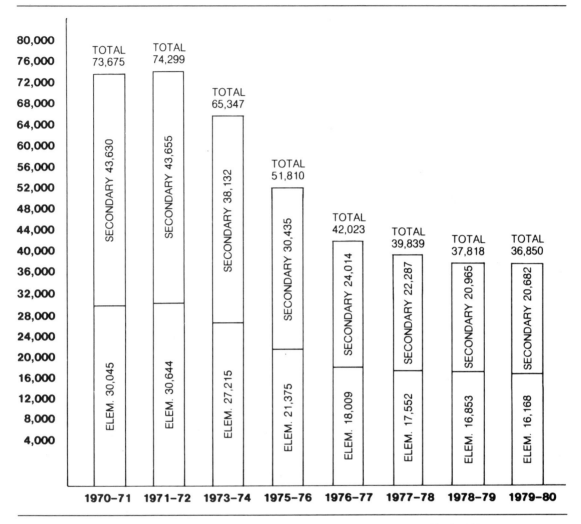

Source: *Teacher Supply/Demand in the United States, 1980,* ASCUS Research Report, Madison, WI., March 1980.

severe during the period 1976–80 as compared to the early 1970s. A comparison of select years for the total supply of new teachers would indicate the following percentage change:

1971–72 vs. 1978–79 = −49.10%
1971–72 vs. 1975–76 = −30.26%
1975–76 vs. 1978–79 = −27.00%
1978–79 vs. 1979–80 = −2.55%

What this reduction in the number of new teachers available has to do with the future employment prospects for new teachers will be directly related to future enrollments in the elementary and secondary schools in the United States. Table 5.2 illustrates the recent ten-year trend in the number of elementary and secondary school classroom teachers. While the total classroom teaching staff has increased 8.5 percent

When will the oversupply of teachers diminish? What factors must be present to influence teacher supply levels?

Table 5.2. Trend in the Number of Elementary and Secondary School Classroom Teachers.

School Year	Elementary School Classroom Teachers	Secondary School Classroom Teachers	Total Classroom Teachers
1969–70	1,106,703	906,605	2,013,308
1970–71	1,127,962	927,256	2,055,218
1971–72	1,126,365	933,537	2,069,838
1972–73	1,142,938	965,908	2,108,846
1973–74	1,175,980	979,468	2,155,448
1974–75	1,169,300	1,001,323	2,170,623
1975–76	1,170,036	1,021,414	2,191,450
1976–77	1,178,481	1,013,486	2,191,967
1977–78	1,176,309	1,022,392	2,198,701
1978–79	1,187,045	1,008,846	2,195,891
1979–80	1,181,713	1,002,610	2,184,323

Source: National Center for Education Statistics, 1980.

Table 5.3. Percent of Change in the Number of Classroom Teachers.

School Year	Percent Change Over 1969–70			Percent Change Over Previous Year		
	Elementary	Secondary	Total	Elementary	Secondary	Total
1969–70	. . .	. . .	. . .	. . .	. . .	. . .
1970–71	1.9	2.3	2.1	1.9	2.3	2.1
1971–72	1.8	3.0	2.8	−0.1	0.7	0.7
1972–73	3.3	6.5	6.5	1.5	3.5	1.9
1973–74	6.3	8.0	8.0	2.9	1.4	2.2
1974–75	5.7	10.4	10.4	−0.6	2.2	0.7
1975–76	5.7	12.7	8.8	0.1	2.0	1.0
1976–77	6.5	11.8	8.9	0.7	−0.8	less than −0.1
1977–78	6.3	12.8	9.2	−0.2	0.7	0.3
1978–79	7.3	11.3	9.1	−0.9	−1.3	−0.1
1979–80	6.8	10.6	8.5	−0.4	−0.6	−0.5

Source: National Center for Education Statistics, 1980.

Table 5.4. Conditions Having an Unusual Influence on Decreasing the Supply of Qualified Teachers in 1979.

Condition Contributing to a Smaller Supply in 1979	Number of States (36) Reporting Condition Contributed		
	To a Small Extent	To a Moderate Extent	To a Great Extent
Better opportunities in other types of employment	6	14	14
Location of vacancies not attractive	7	13	13
Fewer persons completing preparation	2	20	12
Salaries and benefits not attractive to beginning teachers	7	13	8
Fewer QUALIFIED persons completing preparation	6	14	7
Salaries and benefits not attractive to experienced teachers	9	12	7
Working conditions less attractive in teaching	12	9	7
Fewer former teachers applying to reenter active employment	12	11	4
Fewer teachers moving into state	9	7	0

Source: *Teacher Supply and Demand in Public Schools, 1979*, Research Memo, National Education Association, Washington, D.C.

since 1969–70 , the percent changes over previous years has been diminishing since 1976–77. Table 5.3 shows not only the percent change over 1969–70, but also the percent change over the previous year.

Table 5.4 lists several conditions reported by 36 states as having an unusual influence on decreasing the supply of qualified teachers in 1970–80. It should be noted that in addition to the fewer number of persons completing teacher preparation programs, the better opportunities in other types of employment, and the unattractiveness of the location of teaching vacancies were conditions having a strong influence on decreasing the supply of qualified teachers.

Figure 5.1. Total Number of Live Births in the United States, 1960–79.

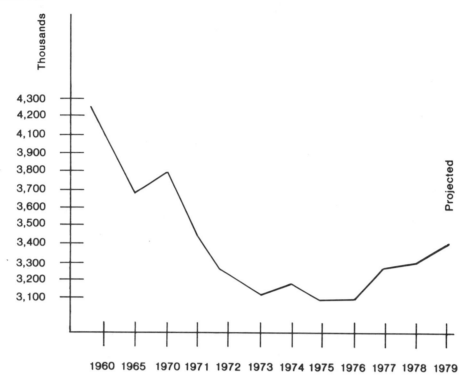

Source: *Teacher Supply/Demand in the United States, 1980,* ASCUS Research Report, Madison, WI., March 1980.

Declining Birthrates

School enrollment is, of course, influenced by birthrates. Figure 5.1 shows the number of live births in the United States from 1960 to 1979. This information, from the Department of Commerce, indicates that the number of live births in the United States peaked in 1960 at an all-time high of 4.25 million. Live births then fell to 3.55 million in 1971. Preliminary data shows only 3.25 million children born in 1971—the smallest number since 1946.

Figure 5.2 illustrates projected school age population in the United States from 1975 to 2000. The 1971–72 school year was the peak K–12 enrollment period. The elementary enrollment peak year was 1970–71, with 1976–77 as the peak year for secondary enrollment. For the elementary schools the current decline in enrollments in the public schools should bottom-out by 1984. Secondary enrollments should not reach the bottom-out position until 1990. College-age enrollments will continue to decline through 1995. These projections are predicated upon the upward trend in live births during the late 1970s and continuing in the 1980s.

Enrollment Trends

More than 3 million American youths graduated from high school in 1972 and 1973. The size of these classes reflects the high birthrate of the 1950s as well as lower dropout rates. About 78 percent of our American youth now finish high

As birthrates continue to decline in the United States, so too does the demand for teachers.

school. About 48 percent of them (or about 62 percent of our high school graduates) enter some type of higher education institution. About 25 percent of our youth now earn a bachelor's degree, 8 percent earn a master's degree, and between 1 and 2 percent go on to earn a doctor's degree.

Enrollment in elementary schools reached a peak in 1971, and is now declining. The U.S. Office of Education projects that elementary school enrollment will continue to decline until the early 1980s, and then begin to increase. Secondary school enrollments, after rising through the mid-1970s, will decline through the 1980s. Figure 5.3 illustrates the projected decline in high school enrollments through 1990. Enrollment in higher education is increasing, and will likely continue this trend until at least 1990.

Figure 5.2. Projected U.S. School Age Population: 1975–2000.

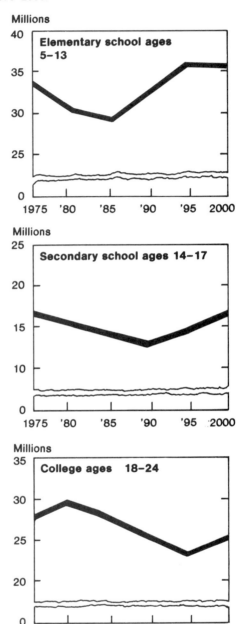

Source: U.S. House of Representatives, Select Committee on Population. *Domestic Consequences of United States Population Change*, 95th Congress, 2nd Session, 1978, p. 45.

Figure 5.3. Decline in High School Enrollment.

Actual and projected enrollments for grades 9–12 in U.S. public schools in selected years.

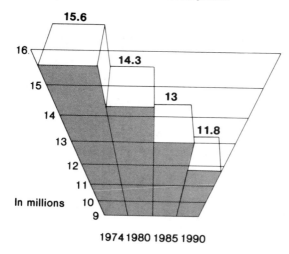

Source: U.S. Bureau of the Census

Needless to say, these projected enrollments have great implications for the employment prospects of new teachers. Elementary enrollment, which increased from 25.8 million in 1963 to 26.4 million in 1973, declined through the remainder of the 1970s to 24.2 million in 1980. Slight increases to 25 million are predicted by 1983. Public secondary school enrollment increased from 14.4 million in 1963 to 15.6 million in 1974, and declined to 14.3 million in 1980. Further declines are predicted to reach 13 million by 1985, and then drop sharply to 11.8 million in 1990. While

the job market for elementary teachers will be slightly improved during the early 1980s, the job market for secondary teachers will remain depressed until after 1990.

In addition to future enrollments, several other factors will affect the demand for teachers. One of these factors, which has been discussed earlier in this chapter, is the number of new teachers entering the market. Class size or pupil-teacher ratio will also influence teacher demand. In 1959 the pupil-teacher ratio for public elementary schools was 28.7 students per teacher. In 1973 this ratio had been lowered to 24 students per teacher. Similar statistics for public secondary schools were 21.5 in 1959 and 20 in 1973, and are expected to continue decreasing to 17.7 in 1983. While the pupil-teacher ratio tends to be somewhat higher in nonpublic elementary and secondary schools, the ratio in these schools, too, has decreased in the past decade. Obviously, the lower the pupil-teacher ratio, the more teachers must be hired. If the pupil-teacher ratio continues its downward trend in the next decade, employment prospects for the new teacher will be brighter. If this ratio levels off or rises, of course fewer teachers will be employed.

Taxpayer Attitude

Taxpayer attitude, also, influences teacher demand. Insofar as people are willing to pay higher taxes to support education, more teachers can be hired. Some authorities have even suggested that the current oversupply of teachers is not really that, but is rather an "underemployment of teachers" brought about by the taxpayers' unwillingness to pay higher taxes to support education. Most educators feel that we need more teachers than the schools can now afford to hire.

Because of inflation and the defensive tactics of organized school employees, falling enrollments do not mean falling budgets. However, they do mean less sharply rising budgets, especially for high schools and higher education. The administration and financing of retrenchment are radically different from those of expansion. There is sure to be a lot of unhappiness in American schools at every level in the next couple of decades as the school-age population declines.

Countless other factors influence the demand for teachers in various ways and to different extents; however, the two main factors that will determine the future employment prospects for new teachers will be the number of new teachers produced and the number of students enrolled in our schools.

Teacher Demand

The conditions discussed to this point in the chapter—teacher production, declining birthrates, enrollment trends, taxpayer attitude—have combined to produce an oversupply of teachers in the United States. However, there are several recent indicators suggesting that the employment op-

Declining enrollments curtail the number of teaching positions available.

portunities for teachers may be much improved by the mid-1980s. The total demand for elementary and secondary school teachers (not employed in the schools the previous year) includes those needed to allow for increased enrollment, additional staff required for lowering pupil-teacher ratios, and those needed for replacement of teachers leaving the profession. Even with declining school enrollments, approximately 1.5 million new teachers or returnees to the profession were employed by the public schools during the 1970s period of heaviest oversupply of available teachers.

Table 5.5 shows another aspect of the current teacher demand analysis. It shows the relative demand for teachers by teaching area. The data presented is summarized from data gathered across the continental United States. The principal subjects taught by departmentalized elementary teachers and secondary teachers are English, mathematics, and the natural sciences, which could be a reflection of curriculum interests in our schools as well as areas of high demand for prospective teachers. The teaching areas in which there will likely be the best employment opportunities can be ascertained by examination of this table.

Table 5.6 gives an indication of the employment opportunities in special education. This figure also shows estimates of the number of elementary and secondary schoolchildren affected by each of the different types of handicaps. Table 5.6 clearly points to a very considerable

shortage of qualified teachers and specialists in the area of special education. Recent state and federal laws are beginning to provide funds for hiring trained special education teachers for the schools.

A comparison of Table 5.6 with Table 5.7 illustrates another aspect of the demand for qualified special education teachers. Whereas over 5 million children are estimated to have different types of handicaps, the number of handicapped children receiving educational services in 1979–80 was 4 million.

Another factor that could lead to a brighter employment picture for beginning teachers is earlier teacher retirement. Since there seems to be a trend toward earlier retirement in all fields of work, it is not inconceivable that a similar trend may occur in the teaching profession. If, for example, states would pass legislation making it possible for teachers to retire with full retirement benefits at age fifty-five, the demand for new teachers would sharply increase.

The advent of compulsory early childhood education would be yet another factor that could create many new teaching jobs. As was pointed out earlier in this chapter, many early childhood educational opportunities are now provided on an optional basis. If states decide to mandate compulsory early childhood education programs, schools will need to hire a great number of teachers to staff those programs.

Table 5.5. Relative Demand by Teaching Area and Year (Continental United States). (Based upon a Survey of Teacher Placement Officers.)

	1981	1980	1979	1978	1976
Teaching fields with considerable teacher shortage . . . . (5.00–4.25): *					
Mathematics	4.79	4.80	4.68	4.40	3.86
Industrial arts	4.72	4.77	4.68	4.65	4.22
Science-physics	4.56	4.28	4.36	3.91	4.04
Special education-LD	4.47	4.48	4.50	4.45	4.00
Vocational agriculture	4.46	4.73	4.67	4.69	4.06
Science-chemistry	4.42	4.18	4.09	3.97	3.72
Science-general	4.31	4.10	4.00	—	—
Speech correction	4.27	4.17	3.83	3.83	3.68
Teaching fields with slight teacher shortage . . . . (4.24–3.45):					
Special education-PSA	4.22	4.36	4.22	3.96	3.42
Special education-reading	4.21	4.23	4.27	4.09	3.96
Special education-MR	4.14	4.23	4.39	3.52	2.87
Special education-multi. handicapped	4.13	3.87	3.24	—	—
Bilingual education	4.10	4.21	4.32	—	—
Special education-gifted	4.10	4.33	4.56	3.95	3.85
Science-earth	4.08	3.64	3.82	3.50	3.44
Science-biology	3.98	3.50	3.49	3.11	2.97
School psychologist	3.70	3.87	3.43	3.68	3.09
Business	3.50	3.80	3.65	3.52	3.10
Teaching fields with balanced supply and demand . . . . (3.44–2.65):					
English	3.37	3.51	2.78	2.30	2.05
Music-instrumental	3.33	3.65	3.33	3.30	3.03
Library science	3.31	3.58	4.26	—	—
Counselor-secondary	3.13	3.76	3.03	3.31	2.69
Music-vocal	3.06	3.32	2.97	3.03	3.00
Counselor-elementary	3.05	3.38	2.96	3.00	3.15
Language, mod.-Spanish	2.95	3.34	2.88	2.84	2.47
Driver's education	2.87	2.98	3.06	2.63	2.44
Journalism	2.77	2.98	2.50	2.54	2.86
Language, mod.-other	2.70	3.33	3.23	—	—
Speech	2.65	2.50	2.47	2.48	2.46
Teaching fields with slight surplus of teachers . . . . (2.64–1.85):					
Language, mod.-French	2.58	2.68	2.49	2.15	2.15
Language, mod.-German	2.58	2.70	2.17	2.28	2.03
Elementary-intermediate	2.56	2.84	2.33	1.97	1.90
Home economics	2.54	2.85	2.67	2.37	2.62
Elementary-primary	2.24	2.77	2.19	1.84	1.78
Health education	2.24	2.17	2.16	2.38	2.27
Social science	2.05	1.98	1.83	1.51	1.51
Art	2.00	2.45	2.06	1.72	2.14
Teaching field with considerable surplus of teachers . . . . (1.84–1.00):					
Physical education	1.80	1.82	1.67	1.86	1.74

*5 = Greatest demand, 1 = least demand

Source: James N. Akin, *Teacher Supply/Demand 1981.* Madison, WI: Association for School, College and University Staffing, January 1981, p. 3.

The larger proportion of teachers are in the basic academic areas.

Table 5.6. Instructors Needed to Educate the Handicapped.

Area of Handicapped	Estimated Children of Elementary and Secondary School Age	Number of Additional Teachers and Specialists Needed
Speech Handicapped	1,833,230	12,733
Emotionally Disturbed	1,047,560	121,791
Mental Retardation	1,204,694	58,406
Specific Learning Disabilities	523,780	22,564
Hard of Hearing	261,890	12,100
Crippled and Other Health Disorders	261,890	5,674
Visually Handicapped	52,378	2,877
Deaf	39,283	823
TOTAL	5,224,705	236,968

Source: Council for Exceptional Children, National Education Association.

Whom, then, do I call educated . . . ? First, those who manage well the circumstances which they encounter day by day, and who possess a judgment which is accurate in meeting occasions as they arise and rarely misses the expedient course of action; next, those who are decent and honourable in their intercourse with all with whom they associate, tolerating easily and goodnaturedly what is unpleasant or offensive in others and being themselves as agreeable and reasonable to their associates as it is possible to be; furthermore, those who hold their pleasures always under control and are not unduly overcome by their misfortunes, bearing up under them bravely and in a manner worthy of our common nature; finally, and most important of all, those who are not spoiled by successes and do not desert their true selves and become arrogant, but hold their ground steadfastly as intelligent men, not rejoicing in the good things which have come to them through chance rather than in those which through their own nature and intelligence are theirs from their birth. Those who have a character which is in accord, not with one of these things, but with all of them—these, I contend, are wise and complete men, possessed of all the virtues.

These then are the views which I hold regarding educated men.

Isocrates

Table 5.7. Number of Handicapped Children Receiving Educational Services, 1979–80.

1.	California	355,533	27.	Washington	54,049
2.	Texas	267,612	28.	Arizona	48,303
3.	Illinois	250,463	29.	Colorado	47,228
4.	New York	218,587	30.	Arkansas	45,027
5.	Ohio	201,352	31.	Oregon	44,145
6.	Pennsylvania	190,244	32.	Mississippi	42,430
7.	Michigan	155,385	33.	Kansas	38,733
8.	New Jersey	149,578	34.	Utah	36,127
9.	Massachusetts	141,869	35.	West Virginia	33,964
10.	Florida	136,963	36.	Nebraska	30,386
11.	North Carolina	114,894	37.	Maine	24,343
12.	Georgia	101,847	38.	New Mexico	20,479
13.	Indiana	98,818	39.	Idaho	18,066
14.	Missouri	98,134	40.	Rhode Island	16,071
15.	Maryland	93,763	41.	Delaware	14,434
16.	Tennessee	93,004	42.	Montana	12,781
17.	Virginia	91,051	43.	New Hampshire	12,627
18.	Louisiana	85,640	44.	Vermont	12,424
19.	Minnesota	82,346	45.	Hawaii	11,382
20.	Alabama	72,378	46.	Nevada	11,207
21.	South Carolina	71,466	47.	Alaska	10,242
22.	Kentucky	67,087	48.	Wyoming	9,873
23.	Wisconsin	65,611	49.	South Dakota	9,850
24.	Connecticut	62,551	50.	North Dakota	9,776
25.	Oklahoma	60,997	51.	District of Columbia	5,217
26.	Iowa	58,969			
				UNITED STATES	4,036,255

Source: HEW, Bureau of Education for the Handicapped, unpublished data, May 1980.

The message in the current teacher supply and demand picture for students considering a career in teaching is that teaching is going to continue to be one of the nation's largest enterprises. Teacher education graduates with good credentials who are willing to accept teaching positions where they occur are going to continue to get jobs. As we move into the 1980s, the employment prospects for prospective teachers appear to be improving considerably.

Probably out of every ten graduates of teacher training programs, only four are very interested in teaching and actively seeking teaching jobs. Another three of the ten will teach only if they get a position that suits them where they want it, and another three are not interested in teaching. The latter three are those who want the courses and experience teacher training provide, but they are not part of the 'surplus,' because they are using the training as a general education option and have no intention of making teaching a career.

John Palmer

Obtaining a Position

For those who are trying to decide whether or not to pursue teaching as a career, and those who are nearing the completion of a teacher education program, considerations about obtaining a teaching position are of utmost importance. While first presented over a decade ago, the following discussion contains excellent and currently relevant suggestions about selecting a teaching career direction and obtaining a teaching position:

The first basic decision you must make which definitely affects how you go about selecting a teaching position is determined by looking inward. Considering you—yourself—honestly, dispassionately, objectively, you ask yourself the question, "Am I looking for a position where there is the greatest need for help, where I can do the greatest good for society, where my abilities will be challenged to the utmost by difficult situations or am I looking for a position which will be most beneficial to me—gives me the greatest opportunity to travel, pays the highest salary, contains the pleasantest environment, commands the strongest resources, and includes the most stylish and compatible faculty?" Your choice is a very personal one and to be happy and successful in your first professional experience it must be fought through with yourself honestly and dispassionately for the good of your own mental health and the goodness of society. Dedicated, superior teachers are needed desperately in the slums, ghettos, in poverty-stricken outlying areas and in developing countries—but what we don't need is more frustrated, unhappy, and inept teachers who may do more harm than good. Nor do we need the "do-gooder" who is impervious and unconscious to the real problem.

You must face yourself honestly in regard to this question and not feel guilty for the direction you choose. There are many legitimate reasons why you should not seek out trouble in your first experience. One important consideration is that in the safe sanctity of the suburb you may find opportunity to gain needed experience before facing more difficult teaching experiences.

Now that you have faced the more personal and philosophical question of how far you are ready to go in helping society, the next step of decision-making is simpler in terms of establishing an objective list of pros and cons.

Selecting implies choosing, making comparisons, evaluating and carefully arriving at a final decision. While you can make this next phase of the selection process quite simple and mechanical, it does take time. You should not relegate it to a last-minute activity during your senior year. The task is too crucial. Do not think you are just choosing a job for one year but rather you are beginning a career.

To keep the choice of the first teaching position from becoming a near-perfunctory one, you might ask significant questions such as the following:

What do I look for in the school system with which I wish to be associated?

How important are working conditions?

What are the opportunities for professional growth?

What are the positions for orientation and induction of new teachers?

Can I make a contribution to this school and community?

Is recognition given to staff achievement and contributions?

How will I be evaluated?

Many of the answers to questions like these can be secured by early and persistent investigation of numerous and various sources of information available to you. Talk with teachers already employed in school

Dedicated, superior teachers are desperately needed: frustrated, inept teachers may do more harm than good.

systems in which you are interested. Talk with your college and university instructors and the people in the placement bureaus about the local schools or schools in another state. Even more valuable would be visits to these schools during semester breaks. These visits would permit you to see and appraise firsthand the physical facilities, variety of instructional materials and methods, and also sense the climate of the school and community.

If you are interested in teaching in another state, you can secure additional information about the schools and communities by writing to the state departments of education, the superintendents of the various school systems or to the chambers of commerce. State educational associations and state departments of education very often publish comparative fact sheets about the schools of their states which would assist you in analyzing a school system. Most school systems publish brochures, pamphlets or handbooks containing information on the school program, salary schedules and prerequisites, teaching and special services staff,

policies pertaining to supervision and tenure, opportunities for professional growth, professional associations, and the history of the community. Some schools publish separate and special materials for new teachers which include very detailed orientation information on daily teaching schedule, classroom discipline, policies regarding homework, procedures for fire drills, location and distribution of instructional materials and resources, samples of forms for reporting pupil progress, checklists of duties and suggested teaching plans for the first few days of school.

A critical examination of all the information you receive through informal discussions or printed materials will enable you to eliminate from future consideration those teaching situations which are least promising or attractive to you. The personal visits that you make to schools and communities recommended by teachers in service or by college staff will reveal whether you can adjust to the situation, and, more important, be stimulated to grow as a member of the profession. Analysis of the content of the printed materials you receive can also help you in selecting the

Good teachers are needed in the inner cities and poverty-stricken areas.

most promising teaching situation. These materials often contain statements about "meeting the needs of pupils of varying interests and abilities" or "providing for the gifted, the mentally retarded and the emotionally disturbed." Are there supportive statements regarding special services personnel, flexibility in the educational program and descriptions of special programs? Take a careful look at the sample report card or reporting form which the school system uses in communicating to parents the growth of the progress of the child. Many educators agree that the pupil reporting forms reflect the operating philosophy of the school, the curriculum and the organizational pattern. Does the report form set forth a list of subject matter areas and a letter or numerical grade for each area? Can this type of reporting be reconciled with statements about "full partnership in evaluating each child's growth," "attainment and uniqueness of each child" or "learning is personal, unique, unstandardized"? Examine the statements concerning supervision and evaluation of probationary teachers. Who is involved in evaluation? Are written records kept? Are these records available to you? What new media or procedures are being used for appraising performance? What support, cooperation and assistance will be given during your beginning years of service? Those school systems which you feel are presenting the most positive or desirable practices in these areas should be included on the list of school systems to which you would apply for your first teaching position.

The personnel in the placement office in your college or university can give you much help in obtaining a teaching position. There are many forms to be completed and records to be filed. Great care should be given to the preparation of these materials. You will also need to write a letter of application. It, too, should be carefully written. Specific suggestions about the form and content of these letters are usually presented by the college director or coordinator of student teaching. Sample letters may be found in publications such as student teacher handbooks or professional texts dealing with the student teaching program. Your letter should include a statement regarding arrangements for an interview.

For most students the interview experience is a strained one. They often report that they were tense, nervous, and uncomfortable. However, if you devoted the necessary time and thought in visiting and inquiring about many schools, and applied only in selected schools, your interview should be an exhilarating experience. The background of information that you will already have about the school system will not only allow you to ask pertinent and meaningful questions but will also facilitate communicating your own dedication to teaching and your sincere interest in the particular teaching position. It will also permit you to respond to questions with confidence and clarity, and serve you well in decisions you will have to make.

The decision regarding the particular position to accept is often a troublesome one, especially when accompanied by a deadline date for acceptance. However, your preliminary research should make your decision an easy one. Since you have applied only in selected systems, any offer should be immediately desirable to you.

When you have signed the contract, you should inform your college placement office that you have accepted a position. It is also in good taste to notify at least the school systems which interviewed you and include some expression of gratitude or appreciation for any consideration they may have given to your application.[1]

An attempt has been made in this chapter to analyze the current teacher supply and demand picture in the United States. Topics such as birthrate trends, teacher production, and school enrollment projections have also been discussed in an effort to help the reader understand the employment prospects for new teachers.

Predicting the future is, of course, a very difficult if not totally impossible task. While one can, as has been attempted in this chapter, analyze different variables and apply logic to a prediction, all predictions must be based on assumptions. If the assumptions do not prove to be accurate, the predictions will be wrong. It therefore behooves you to critically analyze the data and assumptions set forth in this chapter and arrive at your own conclusions concerning the employment prospects for beginning teachers. In so doing, the reader will quickly realize that there are many opinions on this topic.

Point of View

In the past few years, the general economic depression in the United States coupled with declining enrollments has had a startling effect on the concerns of the typical college graduate planning to teach. The general shrinkage of job opportunities across all fields has spawned a strong preoccupation with one question among all college students—What kind of a job can I obtain after I graduate? Even though school district consolidation has greatly reduced the number of districts in the United States, small school districts continue as the dominant form of school organization. In the following statement, Professor Arni Dunathan suggests that nowhere is the growing teacher shortage more of a threat than in the nation's smaller school districts.

Teacher Shortage: Big Problems
for Small Schools

Arni T. Dunathan

For 35 years the swords and plowshares of education in the U.S. have mowed down and plowed under small schools. Districts beyond the metrocenters have been coaxed, badgered, coerced, and beaten to consolidate in the name of equity. There were more than 100,000 school districts in 1946; a scant 16,000 remain.

Yet small, independent districts continue as the dominant form of school organization. Districts with fewer than 2,500 pupils enroll 75% of the U.S. school population. Fifty-four percent of them enroll fewer than 1,000 pupils. Nearly nine million children still attend the kind of schools that most middle-aged Americans recall with affection.

The fight to save the small, the remote, and the indigenous has been heroic. Time and again, as the forces for consolidation built up, unwavering community support kept small districts intact. Denied a fair share of outside funding, discriminated against by classification systems, legislated against by lawmakers, and virtually ignored by teachers colleges, small schools fought back with the pitchforks and axe handles of local initiative.

But now comes the teacher shortage. It is a problem national in scope, irrational in character—and beyond the control of local initiative. New teacher production has dwindled to little more than half what it was in 1972. There are critical shortages of mathematics, science, vocational/industrial, agriculture, and special education teachers. Shortages in other specialties are being reported with increasing frequency.

Source: Arni T. Dunathan, "Teacher Shortage: Big Problems for Small Schools," *Phi Delta Kappan,* November 1980, pp. 205–206.

In a recent survey, rural school superintendents in nine Midwestern states more often reported shortages than surpluses in all but two teaching subjects.

Smaller percentages of high-ability high school graduates are going to college each year; among those who do, fewer are majoring in education. As college-age populations decrease in the Eighties, so will the supply of new teachers. At the same time, public school enrollments, at a realistic estimate of 2.1 children per family, will rise. Demand for teachers will increase. The tame shortages that nagged superintendents in the Seventies will become shrewish.

Several characteristics of small schools enliven their teacher supply problems. Small schools consume more than their share of new teachers. The average annual employee turnover rate for schools is 6%; the small-school turnover rate is often three to five times that high.

Small schools get fewer applicants for teaching jobs than do large schools. Not only are large-district salaries higher than their smaller competitors, but new teacher graduates predominantly prefer to teach in urban settings.

Small schools increasingly get no fully qualified applicants for teaching vacancies and must resort to some form of provisional certification. In spite of the fact that avenues for obtaining temporary certification are closing in every state, a spot check with certification officers in five Midwestern states confirmed as much as a fourfold increase in requests for such certificates, particularly from superintendents in small districts.

Career teachers in small school districts are often small-town born, small-town bred, and small-college trained. Rising costs of college education may persuade already dubious high school graduates that a college degree isn't worth the price. As college-age populations become smaller and as fewer high school graduates attend college, we can expect termination of teacher preparatory programs in small public and private colleges.

Small schools need teachers who can teach more than one subject. But teacher training and licensing officials have complied with large-district demands for teachers who are highly trained specialists. Today it is all but impossible for a teacher trainee to acquire more than one certificate in four years of college. Newspaper ads placed by desperate small-school districts ("Needed: basketball coach who can teach vocal and instrumental music") are funny only to superintendents who have those subjects covered.

What small schools plan to do about the problem may not work. Educators and patrons are organizing for class-action offensives in the Eighties. They plan to carry their fight for recognition to capitol hills where, as Boston University's Timothy Weaver has pointed out, they may lack the access and experience to win.

But there is little danger that they will lose. If small-school coalitions fight only for the right to exist, they will win an easy battle in the Eighties. Urban outmigration, along with energy, materials, and transportation concerns, militate for, not against, small schools. New evidence from deconsolidation experiments, as well as the financial plight of larger districts, suggests economies of scale far smaller than were previously assumed. National assessment data that indicate no link between school size and pupil achievement are putting to rest the notion that big is better. Trend-sensitive politicians and agencies are paying more attention to small schools and promising greater access to outside support. There is a growing recognition that small schools never lost what large schools are now scrambling to recover.

The real danger is that while class actions protect the hills, the teacher shortage flood will carry off the school in the hollow. In the Eighties, small schools need to get away from the argument that they *ought*

to survive and get on with survival. The real down-home threat is a shortage of teachers trained and dedicated to practice in small schools. Solving that problem will take a massive, well-coordinated effort at every level.

First, by local initiative or state subsidy, the salary differentials favoring large districts must be closed. Annual increments need to be increased, so that small districts can reduce turnover and the inability to find replacements.

Individual small schools must reward superior teaching and recruit their best students for teaching. Future Teachers of America and cadet Teacher Corps should be part of every school program. Recognition of local teacher excellence should be promoted within school and community organizations. Wherever possible, school districts should help train student teachers. New teachers prefer to teach in schools like those in which they student taught. They are more successful there and remain longer.

Small-school interest groups must work collectively to support teacher training programs, particularly in small public and private four-year colleges where the bulk of small-school teachers originate. Small colleges in the Eighties will bear the brunt of declining enrollments. Universities will survive, but it is not they who supply teachers for small schools.

Small-school coalitions should support state and national teacher organization demands for a larger role in training and certifying teachers. They should insist that approved administrators and master teachers at the local level have the right to design, conduct, and assess inservice programs. Unless small-school systems find some way to train their teachers for additional assignments, there is no reasonable hope of acquiring the multiskilled faculty small schools need.

For their own and the profession's good, small-school interests should discourage further issuance of temporary, emergency, or other marginal certification unless each is accompanied by a bona fide plan to train such persons to full certification in a specified length of time. Escalation of charity certificates masks the real shortage of certified teachers and delays solution of the problem.

Small schools cannot allow themselves to be the dumping ground for the unfit, the inept, and the outrageous. They must collectively insist that the excess capacity of teacher education programs, particularly in universities, be put to use in training teachers for small schools. They must demand equity in the study of urban and rural school problems in teacher training curricula.

At the same time, small-schoolers must call for reallocations in the production of new teachers by specialty. They must ask for a slowdown in the overproduction of teachers for whom there is low demand and a speedup in the production of math, science, vocational/technical, agriculture, and special education teachers.

Collectively, they must lobby for subsidies to students who have the aptitude and desire to serve small schools. They must press for funds to support the installation of small-school education courses in teacher training programs and the retraining of present faculty to teach them.

Finally, they must promote and seed scholarly research about small-school education. Although small-schoolers know best what they are and what they want to become, they need to cooperate with social scientists who can measure, codify, analyze, and transmit the small-school ethos to future educators.

Small-school antagonists may be ready to give up the notion that education equity depends upon the destruction of small schools. They are not, and ought not to be, ready to give up the notion that every child is entitled to the best possible education.

If small schools cannot solve their teacher supply problems, a host of proven technological systems stand ready to deliver teaching without delivering teachers—to keep children on-line instead of in-line.

Questions for Discussion

1. Within the past decade, the number of college education majors has dropped drastically. In your estimation, what will be the effect of this reduction on the supply and demand situation for beginning teachers?

2. How does taxpayer attitude influence the demand for teachers? What other factors influence teacher demand?

3. Several indicators suggest the prospects for beginning teachers will be greatly improved by the early 1980s. What is the basis for this optimism?

4. Many administrators place a great deal of emphasis on the personal interview when hiring new teachers. How do you feel a candidate should act during an interview to make a favorable impression?

5. If you were an administrator, what would you look for when hiring a new teacher?

Supplementary Learning Activities

1. Study an NEA report about the supply and demand of teachers and report on those fields which are least crowded and most overcrowded.

2. Invite a school administrator to your class to discuss what he/she looks for when hiring new teachers.

3. Visit a variety of different schools—nursery, elementary, middle, secondary, trade, and/or community college. Try to arrange informal discussions with teachers and administrators regarding teaching as a career choice.

4. Prepare a checklist (derived from your reading in this chapter) that you might use to evaluate a school system in which you are considering employment.

5. Make a critical self-evaluation to determine whether you should enter the teaching profession.

Notes

1. William H. Roe and Rose M. Verdi, "Selecting the First Teaching Position," *Teaching Opportunities for You.* Association for School, College and University Staffing, 1969, pp. 19–20. Used by permission.

Selected References

Endicott, Frank S. *The Endicott Report 1980.* Evanston, Ill.: The Placement Center, Northwestern University, 1980.

Gerwin, Donald, ed. *The Employment of Teachers.* Berkeley, Calif.: McCutchan, 1974.

Golladay, Mary A. *The Condition of Education.* Washington, D.C.: National Center for Educational Statistics, 1980.

Illinois Teacher Salary Schedule and Policy Study, 1974–75. Springfield: Research Division, Illinois Education Association.

Munse, Albert. "Comparing School Expenditures." *American Education,* January–February 1975.

Pourchot, Leonard L. "Teacher Supply and Job Demand for the Early 1980s," *Thresholds (Northern Illinois University),* Volume 6, no. 1, 1980, p. 27.

Projections of Teacher Supply and Demand to 1980–81. U.S. Department of Health, Education and Welfare, 1975.

Status of the American Public School Teacher, 1975–76. Washington, D.C.: National Education Association.

Teacher Supply/Demand in the United States, 1980. ASCUS Research Report, Madison, Wisconsin, March 1980.

Toombs, William. "Developing Today's Faculty for Tomorrow's School." *The Educational Forum,* March 1977.

Rewards and Frustrations of Teaching

6

This Chapter
- Discusses teachers' salaries as the prime economic aspect of teaching.
- Lists annual salaries of school system employees in 6 major cities.
- Illustrates purchasing power of 1979–80 average salary of classroom teachers.
- Describes the intangible rewards of teaching in terms of both status and job satisfaction.
- Supplies survey data about conditions that help and those that hinder teaching.
- Identifies basic premises regarding the frustrations of teaching.
- Presents attitudes of the public toward education.
- Provides a rank order list of suggested ways to improve education.
- Presents a point of view regarding the hidden dilemma of teachers in role conflict.

As the 1980s begin much is being written and said about the rewards and frustrations of teaching. Increasing attention is given to teacher burnout, lack of discipline, violence in the classrooms, low salaries, and the teacher shortage, all of which serve as deterrents to the teaching profession. Historically the rewards of teaching focused on community status, the love of working with learners, satisfaction associated with helping students prepare for life, and job satisfaction all of which are often considered "Pollyannish" to the advocates of teacher militancy for gaining long-sought economic rewards. When considering the schools as a place of employment, attention should be given to the words of Professor Diane Ravitch of Teachers College, Columbia University, who postulated the schools as a curious institution in American history. She said:

The schools are a curious institution in American history, curious in the sense that they have been the subject of the most passionate admiration, and simultaneously, the most passionate abuse. They have been applauded as the bulwark of our freedom, the foundation of our republic; but they have also been regularly condemned as useless, extravagant, and incompetent.

The tradition of heaping lavish and unwarranted praise on the schools goes hand-in-hand with the tradition of heaping on them equally unwarranted scorn.[1]

Prospective teachers are urged to carefully weigh the school setting as a place of employment with the rewards and frustrations of classroom teaching. There are more pitfalls associated with teaching in the public schools in the 1980s than there were 25 years ago. But we must remember that there are various problems (frustrations) as well as rewards associated with any vocation. The most attractive professions are those which provide challenges to problems, and a proportionate balance of tangible rewards to the professional who satisfactorily meets those challenges. Teaching as a vocation is presently an attractive profession, and has the potential of becoming increasingly more attractive. Teaching, however, while rewarding in many ways, is hardly a profession free of frustrations.

Many teachers further their professionalism during the summer with travel and other educational activities.

Teachers' Salaries

Salary is the prime economic aspect of teaching. A major reason for the 1960s teacher shortage was the lure of higher salaries provided by both private business and government jobs. While the salary gap has narrowed, teaching has not as yet caught up to all private business and government agencies.

Salary offers to persons who are about to receive bachelor's degrees and enter the labor force provide an indicator of changes in employment practices. Surveys of college graduates over the last several years find that the starting monthly salary for teachers was less than for accounting, chemical engineering, chemistry, and computer science, but exceeded the monthly salary offers for general business, social sciences, and health professions. Comparisons of this kind usually do not allow for the fact that teacher salaries are usually for nine months whereas the other salaries are for twelve months. A potential for increased teacher salaries lies in the expansion of summer teaching opportunities which would permit teachers to earn from their profession on the twelve-month basis.

Teachers' salaries differ from city to city and from state to state. Generally, salaries of school system employees in the major cities are higher than in small systems. Table 6.1 not only shows the salary paid a teacher holding a bachelor's degree with 5 years teaching experience, but also compares the teachers' salaries with other employees of the system. Even though teachers in the large city systems work nine and one-half months instead of the full year like most of the other employees, they still get ridiculous salaries compared to the salaries paid to the building trade union employees. So it is easy to see that a gross inequity in salary levels exists here; teachers should earn at least as much as the other employees because of their training and responsibilities.

One of the questions in the National Education Association's 1980 Nationwide Teacher Opinion Poll asked the teachers to report their annual salary before deductions. Table 6.2 provides the responses of that survey question.

While table 6.2 provides survey data regarding the 1978–79 annual contract salaries reported by teachers, the expression of money in terms of constant dollars would render the salaries more meaningful in this inflationary age. Table 6.3 compares average salaries for teachers in 1970–71, and in 1980–81. During this 10-year period, the average salary of classroom teachers

Table 6.1. Annual Salaries of School System Employees in Six Major Cities.

Position	Cleveland	Detroit	Minneapolis	Los Angeles	New York	Chicago
Teacher, B.A. 5 Years Experience	$14,477	$17,108	$12,312	$14,940	$15,250	$17,200
Custodians	19,867 (average)	18,688 to 26,200	12,708 to 15,348	12,750 *	12,417 *	13,289 to 33,313
Carpenters	25,896	25,188	20,586	22,815	22,600	25,908
Electricians	25,584	25,854	23,925	20,140	20,948	26,800
Painters	22,817	23,462	19,896	20,800	15,360	22,047
Plumbers	25,251	24,169	23,012	27,040	18,530	28,152
Lunchroom Employees	4.75 per hr.	3.59 to 4.66 per hr.	3.61 to 4.10 per hr.	3.71 to 4.62 per hr.	3.94 per hr.	3.86 to 4.05 per hr.
Bus Drivers	6.13 per hr.	*	8.04 per hr.	7.30 to 7.78 per hr.	8.07 per hr.	*

*Set by contract with private agencies.
Source: *Chicago Tribune,* Sunday, January 27, 1980, Section 1, p. 8.

Table 6.2. 1978–79 Annual Contract Salary.

Question	Total	Region North-east	South-east	Middle West	Student Enrollment 25,000 & Over	3,000–24,999	2,999 & Less	Teaching Level Ele-men-tary	Junior High	Senior High
1	2	3	4	5	6	7	8	9	10	11	12
What is your current ANNUAL contract salary (before deductions) as a teacher for the 1978–79 school year? (Percent responding.)										
Less than $12,000	19	13	31	19	14	13	17	30	24	21	15
$12,000–$13,999	21	13	31	19	20	16	22	24	21	22	19
$14,000–$15,999	18	16	22	19	14	13	19	21	17	17	18
$16,000–$17,999	13	17	12	11	15	18	12	11	13	15	15
$18,000–$19,999	11	15	2	13	13	12	12	7	11	9	12
$20,000 and more	18	26	2	19	24	28	18	7	14	16	21
Mean annual contract salary	$15,589	16,975	13,351	15,726	16,404	16,978	15,683	13,974	15,041	15,249	15,627

Source: *Nationwide Teacher Opinion Poll, 1980,* Research Memo, National Education Association, Washington, D.C.

Table 6.3. Average Salary of Public Classroom Teachers, 1970–71 and 1980–81.

	1970–71	1980–81	% Increase Over 1970–71	Purchasing Power in 1970 Dollars*
Average salary of classroom teachers	$9,269	$17,264	86.3	$7,423
Elementary	9,021	16,879		
Secondary	9,568	17,725		

*Author's estimate based on consumer price index 4.3% average loss per year.
Source: Adapted from *Estimates of School Statistics,* 1980–81 (Washington, D.C.: National Education Association, 1980), p. 17.

Teachers are standing up for their right to earn a decent wage after years of being treated as second-class professionals on their paychecks.

increased by $7,995—an average increase of 6.42 percent per year over the 1970–71 average salary of $9,269. But if we estimate an average increase in the consumer price index of 8 percent per year (compounded) for this time period, the annual decrease in buying power for teachers is 1.58 percent per year or—15.8 percent for these 10 years. In 1979 dollars, this amounts to $7,804—a loss of $1,465 in purchasing power. Projections for the future also appear bleak with regard to teacher salaries keeping up with cost of living increases. Continued bleak prospects will put pressure on teachers' organizations to resort to strikes for improved salaries.

Fringe Benefits for Teachers

Fringe benefits accrue to teachers in the forms of paid insurance premiums, sick leave, emergency or personal leave, and sabbatical leave. In addition to examining the salary provisions, beginning teachers would be wise to investigate the nature of the fringe benefit program in the district wherein they are seeking employment. Districts vary greatly in this regard, with fringe benefits often worth considerable amounts.

Intangible Rewards of Teaching

Generally, being a teacher carries reasonably high community status, which is an important dimension of career selection for most of us. In addition, teachers are typically highly motivated

and well-educated persons, and tend to derive considerable job satisfaction from being privileged to work with motivated and well-educated peers. Teachers benefit from assorted intangibles associated with working with youth. A kind of pride is generated within teachers from feelings that they are contributing to the future of their nation through helping to educate the young. Only in the United States has universality of educational opportunity come to be a part of the national tradition. Whatever the tangible problems and rewards, certain intangibles of teaching as a career are well worth considering.

All the intangibles of teaching are not so positively idealistic. Teachers are often hard pressed to produce evidence of their accomplishments. The accomplishments of teachers are not readily given to visual assessment. Therefore, teaching is accompanied by a kind of personal mental anxiety brought on by the lack of knowledge that what you are doing as a teacher is productive. Because of this aspect of teaching, the ego gratification afforded teachers through their job is at a minimum.

Thus, the rewards and problems of teaching are both tangible and intangible. Certainly, there are times when an individual teacher might feel that the problems and frustrations of teaching outweigh the rewards. However, the overall attractiveness of the teaching profession steadily improves. Tangible rewards are increasing while tangible problems are being solved. The intangible rewards continue to provide teachers with drives for professional improvement. Teaching as

Teachers benefit from the intangibles associated with working with youth.

a career offers much to those who enter the profession well prepared in their chosen area of specialty. Further, prospective teachers who orient their preparation toward those specific areas of teacher shortage can be assured of finding employment opportunities throughout the United States.

Helping Conditions for Teaching

In a 1975–76 NEA survey, teachers identified the types of conditions which helped them render their best service as teachers. Those factors which were most helpful in rendering better service were training, education, and knowledge of subject matter (17.6 percent), staff cooperation (17.5 percent), and interest in children (16 percent). Also identified as moderately helpful were administrators (9.6 percent), adequate facilities, equipment, and resources (8.2 percent), independence in the classroom (6.5 percent), and personality (5.2 percent). In previous surveys, adequacy of resources and excellence of administrators were frequently mentioned as being of the greatest help to teachers. From 1971 to 1976, the percentage of teachers who had satisfying conditions to report rose from 67 percent to 88 percent. Hopefully, this change in teacher response is an indicator of increasing satisfaction among teachers regarding their work.

Table 6.4. Ranking of Helping and Hindering Conditions for Teaching.

Rank	Helping Condition	Rank	Hindering Condition
1	Interest in Children (29.0%)	1	Heavy Workload (21.0%)
2	Help from Administrators and Specialists (14.4%)	2	Discipline, Student Attitude (18.3%)
3	Cooperative, Competent Teacher Colleagues (11.9%)	3	Incompetent or Uncooperative Administrators (17.5%)
4	Interested Students, Community (9.8%)	4	Negative Attitudes of Public (11.7%)
5	School Environment, Organization, Freedom to Teach (9.4%)	5	Lack of Time to Teach (7.1%)
6	Training and Knowledge of Subject Matter (9.1%)	6	Lack of Materials (5.9%)
7	Good Materials, Resources, and Facilities (5.2%)	7	Lack of Preparation Time (3.6%)

Source: Adapted from *Status of the American Public School Teacher (1979-80)* (Washington, D.C.: National Education Association).

Hindering Conditions for Teaching

The percentage of teachers reporting problems rose only slightly—from 81 percent (1971) to 87 percent (1976). Teachers reported that student attitude and discipline (17.1 percent), poor administration (17.1 percent), and heavy work load (13.9 percent), were the three areas of greatest concern. Of moderate concern were lack of materials, resources, and facilities (9.7 percent), preparation time (9.3 percent), extra responsibilities (8.6 percent), and negative attitude of the public (5.7 percent). Table 6.4 gives a ranking of the helping and hindering conditions for teaching. Of particular concern in table 6.4 is the appearance of Administrators, Materials and Student and Public attitudes as common conditions for both helping and hindering teachers in rendering their best services.

Frustrations of Teaching

The word *frustrate* implies a deprivation of effect or a worthless rendering of efforts directed toward some end. Teachers may often feel frustrated in their work. Much of this frustration comes about from the very nature of teaching. Many teachers enter the profession filled with a high degree of idealism, anxious to be doing such a socially important job. Such idealism would probably survive if each of the teachers' classes consisted of one, or at most, a very small number of pupils. However, the problem of large class size and other problems previously cited demoralize the teacher almost from the start. It becomes quite easy for teachers to feel that their best-meant efforts are rendered worthless, and are not related to some desirable end.

Teaching is also accompanied by a sense of frustrating lonesomeness. When faced with problems in the classroom, it seems logical that a teacher would seek assistance from peer professionals. More often than not, such assistance is not meaningful to the teacher's situation; often outside assistance is not available at all, with frustration as a result.

Evaluation of teaching effectiveness usually does not exist. Building administrators, department chairpersons, and teaching colleagues are reluctant to attempt to evaluate teacher effectiveness, since the criteria for evaluation are nebulous. Consequently, a teacher has little feedback regarding effectiveness and is, therefore, frustrated by this vague aspect of teaching. Most of us like to know when we are effective in our

Teachers often feel that their best-meant efforts are rendered worthless.

work, and our jobs are less frustrating when we realize that our work is effective. The results of a teacher's efforts are for the most part unknown. Those who take the frustrations as continuing challenges of the profession often use those frustrations as the driving forces for improvement in their teaching skills. For those whose personality disposition requires constant reinforcement through feeling that their work is effective, the frustrations are often cause enough for leaving the teaching profession.

The 1980 Nationwide Teacher Opinion Poll conducted by NEA Research included several questions asking about job satisfaction. Of the 1,738 teachers who responded to the questionnaires, the percent responding to the two questions which asked about job satisfaction and the positive or negative effects on job satisfaction are presented in table 6.5. More than one-third (35 percent) are dissatisfied with their current job as a teacher, with almost 9 percent of those very dissatisfied. Teachers in city school systems—systems with 25,000 or more students—and in high schools are a little more dissatisfied than other teachers.

Those areas selected by a majority of teachers as having a negative effect on their job satisfaction are public attitudes toward the schools (66 percent), treatment of education by the media (60 percent), student attitudes toward learning (60 percent), and salary (58 percent). About half say status of teachers in the community (52 percent), and student behavior (49 percent) have negative effects. Less than half indicate that class size (42 percent), opportunities for professional growth (37 percent), physical facilities/environment (36 percent), relationships with parents (25 percent), job security (23 percent), intangible rewards from teaching (20 percent), and relationships with other teachers (9 percent) affect their job satisfaction negatively.

Table 6.5. Satisfaction with Teaching/Effects on Job Satisfaction.

Question	Total	Region				Student Enrollment			Teaching Level		
		North-east	South-east	Middle West		25,000 & Over	3,000–24,999	2,999 & Less	Ele-men-tary	Junior High	Senior High
1	2	3	4	5	6	7	8	9	10	11	12
To what degree are you satisfied or dissatisfied with your current job as a teacher? (Percent responding.)											
Very dissatisfied	9	10	7	10	8	12	8	6	8	8	8
Somewhat dissatisfied	26	26	27	24	28	30	23	28	24	25	30
Somewhat satisfied	39	37	44	38	37	36	41	37	38	42	38
Very satisfied	27	27	22	29	27	22	28	29	30	25	23
Each of the following affects teacher morale. Has each had a positive or negative effect on your job satisfaction? (Percent responding "negative.")											
a. Salary	58	49	70	52	61	58	59	57	51	63	65
b. Class size(s)	42	42	43	37	48	51	44	30	43	43	38
c. Physical facilities/environment	36	39	37	33	37	39	37	33	33	39	41
d. Job security	23	27	16	26	22	24	24	19	21	24	27
e. Public attitudes toward schools	66	74	60	63	67	70	66	62	62	68	71
f. Status of teachers in the community	52	61	43	52	52	54	52	49	49	52	55
g. Treatment of education by the media	60	66	56	56	63	68	60	51	58	60	63
h. Relationships with parents	25	29	32	21	21	30	25	22	23	27	28
i. Student behavior	49	51	52	44	49	57	47	44	44	53	50
j. Student attitudes toward learning	60	62	61	57	61	65	58	59	48	70	73
k. Relationships with other teachers	9	10	8	9	8	9	9	9	8	9	10
l. Intangible rewards from teaching	20	23	24	18	17	26	18	17	17	22	22
m. Opportunity for professional growth	37	42	33	37	36	39	36	38	32	41	43

Source: *Nationwide Teacher Opinion Poll 1980,* NEA Research Memo, September 1980, p. 14. Washington, D.C.: National Education Association.

Good teachers use their frustrations as driving forces to come up with fresh solutions to the problems they encounter.

Public Attitudes toward Education

While most of the rewards and frustrations of teaching can be viewed within the context of the teacher's world of work, public attitudes toward education can provide other kinds of considerations. The "Twelfth Annual Gallup Poll of Public Attitudes Toward Education" (1980) surveyed 1,547 adults in every area of the country, and in all types of communities.[3] The survey involved personal, in-home interviewing. When the respondents were asked to name the most important problems confronting the public schools, the following list of problems in order of mention was formulated:

1. Lack of discipline
2. Use of dope/drugs
3. Poor curriculum/poor standards
4. Lack of proper financial support
5. Integration/busing (combined)
6. Size of school/too many classes
7. Difficulty of getting "good" teachers
8. Parents' lack of interest
9. Teachers' lack of interest
10. Pupils' lack of interest

The Twelfth Annual Gallup Poll of Public Education asked the respondents about their suggestions for improving education in their own communities. The suggestion for improving education that received top priority was "well-educated (trained) teachers and principals," with second in importance being "emphasis on basic education." Perhaps the greatest surprise in the public's selection is the relatively low priority given to "small classes" as a way to improve education. Table 6.6 lists in rank order the fourteen suggestions for improving education with the

Table 6.6. Ways to Improve Education in Your Community.

	National Totals	No Children in Schools	Public School Parents	Parochial School Parents
	%	%	%	%
1. Well-Educated Teachers and Principals	50	50	48	64
2. Emphasis on Basics Such As Reading	49	48	52	52
3. Teachers and Principals Personally Interested in Progress of Students	44	43	48	38
4. Good Parent/Teacher Relationships	40	39	42	44
5. Careful Check on Student Progress and Effort	32	32	32	39
6. An Orderly but Not Rigid Atmosphere	27	26	28	38
7. Useful Materials and Adequate Supplies	25	25	27	16
8. Small Classes	25	24	28	20
9. Special Classes for Handicapped Students	24	25	21	17
10. High Goals and Expectations on Part of Students	19	19	17	25
11. Wide Variety of Vocational Courses	18	17	19	20
12. Advance Classes for the Gifted	12	12	11	14
13. Extracurricular Activities	6	5	7	7
14. Successful Athletic Teams	6	7	4	1
Don't Know/No Answer	6	7	4	1

Source: George H. Gallup, "Twelfth Annual Gallup Poll of Public Education," *Phi Delta Kappan*, September 1980, pp. 35–36.

percent response for the entire national sample, for adults with no children in schools, for public school parents, and for parochial school parents.

Since most of us intend to spend much of our lives working for organizations we naturally seek information about the organizational work we are considering. The previous discussions related to salaries and fringe benefits, intangible rewards, helping and hindering conditions, frustrations, and public attitudes toward education provided such information about teaching. Prospective teachers, and practicing teachers as well, might lose sight of the presence of a reward side of teaching when attention seems most frequently focused on the frustrating aspects. There obviously must be associated with the work of teachers rewards of all kinds that attract and hold highly competent persons in the vocation. Certainly the monetary rewards are important considerations. In addition, there are personal and professional rewards and frustrations that ought to be examined by prospective teachers.

Point of View

When a person accepts employment as a teacher within the public school system, there exists a hidden dilemma of serious role conflict which could result in teaching problems. One could argue that employment within the private business community would involve less inherent role

Teachers must be executive and counselor oriented.

conflicts since the business world's work routine would be more clearly delineated than the work routine of teachers. Teachers are executive (supervisory, directive, critical) and counselor (supportive, advisory, knowledge) oriented. But these are often contradictory roles, and together can result in anger and frustration. Is a resolution possible? In the view of Susan Ketchin Edgerton, former high school English teacher in Chapel Hill, North Carolina, the usual psychological orientation in education is not enough, for there are still personality shortcomings which account for tension and conflicts. Her article considers several reasons which suggest that teacher education must include not only study of learning theory and methods, but also a systematic examination of the social nature of the school.

Teachers in Role Conflict: The Hidden Dilemma

Susan Ketchin Edgerton

Nearly every time they get together, teachers seem compelled to exchange war stories and complaints. They emerge with the same old soul-numbing conclusion: Teaching must be the most frustrating, harrowing, and futile job this side of Purgatory.

They may be right. Let us assemble a bill of particulars.

Throughout the day a teacher must deal with a huge catalogue of expectations, rules, and duties. She must sign admission slips, issue hall passes, take attendance, make announcements, upbraid tardiness, supply four or five pencils, collect late assignments, disarm spitballers, and frown down screechers. At the same time, she must (and wants to) acknowledge each student, custom-tailor her compliments, encourage the timid, guide the bold, individualize instruction, implement behavioral objectives, and foster creative thinking. She wants to experiment, to be innovative, to motivate her students. Meanwhile, she must administer discipline fairly and consistently, using her knowledge of the wayward student's psychological past and remembering the needs of other students. Sometime during each day she is expected to accept her share of at least two of the following: bus duty, lunch duty, hall monitoring, ditto making and duplicating, paper grading, homeroom duties, and the completion of state attendance registers. She must help colleagues, devise lesson plans, assemble materials, and clean up her room. Each week she must talk with parents, sponsor extracurricular activities, and attend departmental meetings, faculty meetings, and committee meetings. Once a month PTA meetings, parent nights, and staff development workshops appear on her list of things to do.

Source: Susan Ketchin Edgerton, "Teachers in Role Conflict: The Hidden Dilemma," *Phi Delta Kappan*, October 1977, pp. 120–22. Reprinted by permission.

Underlying each expectation and requirement is the teacher's desire to help people learn, cope, and create.

Over the past few years a series of changes (smaller class size, teacher aides, improved curriculum) have been instituted to alleviate work loads and bolster morale in many schools. Yet, no matter what reforms have been made, conscientious teachers still emerge from the building each day discouraged, angry, and depleted. It seems that external changes, though desirable and sometimes even necessary, cannot solve the problem. It's like taking new crew members on board the *Titanic*. Useful but hardly basic. The iceberg was the problem. What is the nature of the problem in teaching?

I think it is this: Not only do extraneous duties compete for the teacher's time (there is literally not enough time in the teacher's day to perform all of these duties even minimally), but more important, many of the roles assigned to teachers are mutually exclusive. They are inherently contradictory, continually in conflict. By the very nature of her work, the teacher finds herself in an impossible bind. It is this bind, more than lack of time or help, that accounts for the teacher's chronic sense of absurdity, anxiety, and defeat.

In its acute stages the dilemma is like the one you would experience if your brother, a bank robber, should ask you to hide him from the police. What would you do? Whatever you decide, you are left with an uncomfortable and undefined sense of regret and anger.

Of what is this dilemma composed? The contradictory roles teachers fulfill can be divided into two categories. One, the executive,[1] is essentially supervisory, directive, and critical. The other, counselor, is essentially supportive, advisory, and oriented toward the pursuit of knowledge. These two general types are supported by a constellation of supplementary roles.

1. Willard Waller, *The Sociology of Teaching* (New York: John Wiley and Sons, 1967), p. 325.

(The paper-pushing functions, fulfilled by the teacher as "supply clerk," are merely tangential to the executive/counselor dichotomy.)

In her executive role the teacher enforces rules and in general maintains her authority in and out of the classroom. She may interpret this role as kindly adult ("O.K., kids, let's get to class"), as petty tyrant or battle ax ("I don't want to hear any backtalk from you, young man; get to class now"), or as policeman ("All right, move on to class, or I'll have to turn your name in").

A closely related executive role, fraught with conflicts and "guilt pangs," is that of evaluator. The teacher not only evaluates academic performance but, less overtly, "character development." The student must be judged not only on how well he knows the material but also on abstract and subjective criteria such as how hard he tries, how quiet or funny he is, and how well he gets along with everyone.

A third part of the executive role is that of organizational spokesman and mediator.[2] In this role the teacher represents the system in explaining school policy to students. And since all the rules cannot be followed (much less enforced), the teacher also communicates what *really* is expected. When a student becomes tangled in bureaucratic red tape, the teacher has the power to talk (or refuse to talk) to the right administrator or to modify policies ("make an exception") to fit the student's situation.

These roles of executive, enforcer, and spokesman complement and support each other in theory and in execution.

Another set of roles, however, directly contradicts these basically authoritarian functions. The primary role espoused in student teaching and cherished by teachers is that of intellectual guide[3] and counselor. In this capacity the teacher expects to provide intellectual leadership—to be a resource person who discusses ideas, suggests thought-provoking books to read, and makes interesting and challenging assignments.

As counselor, the teacher is expected to be involved in student interests, activities (the bake sale, the big game), and personal problems ranging from failing a test to handling the private terror of drug addiction or unwanted pregnancy.

The chronic rub comes from the constant tension between the contradictory expectations of executive and counselor. Taoist monks may welcome the prospect of infinite paradox, but teachers break down under the strain. Continually trying to cope with the unresolvable uses up a great deal of energy.

Perhaps a brief look at Mary Lou Teacher's life in the classroom will help illuminate the problem. Mary Lou, intellectual guide, enters the classroom ready to get her students excited about William Faulkner. But first she must pass out materials, give Joe a pencil, and call the roll. Switch to supply clerk. Then Johnny, who has cut three classes, slides in. Switch to policeman. "Johnny, do you have a note? . . . Why not? . . . Stay after class."

Then she begins her lesson. Switch to intellectual guide. Luckily, she is able to continue for about five minutes in the role she loves, answering questions, offering insights, doing all the stuff she learned in EDCI 223 at the university. Then she notices tears on a haggard face in the back row. Switch to counselor. "Pat, will you see me after class?" But Pat thinks Mary Lou has switched to policeman: "What for? I didn't do nothing." Although there is some slippage, Mary Lou manages to remain in the counselor role. "Yes, of course you didn't. I just need to see you about something."

By this time the class has begun to mumble. Switch to intellectual guide *and* policeman, "Now class, quiet down or I'll have to . . . uh, Janie, what did I say about Faulkner's use of symbolism? . . . . You don't know? Bill, do you?" Switch to evaluator.

2. Philip Schlechty, *Teaching and Social Behavior: Toward an Organizational Theory of Instruction* (Boston: Allyn and Bacon, 1976), p. 154.
3. Ibid., p. 159.

"O.K., I'm going to test you on this, so pay close attention." Poof—out with free inquiry about Faulkner and in with executive coercion:

"Learn this because I'm going to grade you on it."

With that announcement, Mary Lou notices a subtle change in her class. Some students perk up and begin taking notes. Mary Lou, now intellectual guide-evaluator, has mixed emotions: "I'm glad they're finally showing some interest," she thinks, "but isn't it too bad that they're so grade-conscious?" She blames her students, or the grading system, or pressure-dealing parents, and herself for making grades the condition of learning. She is therefore slightly angry. Switch to organizational spokesman. "You kids shouldn't worry so much about grades; it's learning that is important." The kids, of course, know the difference between that party line and the reality of the report card.

Other kids in Mary Lou's "changed" class had immediately switched off when Mary Lou said "grades." Several of them in one corner scrunched down in their seats and began to talk. "Switch to policeman? counselor?" Mary Lou wonders (but not in those words). After all, these kids need help, not censure. So Mary Lou, counselor, says: "Boys, give this a chance and see if you can tell me. . . ."

"Man, what's she jabbering about?" Johnny snarls to his buddies and follows with a barrage of abusive language. Mary Lou snaps. Counselor switches to policeman to petty tyrant: "You, you, and *you*—OUT!" Johnny, of course, resists; tension builds. His buddies leave the room muttering, "It ain't fair! I wasn't talking."

By the end of class everyone's resentment or fear and frustration are deeply interfering with any curiosity or enjoyment there might have been. Mary Lou, gentle intellectual guide, has watched herself being transformed into a shrew. She feels defeated again. She blames herself and Johnny.

How do teachers cope with these conflicts? The consequences of such role incompatibility for teacher morale and effectiveness are significant. Quite often teachers become ultracritical of the administration, students, and parents. They develop distinctly unpleasant personality characteristics. Many become acutely ambivalent toward teaching itself and either literally or figuratively resign. How many of us begin the school year with optimism and good will only to become more distrustful and petty as the year wears on? How many of us have felt a surge of self-hate after screaming at a student, secretly realizing that we don't like the kind of person we are becoming? A surprising number of first- and second-year teachers become convinced that they do not want to remain in the classroom because of frightening behavioral changes they see in older teachers.[4]

These unfortunate coping mechanisms are well documented in sociological studies of employees in role conflict. They are not unusual. The tragic fact is that a person who has coped in these ways is not an effective teacher. Even the rare souls who manage to carve out a niche of personal influence in the classroom could be much more effective and exciting leaders were they not severely hampered by contradictory role expectations.

The fact that role conflict is a sometimes devastating but little recognized phenomenon has several compelling implications for educators interested in school reform.

Teacher education must include not only study of learning theory and methods but also a systematic examination of the social nature of the school, with special emphasis on the organizational structure of the school and the roles implicit in it. Student teachers, having examined school problems from a sociological perspective, will be less traumatized by the "unknown" forces they confront during their first teaching experience. As they remain in the classroom, an understanding of role conflict will enable them to be aware

4. Seymour B. Sarason, *The Culture of the School and the Problem of Change* (Boston: Allyn and Bacon, 1972), p. 165.

that the debilitating problems and tensions they experience are not due solely to their own personal weaknesses or inadequacies. Principals, superintendents, and other administrators who understand sociological problems of the school and classroom can speak in a language that rings true to classroom veterans.

The study of teacher role conflicts is only one dimension of a useful sociological orientation—an orientation educational researchers must at least include in efforts to understand and solve serious school problems. Until structural sources of tension are recognized and managed, merely personal resolutions of tensions remain illusory and transitory.[5] In other words, the usual psychological orientation in education that accounts for tension and conflict strictly in terms of personality shortcomings is not enough.

Questions for Discussion

1. What do you consider to be the three most important problems related to inadequate teaching conditions? Why?

2. While average teacher salaries have gone up over the last several years, salary averages for other jobs have risen even more. In your estimation, what is the impact on motivation for teaching so far as salary is concerned? What other factors are important for influencing a person to seek a teaching position?

3. Are women discriminated against in teaching opportunities? To what extent has the women's liberation movement opened up further opportunities for women in education?

4. To what extent should teachers adjust their methodology to satisfy community desires? How can teachers help educate communities toward the acceptance of newer procedures?

5. This chapter listed school problems identified from the Gallup Poll of public attitudes toward education. How would you (as a teacher) strive to modify your pedagogy to minimize such problems in your classes?

Supplementary Learning Activities

1. After reading several articles on the topic, prepare a set of symptoms that teachers might use in establishing an argument in support of corporal punishment in schools.

2. Conduct interviews with teachers who have a varied length of experience for the purpose of discussing the tangible and intangible rewards and problems of teaching. Formulate a summary of the interview findings.

3. Let each class member report the qualities of the best teacher he/she has had. Formulate a list of the most common "excellent teacher" qualities.

4. Organize a brief survey questionnaire about attitudes toward education. Use your questionnaire to conduct a poll among your classmates. Compare your classmates' attitudes toward education with the results of the public attitudes toward education presented in this chapter.

5. Give some of the important court decisions (of both state supreme courts and the U.S. Supreme Court) that have affected education.

Notes

1. Diane Ravitch, "In Defense of the Schools," *American Educator,* October 1977, p. 15.

2. George H. Gallup, "Twelfth Annual Gallup Poll of Public Education," *Phi Delta Kappan,* September 1980, p. 34.

5. Schlechty, op. cit., p. 191.

Selected References

Banas, Casey. "A Primer for Teachers on Maintaining Discipline." *Chicago Tribune,* September 10, 1980.

Bell, Terrel H. "What Makes a Good Leader?" *American Educator.* Washington, D.C.: American Federation of Teachers, Winter 1977.

Carter, David G., et al. "Student and Parents Rights: What Are Their Constitutional Guaranties?" *NOLPE School Law Journal,* 1976, pp. 45–60.

Discipline and Learning: An Inquiry into Student-Teacher Relationships. West Haven, Connecticut: NEA Distribution Center.

Estimates of School Statistics 1979–80. Washington, D.C.: National Education Association, 1980.

"Help!! Teacher Can't Teach." *Time,* June 16, 1980, pp. 54–63.

Kovacs, Frank W. (Director). *Nationwide Teacher Opinion Poll, 1980.* Washington, D.C.: National Education Association Research Memo, September 1980.

National Task Force for High School Reform. *The Adolescents, Other Citizens, and Their High Schools.* New York: McGraw-Hill, 1975.

Ornstein, Allan C. "Teachers' Salaries: Past, Present, Future." *Phi Delta Kappan,* June 1980, pp. 677–79.

Valente, William D. *Law in the Schools.* Columbus, Ohio: Charles E. Merrill Company, 1980.

THE TEACHERS' UNION

Teacher Organizations

7

This Chapter
- Outlines the functions of teacher organizations through the use of graphs, charts, and current publications.
- Focuses on the objectives conflict between the American Federation of Teachers (AFT) and the National Education Association (NEA).
- Presents the data and sequences the events that dim the prospects for a merger of AFT and NEA.
- Identifies the manifestation of teacher power as resident with the local teacher organization.

- Translates the emotions and issues of teacher strikes into understandable teacher concerns.
- Generalizes about the efforts of teacher organizations to offer benefits for members.
- Provides the National Education Association's Bill of Teacher Rights.
- Provides the American Federation of Teachers' Bill of Rights.
- The chapter point of view centers on Gallup Poll findings regarding teacher strikes and required union membership.

Membership in teacher organizations may be considered as an important determinant of social success, and even physical survival in certain situations. Organizations are prized by some members in terms of what the organization can do for them. Often the pressures of special interest groups, such as teacher organizations, have a significant influence on the operations of school government. In this way teacher organizations are effective agents in dealing with teacher concerns.

Teachers are solicited for membership in numerous types of organizations. The most popular types of organizations are those which bring members of an occupational group together for the advancement of their mutual purposes. The two major teacher organizations are the (1) American Federation of Teachers, a union affiliated with the American Federation of Labor—Congress of Industrial Organizations (AFL-CIO), and (2) the National Education Association (NEA). The NEA membership population is 1,709,673, and consists of teachers in large metropolitan schools, suburban schools, and rural schools throughout the United States. The AFT members number over one-half million

(519,279), and are drawn mostly from teachers in large metropolitan schools. Since the social milieu of the metropolitan teachers is similar to that of lower level employees of mass industry, the union identification of the AFT with the AFL-CIO is perceived by metropolitan teachers as the best means of attaining their goals. In the last decade, as the NEA has become more and more unionistic in identification, additional members have been attracted from the large metropolitan school systems. At the same time, the NEA has kept a professional association image which helps to sustain membership among teachers outside the large metropolitan centers. While there are other organizations for teachers in the private schools, independent city organizations, and for other local teacher groups, the National Education Association (NEA), and the American Federation of Teachers (AFT) are the two largest and most powerful teacher organizations. Chances are very good that most beginning teachers will be solicited to join either the NEA or the AFT during their first year of teaching.

Teacher organizations give teachers a collective voice.

National Education Association (NEA)

The NEA was originally founded in 1857 as the National Teachers Association. In 1870 the National Association of School Superintendents and the American Normal School Association merged to form the National Education Association (NEA). The two purposes stated in the charter are "to elevate the character and advance the interests of the profession of teaching, and to promote the cause of education in the United States."

In 1966, black and white educators demonstrated their concern for the unity and integrity of the teaching profession by arranging a merger of the National Education Association with the American Teachers Association. The merger of NEA and ATA paved the way for merger agreements between black and white associations in state and local affiliates throughout the South.

It also signaled NEA's great leap forward in terms of promoting civil and human rights of educators and children. For decades the ATA had sought to eliminate discrimination in education; to eradicate racism in American society; to improve the education of children; and to strengthen the educational systems of communities.

Today, the NEA is governed by the annual Representative Assembly composed of 7,604 delegates from affiliated state and local associations. This body develops policy resolutions which are interpreted by a Board of Directors, which consists of one director for each state affiliate plus an additional director for each 20,000 active NEA members within that state affiliate, and the Executive Committee, made up of the three executive officers and six members elected at large by the Representative Assembly.

Tied into the NEA are a number of standing committees and special committees. While a part

Teachers are encouraged to take part in conferences and conventions.

of the parent NEA, these committees often represent the major organizational affiliation for the teachers. These committees are self-governing groups within the profession, with some serving general interests. The standing committees facilitate operations and advise NEA's governing bodies in various program areas. Special committees are established to accomplish specific tasks. Created by the Representative Assembly and financed by the Association, a number of national commissions also develop their own programs. Typical of these commissions are the National Commission on Professional Rights and Responsibilities (PR&R) and the National Commission on Teacher Education and Professional Standards (TEPS). The NEA also organizes a number of standing committees, which are charged with developing specific programs in such areas as citizenship and ethics. The organization chart of the NEA, as outlined in figure 7.1, shows the

various standing committees of the representative assembly, standing committees relating to programs, and special committees within the NEA.

The income of the Association is derived almost entirely from membership dues, with a small amount returning from the sale of publications. Budgeted expenditures for 1980–81 will exceed $60 million.

Headed by the Executive Director, who is chosen by the Executive Committee, a staff of several hundred individuals serves in the NEA Center (1201 Sixteenth St. N.W., Washington, D.C. 20036), and in eleven regional offices. The Association is an affiliate of the World Confederation of Organizations of the Teaching Profession (WCOTP), which includes national teacher organizations in practically every country of the free world.

Figure 7.1. Organization Chart of the National
Education Association of the United States.

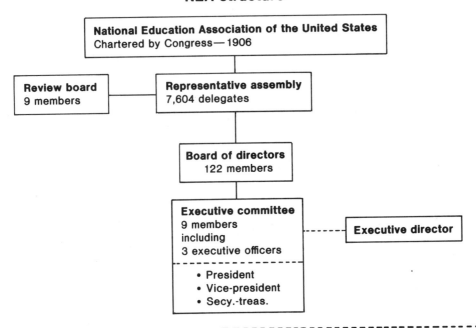

NEA structure

National Education Association of the United States
Chartered by Congress—1906

Review board
9 members

Representative assembly
7,604 delegates

Board of directors
122 members

Executive committee
9 members
including
3 executive officers

- President
- Vice-president
- Secy.-treas.

Executive director

Standing committees of the representative assembly	Standing committees related to program	Special committees
• Constitution, bylaws, and rules • Program and budget • Resolutions • Credentials • Elections	• Affiliate relationships • Human relations • Instruction and professional development • International relations • Legislative and financial support for public education • National public relations • Teacher benefits • Teacher rights	• Minority affairs (1975–81) • Vocational and practical arts educators (1978–81) • Education of the handicapped (1979–81) • Women's concerns (1980–82)

Note: This chart does not include
ad hoc internal committees of
the Board of Directors and
Executive Committee.

Source: *NEA Handbook, 1980-81* (Washington, D.C.: National Education Association), p. 10.

A pamphlet published by the National Education Association entitled *Your Future in a Great Profession* lists a few things which the members need to do at the local, state, and national levels.

LOCALLY

Meet your faculty representative at once. He/she is your faculty's professional leader, and will introduce you to professional members and friends. He/she will help you, or secure help for you, during those hectic first weeks of school. . . . He/she is your source of information about your professional associations.

Read the newsletters published by your local association, and become familiar with events and issues which concern you.

Attend meetings. Meet your fellow teachers who serve as association officers and chairpersons. Become acquainted with your professional coworkers who volunteer to work for you. Conscientiously use your influence and vote.

Learn about the activities of committees, and meet the committee members who are working voluntarily to improve your salary, and gain other welfare benefits for you.

Volunteer to work in your local education association in some capacity. Take full advantage of your local association's services, savings, and social events.

STATEWISE

Read your state journals. Inform yourself about educational and professional affairs in your state. They concern you.

Learn about special state association services such as insurance programs and others. Plan to make full use of them.

Attend state institutes, conferences, conventions, and workshops.

Plan to meet association officers and leaders who serve and represent you on the state level.

Keep informed about, and do your part to support, state legislative campaigns.

NATIONALLY

Read *Today's Education*—mailed to members monthly. Take full advantage of its professional articles, classroom aids, guides to publications, instructional tools, and many other special features. Read, also, the NEA Reporter which will keep you up-to-date on NEA accomplishments and plans.

Secure a copy of NEA's Publications Catalog, arranged by subject matter and available to members on request. NEA is the world's largest publisher of professional materials. Obtain and use them to meet your needs.

Write the NEA for information or resources that will help you to meet your classroom needs, improve your relations with parents, help you function well in local association activities, or guide you in your advanced studies.

Plan to spend a day at the NEA Center when you visit Washington, D.C. At the NEA Center you will meet staff employees who work for you on the national level: they produce your publications; represent you before Congress; maintain contacts with the press and with national lay organizations; and provide many kinds of information and service.

Plan to attend an NEA Convention, held annually during the summer in some large city. At NEA conventions about 20,000 members of your profession and visitors from every state and many foreign countries meet, exchange ideas, share experiences, and learn. Some 7,000 delegates from local and state affiliated associations vote to determine NEA's program of activities for the coming year.

Take full advantage of NEA materials to help you to participate effectively in NEA-originated events such as American Education Week.

Learn to use NEA's many special services, such as NEA's field representatives; NEA's salary and negotiation consultants; NEA's consultants in instruction; NEA's research in all areas of educational practice and teacher welfare; NEA's publications and aids with such classroom problems as discipline and the use of TV and teaching machines; and NEA's regional instructional conferences in basic and in special subject matter areas.

Avail yourself of savings and advantages made possible by NEA, such as NEA's Life Insurance programs; NEA Accidental Death program; NEA tours—U.S. and foreign—some with opportunities to earn college credits enroute; NEA-secured deductions on your federal income taxes for your advanced-educational expenses; and quantity discounts for NEA's professional publications.

American Federation of Teachers (AFT)

The American Federation of Teachers is not a new organization. It was organized on April 15, 1916, affiliated with the American Federation of Labor May 9, 1916, and has grown in membership and influence every year since. While the AFT is the largest teachers' union in the United States, the general membership of 519,279 as of May 1, 1979, is small compared to the 1,709,763 members of the NEA. However, the AFT functions as the dominant teachers' organization in some of our largest cities.

In the fall of 1961, an election was held among New York City teachers to elect an agent to bargain with the Board of Education. In the election, the United Federation of Teachers (AFL-CIO) defeated the Teacher's Bargaining Organization which was supported by the National Education Association. This election has been referred to as the opening skirmish of what has grown to be a noisy battle for the loyalties of American teachers. The New York election is cited as a major factor in the rise of the AFT to a position of national prominence.

A pamphlet entitled *Questions and Answers about AFT* published by the AFT provides information regarding organizational structure and affiliation with organized labor. The American Federation of Teachers comprises more than 650 local unions of teachers in the United States, the Canal Zone, Guam, and in Armed Forces Overseas Dependents Schools. State federations of teachers exist in a majority of the states, and are active in legislative and organizational work. The national headquarters of the AFT is located at 11 Dupont Circle N.W., Washington, D.C. 20036. The president, secretary-treasurer, and administrative and office staffs, from here, supply organizational, membership, and other aid to local unions and members as requested.

The general offices include those of the president, secretary-treasurer, administrative staff, and the following departments: financial, organizational, legal, research, publications, public relations and publicity, civil rights, state federations, colleges and universities, membership, and mailing.

Figure 7.2. Organization Chart of the American Federation of Teachers.

Table of organization

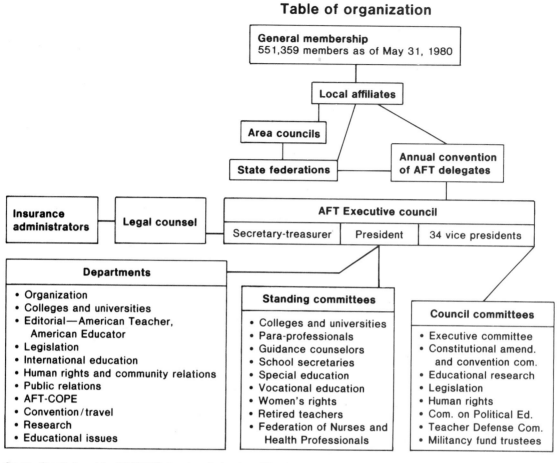

Source: *Constitution of the AFT* (1980), American Federation of Teachers, AFL-CIO, Washington, D.C. Used by permission.

The annual convention functions as the AFT's governing body. Delegates to this convention are elected by local union members. Each affiliated local is entitled to one delegate for 25 or fewer members, and one delegate for each 100 additional members.

The interim governing and administrative body is the Executive Council of 30 vice-presidents, and the president, who is a full-time officer. The president and vice-presidents are subject to election every two years. Vice-presidents, who are assigned to specific geographical areas, serve without remuneration (see figure 7.2).

Organized labor was a major driving force in establishing our system of free public schools, and has actively backed every practical public school improvement at local, state, and national levels. The objectives of the American Federation of Teachers coincide with labor philosophy on the importance of public education.

Labor affiliation gives the AFT and its members the support of the more than 15 million members of unions in the AFL-CIO. Local and state teachers' federations can rely on the support of state and local central labor bodies. AFT local

Figure 7.3. Relationship of American Federation of Teachers to AFL-CIO.

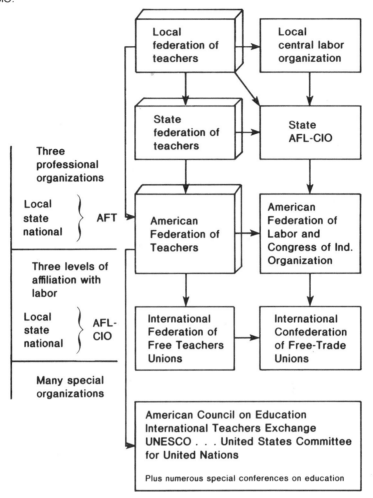

Source: American Federation of Teachers, Washington, D.C. Used by permission.

unions have often won better salaries and other benefits for teachers with the aid and support of local labor trades and labor councils, after teachers' organizations outside the labor movement failed to accomplish these objectives.

Labor affiliation does not impose any obligations on union teachers that would deter them from the best professional service they can render and the highest professional ethics they can command. Labor affiliation, by emphasizing the dignity of the teaching profession, makes it easier for teachers to act, on the job, as the professionals they are. Figure 7.3 outlines the relationship of the American Federation of Teachers to the American Federation of Labor—Congress of Industrial Organizations.

Membership in the AFT includes principals, supervisors, department heads, and teachers, but does not permit superintendents to join on the grounds that superintendents represent the interests of the employer. As with the NEA, a Student

Local and state teacher delegates vote to determine national policies and programs.

Federation of Teachers may be chartered in any college or university under the auspices of the parent AFT.

The AFT boasts that John Dewey held Membership Card Number 1 in the American Federation of Teachers. Dr. Dewey, who died in 1952 at the age of 93, was professor of philosophy at Teachers College, Columbia University. In an address by Dr. Dewey, published in the *American Teacher,* a publication of the AFT, January, 1928, he said:

The very existence of teachers' unions does a great deal more than protect and aid those who are members of it; and that, by the way, is one reason the teachers' union is not larger. It is because there are so many teachers outside of it who rely and depend upon the protection and support which the existence and the activities of the union give them, that they are willing to shelter behind the organization without coming forward and taking an active part in it.

And if there are teachers . . . who are not members of the union, I should like to beg them to surrender the, shall I call it, cowardly position, and come forward and actively unite themselves with those who are doing this great and important work for the profession and teaching.

Total membership in the AFT at the time of Dr. Dewey's address (1928) was approximately 5,000. The steady rise in membership had reached approximately 60,000 at the time of the

1961 New York City teacher election won by the United Federation of Teachers supported by the AFL-CIO labor union. From May 1, 1968, to May 1, 1979, the membership in the teachers' unions affiliated with AFL-CIO rose to 519,279, which represented a gain of approximately 356,000 during a five-year span. While the rivalry for membership strongly continues between the NEA and the AFT, the total membership of the two organizations combined represents only slightly more than 50 percent of all teachers. Obviously, then, many teachers elect to join local teacher groups or do not join any teacher organizations.

NEA versus AFT

During the past decade the tactics and behaviors of the AFT have greatly influenced the tactics and behaviors of the NEA, and vice versa. While the two organizations have differences, such differences are becoming less and less obvious. Table 7.1 illustrates that so far as stated objectives of the AFT and the NEA are concerned, the two organizations are not in basic conflict. In view of the general similarities of purposes which continue to evolve, considerable speculation also evolves regarding the possible merger of the AFT and NEA to form a single, more representative organization for all teachers in the United States. David Selden was elected president of the AFT in August 1968 on a "merger" platform. On October 4, 1968, the AFT extended an invitation to

the NEA to enter into discussions of merger. On October 11, 1968, the NEA Executive Committee declined the AFT invitation to discuss merger prospects.

After nearly five years of informal discussion both the NEA and the AFT confirmed future merger considerations. In June 1973, the NEA's annual Representative Assembly reversed its opposition to merger talks and voted to authorize discussions for the fall of 1973, despite its coolness to ties with the AFL-CIO. The AFT quickly followed suit. At the AFT convention in Washington, D.C., in August 1973, delegates voted to support merger talks aimed at bringing members of the AFT and NEA into one organization affiliated with the labor movement. Seemingly, the major deterrent to the prospects of merger is the issue of affiliation with the labor movement. Nonetheless, the first day of discussions on merger between top Federation and Education Association officers was concluded in Washington, D.C., on October 2, 1973, with agreement on procedural rules for future meetings. AFT President David Selden and NEA President Helen Wise issued a joint press conference statement on October 3, 1973, confirming that talks were held under authorizations from the preceding conventions of the two organizations.

On February 1, 1970, teachers in the Los Angeles school district merged their two rival professional organizations (NEA and AFT) into a single teachers' group. The new teachers' unit, to be called United Teachers—Los Angeles, was approved on a 8,999—5,042 vote by members of the Association of Classroom Teachers, and

Table 7.1. Objectives: AFT and NEA.

AFT Objectives	NEA Objectives
1. To obtain exclusive bargaining rights for teachers and other educational workers, with the right to strike.	1. Economic and Professional Security for All Educators (Collective Bargaining Support System • Exclusive Bargaining Support System • Effective Negotiated Contracts • Contract Enforcement Assistance • Teacher Retirement and Benefits).
2. To bring local and state Federations of teachers and other educational workers into relations of mutual assistance and cooperation.	2. Significant Legislative Support for Public Education (Federal Aid • Federal Bargaining Bill • Enactment of NEA Legislative Priorities • Implementation of Legislation • Election of Pro-Education Candidates).
3. To obtain for teachers and other educational workers all of the rights to which they are entitled in a free society.	3. Human and Civil Rights in Education (Legal Defense System • Coordination of Rights Enforcement • Professional Liability Insurance • Attorney Referral Program • Involvement of Minorities and Women).
4. To improve standards for teachers and other educational workers by promoting better preparation, encouraging relevant in-service training, and securing the working conditions essential to the best performance of professional service.	4. Leadership in Solving Social Problems (Migrant Education and Rights • Violence Within the Schools • American Indian/Alaska Native Education • Desegregation and Integration).
5. To encourage the hiring and retention of competent teachers and other educational workers, the maintenance of modern well-equipped schools, and the promotion of such educational programs and conditions in American schools, as will enable their students to equip themselves better to take their places in the economic, social, and political life of the community.	5. An Independent, United Teaching Organization (Secure and Maintain Membership • Organizational Training • Constitutional Compliance • Coordination of Service to Affiliates).
6. To promote the welfare of children, by providing progressively better educational opportunities for all, regardless of race, color, creed, sex, and social, political or economic status.	6. Professional Excellence (Relevant Preservice and In-service Education • Educational Research Responsive to Practitioners • Influence Public Policies on Education • Information on Curriculum and Instruction).
7. To fight all forms of bias in education due to race, creed, sex, social, political or economic status, or national origin.	
8. To support and promote the ideals of democracy as envisioned in the Constitution of the United States of America, its Bill of Rights and other Amendments, to work for passage and retention of just laws which will improve the educational climate for students, teachers and other workers in education, and to encourage them to exercise their proper rights and responsibilities under these laws.	
9. To encourage locals to organize chapters of retired members within their jurisdiction.	

Sources: *Constitution of the American Federation of Teachers,* Article II, 1979; "NEA Program Goals and Objectives, 1979–80," *NEA Handbook* (Washington, D.C.: National Education Association, 1979). Used by permission.

members of local 121, AFL-CIO. The merger was the first ever of major urban locals of the rival National Education Association and the American Federation of Teachers. The only other merger occurred in October 1969, in Flint, Michigan, where 1,800 teachers joined together. The Los Angeles merger was regarded as a major breakthrough, and potentially the harbinger of a single national teachers' group. Since the Los Angeles merger, mergers have also occurred at the state or local level in New York State, New Orleans, and Gibraltar, Michigan. In November 1973, in Dade County (Miami), Florida, teacher unity discussions began in November 1972 among state affiliates of the AFT and NEA. While the negotiations did not bring about a statewide merger, they did produce a favorable climate for further discussions in Dade County and other parts of Florida. In July 1973 both organizations in Dade County agreed to enter into joint activities to resolve problems. Negotiations were held and, in August 1973, representatives of the two groups—the national and state AFT and the Florida Education Association—signed an agreement spelling out general conditions and a timetable for merger.

By the late 1970s much doubt again arose regarding the prospects for a national merger between the NEA and AFT. In March 1976, delegates to the New York State United Teachers (NYSUT) Convention voted to leave the NEA and remain with the AFT, thus breaking the 1973 New York State merger. Terry Herndon, executive director of the NEA, committed $1.5 million to the New York struggle with a goal of winning back 50,000 NYSUT members. Since AFT president Albert Shanker built the AFT local in New York City into a political and economic powerhouse, his expected leadership of the New York membership struggle should set off strong competitive fireworks once again. Most of the old issues centering on labor union affiliation are being heard once again. However, to a lot of teachers the reasons for merging appear to be better than those for fighting. Several local officers of both the NEA and AFT seem to agree that teachers are not against merger, but state that the national leaders are against merger. At this point, it appears that the prospects for a national merger of the NEA and AFT are remote.

National, State, and Local Affiliation

In the early years of the sixties decade, the NEA was viewed philosophically and operationally as the national organization that served as an umbrella under which the state and local associations were sheltered. Each of the three levels of affiliation could remain as autonomous as desired by their respective memberships. Individual teachers could pay membership dues for local membership only, for both state and local membership, or for national, state, and local membership. This mutually autonomous organizational structure and membership dues arrangement was espoused as a desirable feature in membership recruitment announcements by the NEA and state affiliates. During the mid-sixties teacher militancy increased sharply, lending to the concept of teacher power. Concomitant with the expansion of teacher power was a new need for unification of the three levels of affiliation. Local associations sought increased support from state associations, and state associations sought increased national unity. The need for unity across state and local levels of membership to build teacher power prompted an alteration in the NEA point of view regarding the independent organizational and dues structures. The later years of the sixties found the NEA espousing the desirability of a unified dues approach in which members would pay a single membership fee to cover all three levels of association affiliation. Several state associations have taken direct unification steps by amending their bylaws so that their dues include membership fees for both the state and national associations. The National Education Association has taken indirect steps toward unified membership by requiring both state and national association membership as criteria for eligibility for various fringe benefit programs, such as insurance programs, which are NEA sponsored. The AFT has always had a single dues arrangement whereby AFT members were automatically members at the local, state, and national levels. Under the NEA unified dues approach, a teacher in a given association would pay set yearly dues which would cover national, state, and local costs. As indicated earlier, the AFT has always had a unified dues arrangement.

The Local Association and Teacher Power

Teacher power is manifested at the local school district level by the use of a local organization to press for negotiations. Since the local school district is the quasi-municipal governing agency, the decisions of the local board of education are the decisions that affect the teachers directly. Thus, the most powerful voice for teachers to use regarding the decision-making process that affects them is the collective voice of a strong teacher association. The state education associations and the state federations of teachers provide organizational assistance to the local teacher groups, ranging from formalized procedural information, printed materials, and consultant services—to legal services. Generally, the local teacher organizations in the rural and small town school districts are affiliated exclusively with the state affiliate of the National Education Association. The National Education Association also has considerable strength through suburban and large city local chapters. The strength of the American Federation of Teachers is mostly associated with local affiliates in suburban and large city schools. In a few districts, strong local teacher associations exist independent of affiliation with either the NEA or the AFT.

The primary objective of a local association, whatever the state affiliation, is to vie for direct negotiation rights with the local board of education. In many school districts, two or more local organizations exist, each competing to become the sole negotiations agent for the district. Both the NEA and AFT recognize that a single negotiating agent gives maximum power to the local teachers. In school districts that have more than one strong local teacher association, elections are usually held to determine which organization will be the negotiations agency to meet with the local board of education.

After the negotiation process has been affirmed, the local teacher associations exercise their teacher power through the kinds of matters which they negotiate with the local boards. In addition to salary, negotiation items include curriculum matters, textbooks, teacher assignments, class size, in-service training, student teaching programs, faculty participation in the retention and selection of personnel, academic freedom, and fringe benefits.

Teacher Strikes

Teacher strikes occur when negotiations between a local teachers' organization and the local board of education do not produce acceptable resolutions to the teachers' demands. The use of the strike by teachers became the vehicle of teacher power in the latter part of the sixties decade. A summary of teacher strikes for the 1967–68 school year showed that a total of 114 work stoppages (strikes) occurred, which was considered a veritable explosion in teacher strikes. These 114 strikes accounted for over one-third of the number of teacher strikes in the twenty-seven years since 1940. Following the record number of 194 teacher strikes in 1975–76 there seemed to be a

trend for fewer strikes in the late 1970s. However, in September 1981, teacher contract disputes in several large cities and smaller districts once again threatened massive strikes throughout the United States. While boards of education are tightening control, teachers apparently are not willing to settle for less than what they desire.

Political Clout

Both the NEA and the AFT entered presidential politics in 1976 with active support for their candidate Jimmy Carter. President Carter's election identified the national teacher unions as potent forces in the Democratic Party. When President Carter announced a $13 billion cut in the federal budget for 1981, AFT president Albert Shanker called the proposed cuts a betrayal of the people who elected Jimmy Carter in 1976. In March 1980, AFT president Shanker announced the AFT's executive council endorsement of Edward Kennedy's presidential candidacy. Following President Carter's nomination for re-election, the AFT Democratic Party support prevailed, but with less active direct support for President Carter. The continued active support of the NEA was obvious on national television coverage of the Democratic convention through NEA slogan banners and caps on the convention floor. In earlier times when teacher unions were weaker, they preferred bipartisan politics, rather than risk disfavor by a non-supported candidate who won the election. Since the teacher unions actively supported the re-election of President Carter and the other Democratic Party candidates generally, the

Figure 7.4. Mutual Concerns of the AFT and the NEA.

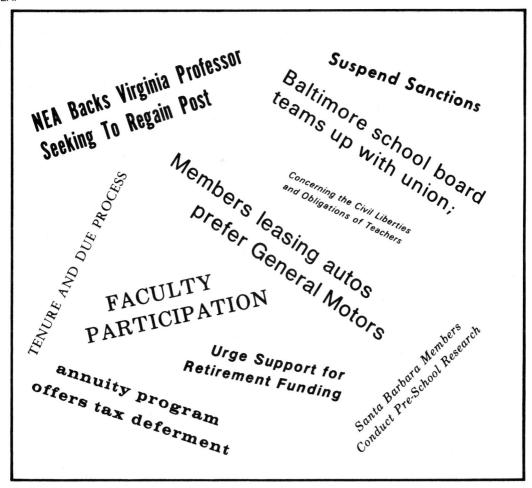

election of Ronald Reagan and the strong support of Republican Party candidates by the voters is being cautiously evaluated by the NEA and the AFT.

Organizational Support Programs

The NEA and the AFT differ in degree in their approaches to specific benefits or programs, but in general terms each organization strives to offer similar benefits to its members. Figure 7.4 illustrates the kinds of fringe benefits and support programs that are of mutual concern to both organizations.

Affiliate publications come to the members of the teacher associations. These usually consist of national journals and state journals, newsletters, handbooks, research studies, and various booklets and reports.

The benefits of research services come to members in the form of reports, such as salary studies, estimates of school statistics, negotiations information, summaries of court decisions, leaves of absence, and fringe benefit programs that exist.

Each of the parent associations have legislative committees at both the state and national levels. These legislative committees work on improving certification standards and improving the laws that relate to teaching.

Teacher welfare is an area of prime importance to the parent associations. Many kinds of programs that focus on advancing and protecting the welfare of members are sponsored by the parent organizations. The NEA and her state affiliates have considerably outdistanced the AFT in this area. Consequently, many teachers have been members of both organizations simultaneously in order to be eligible for teacher welfare-oriented programs. The AFT is steadily increasing research services, publications, printed materials, insurance programs, and consultant services for their members. Among the state educational association teacher welfare programs are: teacher placement services, investment programs, retirement benefits, insurance programs, liability protection, auto leasing programs, and regional service centers. Similar programs are sponsored by the NEA, but to be eligible for their programs the teacher must also belong to the state association. The requirement of state membership is consistent with the unified dues emphasis of the NEA, and prevents the teacher from paying only the national dues in order to profit from the nationally sponsored NEA welfare programs.

Bill of Teacher Rights—Bill of Rights

The philosophical statements of the two major national teacher associations are expressed in the form of the Bill of Teacher Rights (NEA) and the Bill of Rights (AFT). The two statements are included here in their entirety.

Bill of Teacher Rights

National Education Association

Preamble
We, the teachers of the United States of America, aware that a free society is dependent upon the education afforded its citizens, affirm the right to freely pursue truth and knowledge.

As an individual, the teacher is entitled to such fundamental rights as dignity, privacy, and respect.

As a citizen, the teacher is entitled to such basic constitutional rights as freedom of religion, speech, assembly, association and political action, and equal protection of the law.

In order to develop and preserve respect for the worth and dignity of man, to provide a climate in which actions develop as a consequence of rational thought, and to insure intellectual freedom, we further affirm that teachers must be free to contribute fully to an educational environment which secures the freedom to teach and the freedom to learn.

Believing that certain rights of teachers derived from these fundamental freedoms must be universally recognized and respected, we proclaim this Bill of Teacher Rights.

Article I Rights as a Professional

As a member of the teaching profession, the individual teacher has the right:

Section 1. To be licensed under professional and ethical standards established, maintained, and enforced by the profession.

Section 2. To maintain and improve professional competence.

Section 3. To exercise professional judgment in presenting, interpreting, and criticizing information and ideas, including controversial issues.

Section 4. To influence effectively the formulation of policies and procedures which affect one's professional services, including curriculum, teaching materials, methods of instruction, and school-community relations.

Section 5. To exercise professional judgment in the use of teaching methods and materials appropriate to the needs, interests, capacities, and the linguistic and cultural background of each student.

Section 6. To safeguard information obtained in the course of professional service.

Section 7. To work in an atmosphere conducive to learning, including the use of reasonable means to preserve the learning environment and to protect the health and safety of students, oneself, and others.

Section 8. To express publicly views on matters affecting education.

Section 9. To attend and address a governing body and be afforded access to its minutes when official action may affect one's professional concerns.

Article II Rights as an Employee

As an employee, the individual teacher has the right:

Section 1. To seek and be fairly considered for any position commensurate with one's qualifications.

Section 2. To retain employment following entrance into the profession in the absence of a showing of just cause for dismissal or nonrenewal through fair and impartial proceedings.

Section 3. To be fully informed, in writing, of rules, regulations, terms, and conditions affecting one's employment.

Section 4. To have conditions of employment in which health, security, and property are adequately protected.

Section 5. To influence effectively the development and application of evaluation procedures.

Section 6. To have access to written evaluations, to have documents placed in one's personnel file to rebut derogatory information and to have removed false or unfair material through a clearly defined process.

Section 7. To be free from arbitrary, capricious, or discriminatory actions affecting the terms and conditions of employment.

Section 8. To be advised promptly in writing of the specific reasons for any actions which might affect one's employment.

Section 9. To be afforded due process through the fair and impartial hearing of grievances, including binding arbitration as a means of resolving disputes.

Section 10. To be free from interference to form, join, or assist employee organizations, to negotiate collectively through representatives of one's own choosing, and to engage in other concerted activities for the purpose of professional negotiations or other mutual aid or protection.

Section 11. To withdraw services collectively when reasonable procedures to resolve impasse have been exhausted.

Article III Rights in an Organization

As an individual member of an employee organization, the teacher has the right:

Section 1. To acquire membership in employee organizations based upon reasonable standards equally applied.

Section 2. To have equal opportunity to participate freely in the affairs and governance of the organization.

Section 3. To have freedom of expression, both within and outside the organization.

Section 4. To vote for organization officers, either directly or through delegate bodies, in fair elections.

Section 5. To stand for and hold office subject only to fair qualifications uniformly applied.

Section 6. To be fairly represented by the organization in all matters.

Section 7. To be provided periodic reports of the affairs and conduct of business of the organization.

Section 8. To be provided detailed and accurate financial records, audited and reported at least annually.

Section 9. To be free from arbitrary disciplinary action or threat of such action by the organization.

Section 10. To be afforded due process by the organization in a disciplinary action.[1]

Bill of Rights

American Federation of Teachers

The teacher is entitled to a life of dignity equal to the high standard of service that is justly demanded of that profession. Therefore, we hold these truths to be self-evident:

I

Teachers have the right to think freely and to express themselves openly and without fear. This includes the right to hold views contrary to the majority.

II

They shall be entitled to the free exercise of their religion. No restraint shall be put upon them in the manner, time or place of their worship.

III

They shall have the right to take part in social, civil, and political affairs. They shall have the right, outside the classroom, to participate in political campaigns and to hold office. They may assemble peaceably and may petition any government agency, including their employers, for a redress of grievances. They shall have the same freedom in all things as other citizens.

IV

The right of teachers to live in places of their own choosing, to be free of restraints in their mode of living and the use of their leisure time shall not be abridged.

V

Teaching is a profession, the right to practice which is not subject to the surrender of other human rights. No one shall be deprived of professional status, or the right to practice it, or the practice thereof in any particular position, without due process of law.

VI

The right of teachers to be secure in their jobs, free from political influence or public clamor, shall be established by law. The right to teach after qualification in the manner prescribed by law, is a property right, based upon the inalienable rights of life, liberty, and the pursuit of happiness.

VII

In all cases affecting the teacher's employment or professional status a full hearing by an impartial tribunal shall be afforded with the right to full judicial review. No teacher shall be deprived of employment or professional status but for specific causes established by law having a clear relation to the competence or qualification to teach proved by the weight of the evidence. In all such cases the teacher shall enjoy the right to a speedy and public trial, to be informed of the nature and cause of the accusation; to be confronted with the accusing witnesses, to subpoena witnesses and papers, and the assistance of counsel. No teacher shall be called upon to answer any charge affecting his employment or professional status but upon probable cause, supported by oath or affirmation.

VIII

It shall be the duty of the employer to provide culturally adequate salaries, security in illness and adequate retirement income. The teacher has the right to such a salary as will: a) Afford a family standard of living comparable to that enjoyed by other professional people in the community b) To make possible freely chosen professional study c) Afford the opportunity for leisure and recreation common to our heritage.

IX

No teacher shall be required under penalty of reduction of salary to pursue studies beyond those required to obtain professional status. After serving a reasonable probationary period a teacher shall be entitled to permanent tenure terminable only for just cause. They shall be free as in other professions in the use of their own time. They shall not be required to perform extracurricular work against their will or without added compensation.

X

To equip people for modern life requires the most advanced educational methods. Therefore, the teacher is entitled to good classrooms, adequate teaching materials, teachable class size and administrative protection and assistance in maintaining discipline.

XI

These rights are based upon the proposition that the culture of a people can rise only as its teachers improve. A teaching force accorded the highest possible professional dignity is the surest guarantee that blessings of liberty will be served. Therefore, the possession of these rights imposes the challenge to be worthy of their enjoyment.

XII

Since teachers must be free in order to teach freedom, the right to be members of organizations of their own choosing must be guaranteed. In all matters pertaining to their salaries and working conditions they shall be entitled to bargain collectively through representatives of their own choosing. They are entitled to have the schools administered by superintendents, boards or committees which function in a democratic manner.[2]

Point of View

Teacher militancy continues to manifest itself in the form of vote procedures for negotiation representation, negotiated teacher contracts, teacher strikes, teacher involvement in political arenas, and various other activities and events. In some communities teachers have been threatened with dismissal or jail sentences, or both, as a result of their participation in such activities. Among the outcomes of this kind of tense climate are increasing salaries and fringe benefits for teachers, advocacy of stronger teacher organizations by more active membership drives and the merger of competing organizations, and more and more demands by teachers for improved conditions of work.

During the last few years, the objectives of the two largest teacher organizations (AFT and NEA) have drawn closer together. *Teacher unions* as a description of teacher organizations is much more acceptable than a decade ago. The teacher organization as an informal group within the structure of a school system is now viewed as a powerful force in most districts.

Earlier in this chapter it was suggested that "the use of the strike by teachers became the vehicle of teacher power in the latter part of the sixties." During the seventies, not only did the number of teacher strikes increase nationwide, but also the strike strategy reached many smaller districts as well as the large urban and suburban districts. Indications that many educators continue to question the use of unionized labor tactics in the schools were illustrated by the inclusion of questions about teacher strikes and required payment of union dues by teachers in *The 12th Annual Gallup Poll of the Public's Attitudes toward the Public Schools.* This survey, which measures the attitudes of Americans toward their public schools, makes a great effort each year to deal with issues of greatest concern to both educators and to the public. To be sure that the survey would embrace the most important issues in the field of education, the Kettering Foundation sent letters (a survey) to educators across the nation asking for their ideas. The final survey format was designed by an executive committee including representatives of the Kettering Foundation and George M. Gallup who discussed issues, evaluated proposed questions, and added new questions for the survey. While teacher unions, especially the NEA and the AFT, will continue to actively solicit members from the new teachers' ranks, prospective teachers may also

Source: George H. Gallup, "The 12th Annual Gallup Poll of the Public's Attitudes toward the Public Schools," *Phi Delta Kappan,* September 1980, pp. 40, 41, and 43.

find interest in the attitudes of the public concerning teacher strikes and union membership as expressed in the recent Gallup Poll.

Should Public School Teachers be Permitted to Strike?

A conservative trend in most areas of American life evidenced by survey findings parallels increasing public opposition to strikes by public school teachers. In 1975, when this question was last put to the public in this series, a slight majority opposed strikes. The vote then was 48% opposed to strikes and 45% in favor, with 7% having no opinion. When the same question was asked in the present survey, 52% opposed strikes, 40% favored them, and 8% had no opinion.

The question:

Should public school teachers be permitted to strike or not?

	National Totals %	No Children In Schools %	Public School Parents %	Parochial School Parents %
Yes	40	39	43	41
No	52	53	49	51
Don't know	8	8	8	8

The greatest changes were found among college-educated respondents, a group that favored strikes five years ago by a 52% to 44% margin and now opposes strikes by nearly the same margin, 51% to 43%.

In the Eastern states opinion was equally divided in 1975. A total of 46% favored strikes; 46% opposed them. Today the comparable figures are 34% in favor, 58% opposed.

Interestingly, parents of children attending the public schools have less objection to strikes than do those who have no children of school age.

Further breakdowns follow:

Permit Teachers to Strike?

	Yes %	No %	Don't Know %
NATIONAL TOTALS	40	52	8
Sex			
Men	40	54	6
Women	39	51	10
Race			
White	38	54	8
Nonwhite	53	39	8
Age			
18 to 29 years	57	40	3
30 to 49 years	42	49	9
50 & over	25	64	11
Community size			
1 million & over	39	49	12
500,000–999,999	43	51	6
50,000–499,999	46	48	6
2,500–49,999	38	53	9
Under 2,500	35	58	7
Education			
Grade School	31	57	12
High school	41	51	8
College	43	51	6
Region			
East	34	58	8
Midwest	44	50	6
South	40	51	9
West	43	48	9

Requiring Nonunion Members To Pay Union Dues

The public is fairly evenly divided on the question of whether teachers—in districts where there are teacher unions—should be required to pay union dues even though they do not belong to the union. A slight plurality is found on the side of requiring them to pay dues. The public's ambivalence on unions has been evidenced in earlier surveys indicating that, while our respondents favor unions for teachers, they are opposed to strikes.

The question:

In schools where there are teacher unions, should those teachers who do not belong to the union be required to pay union dues, since they share the benefits of union bargaining?

	National Totals %	No Children In Schools %	Public School Parents %	Parochial School Parents %
Yes, should be required to pay	47	47	49	51
No, should not	44	44	43	47
Don't know	9	9	8	2

Differences are found on this issue by sections of the nation. Residents of the South oppose requiring teachers to pay union dues when they do not belong by a vote of 54% opposed to 37% in favor. Sentiment is evenly divided in the small cities and rural communities. The college educated, who are found largely in the upper-income levels, vote against this requirement by 58% to 35%.

Further breakdowns:

	Yes, Should Be Required to Pay %	No, Should Not %	Don't know %
NATIONAL TOTALS	47	44	9
Sex			
Men	44	47	9
Women	50	41	9
Race			
White	47	45	8
Nonwhite	52	37	11
Age			
18 to 29 years	56	40	4
30 to 49 years	44	46	10
50 & over	44	44	12

	Yes, Should Be Required to Pay %	No, Should Not %	Don't know %
Community Size			
1 million & over	47	43	10
500,000–999,999	53	38	9
50,000–499,999	49	42	9
2,500–49,999	44	45	11
Under 2,500	46	47	7
Education			
Grade school	45	39	16
High school	55	37	8
College	35	58	7
Region			
East	54	39	7
Midwest	54	37	9
South	37	54	9
West	46	43	11

Questions for Discussion

1. What is an operational difference between the NEA and AFT?

2. Why are teacher organizations actively engaged in attempting to have state laws passed that sanction the negotiations process?

3. Do you think it is a good idea to have teachers running for political office? Should teachers be permitted to serve on boards of education?

4. Would a merger of the AFT and the NEA be advantageous or not? Discuss.

5. In what way does teacher militancy do a disservice to the teaching profession? Discuss.

Supplementary Learning Activities

1. Invite representatives of the state affiliates of the NEA and the AFT to class sessions to discuss their respective organizations.

2. Interview the officers of a local teacher association regarding their relationships with their board of education.

3. Invite a negotiator for school boards to class to discuss his or her views regarding the role of teacher organizations and the negotiations process.

4. Invite an elected political figure to a class session to discuss his or her views regarding the role of teacher organizations.

5. In your own terms, list the factors that are similar and those that are different, in a comparison of the Bill of Teacher Rights (NEA) with the Bill of Rights (AFT).

Notes

1. National Education Association, "Bill of Teacher Rights" (Washington, D.C.: National Education Association Publications). Used by permission.

2. American Federation of Teachers, *Bill of Rights* (Washington, D.C.: American Federation of Teachers). Used by permission.

Selected References

AFT/NEA: The Crucial Difference. Washington, D.C.: American Federation of Teachers.

Cheng, C. W. "Community Participation in Teacher Collective Bargaining: Problems and Prospects." *Harvard Educational Review,* 46: 153–74, 1976.

Collective Negotiation Agreements for Administrators. Arlington, Va.: Educational Research Service, 1978.

Constitution of the AFT. Washington, D.C.: American Federation of Teachers, AFL-CIO, 1980.

Luke, Robert. "Collective Bargaining and Inservice Education." *Phi Delta Kappan,* March 1976.

NEA Handbook for Local, State, and National Associations. Washington, D.C.: National Education Association, 1979–80.

Odden, Allan. "School Finance Reform." *The Education Digest,* September 1978, pp. 14–17.

Riccio, Alfred T. "Seven Questions (with answers) that Boards are Asking About Bargaining." *American School Board Journal,* November 1977, pp. 36, 54.

"A Teachers' War That's Costing Millions." *U.S. News and World Report,* 5 April 1976, pp. 90–91.

Walter, Robert L. *The Teacher and Collective Bargaining.* Lincoln, Nebraska: Professional Educators Publications, Inc., 1975.

Montana
N. Dakota
S. Dakota
Minn.
Wis.
Wyo.
Nebraska
Iowa
Ill.
Ohio
Utah
Col.
Kansas
Mo.
Kentucky
N Mex
Oklahoma
Arkansas
Miss.
Texas

The Role of Education in the United States

The role of education, of which our schools are the very essence, is becoming increasingly important as our society becomes more complex. This section of the book explores education's role from sociological, historical, and philosophical points of view.

American society is a reflection of our representative form of government, and as such, it professes the ideal precepts of a democracy. The basis of these ideals is freedom: freedom of expression, freedom of opportunity, and the freedom of the people to determine their own destinies. A high premium is placed on the worth of the individual and his or her opportunities for education. A major function of education in a democracy is to develop individuals to their fullest capacities so that they in turn may contribute to the achievement of a democratic society's ideals.

Society's expectations for education are numerous, but among them two readily recognized goals come to the fore: the perpetuation of certain knowledge elements of our culture, and the refinement of our actual ways of living to cause them to become more congruent with our ideals. The second of these gives rise to expectations for the schools to be instrumental in resolving some of our social problems.

Individual expectations for education are also numerous. All Americans, in their own individual ways, have ideas of what they want the schools to do for them and for their children. Their expression of these expectations is reflected by our school programs. Individual voices join to form societal choruses to be heard by those who are charged with directing education. While the size and complexities of our society make it increasingly difficult for the individual to be heard, our form of government and our educational systems are committed to the protection of the right of individuals to be heard.

Historically, expectations for education have changed as our nation has evolved. And generally, our educational system has responded to the demands of individuals and to the demands of society. But in the future the needs of individuals and of society are not likely to be met by schools that take merely a reflective or responsive posture. The schools must assume a leadership stance.

Individuals from all walks of life hold beliefs about education. Philosophers, scholars, professional educators, and lay citizens in either a very formal or informal way function from a set of beliefs about the basic purposes of education, including what should be taught and the methodologies of instruction. These beliefs have had a powerful influence on education and will continue to do so in the future. The last chapter (11) in this section provides a brief introduction to the relationship of beliefs, or philosophies, to American education.

Education's Purpose in Our Society

8

This Chapter
- Presents a variety of expectations that Americans hold for their schools.
- Explains the nature of culture, subcultures, and the concept of cultural pluralism.
- Discusses values, and raises questions about the values that schools should transmit.

- Lists and questions the relationships of many activities that have been relegated to the schools over the years.
- Raises the question of whether our schools should transmit, respond, or lead in our society.
- Provides a point of view dealing with the changing nature of American families.

Society expects many things from its schools. Most of these, however, can be grouped into two major categories: (1) the transmission of culture, and (2) helping to solve our social problems.

Transmission of Culture

Culture may be defined as the ways of living that societies have developed as their members have encountered and interacted with themselves and their environment. As such it includes knowledge, beliefs, arts, morals, values, laws, languages, tools, institutions, and ideas. Every individual is cultured—has a way of living; however, rarely, if ever, would one know the complete culture of one's own society. For example, while most citizens of the United States enjoy and use plumbing facilities, they do not have the specialized knowledge of plumbers. Nor do most citizens have a complete knowledge of medicine, yet they benefit from its advanced state in our culture. Individuals learn the culture of their societies beginning at infancy; much of it they gain from imitation and by osmosis. With maturity, individuals consciously or unconsciously choose for their pur-

poses that which they value from the dominant culture.

The United States, because of its multiethnic origins, contains many subcultures. Most large cities have neighborhoods which reflect immigrant cultures. These neighborhoods feature the foods, arts, and handicrafts of the ancestoral backgrounds of the inhabitants.

Frequently, the neighborhood residents sponsor festivals featuring facets of their ethnic culture. Cultural elements with a distinct uniqueness also develop in geographic regions of our nation, and in the rural, suburban, and urban demographic groups. From these fertile milieus, which have been accumulating, admixing, and altering for the past three and one-half centuries, Americans seek to identify the uniqueness of their total culture.

Schools in our society have been given the responsibility of transmitting culture. They are expected by the citizenry to accomplish this task. What shall they transmit? While a clear and specific answer to this question cannot be given, history has provided some guidelines.

Culture is a human production, and man differs from animals because he creates culture, and because he transmits what he has learned and what he has created from one generation to the next.

Robert J. Havighurst

Learning to read is a necessary early step toward inculturation.

There is little question that the schools are expected to transmit the knowledge element of culture. Historically in our early colonies this meant to teach the young to read, write, and cipher, using the Bible as the basic textbook. As the colonies grew and became a nation and the westward movement began, knowledge came to include vocational skills necessary for our growth. During these periods the secondary schools came into existence, partly in recognition of the added knowledge necessary to foster the development of our growing nation. Today, one need look only at the curriculum of a modern secondary school to realize that "knowledge" has become an increasingly comprehensive term. It still represents reading, writing, and ciphering, but it also represents social studies, biological and physical science, agriculture, home economics, industrial education, languages, business, art, and a multitude of other specialties ranging from automobile body repair to contract bridge.

The "knowledge explosion" has caused many educators to seriously consider what knowledge the school should transmit. It is obvious that in the amount of time customarily dedicated to formal schooling, only a small portion of the total knowledge that humanity now possesses can be passed on to the student. If one could conceptualize knowledge as being of a material nature, such as books, and then try to imagine the size of the mountain it would make, the immensity of the task can be partly realized. Selectivity is necessary as decisions are made regarding which portions of the total knowledge available are to be transmitted by the schools. Americans seem to have said: first of all, let us make certain that each individual is required to learn what knowledge is necessary for one's survival in our society; secondly, let us permit individuals to determine what they want to learn that will assist themselves and perhaps, incidentally, advance our society; and thirdly, let us plan and hope that in the process, skills will be mastered to foster and enhance the development of more knowledge to the betterment of our way of life. So certain parts of the "mountain" are parcelled out to all young people, after which they can select some more if they want to, while the mountain gets larger and larger simultaneously.

Social studies is an important part of the curriculum, and often is a means of teaching good citizenship.

Knowledge transmission, through the American school system, has undoubtedly contributed to the relatively high leadership position of the United States in materialistic manifestations of cultural accomplishments. Our standard of living is closely related to the United States' commitment of knowledge for all citizens through public education. Level of education is definitely a fourth variable in the land, labor, and capital economic formula.

A second traditionally accepted responsibility of the schools in terms of cultural transmission is that of citizenship education. The schools are expected to, and do, make efforts to enable children to appreciate and understand our system of government. An educated citizenry is one that not only has knowledge, but one that is composed of individuals who will use this knowledge to foster an effective scheme of government, of, by, and for the people. In addition to formal instruction in our schools, youngsters also learn about good citizenship by participating in various forms of student government simulating our local, state, and national systems. Student councils, mock elections, and student government days are examples of these activities. While specific societal expectations for citizenship education will vary, perhaps from blind indoctrination to the advocacy of laissez-faire behavior, the most common

> Because our schools help shape the mind and character of our youth, the strength or weakness of our educational system today will go far to determine the strength or weakness of our national wisdom and our national morality tomorrow. That is why it is essential to our nation that we have good schools. And their quality depends on all of us.
>
> *Dwight D. Eisenhower*

position of the schools has been that of enabling mature students to critically analyze, and then to participate in improving our system.

Our overall society has prescribed democratic ideals—ideals toward which our society is striving, and which the schools are expected to exemplify, practice, and teach. A democratic society places a high premium on the worth of the individual.

It is important to note that a major responsibility for achieving the societal goal of equality, particularly with reference to the elimination of racial discrimination, has been placed on the schools. The U.S. Supreme Court in their 1954 *Brown v. Board of Education of Topeka* decision marked the beginning of an era of efforts to eliminate racial segregation. Race relationships will be discussed in the next chapter.

In citizenship education, the schools are expected to bring about a congruency between American ideals and real life circumstances. Some of the dissension apparent in young people today can be attributed to this lack of congruency. Students seem to be saying, "Your actions speak so loudly that I can't hear your words." They have accused the older generations of professing peace and practicing war, espousing equality of opportunity and perpetuating inequality, and advocating participation in political and school decision making while at the same time castigating those who would dare raise a

dissenting voice. Some persons seem to have lost faith in the American system, advocating its destruction, while still others strive to work from within to improve it. Schools today, particularly at the levels of secondary and higher education, in response to student dissent and protest, are changing their traditional ways of participatory student citizenship education.

While American society in general recognizes the necessity of, and subscribes rather unanimously to, the transmission of knowledge and training for citizenship in our schools, the unanimity begins to fragment as subcultural elements are considered. The influence of community subcultures can be observed as local schools decide what they shall teach. The increase of Afro-American studies in many urban schools is indicative of this phenomenon.

Pluralism, Democracy, and Values

As has been indicated, America is a pluralistic society consisting of many different subsocieties. This is a result not only of our multiethnic origin, but also of our emphasis on the protection and enhancement of individual freedoms, as specified in the United States Constitution and as practiced in our daily life. Thus, the democratic form of government fosters pluralism. Gans has suggested that American democracy needs to be modernized so as to accommodate itself to pluralism.

Should schoolchildren be taught to respect the United States flag?

I believe that the time has come to modernize American democracy and adapt it to the needs of a pluralistic society; in short, to create a pluralistic democracy. A pluralistic form of democracy would not do away with majority rule, but would require systems of proposing and disposing which take the needs of minorities into consideration, so that when majority rule has serious negative consequences, outvoted minorities would be able to achieve their most important demands, and not be forced to accept tokenism, or resort to despair or disruption.

Pluralistic democracy would allow the innumerable minorities of which America is made up to live together and share the country's resources more equitably, with full recognition of their various diversities. Legislation and appropriations would be based on the principle of "live and let live" with different programs of action for different groups whenever consensus is impossible. Groups of minorities could still coalesce into a majority, but other minorities would be able to choose their own ways of using public power and funds without being punished for it by a majority.[1]

What values should children be taught?

The National Coalition for Cultural Pluralism, a newly formed group, has issued the following statement calling for action to help bring about a truly multicultural society:

America has long been a country whose uniqueness and vitality have resulted in large part from its human diversity. However, among all the resources formerly and currently used to insure physical and social progress for this nation, the human resource with its myriad ethnic, cultural, and racial varieties has not been used to its fullest advantage. As a result, the American image that has been delineated by its governmental, corporate, and social structures has not truly reflected the cultural diversity of its people.

There should be no doubt in anyone's mind that America is now engaged in an internal social revolution that will thoroughly test her national policies and attitudes regarding human differences. This revolution manifests itself in many ways, through many movements. Blacks, Spanish Americans, women, college students, elderly people, etc., are all finding themselves victimized by technological and social systems which look upon significant differences among people as unhealthy and inefficient. But, whether the society likes it or not, many individuals and groups will never be able to "melt" into the American "pot." And it is these groups who are now gearing themselves up to be more self-determining about their own destinies. For them it is a simple matter of survival in America.

In the future, surviving in America will of necessity be the major concern of every citizen, regardless of his wealth, heritage, race, sex, or age. This has already been made abundantly clear by the developing crisis in ecology. The national concern over pollution, overpopulation, etc., will probably be solved through our technological expertise. But the social crisis facing this country will require a different solution concept, one which will provide unity with diversity where the emphasis is on a shared concern for creating and maintaining a multicultural environment.

The concept of cultural pluralism, therefore, must be the perspective used by the different social groups in their attempt to survive as independent, yet interdependent, segments of this society. Pluralism lifts up the necessary and creative tension between similarity and difference. It strongly endorses standards of variety, authentic options, diverse centers of power, and self-direction.

It is the institutions of our society which provide the supports for some individual and group attitudes, values, and standards which, when applied, are clearly discriminatory against others. It is these same institutions which can reverse many of the current social trends by establishing supports for a culturally pluralistic society—where everyone recognizes that no single set of values and standards is sufficient to inspire the full range of human possibilities.

The creation of a truly multicultural society will not happen automatically. There must be established a plan of action, a leadership, and a cadre of supporters that will effectively implement the concept of cultural pluralism throughout the length and breadth of every community in America. Institutions, groups, and individuals must be actively engaged in working toward at least three goals, which are:

- The elimination of all structural supports for oppressive and racist practices by individuals, groups, and institutions.
- The dispersal of "power" among groups and within institutions on the basis of cultural, social, racial, sexual, and economic parity.
- The establishment and promotion of collaboration as the best mechanism for enabling culturally independent groups to function cooperatively within a multicultural environment.

The accomplishment of these and other goals can be facilitated only through a national effort. Therefore, the emergence of the National Coalition for Cultural Pluralism is an important first step in the right direction. . . .[2]

The fostering of pluralism encourages the perpetuation and development of many different value systems. What are values? Phenix has recognized two distinct meanings of the term *values:* ". . . a value is anything which a person or persons actually approve, desire, affirm, or expect themselves to obtain, preserve, or assist. According to the second meaning, a value is anything which *ought to be* approved, desired, and so forth, whether or not any given person or persons in fact do adopt these positive attitudes toward it."[3] Schools must be concerned with both definitions—they operate in "what is" and are expected to create "what ought to be," and have some difficulty being certain of the values in either case. The United States Constitution has set forth some values, and a body of case law seeks to define them. What of issues not so clearly defined? What, for example, are the value preferences of different groups of people regarding honesty, cleanliness, manners, loyalty, sexual morality, and punctuality? As one reflects upon this problem it becomes clear that people cherish different viewpoints. Whose viewpoints should be perpetuated? When must individual freedom be sacrificed to the needs of society? Are there absolute values that must be accepted and adhered to by all for the success and vitality of our society? Or, are values relative in nature depending upon circumstances?

Absolutists believe that there are time-honored *truths,* upon which value systems can be

Democratic nations care little for what has been, but are haunted by visions of what will be; in this direction their unbound imagination grows and dilates beyond all measure. . . . Democracy, which shuts the past against the poet, opens the future before him.

Alexis de Tocqueville

Americans need to acquire a great variety of skills and values to function effectively in their increasingly complex society.

based. These truths are generally thought of as being derived from either God or Nature.

The search for universal values continues while the trend is currently toward relativism. Sorokin has said:

We live in an age in which no value, from God to private property, is universally accepted. There is no norm, from the Ten Commandments, to contractual rules and those of etiquette, that is universally binding . . . What one person or group affirms, another denies; what one pressure group extols, another vilifies . . . Hence the mental, moral, religious, social, economic and political anarchy that pervades our life and culture. . . .[4]

Yet, it seems that if we are to survive in a pluralistic society some agreement on major or superordinate values must be reached. Further, these values must then be learned by children of that society. Such a system would certainly not preclude the holding of different values so long as they did not conflict with the overall values.

The task of the schools in doing their part in educating youth for citizenship in pluralistic urban America is both complex and immense.

Increasing Demands on Our Schools

Nearly half a century has passed since Chapman and Counts submitted the above dialogue, which illustrates individual learning needs and desires for other than "book larnin'." How well have we done in meeting such individual learning needs?

Greeting his pupils, the master asked: "What would you learn of me? And the reply came: How shall we care for our bodies? How shall we rear our children? How shall we work together? How shall we live with our fellowmen? How shall we play? For what ends shall we live?". . . And the teacher pondered these words, and sorrow was in his heart, for his own learning touched not these things.

Chapman and Counts

Daily newspapers yield indications that these learning needs have not as yet been satisfactorily met. During the decade of the sixties, the criticism of irrelevance was leveled against existing operations of the schools. The seventies have shown the American experiment struggling for survival in an era marked by misplaced loyalties in the political realm, by deprivation and material scarcities, by high crime rates, and by a myriad of other urgent human problems. It seems likely that today's pupils would respond to the master's question in much the same way that pupils responded half a century ago.

One challenge for today's teachers assisting their pupils in finding individual answers to such questions lies in keeping abreast of the times. Pupils prefer those teachers who possess current knowledge, who have an outlook on life that goes beyond the knowledge domain, and who demonstrate attitudes that are flexible to the stresses of the times. Consider just one of the pupils' questions—How shall we rear our children? During the last half century the answers to that question have been dealt with primarily within the home. Since the family unit served as the general environment within which to raise children, the schools were not expected to be deeply involved with the question of rearing children.

It has been suggested that recent social changes—including more women in the work force, lesser numbers of relatives living in the household, and greater geographic mobility of families—have combined to make the family a less effective environment within which to raise children.[5] These changes in the family are directly related to changes in the ways children are raised today. However, many teachers obtained their knowledge and attitudes regarding the rearing of children within the traditional family setting. Therefore, some teachers are still likely to feel that the family should be the agent for providing child-rearing knowledge. But, *if* the family setting today is truly a less effective agent in rearing children than when our teachers were raised, then such teachers are likely to have difficulty accepting contemporary attitudes regarding the basic question—How shall we rear our children?

During the past half century the schools have adjusted in many ways to the shift of many former family responsibilities onto the school. Teachers have inherited many of the responsibilities formerly reserved for the home. Today's schools and teachers are very much expected to be involved with various responsibilities related to rearing children. A significant aspect of the operations of the schools deals with pupil personnel services, including health and dental care, sex education, guidance, discipline, manners, and codes of dress. Increasing emphasis is being placed on early childhood education. Some programs propose parental involvement extended as far back as prenatal care. At the same time, much attention is being directed toward the adult and continuing education aspect which stresses education as a lifelong process.

Children must learn to acknowledge and respect the cultural differences in our pluralistic society.

Educators are now questioning—Where does all this end? Who decides what the limits are? What are or should be the actual responsibilities of the teacher in this regard? Our schools have made valiant strides in attempting to meet the various student needs that were formerly within the province of the family household. By high school age, many of today's pupils are sophisticated enough to be able to determine their own unique needs, and the schools should be flexible enough to meet individual needs regarding things other than subject matter. Perhaps the most relevant questions are those that ask individuals

what it is that *they* desire or need assistance with as related to their own individual health, sex education, guidance, or manners.

Many other persistent needs exist that pupils expect their education to satisfy, whatever the societal setting. The task of the teacher becomes that of constantly examining the ways in which individual expectations can be satisfied within the framework of the school system that has been typically group-oriented (primary attention given to societal needs). The current acceptance of the interaction of societal and individual needs is a recent development that has generated new excitement within the school setting as related to individual needs. The general axiom that new teachers tend to teach as they have been taught needs careful examination in light of increased emphasis on individual expectations with regard to education. Teachers, particularly new teachers, must find the appropriate means for directing knowledge and understanding gained from their own educational experiences toward the individual expectations their pupils have regarding their own education.

Parental and Pupil Expectations

Both parents and pupils expect the schools to satisfy a wide variety of individual needs. When parents and pupils are asked "What are the most important reasons for going to school?" their responses concur, for the most part, with the major societal expectations of the schools as previously discussed. For example, pupils of all ages are quick to suggest that intellectual development is the highest expectation within their educational experiences. Likewise, individuals expect the schools to provide meaningful school experiences with regard to citizenship, personality, vocational training, recreation, and health.

Loss of Public Confidence

Parents have historically felt that the public schools provided their children with the essential ingredients for a successful life. Unfortunately, this public confidence in our schools has gradually dwindled in recent years.

This change is reflected in the 1980 Gallup Poll of the Public Attitudes Toward the Public Schools, which asked:

Students are often given the grades A, B, C, D, and FAIL to denote the quality of their work. Suppose the *public* schools, themselves, in this community, were graded in the same way. What grade would you give the public schools here—A, B, C, D, or FAIL?[6]

In 1974, 18 percent awarded the schools an A, but in 1981, only 9 percent did so. By the same token, in 1974 only 6 percent gave the schools a D, but this grade rose to 13 percent in 1981.

Education for Citizenship

One's attitudinal development is considerably influenced by the person's environment, including the influences of various societal institutions. In turn, an individual's attitudes and values influence that person's behavior. Each individual is ultimately privately responsible for determining what his or her citizenship behavior shall be. The individual elects to vote or not, to violently protest or not, to accept normative standards or not. Notwithstanding these many influences upon an individual, as a participatory citizen, that individual eventually stands alone and practices the act of citizenship in his or her own unique way.

One of the functions ascribed to the public schools has been that of helping students become "good citizens." Parents, board of education members, school administrators, teachers, and

Above all things, I hope the education of the common people will be attended to; convinced that on their good sense we may rely with the most security for the preservation of a due degree of liberty.

Thomas Jefferson

Many subcultures must learn to live in harmony in the United States.

legislators have given much attention to citizenship as a dimension of an individual's education. Most states have laws which direct the schools to engage in specific teaching tasks aimed at developing citizenship behavior in students. For example, an Illinois law states that every public school teacher shall teach the pupils honesty, kindness, justice, and moral courage for the purpose of lessening crime and raising the standard of good citizenship. Implied in this law is that honesty, kindness, justice, and moral courage are criteria for lessening crime and, therefore, contribute to the promotion of good citizenship. Terms such as honesty, kindness, justice, and moral courage are not only difficult to define, but are also difficult to teach within the school setting. In spite of such difficulties, schools (that is, teachers) are expected to accept the challenge of providing individual pupils with learning experiences which will help each of them to develop alternatives for solving the moral problems of life. The schools are also expected to help enable youth to understand the desirability of being kind and just individuals even if some adults they know are unkind and unjust. Individual moral courage, while an admirable attribute of character, and important to citizenship, is difficult to attain in a formalized school setting.

Teaching as related to these aspects of good citizenship draws heavily from an idealistic premise that charges teachers to serve as models in their manner of participation as citizens. Likewise, this idealistic approach draws heavily upon the character analysis of great citizens past and present. The risk of this latter kind of teaching is that the "gospel" becomes Pollyannaish and at times unreal. One aspect of the teaching task is to enlarge upon the dimensions of this idealism and "tell it like it is" so that the students have several alternatives to model, choose from, or modify for their own personal life-style.

Since the early 1930s the American public schools have also been charged with the responsibility for developing other aspects of citizenship. American patriotism, the principles of representative government as enunciated in the American Declaration of Independence, and the Constitution of the United States of America have been emphasized in citizenship training. For many years, teachers have taught that all citizens should demonstrate their patriotism by serving their country in peace as well as in war, by respecting the United States flag, and by voting in elections. A kind of nationalistic idealism was assumed when good citizenship was taught in this manner. This form of idealism seemingly held true in an era when our society was closer knit, less complex, and agrarian-oriented. Many living Americans coming from this heritage continue to operate from such a basis of idealism, not being cognizant of the conflicts resulting from the impersonal, complex, and multigroup influences of the contemporary, urban, pluralistic, machine-oriented society. Our younger people tend to utilize bold dramatic methods in their desire to be heard, whereas older people believe the way to be

Children bring many different values and cultural heritages with them to school.

heard is through more traditional, "good ol' days" procedures. In the reality of today, when one pursues the traditional channels of expression, that person is frequently overwhelmed by the massiveness and complexity of our contemporary society. With all of our technological sophistication, communication problems are still manifest among us. A small voice is practically unheard, and a letter to an elected governmental representative is likely to be of minor importance in and of itself. Thus, an increasing number of young people seem to find it necessary to pool their efforts for the purposes of being heard. Consequently, a tense climate has developed between the active, impulsive, "tell it like it is," *now*-oriented young citizens and their dramatic ways of communicating, and the less active, deliberate, "it was good enough for me," traditionally oriented older citizens. All are involved in a kind of trial-and-error reexamination of the dimensions of good individual citizenship. Obviously, each individual must ultimately make a choice as to what kind of citizen to be.

Education for Personal Growth

Individuals are unique with regard to personality. In fact, no two personalities are exactly alike. One's *personality* is considered to be the habitual patterns and qualities of behavior as expressed by physical and mental activities and attitudes, and also the distinctive individual qualities of a person considered collectively.

Many differing experiences affect the personality development of an individual. Since the experiences of life vary among individuals, it follows that personalities also differ among individuals. Behavioral scientists have observed that, in addition to the influences of heredity, similar personality characteristics in individuals are related to the similarities of life experiences of the individuals. In essence, this line of reasoning assumes that personality characteristics are learned from experience. Thus, particularly with peers, school experiences do in fact contribute to the development of one's personality. One's peer group identity and experiences with the peer group are strong influences on that individual's personality development. Therefore, it appears to be a reasonable expectation of parents that schools should provide experiences that will enhance the

All youth need to develop salable skills and those understandings and attitudes that make the worker an intelligent and productive participant in economic life.

Education Policies Commission
Education for All American Youth
(Washington, D.C.: National
Education Association, 1944), p. 26.

personality development of their children. As pupils mature, they become increasingly aware of many dimensions of their own personality and often select activities and courses that they believe will help develop their personality.

Biological qualities such as age, sex, stature, and pigmentation also influence one's personality. Various ethnic and racial groups influence the behavior patterns of their young through the sharing of similar experiences. Characteristics of an individual's personality are in part reflections of the individual's age group, sex group, and racial group. One's behavior is partially adjusted to the forces of these impinging biological qualities.

An individual's behavior is affected by the total impact of that person's life's experiences. Heredity and environment interact to make each individual a distinct and unique person.

Should the Schools Transmit, Respond or Lead?

What should be the posture of the school in American society? Historically, and into the present, schools have been responsible for the transmission of culture. In this role, as has been indicated, they have assumed a passive and reflective posture. What society deemed as being the "good" of the past and that which is worth preserving, even if not utilitarian or relevant, was presented to children in school for their use and for posterity. In many schools today, transmission is still the primary goal. However, schools have also added another role, a different posture: that of *responding*. As society changes, and needs are recognized in society that can be fulfilled by the school, the school responds or adjusts to these needs. For example, as computers were developed and operators were needed, the schools began to train the specialists necessary. Much of the schools' reactions to social problems fall into the response posture. As poverty was recognized as a problem, and children came to school hungry, the schools fed them. A third posture is possible—that of *leading*. In this posture the schools would strive to achieve the ideal society as it has been envisioned. In this role, the school would act as the agent of change for society, attempting to mold and shape it to desired ends. While schools have not served as initiator, they have been placed in a position of leadership in building an integrated society. It appears that they may be increasingly called upon to take the leadership role. Schools assume all three postures (transmit, respond, lead) in their various responsibilities. The blend of these postures changes as societal expectations change.

In summary, this chapter has pointed out that our society has come to expect a multitude of things from our schools. It has also shown that there are differing opinions about the role that our schools can and should play in our society.

Each student is a unique individual who desires
different things from his or her education.

Point of View

The following interesting article deals with that
American institution which affects our nation's
youth more than any other—the family.

The American Family: Bent—but Not Broken

Challenged and buffeted as rarely before, the American family once again is changing to survive in a
changing world.

The latest accommodations—heartening to some,
while alarming to others—underscore the resilience of
an institution that has repeatedly withstood predictions
of an early demise.

Source: "The American Family: Bent—but Not Broken,"
U.S. News & World Report, Inc. June 16, 1980, pp. 48–50.

Mankind's most basic and oldest social unit, the
family, has "taken many forms over history and con-
formed to the social forces of that era," observes John
P. Vincent, associate professor of psychology at the
University of Houston. "We're seeing a natural evolution now."

Cries of crisis, Vincent says, only document the
family's "growing pains."

Sacred, mysterious and sometimes misunderstood, the family today is assuming a variety of forms,
each reflecting an adjustment to the revolutionary social changes that have swept the nation in the past
generation. Few realize just how far-reaching the ad-
aptations have been.

The "traditional" American family, for example,
still portrayed by advertising, children's literature and
popular movies now is in a minority. A scant 13 percent
of the nation's families include a working father, stay-
at-home mother and one or more children.

Broad meaning. Today, the definitions of family
are as varied and pragmatic as the nation itself. "It's
dangerous," notes Mary Margaret Carr, executive di-

rector of the Children's Service and Family Counseling Center in Atlanta, "to say that the only strong family is one that meets my narrow concept or your narrow concept."

Behind the changes lie new economic conditions and widening horizons for women. More than half the nation's mothers work outside the home. Six out of 10 married women with school-age children work. Of married women with children under 6 years old, 43 percent work.

Millions of preschool children now are cared for in day-care centers—a development that still sparks controversy. One expert estimates that 64 percent of all children between the ages of 3 and 5 spend part of their day in facilities outside their home.

Says Alfred J. Kahn of the Columbia School of Social Work: "All the research we have suggests that it doesn't do anything to a child. They grow up like everybody else."

Traditionalists insist, however, that it may take years for the long-term effects of such care to become clear.

Contributing to use of day-care facilities is the growing number of children who live with single parents. Eighteen million children live in what once were called "broken homes" before divorce became so rampant that one marriage ends for every two that begin. According to one Census Bureau expert, fully 45 percent of the children born in 1978 may spend at least part of their childhoods with only one parent.

Financial boon. Still another milestone of change is the birth of the two-career marriage—a partnership that pays off financially. The more than 19 million families that had at least two wage earners in 1979 made an average of $509 a week—more than $26,000 a year—compared with $305 a week for families with single breadwinners.

Economic hardship accounts for the number of mature children returning home after college. "I couldn't afford to live away from home," says Michele Duwelius of Des Moines, who graduated last year from Iowa State University.

The "refilled nest," cautions Drake University sociologist Lewis McNurlen, is not always a happy home, noting: "The tension can get much deeper than questions about whether mom still picks up the towels."

Adds one couple whose children came home: "We ate what we wanted when we wanted. We enjoyed these new freedoms, and then suddenly somebody came home with an appetite."

The proliferation of family forms underscores their adaptability. "The family is not in a state of disrepair," says Bertram Cohler of the University of Chicago. "Not only is the family alive and well, it is aliver and weller."

So sweeping are the changes that many living arrangements once considered immoral, if not illegal, now are accepted as "families." More than 2.7 million men and women live together unmarried, buying and selling houses and even raising the children of one or both partners' previous marriages. Homosexuals openly share households and take marriage vows. Communal living is enjoying acceptance.

The law, too, is changing to match such sweeping social developments. Live-in companions now qualify for "palimony." Moreover, courts are awarding alimony to husbands as well as wives, contending that to bar such payments to men is sex discrimination.

Welcomed by some, resisted by others, none of these transformations has been without cost. Gained has been a robust era of individual freedom. But lost in many cases has been that fragile sense of family that for so long provided Americans a haven of last resort.

Cautions Prof. Urie Bronfenbrenner of Cornell University: "One of these days our pragmatism is going to catch up and we'll realize that we're paying too high a cost for our individualism."

Growing apart. Communication between relatives has waned amid changes in family structure as members spend less time with each other than perhaps at any time in history. Fewer than half the families surveyed in one study in the Detroit area, for example, ate together three nights a week.

"There's a lack of family cohesion now, a product of the celebration of the individual," notes Dr. Greer Litton Fox, director of Wayne State University's Family Research Center in Detroit. "As a result, we're almost like strangers living in the same household."

The elderly grow old alone, cared for by the state or private institutions without the solace of an extended family. Violence jolts millions of households, leaving society to bear the long-term costs of battered wives and physically or sexually abused children.

"If society continues to encourage parents and kids to live out their own lives," warns Fox, "we're going to start seeing some dire results."

Taxpayers shoulder the burden, as well, for vandalism in schools and the soaring number of pregnancies among unmarried teen-agers—symptoms of eroding values that some trace to the breakdown of the American family.

Trouble stalks the family on other fronts, too. TV's impact on children is more pervasive than ever. And rising unemployment spells future difficulty.

What is needed, many specialists contend, is greater openness. "Close ties don't just come by definition," says one expert. "Families have to work toward these relationships."

Spending time together—a family night, for example—is the best method of strengthening ties, experts suggest.

Cornell's Bronfenbrenner proposes that each person work three quarters of the time and devote the remainder to "living, to being a parent, to being a friend, to being a neighbor, to being a participant in other things besides work."

Games are available to help family members open up communication. "The point," says Joan Hoxsey, a director of family life for the Catholic diocese in Youngstown, Ohio, "is to tell it like it is. It's an opportunity for everyone to tell what's going on inside them."

Outside the family, steps are under way to strengthen family bonds in an era of change. Temple Sinai in Atlanta has formed "Havurah," or friendship groups, to provide added support.

"We wanted to develop an extended family for the church," says Ben Walker, the temple's education director. "It's made people closer. People feel like they belong."

In Council Bluffs, Iowa, parents are joining children in a program to reverse academic failure by junior-high-school students. "An hour or so on Saturday may not be enough to turn it around," says school official Ted Stilwell, "but when the child sees the parent has the commitment to come, it may have an effect."

Family therapy is gaining acceptance as people begin to recognize that maintaining close family relationships takes work. "Like anything else that has meaning," says one specialist, "a satisfying marriage and family life won't come until you put a lot of work into it."

What lies ahead for the American family? The willingness to innovate and adapt clearly highlights widespread yearning for the benefits of family. Interest in it is flourishing. Millions watch television programs such as "All in the Family" and "One Day at a Time" that detail changing patterns of family life.

Public concern has surfaced during the preparatory stages of the 3-million-dollar White House Conference on Families that is now holding its final conferences in Baltimore, Minneapolis and Los Angeles. "Our task," says Chairman Jim Guy Tucker, "is to insure that when government touches families, it helps instead of hurts."

Government and industry are beginning to face pressure to accommodate the changes in the family. Congress is at work on the tax code to reverse a penalty on married couples. Social Security laws soon may

Living Arrangements

Composition of U.S. Households

Married Couple, Children

1970
40.3%

Latest
32.4%

Married Couple, No Children

1970
30.3%

Latest
29.9%

One Parent, Children

1970
5.0%

Latest
7.3%

Persons Living Alone

1970
17.1%

Latest
22.0%

Other Living Arrangements

1970
7.3%

Latest
8.4%

USN&WR table—Basic data U.S. Dept. of Commerce

change to more equitably compensate women who stay at home to raise children.

Workers are negotiating for workplace day-care centers, flexible hours and even paternity leave to help ease the burden of family responsibilities.

Businesses in one Chicago suburb can turn to the Niles Family Service to get guidance on helping workers with family problems. "The program is an early-detection program," says psychologist Ronald Martin. "I train supervisors not to become amateur psychologists, but to document declining work performance" so that professional help can be brought in.

Still, authorities contend that much needs to be done. A recent study by a pair of specialists at the Columbia School of Social Work warns that efforts by government to advance the interests of families are "unlikely to yield much or even be launched unless there is greater determination expressed outside the government that family well-being be guarded in the course of general policymaking."

Yet families hunger for action. A Gallup Poll conducted for the White House Conference on Families found that 61 percent of families polled considered their family the most important element in their lives, but nearly half said family life had gotten worse.

And George Masnick and Mary Jo Bane of the Joint Center for Urban Studies of the Massachusetts Institute of Technology and Harvard University report in *The Nation's Families: 1960–1990* that society needs to adjust to fewer married couples, more unattached individuals and the growing variety of family relationships that Americans encounter through life.

Reason for optimism exists, however. "We're a little behind most of the world because America tends to be afraid to tamper with the family," notes Columbia's Kahn. "But it's going to discover that since families are precious and children are precious, it's going to have to do something about it so that children can be reared and adults can work."

10 Ways Families Have Changed

	1970	Latest		Percent Change
Marriages performed	2,159,000	2,317,000	Up	7.3%
Divorces granted	708,000	1,170,000	Up	65.3%
Married couples	44,728,000	47,662,000	Up	6.6%
Unmarried couples	523,000	1,346,000	Up	157.4%
Persons living alone	10,851,000	17,202,000	Up	58.5%
Married couples with children	25,541,000	24,625,000	Down	3.6%
Children living with two parents	58,926,000	48,295,000	Down	18.0%
Children living with one parent	8,230,000	11,528,000	Up	40.1%
Average size of household	3.3	2.8	Down	15.2%
Families with both husband and wife working	20,327,000	24,253,000	Up	19.3%

USN&WR table—Basic data U.S. Dept. of Commerce

Change for the better. While the years of transition may be difficult, many observers foresee both society and the family emerging better prepared to deal with the 1980s.

As Masnick and Bane conclude in their recent study, "We expect changes in households and families to be accompanied by new relationships within families and among households, the community, the economy and the government."

Indeed, the American family may be different—but it is far from dead. As one specialist puts it: "I think people will think the family unit is an important one to maintain. It has something to do with their identity, practical reasons like support systems, and it can provide a richness to life."

Questions for Discussion

1. What elements of the culture of the United States are particularly essential to the survival of representative democracy as a form of government?

2. What values should the school transmit as being representative of our culture?

3. Should the schools be used as agents of planned social change?

4. What provisions, if any, should be made for the schools to transmit the cultural elements of local ethnic subgroups?

5. How valuable is vocational education today? Why?

Supplementary Learning Activities

1. Gather and analyze demographic and sociological data in the area of the institution that you attend, looking specifically for cultural diversity.

2. Devise a questionnaire designed to secure societal expectations for schools and use it to interview individuals selected in a random fashion.

3. Invite persons of differing cultural backgrounds and different socioeconomic group levels to your class to gain their perceptions of American education.

4. Visit a vocational school in your geographical area to better understand the work done there.

5. Visit a school that has a well-developed college prep curriculum.

Notes

1. Herbert J. Gans, "We Won't End the Crisis Until We End 'Majority Rule,' " from *More Equality.* Copyright Pantheon Books, 1973. Used by permission.

2. Madelon D. Stent, William R. Hazard, and Harry N. Rivlin, *Cultural Pluralism in Education,* pp. 149–50. Copyright 1973 by Fordham University. Reprinted by permission of Prentice-Hall, Inc., Englewood Cliffs, New Jersey.

3. Philip O. Phenix, "Values in the Emerging American Civilization," *Teachers' College Record* 61 (1960): 356.

4. Pitirim Sorokin, *The Reconstruction of Humanity* (Boston: Beacon Press, 1948), p. 104.

5. James S. Coleman, "Social Change," *Bulletin of National Association of Secondary Principals* 49, pp. 11–18.

6. George H. Gallup, "Gallup Poll of the Public's Attitudes Toward the Public Schools," *Phi Delta Kappan,* September 1981, p. 35.

Selected References

"The American Family: Bent—but Not Broken," *U.S. News & World Report, Inc.* June 16, 1980, pp. 48–50.

Bailey, Stephen. *The Purposes of Education.* Bloomington, Ind.: Phi Delta Kappa, 1976.

Bowles, Samuel, and Gintis, Herbert. *Schooling in Capitalist America.* New York: Basic Books, 1976.

Brown, B. Frank. "A Study of the School Needs of Children from One-Parent Families," *Phi Delta Kappan,* April 1980, pp. 537–40.

Bryant, Bunyan I.; Chesler, Mark A.; and Crowfoot, James E. "Barometers of Conflict," *Educational Leadership* 33, October 1975, pp. 17–20.

Cobbs, Price M., and Winokur, Diane K. *Education for Ethnic and Racial Diversity.* Los Angeles: Western Teacher Corps, Recruitment and Technical Resources Center, 1977.

Gallup, George H. "The 12th Annual Gallup Poll of the Public's Attitudes Toward the Public Schools," *Phi Delta Kappan,* September 1980, pp. 33–48.

Hall, Brian P. *The Development of Consciousness: A Confluent Theory of Values.* New York: Paulist Press, 1976.

Hawley, Robert, and Hawley, Isabel. *Human Values in the Classroom.* New York: Hart Publishing Co., 1975.

Hechinger, Fred M., and Hechinger, Grace. *Growing Up in America.* New York: McGraw-Hill, 1975.

Leeper, Robert R. *Emerging Moral Dimensions in Society: Implications for Schooling.* Washington, D.C.: Association for Supervision and Curriculum Development, 1975.

Lerner, Max. *Values in Education.* Bloomington, Ind.: Phi Delta Kappa, 1976.

St. John, Nancy H. *School Desegregation, Outcomes for Children.* New York: Wiley, 1975.

Sexton, Patricia. *Women in Education.* Bloomington, Ind.: Phi Delta Kappa, 1976.

Critical Social Problems in Our Schools

9

The United States has many unresolved problems, foreign and domestic—problems that affect groups and individuals; problems that individuals expect society to help them solve. In many cases these problems are so complex that an individual facing them may feel utterly helpless. The days of the American pioneer resolutely and individually making his or her way through life are fast fading. Today, a person's destiny is strongly interdependent on that of others; basic necessities of life, such as food, shelter, and clothing are difficult to create by oneself. The American citizen today exists in a complicated environmental system over which an individual has very little control. Therefore, individual problems become social problems that depend upon the organized efforts of society for solutions. Schools as agencies of society are looked to as one resource for solving these problems. Let us briefly examine some of these social problems that affect our schools.

School Integration

A persistent major social problem throughout history, and one that has received stepped-up attention in the United States during the preceding quarter of a century, has been that of race relations. In 1954 the United States Supreme Court in *Brown v. Board of Education of Topeka* reversed prior decisions supporting the separate but equal doctrine, and said that separate but equal facilities in education were inherently unequal. The Court based its reasoning on the idea that while schools may be equally excellent educationally, with highly qualified staff members and superior facilities, they will differ because of the composition of the student population. This difference, if based on racial segregation, will have an adverse effect upon black students. Since the *Brown* decision, some progress has been made in integrating schools in both the South and the North. School segregation in the North has been most often termed *de facto* segregation. This type of segregation is considered to be of the fact and not "deliberate," resulting primarily from neighborhood residence patterns and neighborhood schools. The *Brown* decision made *de jure* or "deliberate" segregation illegal. The legal status of de facto segregation is still in question. Courts have ruled that attendance center (neighborhood school) lines are illegal if drawn in such a way to promote segregation (*Taylor v. Board of Education in New Rochelle, New York*). They have

The courts instituted racial integration in the public schools.

also ruled that de facto segregation in and of itself is not illegal. The issue becomes further complicated when an entire school population of a district or city becomes predominantly black. In these circumstances, arrangements involving complex legal problems would have to be made to transport students from one school district to another, and in some instances from one state to another. Some plans involving voluntary exchange of students to foster integration have been made. Other programs which attempt to resolve the problem of segregated schools have included busing, open enrollment, redistricting, creation of educational parks, and consolidation. Busing plans involve the transportation of students, both white and black, from one school to another in order to bring about racial balance. Theoretically, open enrollment basically permits students to enroll in any school of their choice. Redistricting involves the redrawing of school attendance boundary lines to facilitate racial balance. Consolidation plans are designed to merge smaller school districts into larger ones, and thus permit a more desirable racial balance. Educational parks represent an attempt to group elementary and secondary school facilities in planned locations so that the pupils who attend come from a wide area, thus avoiding segregation that results from neighborhood schools. Recent complication to the resolution of the problem has been a growing tendency for black separatism, in which black leaders have opposed integration as strongly and vociferously as white segregationists have.

The Civil Rights Act of 1964 resulted in the Department of Health, Education, and Welfare being charged with the responsibility of enforcing those portions of the Act that pertained to education. This agency set about monitoring school districts' desegregation efforts, and brought pressure to bear on districts and states that did not make sufficient progress in this area.

In 1969, the U.S. Supreme Court ruled that "all deliberate speed" was no longer sufficient as the standard for desegregation. The decision called for immediate integration in all school districts.

Since that time there have been many court rulings, laws, and regulations handed down in an attempt to regulate school integration and promote equal educational opportunity. Some of the most recent of these include the following:

– In 1975, the U.S. Supreme Court upheld a lower decision calling for urban-suburban desegregation of the Wilmington, Delaware, area school districts.
– A 1975 Circuit Court of Appeals required schools in the Louisville area to integrate, an action that ultimately led to school district reorganization to accomplish "metro" desegregation.
– In 1977, the U.S. Supreme Court decided that segregation in the Dayton, Ohio, public schools did not justify a statewide remedy. In other words, this action suggests that just because segregation exists in one school district, it may not necessarily mean that other nearby school districts must become involved to facilitate racial integration in the segregated district.
– A 1977 Supreme Court decision held that the courts can even order a school district to provide remedial educational programs for schoolchildren who have been subjected to *de jure* segregation.

These are but a few of the many court findings that, along with agency regulations, are helping to mold racial desegregation in our schools at the present time.

Figure 9.1, which shows, by race, the history of school enrollments and years of school completed, indicates that there has been progress made in providing more, and hopefully better, education for children of all races.

School busing to promote racial integration in our schools is a hotly debated issue.

Figure 9.1. School Enrollment and Median School Years Completed.

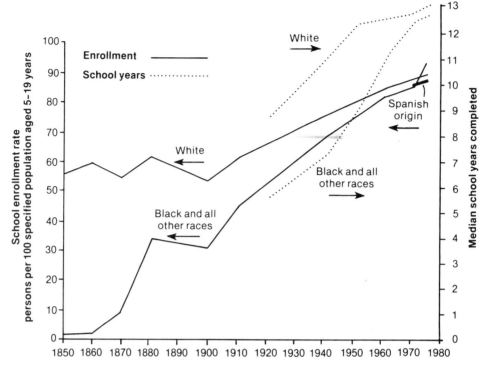

Source: U.S. Office of Education.

While there has been much progress made in providing better education for children of all races in the relatively brief time that has passed since the landmark Supreme Court *Brown* decision in 1954, much remains to be done if we are to reach the goal of providing true equal educational opportunity for all children. Accomplishing this goal will be extremely difficult because of factors such as:

– Misunderstanding of, or lack of information about the purposes and techniques necessary to achieve quality education in integrated settings.
– Failure to commit the staff, time, and resources necessary.
– Misunderstanding or misinterpretation of changing legal requirements.
– Lack of administrative or school board support for positive change.

– Inability or unwillingness to secure competent professional help in bringing about the desired changes.
– Community opposition.
– Apathy.
– Lack of good faith and intent on the part of one or more of the parties involved, including local and state officials, school administrators, school boards, and teachers.[1]

These and other problems must be overcome if our schools are to be integrated, and if equal educational opportunity is to be provided for all.

It should be recognized that race problems in the United States have many causes, and that the efforts to promote integration, while concentrated heavily on the schools, cannot be completely resolved by the schools. The resolution of racial issues resides in the attitudes of citizens, yellow, black, and white. While these attitudes

The human mind is our fundamental resource. . . . The Federal government's responsibility in this area has been established since the earliest days of the Republic—it is time now to act decisively to fulfill that responsibility for the sixties.

John F. Kennedy

Poverty underlies most serious social problems in the United States.

are formulated under strong influences within the home and within peer group associations of the child, the school can and must continue to be a strong influence on the attitudes developed by the pupils.

Problems of Poverty

Another domestic social problem that is ultimately related to education is that of poverty. While the United States is one of the richest nations on earth in terms of material wealth, some of its people suffer from extreme poverty.

Many individuals and families in the United States fall below the poverty level and thereby receive public aid. These numbers have increased in recent years, and now include over 11 million individuals in over 3.5 million families.

There is a far greater percentage of nonwhite people affected by poverty than white people. Approximately 20.1 percent of the nonwhite and 7.5 percent of the white families in our country are now living in poverty. While there is a higher percentage of nonwhite families living in poverty, numerically there are many more impoverished white families.

Figure 9.2 shows yet another subtle result of poverty in the United States. Nonwhites have had historically, and still have to this day, significantly shorter life expectancies at birth than do whites. This fact is attributed to poorer nutrition and health care, both of which are, in turn, related to poverty as well as poorer education.

Many more statistics could be cited to further delineate the problem. Let it suffice to conclude that poverty in America is a very serious problem; that while poverty affects both whites and nonwhites, the problem percentage-wise is much more serious for nonwhites; that it is widely distributed throughout both metropolitan and farm areas; and that with the exception of the suburban area, approximately one of every four children is being reared under conditions of poverty.

How does the poverty problem relate to education? Children of poverty, sometimes inaccurately labeled as "culturally deprived" or

Figure 9.2. Life Expectancy at Birth.

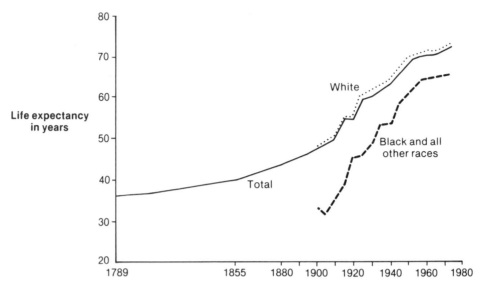

Source: U.S. Department of Health, Education, and Welfare.

"disadvantaged," simply do not possess at the time of entrance into school as many of the skills needed for success in school as those children who have not been impoverished. This is caused by combinations of many factors, among them physical debilitation, lack of intellectual stimulation, different cultural background, negative self-concept, and many other factors related to their environmental background. Further, and perhaps more significantly, many schools have not developed the kinds of programs necessary to enable these students to succeed. As a result, their poverty background is reinforced by failure in school. Many teachers, either having been of the middle class originally, or having become a part of the middle class due to upward social mobility, have difficulty in relating to, and therefore teaching impoverished children. The schools then have the task of adjusting their programs, changing their techniques, and doing their very best to enable their students to obtain the skills necessary to

compete favorably in our society. The federal government has recognized this task, and is endeavoring to help. Title I, in particular, of the Elementary and Secondary Act of 1965, provides funds to state education agencies specifically for the purpose of improving education programs for the poor. Under Title I, local school districts design programs, ranging from those providing physical necessities such as eyeglasses and shoes to those providing counselors and remedial reading specialists to supplement their existing programs. Funds are allocated on the basis of the number of poor families in a school district. Other federal programs such as Head Start, National Teacher Corps, and Upward Bound are aimed at improving the opportunities of the poor.

Jencks and Bane in their controversial essay "The Schools and Equal Opportunity" challenged the assumption that the primary reason poor children cannot escape from poverty is that they do not acquire basic cognitive skills. Other evidence points out the fact that there is almost as much economic inequality among those who

Poverty can seriously affect a child's well-being and performance in school.

score high on standardized tests as there is in the general population. Jencks concludes:

In America, as elsewhere, the long-term drift over the past 200 years has been toward equality. In America, however, the contribution of public policy to this drift has been slight. As long as egalitarians assume that public policy cannot contribute to equality directly but must proceed by ingenius manipulations of marginal institutions like the schools, this pattern will continue. If we want to move beyond this tradition, we must establish political control over the economic institutions that shape our society. What we will need, in short, is what other countries call socialism. Anything less will end in the same disappointment as the reforms of the 1960's.[2]

Unemployment and Underemployment

Closely related to problems of poverty are the problems of unemployment and underemployment (that is, individuals working at jobs who are qualified for better jobs). It has been estimated that today there are about 10 million underemployed, 6.5 million of whom work full-time and earn less than the annual poverty wage. Approximately 500,000 of the unemployed are "hardcore" unemployed who lack the basic education necessary to secure and hold a job.

While unemployment statistics such as these vary considerably from month to month (due to seasonable work), and from year to year (due to general economic conditions), even in the best of times many Americans are unemployed or underemployed.

Figure 9.3. Median Annual Money Income in Constant (1975) Dollars of Families, by Race: 1960 to 1975.

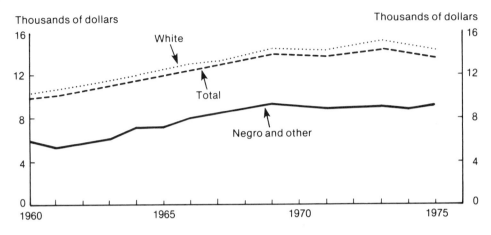

Source: U.S. Bureau of the Census.

As one might suspect, high percentages of those who are unemployed or underemployed are nonwhite. This fact helps to explain, at least in part, the difference in annual income between white and nonwhite Americans. This difference is documented in figure 9.3, which shows the median annual income of American families by race. There is a relationship between unemployment rates and years of school completed. While the relationship is not perfect, undoubtedly because of other variables, the positive correlation between increased level of education and reduced unemployment rate is evident. Further, with the exception of the elementary level of education, and exclusive of eight years of education completed, the nonwhite rates of unemployment are higher than those for whites. Also, the unemployment rates for women tend to be higher than those for men. Recognizing that relationships are not indicative of "cause and effect," one possible explanation of the data in respect to nonwhites and women could, nevertheless, be discrimination.

Do the schools have a societal role in solving the problem of unemployment and underemployment? They certainly do, from basic reading and writing skills to vocational and technical training programs for adults. Efforts are being made in these directions in high schools through day and night programs, technical and trade schools, and community colleges. Further, schools must continue to urge equal opportunity for education and employment in society. Again, though, the schools cannot completely resolve the problem; they can, however, as one agency of society, make a major contribution.

Crime and Violence

The extent of the current crime and violence problem in our country is revealed in the following data:

- Serious crime rose by a record 17 percent in the United States in one recent year.
- Youth under eighteen years of age now account for over one-fifth of our total arrests.

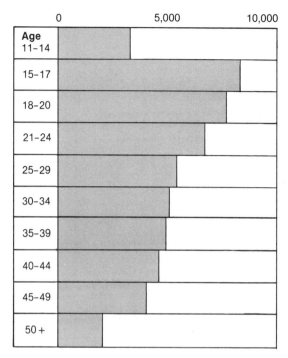

Figure 9.4. Arrest Rate per 100,000 Population, by Age.

Age		
11–14		
15–17		
18–20		
21–24		
25–29		
30–34		
35–39		
40–44		
45–49		
50 +		

- Arrests are made for fewer than one-fourth of our serious crimes.
- About 65 percent of all persons arrested for crimes have records of previous arrests.
- Crimes by females have increased by over 80 percent in the past decade.
- Between 1970 and 1973, school homicides jumped 18 percent, school rapes 40 percent, school robberies 37 percent, assaults on students 85 percent, and assaults on teachers, 77 percent.

It is sad reality that, in one way or another, crime and violence touch the lives of all of our students, and all of our schools. Figure 9.4 points out this fact vividly by showing the arrest rate per 100,000 population by age.

Drug Abuse

Senator Harold E. Hughes, as chairman of the Senate subcommittee on alcoholism and narcotics, in referring to drug abuse said: "The truth is that we have a cancerous problem that has the capability of destroying our society. By and large, we have not begun to awaken to its magnitude."[3]

Data that indicate the magnitude of the problem include:

- Of the 18 million public secondary students, 6 million are taking drugs illegally.
- Twelve to fifteen percent of the public secondary students are using marijuana and other soft drugs on a regular basis.
- From two percent to three percent of the public secondary students are hooked hopelessly on hard drugs like heroin.
- Nationwide, arrests of persons under eighteen for narcotics violations grew an almost unbelievable 1860% from 1960 to 1968, according to the Federal Bureau of Narcotics Director Ingersoll.[4]

Student Use of Alcohol and Tobacco

While there are encouraging indications that student use of drugs may be declining to some extent, there are, unfortunately, corresponding discouraging indications that student use of alcohol and tobacco is increasing.

Our schools need to develop more viable programs for youth who have been involved with crimes and/or drug abuse.

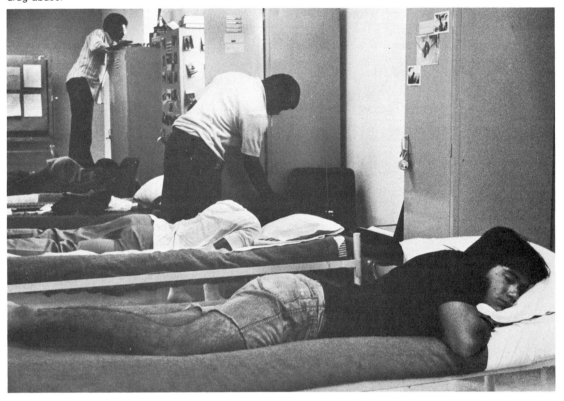

Statistics show that mortality from lung cancer (largely attributed to smoking), continues to skyrocket—from 72,000 in 1973, to 81,000 in 1975, to an estimated 100,000 this year.[5] While there has been a slight decrease in the number of adult smokers in recent years, there has been a disappointing increase in the number of student smokers. Figure 9.5 reveals information regarding teenage smoking. The percentage of girls who smoke is increasing much faster than that of boys. Many schools have initiated vigorous smoking-education programs in an effort to stem the rising tide of student smokers. A good example of such a program is one in New York State initiated by McRae and Nelson.[6] This particular program was based on the assumptions that the bulk of students smoke because their friends smoke, and that students wish to be independent and develop their own life-style. The program depended on youth-to-youth communication and was designed and carried out by a teenage youth committee. Students in seventy-five schools participated in the program. The plan also involved corresponding units of instruction in certain classes on topics such as cancer.

A recent Department of Health, Education and Welfare task force found that teenage drinking is commonplace in our country—93 percent of our high school senior boys and 87 percent of the girls use alcohol in varying amounts. Dr. Morris E. Chafety, director of the National Institute on Alcohol Abuse and Alcoholism, recently stated that half the tenth graders drink in cars at night, 60 percent of our traffic fatalities among youth involve alcohol, and the number of

Smoking is yet another serious social problem that affects the health of many American youth.

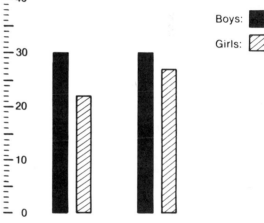

AREN'T YOU A LITTLE OLD TO BE SMOKING?

You look like you're old enough to read. And if you're old enough to read, why don't you sit down and read that pack of cigarettes. Especially the warning.

AMERICAN CANCER SOCIETY ®

THIS SPACE CONTRIBUTED BY THE PUBLISHER

Figure 9.5. Teenage Cigarette Smoking: Current Regular Smokers by Age and Sex.

Source: U.S. Department of Health, Education, and Welfare.

high school students who have ever used alcohol was up 90 percent in a recent three-year period. A recent study in New York shows that almost 10 percent of that city's junior and senior high school students are already, or are potential alcoholics. A Houston "drying out" program for teenage drinkers has increased its clientele from 6 to 1,200 in three years.

These statistics vividly point out the problems that our schools and our society face regarding student use of alcohol and tobacco. Most

Alcohol abuse among youth is increasing with no end in sight.

authorities believe that our schools alone will not be able to solve this problem, so both our schools and our society will undoubtedly have to devote more attention to these areas in the future.

Truancy

Students are "skipping school" more frequently and in increasing numbers. Richard Benedetto captures the essence of this problem when he writes:

When a high school student is absent in Tallahassee, Fla., a parent has 48 hours to call the school with an excuse.

"They used to have them write notes," says teacher Pat Faircloth, "but too many kids were forging the notes."

In another room in the same school, teacher Ionia Smith holds up a book saturated with red marks. "Those are for the tardies and unexcused absences for this semester alone," she says.

In Sacramento, the police have become truant officers. If a teenager is seen out of school without a written excuse, he or she is picked up and released only to a parent or school official.

In Charlotte, N.C., high school principal Richard Cansler says he's ready to drop the perfect attendance award because nobody ever wins it. His school's average daily attendance is 85 percent. Ten years ago it was 96 percent.

As one New York City school official put it: "It's tough enough to teach these kids how to read and write. You can't teach them if they're not in school."

Average attendance in New York's 1,000 public schools is about 84 percent. That means that 160,000 are absent every day.

School officials can tick off a long list of reasons why children don't show up. They include lack of parental concern, the need to take care of younger children in the family, teenage pregnancy, emotional and economic problems, boredom, failure to achieve and a growing belief that school isn't a key to success.

Urban school districts throughout the country report similar trends, and it now appears the disease is spreading to the suburbs and beyond.

At White Oak Junior High in the suburbs of Cincinnati, parents of absent students receive a phone call to determine whether the absence is legitimate. If there is no answer at home, a parent is called at work.

Terry Byrne, the White Oak principal, says the call-a-parent program has been used for five years "because it's effective." The school's average attendance is 93 to 94 percent.

At Schoharie Central High School in rural upstate New York "there was a lot of cutting going on, so we had to start taking attendance in every class," says principal Edward Reid. "It's like an hourly bed check."

Reid says his attendance rate is about 93 percent, but on Fridays and Mondays it drops below 90 percent when there are farm chores to be done.

"Nobody's afraid of the truant officer anymore," says Tim Wendt, assistant to the deputy chancellor of the New York City schools who is working on an attendance improvement program there.

He noted that New York has attractions like Yankee Stadium, Coney Island and Times Square where students gather when they skip school. The schools have set up satellite centers in those areas where truants picked up by police are taken. The schools are then notified, and the students are sent back. "But many don't come back," says Wendt.

One attendance aide called a mother to find out why her daughter hadn't been in school for a week. "I haven't seen her in a month," the mother replied.

Sarah Pearlmutter, a teacher at Louis Brandeis High School in Manhattan, said she has improved attendance by posting pictures of students who show the greatest attendance improvement. "These children just like to know someone cares," she said.[7]

Sexism in Education

Yet another pressing social problem of a slightly different nature that currently affects our schools is that of sexism. This problem is far-reaching in its implications, touching on such things as equal educational opportunity for females, new federal legislation such as Title IX discussed elsewhere in this book, equal employment opportunities for women, sex stereotyping, and, in fact, the civil rights and quality of life of American females. Space permits only a brief discussion of one aspect of this larger problem—that of sexism in our schools.

Some authorities feel that we would take a large step toward solving this problem if we could find a way to provide true sex equity in our language. They argue that language is the key element in human interaction and that any language which is oriented in favor of one sex will inevitably result in that sex having a dominant role in the society.

One need not ponder long to determine that common language usage in America is male-oriented and filled with sex stereotyping. Authors commonly use "he" when referring to people in general; we call the person in charge of a meeting a "chairman" even if it happens to be a female; and we address unknown persons as "Dear Sir" in correspondence. In our schoolbooks, doctors, lawyers, merchants, police, soldiers, and people in charge such as the school principal are usually male; while nurses, waitresses, elementary school teachers, and persons who clean, cook, sew, and generally do lower level and lower paying work are female. Also, males are often depicted as tough, smart, and aggressive while females are assigned roles that are weak, docile, and subservient.

Even though most people today fully realize that females are as capable and competent as

Students must have an opportunity to develop
acceptable sexual attitudes and behaviors.

males, and also believe that females should have
equal opportunities in all aspects of life, they
don't realize the subtle influence and damage that
language can do to the young. Unfortunately,
most people do not realize that our sex-oriented
language is probably just as damaging to boys as
it is to girls.

Developing sex equity in our language will
probably take a good deal of time and will certainly take the concerted hard work of a great
many people (including educators) in our society.
Helping people become aware of the problem is
undoubtedly one of the early necessary steps in
this process.

Table 9.1 entitled "Practical Suggestions for
Fairness in Language," represents yet another
kind of step that must be taken to eventually
resolve this problem.

This chapter has but briefly touched on only
a few of the social problems that affect the lives
of our nation's youth, and also our schools. These
are pressing problems that our schools and society at large must join hands to solve if our youth
are to be served.

Point of View

Child abuse and neglect is a growing problem in
our society. A growing debate centers around the
school's role in helping to deal with this problem.
The following essay by Lynn Fossum and Lauralee Sorensen suggests that teachers may be the
very key ingredients in breaking the vicious cycle
that perpetuated this problem.

Table 9.1. Practical Suggestions for Fairness in Language.

After assumptions have been clarified and new perspectives considered, many people still have a problem with sex bias in language: How can I speak and write fairly and clearly, without tripping over myself?

The following examples offer alternatives to traditional forms. Each is intended to be inclusive, convenient, and clear. These resources can suggest further possibilities for bias-free language; a great many inventive solutions remain to be explored.

Avoid a choice of gender
1. By plural forms
   Instead of: A student can choose his adviser as late as his senior year.
   Try: Students can choose their advisers as late as their senior year.
2. By rephrasing to omit pronouns or the necessity to choose a male or female noun
   Instead of: When a youth gets a part time job, he is likely to face increased stress.
   Try: When getting a part time job, you are likely to face increased stress.
3. By using labels that show the activity, not the gender of the actor
   Instead of: mailman, stewardess, lineman, housemother
   Try: mail carrier, flight attendant, line worker, house parent
4. By using common gender "they" in writing as well as in oral communication
   Instead of: Everyone who wants to play should bring his instrument to tonight's informal concert.
   Try: Everyone who wants to play should bring their instruments to tonight's informal concert.

Choose inclusive forms
1. By using "he or she," "she or he," s/he," or "he/she"
                        These forms work best when used in combination with the suggestions above. A large number of "he or she" forms in a short passage will be less smooth to read or hear than one such form in the context of a variety of nouns and noun phrases.
   Try: A student can choose an activity as late as his or her senior year.
2. Alternating female and male pronouns
                        This strategy can help raise the awareness of others when customary sex role references are avoided.
   Try: A professor . . . she; the housekeeper . . . he; the attorney . . . she.
3. By using as examples persons of both sexes

   Try: Researchers such as Margaret Mead and Franz Boas have revealed how people live in widely varying cultures around the world.

Try to avoid these things
1. Stating that you mean "he" generically and continuing to use only "he" to refer to unspecified persons.
   Problem: Whatever you say, listeners are still more likely to receive images of males.
2. Saying inclusive pronouns with long pauses or heightened vocal emphasis.
   Problem: Some listeners will interpret these behaviors as antagonistic toward women or feminism. Others will simply lose your train of thought.

When in doubt
1. Ask people what they prefer to be called.
2. Assume that people are human beings first and that women and men are presumed worthy of respect in whatever they are choosing to do.

Last lines about letters
Several methods for beginning a letter can avoid sex-biased wording
     Dear Director of Education:
     Dear *Village Voice* Staff:
     Dear Barbara Bates:
     Dear people:

All of these suggestions for practical fairness in language are based on a single belief. The belief is that language can affect human experience both positively and negatively. Words can limit, confuse, and stereotype. But words can also communicate the encouraging conviction that what is possible for any human being is possible for oneself as well.

Source: Barbara Bates, "Sex Bias in Language: An Issue Worth Talking About," *Thresholds in Education,* February 1978, pp. 28-29.

The Schools See It First: Child Abuse/Neglect

Lynn Fossum and Lauralee Sorensen

Project HELP, federally funded by the Elementary and Secondary Education Act, Title IV-C, and officially designated "Child Abuse and Neglect: A Training Model for Identification," was developed in the Cupertino (California) Union School District. It followed the premise that, because a teacher sees a child more regularly than the public health nurse, juvenile probation officer, social worker, children's protective service worker, or any other outside person, the teacher may readily sense when something is wrong. The project suggests roles that many other schools may wish to adopt in the amelioration of child abuse and neglect, which are serious national problems.

The school is a focus of attention—the community center—for many people. They seek out the school principal or a teacher for help in a variety of situations, some of which are critical to a child's well-being. Obviously, the school cannot be all things to all people. But it is a focal point. Thus the school can become a clearinghouse or resource center in child abuse/neglect cases.

In Project HELP we found that the school can not only recognize abuse and neglect before a child is battered or emotionally scarred; it can also intervene. When we see stresses developing for a child and family, we assist the family with referrals to appropriate agencies. We identify resources to help the family. And we make observations and gather data to help the agency and family monitor the child's progress. To accomplish this, it is necessary for the school, family, and agency to work together for the welfare of the child. The

school, then, becomes an intermediary prevention system, providing much help to children and families before abuse and neglect are severe and the damage irreparable.

In conjunction with Public Law 93–247, the Child Abuse Prevention and Treatment Act, all 50 states have enacted some form of legislation requiring reporting of child abuse/neglect. In 42 of these states teachers and other school personnel are mandated reporters. This means that they must report to the legally designated authorities any situation in which they *suspect* a child is being abused or neglected. Teachers are not required to investigate; they merely report their concerns. Children's Protective Service workers and police have the responsibility for investigation. However, a teacher or schoolperson can offer much to the child and family during stressful periods.

Through knowledge of community agencies and resources, the school can help families find needed assistance. Through daily interactions with the child, the teacher can offer support and monitor the child's behavior for signs of stress. Through parent conferences, the school can discuss parent/child interactions and be alert to signs that additional support is needed for the family.

However, for schools to accomplish this intermediary function, there are several requisites:

1. School personnel must be aware of the signs of potential child abuse/neglect. This can usually be accomplished through a sensitive, carefully planned inservice training program for mandated reporters within the school district.

2. School personnel must be aware of the resources available within the community. This awareness can be achieved in several ways: Public agencies may publish a compendium of services; community members and school and agency personnel may create a council to plan for the handling of child abuse/neglect situations; individuals in agencies and schools may assume personal responsibility for building intraprofessional relationships.

Source: Lynn Fossum and Lauralee Sorensen, "The Schools See It First: Child Abuse/Neglect," *Phi Delta Kappan,* December 1980, p. 274.

3. School boards should adopt policies and regulations that acknowledge the school's responsibilities for intervention in child abuse/neglect cases.

4. Public agencies and schools must recognize their common need to cooperate in providing maximum assistance to the families they serve.

We know that child abuse and neglect are self-perpetuating. Resources must be brought together to disrupt cyclical patterns before they affect the next generation. Working closely with the community and other agencies, schools can provide the early intervention necessary to break the vicious cycle.

Questions for Discussion

1. How, and to what degree, have the schools you attended helped you to deal with the social problems you have faced?

2. What do you believe are our country's major social problems, and how do you feel our schools might help to solve these problems?

3. How, do you believe, should our schools attack the problem of providing equal educational opportunity for all students?

4. Discuss the pros and cons of school busing.

5. What are some viable plans that schools could use to reduce student use of drugs, alcohol, and tobacco?

Supplementary Learning Activities

1. Poll some public school teachers regarding the kinds of competencies teachers must have to assist students in meeting the needs suggested in this chapter. Formulate a list of these competencies in collaboration with your classmates.

2. Survey your community's social services. In what ways could the schools and these agencies cooperate to better provide for the needs of youth?

3. Obtain copies of available documents on social problems that affect our youth today. Analyze and critically appraise one or more of these documents.

4. Invite authorities from various social service agencies in your area to discuss what they perceive the functions of schools to be in relation to the social problems with which they are concerned.

5. Arrange for interviews with practicing front-line school social workers, both those who work in cities and in rural areas, to gain their perceptions of the role that schools can play in solving social problems.

Notes

1. *Desegregation/Integration: Planning for School Change* (Washington, D.C.: National Education Association, 1974), p. 5.

2. Christopher Jencks and Mary Jo Bane, "The Schools and Equal Opportunity," *Saturday Review,* September 16, 1972, pp. 37–42.

3. National School Public Relations Association, *Drug Crisis: Schools Fight Back with Innovative Programs* (Arlington, Va.: National School Public Relations Association, 1971), p. 3.

4. Ibid., pp. 3–4.

5. R. L. Neeman and M. Neeman, "Complexities of Smoking Education," *The Journal of School Health* 45, no. 1 (January 1975): 17–23.

6. C. F. McRae and D. Nelson, "Youth to Youth Communication on Smoking and Health," *The Journal of School Health* 41 (1971): 445–47.

7. Richard Benedetto, "Truancy: A Disease that's Now an Epidemic," *Special Report on American Education in the 1980's.* Washington, D.C.: Gannett News Service, 1980.

Selected References

Bachman, Jerald G.; Green, Swayzer; and Wirtanen, Illona. *Dropping Out—Problem or Symptom?* Ann Arbor, Mich.: Institute for Social Research, The University of Michigan, 1972.

Blyth, Dale A.; Thiel, Karen; Bush, Diane; and Simmons, Roberta. "Another Look at School Crime," *Youth & Society.* Vol. 11, no. 3, March 1980, pp. 369–88.

Coles, Robert. *Migrants, Sharecroppers, Mountaineers.* Boston: Atlantic-Little, Brown, 1972.

Eddy, John. *The Teacher and the Drug Scene.* Bloomington, Ind.: Phi Delta Kappa, 1973.

Gentry, Atron; Jones, Byrd; Peedle, Carolyn; Philips, Royce; Woodbury, John; and Woodbury, Robert. *Urban Education: The Hope Factor.* Philadelphia: W. B. Saunders, 1972.

Gold, Milton J., et al., eds. *In Praise of Diversity: A Resource Book for Multicultural Education.* Washington, D.C.: Association of Teacher Educators, 1977.

Grant, Carl A., ed. *Multicultural Education: Commitments, Issues, and Applications.* Washington, D.C.: Association for Supervision and Curriculum Development, 1977.

Green, Robert L. *The Urban Challenge: Poverty and Race,* Chicago: Follett, 1977.

Harrangue, Sr. Rene. "Coping: An Overview," *Educational Horizons.* Vol. 58, no. 3, September 1980.

Johnson, Lloyd. *Drugs and American Youth.* Ann Arbor, Mich.: Institute for Social Research, The University of Michigan, 1972.

Ladd, Edward T. *Students' Rights and Discipline.* Arlington, Va.: National Association of Elementary School Principals, 1976.

Rubel, Robert. *Crime and Disruption in Schools, A Selected Bibliography.* National Institute of Law Enforcement and Criminal Justice, 1979.

Sadker, Myra Pollack, and Sadker, David Miller. *Teachers Make the Difference, An Introduction to Education.* Cambridge: Harper & Row, 1980.

Schlosser, Courtney D. *The Person in Education.* New York: Macmillan, 1976.

Wissot, Jan. "Motivating the Alienated Student," *Humanist Educator.* Vol. 18, no. 3, March 1980, pp. 144–52.

Historical Influences on Education

10

This Chapter
- Provides a chronicle of the historical development of our educational system.
- Points out the various periods in the development of the American educational system.
- Conceptualizes the historical support that Americans have provided for education.
- Emphasizes the concept that education has played a key role in the growth of our American society.
- Traces the evolution of the elementary and secondary school.

- Highlights the historical development of our teacher-training programs.
- Accentuates the dependency of a democratic society on its educational system to produce an informed citizenry.
- Discusses the educational history of minority groups in America.
- Provides a point of view dealing with the history of American education.

Many changes have taken place in American education since the first schools were established in this country. In this chapter, we shall take a brief look at some of these changes.

History permits us to climb to a high place and look back over the road that we have traveled. Once we can see this road clearly, we can avoid some of the mistakes we made before. By the same token, we can capitalize on the successes in our educational past. Moreover, a knowledge of the history of education permits a teacher to appreciate the proud heritage that American educators possess. Let us proceed then with a brief look at the history of American education.

Educational Expectations in Colonial America

When the colonists arrived at Jamestown in 1607, they brought with them their ideas concerning education. Earlier in this book, it was pointed out that Americans today have various expectations of the public schools. Just as con-

temporary Americans have certain expectations of the present-day educational systems, so were there certain educational expectations in colonial America. Colonial America was divided roughly into three geographical areas—the northern colonies in the New England area, the middle colonies centered in New York, and the southern colonies located in the Virginia area. The colonists in each of these three areas had somewhat different expectations of the schools that existed in their respective areas. A New England Puritan, expressing his or her expectations in contemporary language, might have said:

I expect two things from our schools here in the northern colonies. First, my children must learn to read so they can understand the Bible. Secondly, the schools must teach my boys Latin and Greek so that if they wish to go on to college they will be qualified to do so.

This interest in education in the northern colonies coupled with the fact that most of the colonists in that area were of similar religious convictions led to the early establishment of public schools in that area. In fact, by 1635, only fifteen years after Boston had been settled, a Latin Grammar School was established in that area. Grammar schools had existed in Europe for many years prior to their appearance in colonial America. As their name implies, the Latin Grammar Schools included instruction in the classical languages of Latin and Greek. Such instruction was considered to be absolutely essential for the very few colonial boys who went on to a university. The schoolboys—for only boys were admitted—who attended the Latin Grammar School spent most of their time memorizing and then reciting what they had learned to the schoolmaster. Recalling his experiences as a Latin Grammar School student, one graduate recalled:

At ten years of age I committed to memory many rules of syntax, the meaning of which I had no notion of, although I could apply them in a mechanical way. The rule for the ablative absolute, for instance—"A noun and a participle are put in the ablative, called absolute, to denote the time, cause or concomitant of an action, or the condition on which it depends"—I could rattle off whenever I encountered a sample of that construction, but it was several years after I learnt the rule that I arrived at even the faintest conception of what it meant. The learning by heart of the grammar then preceded rather than accompanied, as now, exercises in translation and composition.

The educational expectations of a typical colonist from the middle colonies can be illustrated by the following statement that could have been made by a parent living in that area at that time:

Since there are many different religions represented here in the middle colonies, I want my children to attend a parochial school where they will not only learn to read and write, but also where they will receive instruction in my particular religion.

These middle colonies are sometimes referred to as the "colonial melting pot" because they were settled by people of many different nationalities and religions. These divergent backgrounds made it difficult for the middle colonists to agree upon the curriculum for a public school system, and therefore each religious group established its own parochial school system. It is interesting to note that many of these same educational problems that were found in colonial America still exist today. For instance, there are still many divergent groups in the American society, so that we may still be considered a melting pot (or if you prefer to use more recent popular terminology, a vegetable stew).

Yet another example of an educational problem that has persisted since colonial times is that dealing with parochial education. Just as the middle colonists did, a number of religious groups still feel the need to maintain their own parochial school systems.

The southern colonies consisted of large plantations and relatively few towns. This meant that two rather distinct classes of people—a few wealthy plantation owners, and a mass of poor

A colonial battledore, a variation of the hornbook printed on heavy paper and folded like an envelope.

The earliest known illustration of a secondary school in America. This is the Boston Latin Grammar School founded in 1635. This illustration comes from an old pictorial map of Boston made about 1748, just before this school building was torn down. This was probably not the original building which housed the Boston Latin Grammar School.

black slaves and white indentured servants who worked on the plantations—lived in the southern colonies. This also meant that people lived far apart in the southern colonies. If we could turn back the clock to colonial days, we would probably hear a southern plantation owner explain his educational expectations something like this:

Let me say first of all that we don't really need a public school system here in the southern colonies because, in the first place, the plantation workers do not need any education at all, and in the second place, the children of us plantation owners live so far apart that it would be impractical to have a central public school for all of them to attend. For these reasons, we do not have and do not need a public school system. I hire a tutor to live here on my plantation and teach my children. When my boys get old enough I'll send them back to Europe to attend a university.

The only education available to the poorer people in the southern colonies was that provided by individual parents for their children and that

A colonial hornbook from which children learned the ABCs. It consisted of a heavy sheet of paper tacked to a piece of wood and covered with a thin sheet of cow's horn.

For wisdom is better than rubies; and all things that may be desired are not to be compared with it.

Proverbs (8:11)

A popular Government, without popular information, or the means of acquiring it, is but a Prologue to a Farce or a Tragedy; or, perhaps both. Knowledge will forever govern ignorance: And a people who mean to be their own Governors, must arm themselves with the power which knowledge gives.

President James Madison

provided by certain missionary groups interested in teaching young people to read the Bible. A boy from a poor family who wished to learn a trade would receive his practical education by serving an apprenticeship with a master craftsman who was already in that line of work.

Early School Laws

The first law passed in colonial America dealing with education was passed in Massachusetts in 1642. This law, requiring parents to educate their children, reads as follows:

This Court, taking into consideration the great neglect of many parents and masters in training up their children in learning, and labor, and other implyments which may be profitable to the common wealth, do hereupon order and decree, that in every towne ye chosen men appointed for managing prudentiall affaires of the same shall henceforth stand charged with the care of the redresse of this evil, so as they shalbee sufficiently punished by fines for the neglect thereof, upon presentment of the grand jury, or other information on complaint in any Court within this jurisdiction. And for this end, or the greater number of them, shall have power to take account from time to time of all parents and masters, and of their children, concerning their calling and implyment of their children, especially of their ability to read and understand the principles of religion and the capitall lawes of this country, and to impose fines upon such as shall refuse to render such account to them when they shall be required; and they shall have power, with consent of any Court or the magistrate, to put forth apprentices the children of such as they shall [find] not to be able and fitt to imploy and bring them up.

A photograph of the title page and board back of the oldest known edition (1727) of the New England Primer. It was the most widely used textbook in colonial America.

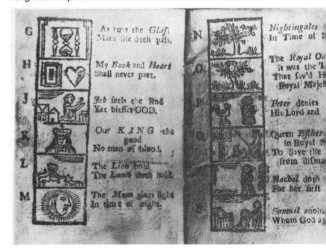

The contents of the New England Primer reflected the religious emphasis of education in colonial America.

In 1647, yet another law dealing with education was passed in Massachusetts. This law, which has come to be known as the "Old Deluder Act," required towns of certain size to establish schools. This law stated:

It being one chiefe project of that old deluder, Satan, to keepe men from the knowledge of the Scriptures, as in former times by keeping them in an unknown tongue, so in these latter times by persuading from the use of tongues, that so at least the true sence and meaning of the originall might be clouded by false glosses of saint seeming deceivers, that learning may not be buried in the grave of our fathers in church and commonwealth, the Lord assisting our endeavors,—

It is therefore ordered that every township in this jurisdiction, after the Lord hath increased their number of 50 householders, shall then forthwith appoint one within their towne to teach all such children as shall resort to him to write and reade, whose wages shall be paid either by the parents or masters of such children, or by the inhabitants in general, . . . and it is further ordered that where any towne shall increase to the number of 100 families or householders they shall set up a grammar schoole, the Master thereof being able to instruct youth so farr as they shall be fitted for the University, provided that if any town neglect the performance hereof above one year, that every such town shall pay five pounds to the next school till they shall perform this order.

In addition to the passage of these laws, further proof of the colonists' early interest in education can be found in the following agreement signed by a number of the citizens living in Roxbury in 1645:

Whereas, the Inhabitantes of Roxburie, in consideration of their relligeous care of posteritie, have taken into consideration how necessarie the education of

The seal of the Society for the Propagation of the Gospel in Foreign Parts. This society, which was the missionary society of the Church of England, was responsible for the support of most of the charity schools in the English colonies during the eighteenth century. The society also furnished books for churches and school libraries.

theire children in Literature will be to fitt them for public service, both in Churche and Commonwealth, in succeeding ages. They therefore unanimously have consented and agreed to erect a free schoole in the said town of Roxburie, and to allow twenty pounds per annum to the schoolmaster, to bee raised out of the messuages and part of the lands of the severall donors (Inhabitantes of said Towne) in several proportions as hereafter followeth under their hands. And for the well

Harvard College buildings constructed in 1675, 1699, and 1720. These buildings were dormitories. Most of the instruction took place in the homes or offices of the president and tutors.

ordering thereof they have chosen and elected some Feoffees who shall have power to putt in or remove the Schoolemaster, to see to the well ordering of the schoole and schollars, to receive and pay the said twenty pounds per annum to the Schoolemaster and to dispose of any other gifte or giftes which hereafter may or shall be given for the advancement of learning and education of children. . . .

Our First Colleges

In 1636, only sixteen years after the settlement of Boston, the first college was established in colonial America. This school was named Harvard College after the man who helped to finance the school's humble beginning. The conditions surrounding the establishment of Harvard, and the school's philosophy and curriculum, are explained in the following document, written in 1643 and entitled *New England's First Fruits,* which is partially reproduced here:

In Respect of the Colledge, and the Proceedings of "Learning" Therein: 1. After God had carried us safe to New England, and wee had builded our houses, provided necessaries for our livelihood, rear'd convenient places for God's worship, and setled the Civil Government: One of the next things we longed for, and looked after was to advance Learning and perpetuate it to Posterity; dreading to leave an illiterate Ministery to the Churches, when our present Ministers shall lie in the Dust. And as wee were thinking and consulting how to effect this great Work; it pleased God to stir up the heart of one Mr. Harvard (a godly Gentleman, and a lover of Learning, there living amongst us) to give the onehalfe of his Estate (it being in all about

1700.1.) towards the erecting of a Colledge: and all his Library: after him another gave 300.1. others after them cast in more, and the publique hand of the State added the rest: the Colledge was, by common consent, appointed to be at Cambridge, (a place very pleasant and accomodate) and is called (according to the name of the first founder) Harvard Colledge.

The Edifice is very faire and comely within and without, having in it a spacious Hall; (where they daily meet at Commons, Lectures and Exercises), and a large Library with some Bookes to it, the gifts of diverse of our friends, their Chambers and studies also fitted for, and possessed by the Students, and all other roomes of Office necessary and convenient, with all needfull Offices thereto belonging: And by the side of the Nolledge a faire Grammer Schoole, for the training up of young Schollars, and fitting them for Academicall Learning, that still as they are judged ripe, they may be received into the Colledge of this Schoole. Master Corlet is the Mr., who hath very well approved himselfe for his abilities, dexterity and painfulness in teaching and education of the youth under him.

Over the Colledge is master Dunster placed, as President, a learned conscionable and industrious man, who hath so trained up his Pupils in the tongues and Arts, and so seasoned them with the principles of Divinity and Christianity, that we have to our great comfort, (and in truth) beyond our hopes, beheld this progresse in Learning and godliness also; the former of these hath appeared in their publique declamations in Latine and Greeke, and Disputations Logicall and Philosophicall, which they have wonted (besides their ordinary Exercises in the Colledge-Hall) in the audience of the Magistrates, Ministers, and other Scholars, for the probation of their growth in Learning, upon set dayes, constantly once every moneth to make and uphold: The latter hath been manifested in sundry of them, by the savoury breathings of their Spirits in their godly conversation. Insomuch that we are confident, if these early blossomes may be cherished and warmed with the influence of the friends of Learning, and lovers of this pious worke, they will by the help of God, come to happy maturity in a short time.

Over the Colledge are twelve Overseers chosen by the generall Court, six of them are of the Magistrates, the other six of the Ministers, who are to promote the best good of it and (having a power of influence into all persons in it) are to see that every one be diligent and proficient in his proper place.

Further insight into the nature of Harvard College may be found in the following entrance requirements published in 1642:

When any scholar is able to read Tully, or such like classical Latine author *extempore,* and make a speak true Latin in Verse and Prose, and decline perfectly the paradigms of nounes and verbes in the Greek tongue, then may he be admitted into the college, nor shall any claim admission before such qualifications.

Harvard was the only colonial college for nearly sixty years until William and Mary was established in 1693. Other colleges which were established early in our history included Yale (1701), Princeton (1746), King's College (1754), College of Philadelphia (1755), Brown (1764), Dartmouth (1769), and Queen's College (1770).

Latin Grammar Schools

The Latin Grammar School was the only form of secondary school found in the colonies until the early 1700s, at which time a few private secondary schools were established. These schools were created out of a need for a more practical form of secondary education than the existing Latin Grammar Schools provided. Insight into the nature of these early private secondary schools can be gained from the following newspaper ad, which was published in the October-November 1723 edition of the *American Weekly Mercury* of Philadelphia:

There is a school in New York, in the Broad Street, near the Exchange where Mr. John Walton, late of Yale-Colledge, teacheth Reading, Writing, Arethmatick, whole Numbers and Fractions, Vulgar and Decimal, the Mariners Art, Plain and Mercators Way; also Geometry, Surveying, the Latin tongue, and Greek and Hebrew Grammers, Ethicks, Retorick, Logick, Natural Philosophy and Metaphysicks, all or any of them for a Reasonable Price. The School from the first of October till the first of March will be tended in the Evening. If any Gentleman in the Country are disposed to send their sons to the said School, if they apply themselves to the Master he will immediately procure suitable Entertainment for them, very cheap. Also if any Young Gentleman of the City will Please to come in the evening and make some Tryal of the Liberal Arts, they may have opportunity of Learning the same things which are commonly taught in Colledges.

The Academy

In 1751 Benjamin Franklin opened a secondary school in Philadelphia which he called an academy. The curriculum in Franklin's Academy included practical training in areas such as surveying, navigation, and printing, as well as courses in English, geography, history, logic, rhetoric, Latin, and Greek.

Franklin's Academy served a real need as the colonies developed a greater need for technically trained citizens. Other academies were quickly established and this type of school flourished for approximately one hundred years. These academies were private schools, and many of them admitted girls as well as boys.

The New Nation and its Educational Needs

One of the great problems facing the United States, after winning her independence from England, was that of welding her people, who had come from many diverse political and religious convictions, into a nation of informed voters. This meant that all citizens should be able to read so that they could keep informed on the issues the country faced. This interest in education found in the new nation was manifested in a number of different ways; for instance, groups of citizens created petitions for better schools. An example of such a petition is the following, which was

A picture of the academy and charitable school of Philadelphia founded by Benjamin Franklin in 1751. It is the first institution in America, so far as present records show, to bear the title of academy. Later on it developed into the University of Pennsylvania.

submitted in 1799 to the General Assembly of Rhode Island:

A PETITION FOR FREE SCHOOL. *To the Honorable General Assembly of the State of Rhode Island and Providence Plantations, to be holden at Greenwich, on the last Monday of February,* A.D. *1799:*

The Memorial and Petition of the Providence Association of Mechanics and Manufacturers respectfully presents—

That the means of education which are enjoyed in this state are very inadequate to a purpose so highly important . . . we at the same time solicit this Honorable Assembly to make legal provision for the establishment of free schools sufficient to educate all the children in the several towns throughout the state. . . .

Another indication of the new national need for, and interest in education is the following comment made by Thomas Jefferson in 1816:

If a nation expects to be ignorant and free in a state of civilization, it expects what never was and never will be . . . There is no safe deposit but with the people themselves; nor can they be safe with them without information.

Despite this new interest in education, the school of the early 1800s was very humble and inadequate. An excellent description of an 1810 New England school is contained in the following reflection of a teacher who taught in this school.

(A) The school building: The School house stood near the center of the district, at the junction of four roads, so near the usual track of carriages that a large stone was set up at the end of the building to defend it from injury. Except in the dry season the ground was wet, and the soil by no means firm. The spot was particularly exposed to the bleak winds of winter; nor were there any shade trees to shelter the children from the scorching rays of the summer's sun, as they were cut down many years ago. Neither was there any such thing as an outhouse of any kind, not even a wooden shed.

The size of the building was 22 × 20 feet. From the floor to the ceiling it was 7 feet. The chimney and entry took up about four feet at one end, leaving the schoolroom itself 18 × 20 feet. Around these sides of the room were connected desks, arranged so that when the pupils were sitting at them their faces were towards the instructor and their backs toward the wall. Attached to the sides of the desks nearest to the instructor were benches for small pupils. The instructor's desk and chair occupied the center. On this desk were stationed a rod, or ferule; sometimes both. These, with books, writings, inkstands, rules, and plummets, with a fire shovel, and a pair of tongs (often broken), were the principal furniture.

The windows were five in number, of twelve panes each. They were situated so low in the walls as to give full opportunity to the pupils to see every traveller as he passed, and to be easily seen. The places of the broken panes were usually supplied with hats, during school hours. A depression in the chimney, on one side of the entry, furnished a place of deposit for about half of the hats, and the spare clothes of the boys; the rest were left on the floor, often to be trampled upon. The girls generally carried their bonnets, etc., into the schoolroom. The floor and ceiling were level, and the walls were plastered.

The room was warmed by a large and deep fire place. So large was it, and so efficacious in warming the room otherwise, that I have seen about one-eighth of a cord of good wood burning in it at a time. In severe weather it was estimated that the amount usually consumed was not far from a cord a week. . . .

The school was not infrequently broken up for a day or two for want of wood. The instructor or pupils were sometimes, however, compelled to cut or saw it to prevent the closing of the school. The wood was left in the road near the house, so that it often was buried in the snow, or wet with rain. At the best, it was usually burnt green. The fires were to be kindled about half an hour before the time of beginning the school. Often, the scholar, whose lot it was, neglected to build it. In consequence of this, the house was frequently cold and uncomfortable about half of the forenoon, when, the fire being very large, the excess of heat became equally distressing. Frequently, too, we were annoyed by smoke. The greatest amount of suffering, however, arose from excessive heat, particularly at the close of the day. The pupils being in a free perspiration when they left, were very liable to take cold.

The ventilation of the schoolroom was as much neglected as its temperature; and its cleanliness, more

Plan of the University of Virginia drawn by Thomas Jefferson in the early nineteenth century. The University was opened in 1825. This plan represents a radical modification of the semimonastic conception of college life held by the earlier colonial colleges. The building facing in the main court is for lectures and recitations; those flanking it are professors' houses; the smaller buildings are dormitories.

The town and church schools of the early colonial period were supplemented by the dame school. In fact, it was a common requirement for that period that children know how to read before entering a town school. Hence, the necessity of these dame schools, which taught the children the alphabet, and possibly the catechism and the rudiments of reading.

perhaps than either. There were no arrangements for cleaning feet at the door, or for washing floors, windows, etc. In the summer the floor was washed, perhaps once in two or three weeks.

(B) The Instructors: The winter school usually opened about the first week of December, and continued from twelve to sixteen weeks. The summer term commenced about the first of May. Formerly this was also continued about three or four months, but within ten years the term has been lengthened usually to twenty weeks. Males have been uniformly employed in winter, and females in summer.

The instructors have usually been changed every season, but sometimes they have been continued two successive summers or winters. A strong prejudice has always existed against employing the same instructor more than once or twice in the same district. This prejudice has yielded in one instance, so far that an instructor who had taught two successive winters, twenty-five years before, was employed another season. I have not been able to ascertain the number of instructors who have been engaged in the school during the last thirty years, but I can distinctly recollect

thirty-seven. Many of them, both males and females, were from sixteen to eighteen years of age, and a few, over twenty-one.

Good moral character, and a thorough knowledge of the common branches, formerly were considered as indispensable qualifications in an instructor. The instructors were chiefly selected from the most respectable families in town. But for fifteen or twenty years, these things have not been so much regarded. They have indeed been deemed desirable; but the most common method now seems to be to ascertain, as near as possible, the dividend for that season from the public treasury, and then fix upon a teacher who will take charge of the school, three or four months, for this money. He must indeed be able to obtain a license from the Board of Visitors; but this has become nearly a matter of course, provided he can spell, read, and write. In general, the candidate is some favorite or relative of the District Committee. It gives me great pleasure, however, to say that the moral character of almost every instructor, so far as I know, has been unexceptional.

Instructors have usually boarded in the families of the pupils. Their compensation has varied from seven to eleven dollars a month for males; and from sixty-two and a half cents to one dollar a week for females. Within the past ten years, however, the price of instruction has rarely been less than nine dollars in the former case, and seventy-five cents in the latter. In the few instances in which instructors have furnished their own board the compensation has been about the same, it being assumed that they could work at some employment of their own enough to pay their board, especially the females.

(C) The Instruction: Two of the Board of Visitors usually visit the winter schools twice during the term. In the summer, their visits are often omitted. These visits usually occupy from one hour to an hour and a half. They are spent merely in hearing a few hurried lessons, and in making some remarks, generally in their character. Formerly, it was customary to examine the pupils in some approved Catechism, but this practice has been omitted for twenty years.

The parents seldom visit the school, except by special invitation. The greater number pay very little attention to it at all. There are, however, a few who are gradually awakening to the importance of good instruction; but there are also a few who oppose everything which is suggested as, at the least, useless, and are scarcely willing their children should be governed in the school.

The school books have been about the same for thirty years. Webster's Spelling Book, the American Preceptor, and the New Testament, have been the principal books used. Before the appearance of the American Preceptor, Dwight's Geography was used as a reading book. A few of the Introduction to the American Orator were introduced about twelve years since, and, more recently, Jack Halyard.

Until within a few years, no studies have been permitted in the day school but spelling, reading, and writing. Arithmetic was taught by a few instructors, one or two evenings in a week, but, in spite of the most determined opposition, arithmetic is now permitted in the day school, and a few pupils study geography.

The Development of the Common School

The national interest in education during the late eighteenth and early nineteenth centuries culminated in a movement to establish free public schools—or common schools, as they were then called—for all children. The man who led this fight for common schools was Horace Mann (1796–1859). Horace Mann became the first secretary (a position we now call the state superintendent of schools) of the Massachusetts state board of education in 1837. In that position, Mann was able to do a good deal to promote the common school cause. Each year, Mann wrote an annual report of his work as the secretary of the state board of education. His twelfth annual report included the following statement about the importance of the common school:

Without undervaluing any other human agency, it may be safely affirmed that the common school, improved and energized as it can easily be, may become the most effective and benignant of all the forces of civilization. Two reasons sustain this position. In the first place, there is a universality in its operations, which can be affirmed of no other institution whatever. If administered in the spirit of justice and conciliation, all the rising generation may be brought within the circle of its reformatory and elevating influences. And, in the second place, the materials upon which it operates are so pliant and ductile as to be susceptible of assuming a greater variety of forms than any other earthly work of the Creator. The inflexibility and ruggedness of the oak, when compared with the lithe sapling or the tender germ, are but feeble emblems to typify the docility of childhood when contrasted with the obduracy

A portrait of Horace Mann—the father of the common school.

and intractableness of man. It is these inherent advantages of the common school, which, in our own state, have produced results so striking, from a system so imperfect, and an administration so feeble. In teaching the blind and the deaf and dumb, in kindling the latent spark of intelligence that lurks in an idiot's mind, and in the more holy work of reforming abandoned and outcast children, education has proved what it can do by glorious experiments. These wonders it has done in its infancy, and with the lights of a limited experience; but when its faculties shall be fully developed, when it shall be trained to wield its mighty energies for the protection of society against the giant vices which now invade and torment it—against intemperance, avarice, war, slavery, bigotry, the woes of want, and the wickedness of waste,—then there will not be a height to which these enemies of the race can escape which it will not scale.

Through his work as secretary to the Massachusetts state board of education, his speaking, and his writing—including his annual reports such as the one just quoted—Horace Mann deserves much of the credit for helping to establish the common school system in the United States. So much so, in fact, that he is now remembered as the "father of the common school."

Another of the many men who did much to help promote education in the United States during the mid-nineteenth century was Henry Barnard (1811–1900). Barnard served as the secretary of the state board of education in Connecticut and then in Rhode Island. Barnard was a prolific writer and his writings were very influential in helping to sell the need for better education. He edited and published the *American Journal of Education* which represented a gigantic compilation of information about education. In 1867 Henry Barnard became the first United States Commissioner of Education.

The work of Horace Mann, Henry Barnard, and many other men of foresight who saw the value—indeed, the essentialness—of a common education for all citizens was firmly established in the United States during the last half of the nineteenth century. Massachusetts, the state that led the way in many facets of education, passed the first compulsory school attendance law in 1852. Other states eventually passed similar laws so that by 1900, thirty-two states required compulsory school attendance.

Laws for the liberal education of youth, especially of the lower class of people, are so extremely wise and useful, that, to a humane and generous mind, no expense for this purpose would be thought extravagant.

President John Adams

The Development of the Public High Schools

It was mentioned earlier in this chapter that the Latin Grammar School was the first form of secondary school that existed in this country. The academy eventually replaced the Latin Grammar School as the dominant secondary school in the United States.

In 1821, a new form of secondary school, one unique to the United States, was established in Boston, Massachusetts. This new secondary school was called the "English Classical School" but three years later its name was changed to the "English High School."

The curriculum of this new English High School emphasized mathematics, social studies, science, and English. The first high schools were for boys between the ages of twelve and fifteen, but later on girls were also admitted.

At about 1900, the high school replaced the academy as the dominant type of secondary school in this country, and, needless to say, remains so today. Figure 10.1 shows, in graphic form, the historical development of secondary schools in the United States.

Education for Minorities

Historically, education was for the most part reserved for white well-to-do boys. With a few notable exceptions, black children, Indian children, children of Spanish descent, and poor white children received very little, if any, formal education.

Likewise, most girls—even many from wealthy families—received little formal education.

Slave owners commonly felt that education and slavery were incompatible. Frederick Douglass, one of the few slaves who managed to educate himself and become a prominent black leader, relates that his master characterized this viewpoint when he said in his own words:

If you give a nigger an inch, he will take an ell. A nigger should know nothing but to obey his master—to do as he is told to do. Learning would spoil the best nigger in the world. Now if you teach that nigger how to read, there would be no keeping him. It would forever unfit him to be a slave. He would at once become unmanageable, and of no value to his master. As to himself, it could do him no good, but a great deal of harm. It would make him discontent and unhappy.[1]

Douglass goes on to point out how he came to realize that education was the "pathway from slavery to freedom." It was not until after the Civil War that any serious attempt was made to provide education for blacks. Even then, many of these efforts were left up to religious groups—whose motive was to teach blacks to read the Bible and gain salvation.

The Freedmen's Bureau was created by congress in 1865 in an attempt to provide basic education to blacks in hopes of helping them to become self-sufficient after receiving freedom from slavery. While many blacks learned to read and write through the efforts of the Freedmen's Bureau, it did little to improve their lot in life. A few black colleges, such as Tuskegee Institute founded by Booker T. Washington, were established prior to 1900, but important as they were, they did little for the masses of black people in America during their early years.

Throughout American history, providing formal schooling and eventual equal educational opportunities for blacks has been an uphill struggle. Some significant dates and events in this uphill struggle are presented in table 10.1. Recent developments in black education are discussed in greater detail elsewhere in this book.

For the American Indian, education had very little utility during the colonial period. The Indian's major concern was retaining the land and eventually simply surviving against the ever increasing encroachment of the whites. A few missionary groups such as the Quakers and the Society for the Propagation of the Gospel attempted to teach some Indians to read and write; however, it was not until late in the 1800s that any serious national effort was made to provide education for American Indians. This happened when the federal government finally provided money as part of its land treaties for educational efforts in the various tribes. This system of federally operated schools for American Indians has existed right up to the present.

The same basic story just told about blacks and Indians can be told about the educational history, or more accurately the lack of it, for other minority groups in America. The Mexican Americans, Puerto Ricans, Japanese Americans, Chinese Americans, and other minority groups simply were not afforded equal educational opportunity in the historical development of America.

Most recently, attention has been brought to the fact that in many respects American women represent yet another group who have not received equal educational opportunity down through American history.

The Development of Teacher Education

As the United States developed a need for better schools and better education, it was inevitable that the subject of better-trained teachers should also receive attention. Citizens of the United States were slow to realize that good education required good teachers. Until the mid-1800s teachers had, for the most part, been very poorly prepared for their work. A teacher's job was not considered very important, and commanded very little prestige. In fact, advertisements that appeared in a Philadelphia newspaper during colonial times show that even indentured servants were sold as schoolteachers.

Since education had a strong religious motive in the colonies, the schools were often conducted in the church by the minister. When the job got too big for the minister to handle by himself, a layperson would be hired to teach at the school. Oftentimes, in addition to teaching the school, the teacher would be required "to act as court messenger, to serve summonses, to conduct certain ceremonial services at the church, to lead the Sunday choir, to ring the bell for public worship, to dig the graves, and to perform other occasional duties."

Table 10.1. Significant Dates in Black-American History.

1619

• The first Negroes to be brought to the American colonies arrived in Virginia as indentured servants.

1661

• Virginia passed the first law making Negroes slaves.

1663

• Slavery was legally recognized in Maryland.

1688

• Quakers in Germantown, Pa., issued the first formal antislavery protest in the Western Hemisphere.

1770

• Crispus Attucks, a runaway slave, was killed in the Boston Massacre.

1775

• The Pennsylvania Abolition Society, the first anti-slavery society in America, was founded.

1776

• The Declaration of Independence was signed, the final version omitting an attack on slavery by Thomas Jefferson contained in the draft version.

1787

• Congress barred the extension of slavery into the Northwest Territory.

1791

• Eli Whitney invented the cotton gin, spurring the expansion of cotton plantations and the demand for slaves.

1800

• Gabriel Prosser, a Virginia slave, led an unsuccessful insurrection and was hanged with 24 conspirators.

1807

• British Parliament abolished the slave trade. Congress barred the importation of new slaves into U.S. territory.

1816

• The American Colonization Society was formed to resettle free American Negroes in Africa.

1820

• Congress adopted the Missouri Compromise providing for the admission of Missouri into the Union as a slave state, and Maine's entry as a free state. All territory north of 36°30′ was declared free; all territory south of that line was left open to slavery.

1827

• The first Negro newspaper, *Freedom's Journal,* began publication in New York City.

1830

• The U.S. Census Bureau reported that 3,777 Negro heads of families owned slaves.

1831

• Federal and state troops crushed a slave rebellion in Southampton County, Va., led by Nat Turner. The rebellion, in which more than 50 whites and more than 100 slaves were killed, ended in the capture and execution of Turner and led to the adoption of more rigid slave codes.

Source: The Hammond Almanac (Maplewood, N.J.: Hammond Almanac, Inc., 1980), pp. 266–68. Used with permission.

Table 10.1. *Continued*

1847

- Frederick Douglass, a former slave and a lecturer with the Massachusetts Anti-Slavery Society, began publishing *North Star,* an abolitionist newspaper.

1849

- Harriet Tubman escaped from slavery in Maryland. She became one of the most venturesome conductors on the Underground Railroad, leading over 300 slaves to freedom.
- Benjamin Roberts filed the first school integration suit on behalf of his daughter. The Massachusetts Supreme Court rejected the suit and established a "separate but equal" precedent.

1850

- The Compromise of 1850 admitted California to the Union as a free state but strengthened the Fugitive Slave Law, giving greater inducement for the apprehension of runaway slaves.

1852

- Harriet Beecher Stowe's novel *Uncle Tom's Cabin,* a vastly popular antislavery work, was published.

1853

- *Clotelle: or the President's Daughter* by historian William Wells Brown was published—the first novel by an American Negro.

1854

- James A. Healy was ordained a priest in Notre Dame cathedral, Paris. He later became America's first Negro Roman Catholic bishop.
- The first Negro college, Lincoln University, was founded as Ashmun Institute in Oxford, Pa.

1855

- The first Negro to win elective office in the United States, John Mercer Langston, was elected clerk of Brownhelm Township, Lorain Co., O.

1863

- The Draft Riots took place in New York City. Blacks and abolitionists were attacked and killed.

1865

- By the end of the Civil War, some 186,000 Negroes had served with the Union forces.
- The Thirteenth Amendment, freeing all slaves, was passed by Congress.
- The Freedman's Bureau was organized to aid and protect newly freed blacks in the South.
- Dr. John S. Rock, a Boston physician and lawyer, was the first Negro admitted to the bar of the United States Supreme Court.
- Southern states passed the "Black Codes" in an attempt to restrict the freedom of emancipated slaves.

1866

- Charles L. Mitchell and Edward G. Walker were elected to the Massachusetts House of Representatives, becoming the first Negroes to serve in a U.S. legislature.

1867

- Morehouse College, Atlanta, Ga., and Howard University, Washington, D.C., were founded.

1868

- Oscar J. Dunn attained the highest elective office held by an American Negro up to that time, becoming lieutenant governor of Louisiana.

1869

- Ebenezer Don Carlos Basset was appointed minister to Haiti, the first Negro diplomat to represent the United States.

Table 10.1. *Continued*

1870

- Hiram Revels was elected to fill the unexpired U.S. Senate term of Jefferson Davis of Mississippi, becoming the first Negro Senator. He served a year.
- Joseph H. Rainey of South Carolina became the first Negro in the House of Representatives. He was subsequently reelected four times.

1875

- Congress passed a civil rights act prohibiting discrimination in such public accommodations as hotels and theaters.

1877

- Henry O. Flipper became the first Negro to graduate from West Point.

1881

- Tennessee passed a "Jim Crow" law instituting segregated railroad travel that set a trend among other states in the South.

1883

- The Supreme Court declared the 1875 Civil Rights Act unconstitutional.

1890

- Mississippi instituted restrictions on voting, including a poll tax and literacy tests, which were designed to disenfranchise Negroes. During the decade, other Southern states followed. Louisiana added (1898) the exclusionary device of the "grandfather clause," which set educational and property qualifications for voting but exempted those whose ancestors had been eligible to vote as of Jan. 1, 1867.

1891

- The Provident Hospital in Chicago—the first such interracial institution in America—was founded by Negro surgeon Daniel Hale Williams.

1895

- Frederick Douglass, the Negro abolitionist whom Lincoln had called "the most meritorious man of the 19th century," died.

1896

- The National Association of Colored Women was organized in Washington, D.C.; Mary Church Terrell served as its first president.

1898

- Four Negro regiments in the regular army compiled an excellent combat record during the Spanish-American War. Dismounted elements of the black Ninth and Tenth Cavalry rescued the Rough Riders from near annihilation.

1905

- Twenty-nine Negro intellectuals from 14 states, headed by Dr. W. E. B. DuBois, organized the Niagara Movement, which demanded the abolition of all racial distinctions. The meeting took place at Fort Erie, N.Y.

1909

- Matthew Henson, a Negro member of Admiral Peary's expedition, placed the American flag at the North Pole.

1910

- The National Association for the Advancement of Colored People (NAACP) was founded in New York.

1911

- The National Urban League was founded. It was originally made up of two groups: The Committee for Improving the Industrial Conditions of Negroes and The League for the Protection of Colored Women.

Historical Influences on Education   223

Table 10.1. *Continued*

1915

- The Association for the Study of Negro Life and History was established by the ''father of Negro history,'' Dr. Carter G. Woodson.

1917

- Ten thousand Negroes marched down Fifth Avenue in New York to protest the many lynchings in the South. The parade was led by W. E. B. DuBois. Race riots broke out in East St. Louis, Illinois.

1920

- The pioneer black nationalist Marcus Garvey inaugurated the International Convention of the Universal Negro Improvement Association (UNIA) in Harlem. UNIA reached its greatest influence during the following two years.

1928

- Oscar De Priest of Illinois was the first black Congressman from a northern state.

1935

- Mary McLeod Bethune organized the National Council of Negro Women.

1936

- Negro track star Jesse Owen won four gold medals in the Olympics at Berlin.

1937

- Joe Louis became heavyweight boxing champion of the world, defeating Jim Braddock for the title.

1939

- Contralto Marian Anderson, denied the use of Constitution Hall in Washington by the Daughters of the American Revolution, sang on Easter Sunday before 75,000 people at the Lincoln Memorial.

1940

- Benjamin O. Davis, Sr., was appointed the first black general in the U.S. armed forces.

1941

- A Negro threat to stage a massive protest march on Washington resulted in the issuance of Executive Order 8802 prohibiting racial discrimination in defense industries or the government (but not the armed forces).

1942

- The Congress of Racial Equality (CORE), an action-oriented civil rights group, was founded by James Farmer in Chicago.

1947

- Statistics amassed by Tuskegee Institute indicated that in the period 1882–1947 3,426 Negroes were lynched in the United States. Of these, 1,217 were lynched in the 1890–1900 decade.

1948

- President Truman issued Executive Order 9981 calling for ''equality of treatment and opportunity'' in the armed forces.

1949

- William L. Dawson became the first Negro to head a Congressional committee.

1951

- Ralph J. Bunche, who won a Nobel Peace Prize in 1950, was appointed Under-Secretary of the United Nations, the highest ranking American employed by the international body.
- Private First Class William Thompson was awarded the Congressional Medal of Honor for bravery in the Korean War, the first Negro to win it since the Spanish-American War.

Table 10.1. *Continued*

1952

- A Tuskegee Institute report indicated that for the first time in 71 years of compilation, no lynchings were reported in the United States.

1954

- In "Brown v. Board of Education of Topeka" the U.S. Supreme Court held that segregation in public education denied equal protection of the laws.

1955

- A bus boycott in Montgomery, Ala., was led by Dr. Martin Luther King, Jr., after Rosa Parks was arrested for refusing to give up her seat to a white man.

1957

- Central High School in Little Rock, Ark., was integrated by nine Negro children, but not until President Eisenhower had called in troops to keep order.

1960

- Four Negro North Carolina A & T College freshmen occupied places at a Woolworth lunch counter, launching a wave of nonviolent sit-ins.

1961

- CORE began "Freedom Rides" that rolled through the South, protesting segregation.

1962

- James Meredith desegregated the University of Mississippi, after President Kennedy dispatched troops and riots killed two persons.

1963

- August 28: The March on Washington in which more than 200,000 Americans from all walks of life converged on the nation's capital constituted one of the largest single protests in American history. The marchers gathered on the steps of the Lincoln Memorial to dramatize discontent with the Negro's plight.

1964

- Three young civil-rights workers—Michael Schwerner, Andrew Goodman, and James E. Chaney—were murdered in Mississippi.

1965

- Malcolm X., former Black Muslim and advocate of black nationalism, was assassinated in New York City.
- Thurgood Marshall was named as the first Negro Solicitor General of the United States.
- President Johnson signed the Voting Rights Act, under which federal examiners are authorized to register black voters who have been refused by state officials.

1966

- Robert Weaver was appointed head of the Department of Housing and Urban Development (HUD), the first Negro ever to serve at cabinet level.
- Constance Baker Motley, former borough president of Manhattan, became the first Negro woman to become a federal judge in American history.
- The U.S. Supreme Court outlawed all poll taxes.
- The concept of "Black Power" was adopted by CORE.

1967

- Solicitor General Thurgood Marshall became the first Negro Supreme Court Justice.
- At a four-day Black Power conference—the largest of its kind in American history—more tha 400 people representing 45 civil rights groups from 36 cities convened in Newark, N.J., expressing viewpoints that ranged from moderate to militant.

Table 10.1. *Continued*

1968

- April 4: While standing on the balcony of a Memphis motel, Dr. Martin Luther King, Jr., was shot and killed by a sniper.
- The Kerner Commission reported that "our nation is moving toward two societies, one black, one white—separate and unequal."

1969

- Educational institutions acceded to demands by black students for more black studies.
- James Earl Ray pleaded guilty to the assassination of Martin Luther King; sentenced to 99 years in prison.

1970

- The killing in December 1969 of a Black Panther leader, Fred Hampton, led to a federal investigation and the subsequent conclusion that the Chicago police had exercised undue force.

1971

- Samuel L. Gravely, Jr., was made the first black admiral in the U.S. Navy.

1972

- The busing of children, both black and white, from one neighborhood school district to another became an important political issue. The Nixon administration supported and signed into law a bill which prohibited busing solely to achieve racial integration.

1975

- Black Muslims agreed to accept white members.

1976

- U.S. Supreme Court outlawed discrimination in commercially operated nonsectarian private schools.

1977

- The TV dramatization of Alex Haley's book *Roots* was seen by the largest audience ever. The story chronicled the black author's family history from mid-eighteenth century African beginnings.

1978

- U.S. Supreme Court ruled that the University of California Medical School at Davis must admit Allan P. Bakke, a 38-year-old white engineer, as the school's minority-admissions plan was inflexible and racially biased. The justices ruled, however, that race could be considered as a university admission factor. Black leaders expressed concern regarding the decision.

Some boys became teachers by serving as an apprentice to a schoolmaster. This method of learning the art of teaching was quite logical since the apprenticeship was a well-established way of learning trades in that day. The following record of such an apprenticeship agreement was recorded in the courts of New York City in 1772:

This Indenture witnesseth that John Campbel Son of Robert Campbel of the City of New York with the Consent of his father and mother hath put himself and by these presents doth Voluntarily put and bind himself Apprentice to George Brownell of the Same City Schoolmaster to learn the Art Trade or Mystery—for and during the term of ten years . . . And the said George Brownell Doth hereby Convenent and Promise to teach and Instruct or Cause the said Apprentice to be taught and Instructed in the Art Trade or Calling of a Schoolmaster by the best way or means he or his wife may or can.

Benjamin Franklin, in proposing the establishment of his academy, claimed that

The direction in which education starts a man will
determine his future life.

Plato

There is a miracle in every new beginning.

Hermann Hesse

a number of the poorer sort [of academy graduates] will be hereby qualified to act as School masters in the Country, to teach children Reading, Writing, Arithmetic, and the Grammar of their Mother Tongue, and being of good morals and known character, may be recommended from the Academy to Country Schools for that purpose; the Country suffering at present very much for want of good Schoolmasters, and obliged frequently to employ in their Schools, vicious imported Servants, or concealed Papists, who by their bad Examples and Instructions often deprave the Morals and corrupt the Principles of the children under their Care.

It is interesting to note that Franklin suggested that the "poorer" graduates of his academy would make good teachers. This wording indicates again the low esteem of teachers at that time.

The first formal teacher-training institution in the United States was a private normal school established in 1823 at Concord, Vermont. This school was established by the Rev. Samuel Hall, and was called the Columbian School. Some insight into the nature of Hall's school can be obtained from the following advertisement, which appeared in the May 20, 1823, edition of the *North Star* newspaper:

COLUMBIAN SCHOOL, CONCORD, VT.

The second term will commence on the third Tuesday (17th day) of June next. The School will be under the direction, and will be principally instructed by the Rev. Mr. Hall.

Books used in the school must be uniform. Hence, arrangements are made so that they may be obtained at either of the stores in town. Branches taught, if required, are the following: Reading, Spelling, Defining, Geography (ancient and modern), History, Grammar, Rhetoric, Composition, Arithmetic, Construction of Maps, Theoretical Surveying, Astronomy, Natural Philosophy, Chemistry (without experiments), Logic, Moral Philosophy, Mental Philosophy, and General Criticism.

It is wished to have the languages excluded.—This will not, however, be strictly adhered to.

TERMS: For Common School studies, $2. per term of 12 weeks. Other branches from $2.50 to $4.

It is intended to have instruction particularly thorough, and hence an additional instructor will be employed, when the School amounts to more than 20. Board obtained near the School room, on reasonable terms.

Application may be made to Mr. Lyman F. Dewey, Mr. John Barnet, or Mr. Hall.

Concord, Vt. May 14, 1823.

This ad points out that the curriculum in Hall's normal school included "Mental Philosophy," which was the forerunner of educational psychology, and "General Criticism" (presumably of the student's practice teaching).

The first public tax-supported teacher-training school in this country was the Lexington Normal School located in Lexington, Massachusetts. This school was opened in 1839. Horace Mann, as secretary of the state board of education, was very influential in the establishment of this state normal school. The curriculum in the Lexington Normal School, and other similar state normal schools which were quickly established, was patterned after similar schools that had existed in Europe since the late 1600s. These early normal schools offered a two-year program designed to prepare their students, many of whom had not attended a secondary school, to teach elementary

What can only be taught by the rod and with blows will not lead to much good; they will not remain pious longer than the rod is behind them.

Martin Luther

To be a schoolmaster is next to being a king. Do you count it a mean employment to imbue the minds of your fellow citizens in their earnest years with the best literature and with the love of Christ, and to return them to their country honest and virtuous men? In the opinion of fools, it is a humble task, but in fact it is the noblest of occupations. Even among the heathen it was always a noble thing to deserve well of the state, and no one serves it better than the molders of raw boys.

Erasmus

An advertisement in a 1735 issue of the Pennsylvania Gazette showing an indentured servant for sale as a schoolmaster. The lower two ads show Negro slaves for sale.

The first high school in the United States, established in 1821 at Boston. This was the counterpart of the Latin Grammar School. The term high school was not applied to it until the school had existed for several years. It was first called an English Classical School.

school. The normal schools eventually developed four-year programs and, during the 1920s, changed their names to "state teachers' colleges." Then later, during the 1950s, many of these institutions expanded their curricula to include liberal arts, and changed their names to "state colleges." During the last decade, many of these same institutions that started as two-year normal schools have begun offering graduate work, including doctoral programs, and have changed their names to "state universities."

It was not until about 1900 that states began passing teacher certification laws which regulated the amount and type of training that a person must have to become a teacher. Prior to the passage of these laws, anyone could legally teach school.

Figure 10.1 The Historical Development of Secondary Schools in the United States.

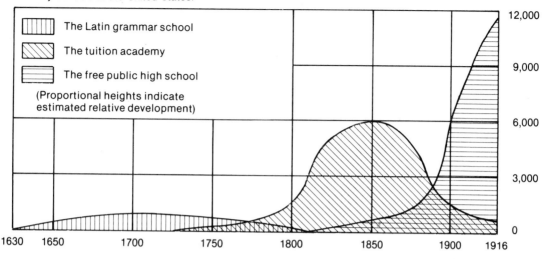

In summary, this chapter has pointed out a number of important concepts concerning the history of education in the United States. These concepts include the following:

- The educational program in colonial America was largely transplanted from Europe.
- The colonists attempted to make educational provisions almost as soon as they set foot on the new world.
- The motive for providing education in colonial America was almost entirely religious in nature.
- Education has played an increasingly important role in the development of the United States, from 1607 when the first colonists settled at Jamestown to the present.
- Many of the educational problems of colonial America have persisted to the present time.
- The role of education in the United States has increased in importance down through time, so

that today education has a larger and more important role to play in our country than ever before.

The chapter has, then, attempted to highlight the historical development of the American educational system. Within this general framework, the concept that education has played a key role, perhaps even *the* key role, in the development of America has been articulated. The well-accepted notion that a democratic society such as ours is totally dependent upon its schools' ability to produce an informed electorate has been developed. The idea that Americans have historically insisted upon an adequate educational system is yet another theme woven throughout this chapter.

A chronology of some of the highlights of the history of American education is presented in table 10.2.

Table 10.2. History of Education—Highlights.

about 4,000	B.C.	Written language developed
about 2,000	B.C.	First schools
479–338	B.C.	Period of Greek Brilliance
445–431	B.C.	Greek Age of Pericles
303	B.C.	Few private Greek teachers set up schools in Rome
167	B.C.	First Greek library in Rome
0		Christ born
31–476	A.D.	Empire of Rome
476	A.D.	Fall of Rome in the West
800	A.D.	Charlemagne crowned Emperor
1100		Turning point in mediaeval history, civilization saved
1150		Universities of Paris and Bologna
1209		Cambridge founded
1295		Voyage of Marco Polo
1384		Order of Brethren of the Common Life founded
1400		Thirty-eight universities; 108 by 1600
1423		Printing invented
1456		First book printed
1500		250 Latin Grammar Schools in England
1517		Luther nails theses to cathedral door, beginning of Reformation
1519–1521		Magellan first circumnavigates the globe
1534		Founding of Jesuits
1536		Sturm established his Gymnasium in Germany, setting the type of the classical secondary school
1601		English Poor Law, established principle of tax-supported schools
1618		Holland had compulsory school law
1620		Plymouth Colony, Massachusetts, settled
1635		Boston Latin Grammar School founded
1636		Harvard founded, first college in North America
1642		Massachusetts law of 1642, compelled inspection
1647		Massachusetts law of 1647, compelled establishment of schools
1662		First newspaper in England
1672		First teacher-training class, Father Demia, France
1684		Brothers of the Christian Schools founded
1685		First normal school, de la Salle, Rheims, France
1697		First teacher-training in Germany, Francke's Seminary, Halle
1751		Benjamin Franklin established first academy in the United States
1762		*Emile* of Rousseau published
1775–1789		Revolution, United States
1785, 1787		Northwest Ordinances
1789		Adoption of Constitution, United States
1798		Lancaster discovered Monitorial plan of education
1804		Pestalozzi's Institute at Yverdon established
1806		First Lancastrian School in New York
1819		Dartmouth College Decision
1821		First American High School established in Boston
1821		Troy Seminary for Women, E. Willard, first higher education for women, United States
1823		Hall, First Normal School in the United States, Concord, Vermont
1826		Froebel's *The Education of Man*
1827		Massachusetts Law compelled high schools
1837		Massachusetts had first state board, H. Mann first secretary
1839		First public normal school, United States, Lexington, Massachusetts
1852		First compulsory school law, Massachusetts
1855		First kindergarten in United States, German, Mrs. Schurz
1857		Founding of the National Teachers' Association (National Education Association)
1861–1865		Civil War
1861		Oswego Normal School (Sheldon)

Table 10.2. *Continued*

1862	Morrill Land-Grant College Act; College of Engineering, military science, agriculture in each state
1868	Herbartian Society founded
1872	Kalamazoo Decision, made high schools legal
1873	First public kindergarten established in St. Louis
1874	Kalamazoo Decision established rights to devote tax money to high schools
1881	Booker T. Washington established Tuskegee Institute
1888	Teachers College, Columbia founded
1890	Second Morrill Act
1892	Committee of Ten established
1902	First junior college established in Joliet, Illinois
1909–1910	First junior high schools established at Berkeley, California and Columbus, Ohio
1914	Smith-Lever Act
1917	Smith-Hughes Act, encouraged agriculture, industry, and home economics education in the United States
1918	Cardinal Principles of Secondary Education
1920	Compulsory education in all states
1932–1940	Eight Year Study of thirty high schools was completed by the Progressive Education Association. Reported favorably on the work of the modern school
1937	George-Dean Act
1944	G.I. Bill of Rights for World War II veterans
1945	UNESCO established
1950	National Science Foundation Act
1952	G.I. Bill's educational benefits extended to Korean veterans
1952	U.S. Supreme Court ruling on released time for religious instruction
1954	U.S. Supreme Court decision required eventual racial integration of public schools
1958	National Defense Education Act
1961	Peace Corps established
1962	U.S. Supreme Court ruling on prayers in public schools
1963	U.S. Supreme Court ruling on Bible reading in public schools
1964	Civil Rights Act (Public Law 88–352)
1965	Elementary-Secondary Education Act (Public Law 89–10)
1965	Higher Education Act
1966	G.I. Bill's educational benefits extended to Southeast Asia War Veterans
1967	Education Professions Development Act
1968	Handicapped Children's Early Education Assistance Act
1972	Indian Education Act passed, designed to help native Americans to help themselves
1972	Title IX Education Amendment outlawing discrimination on the basis of sex
1975	Education for All Handicapped Children: Public Law 94–142 implemented
1978	Supreme Court rules against reverse discrimination in *Bakke* case

Point of View

Raymond Schuessler presents the following "point of view" regarding the historical contributions of Catherine Beecher, who was one of the pioneer women in American education. During the early 1800s, Beecher started several schools for girls and eventually worked to improve teacher training. She was one of our great educational pioneers.

She Rounded Up Teachers for the West

Raymond Schuessler

If you tried to draw a mental picture of a woman who was both a pioneer and a crusader for women's rights, you would never dream up Catherine Beecher.

She went through life with a broken heart—and long curls dangling at her cheeks.

By today's standards, some of her notions about a woman's place in society were almost childish.

She seemed to worship men, believing they were "designed by God" to be dominant. She lectured and wrote against suffrage for women.

In the 1800s, the American frontier was rolling west in a raw, sometimes brutal sweep of humanity. It was followed by another wave—a civilizing wave of quality schools and teachers.

Through her lecturing, teaching and writing, Catherine Beecher played a dominant role in launching and sustaining that second wave.

Source: Raymond Schuessler, "She Rounded Up Teachers for the West," National Retired Teacher's Association (July–August 1978), pp. 29–31.

In the process, she pushed women toward equality by helping to tear down the barriers that had barred them from access to higher education.

Much of her life's work grew from a seed far removed from schools and the frontier—the harsh factory system of the 1830s.

Young men were swarming west, lured by the hope of free land and riches. They left behind thousands of young women. The women, forced to fend for themselves, poured into factories. They toiled long hours at low pay in dirty, dangerous conditions.

Catherine wanted to rescue these women. At the same time, she was fitting together other needs of American society. Women needed better educations; and the West needed schools and teachers.

Above all, she wanted women out of the factories. That was men's work. For women, the factories were eroding the very qualities that made them women.

Today, some would say Catherine, sister of Henry Ward Beecher (noted Protestant clergyman) and Harriet Elizabeth Beecher Stowe (author of "Uncle Tom's Cabin"), left behind a more significant legacy than either of her famous siblings.

Catherine Esther Beecher was born Sept. 6, 1800, at East Hampton, Long Island, the oldest of 13 children. Her father was the hell-and-brimstone Congregationalist preacher Lyman Beecher, described by one contemporary as "the father of more brains than any other man in America."

Her mother taught her reading, writing and arithmetic as well as the domestic arts. Catherine sometimes preferred the teaching of her Aunt Mary, so steeped as it was in fine literature. Her mother's insistence that Catherine learn household duties became a principle that she eventually would adopt as essential to the life of a woman.

At 10, Catherine entered a private girls' seminary only after the headmistress accepted the Beecher children without charge in return for Dr. Beecher's advice in running the school.

Catherine sat primly on the long plank bench, fascinated by the pretty cadence of the teacher's poetry readings. Poetry later would lead Catherine to her greatest joy and also the deepest sorrow of her life. She was taught drawing, painting and music as well. Through private study, she learned the "men's subjects" of Latin, math and philosophy.

At 19, she left home and the following year began to teach at a girls' school in New London, Conn.

A short time later, some of her poems were published in the Christian Spectator. They attracted the attention of Alexander Metcalf Fisher, a young Yale College professor who also wrote poetry. Fisher arranged an introduction through a mutual friend and began courting the plain, but vivacious, Catherine.

Fisher was vibrant and handsome. Described as a mathematical genius at 10, he became the adjunct professor of mathematics at Yale at 23, a full professor at 25. He wrote "A Journey to the Moon and Other Planets," a science-fiction piece of quality and vision.

In a writing, Catherine described Fisher as "the realization of all my favorite dreams of earthly bliss." Fisher proposed; Catherine accepted.

In those days, many American intellectuals took trips to Europe to "broaden their minds." Fisher sailed off—and perished in a violent storm off the coast of Ireland.

Catherine was horrified. She grieved for months.

On top of the rest of the pain, Catherine was hurt by personal notes Fisher left. They revealed he had not accepted God and made no public profession of faith. Her father added to her grief by proclaiming that Fisher was eternally damned because he had not been "technically saved." The thought almost drove her mad.

She sat down and wrote a book, "The Letters on the Difficulties of Religion," to convince herself that Fisher's soul would rise by supernatural influence because of his fine character.

Catherine could never quite stomach her father's religious fervor. And the clergyman, tried three times for heresy, never succeeded in converting any of his three wives or daughters to his fiery beliefs. Harriet, like Catherine, found their father insensitive.

With Fisher gone, Catherine vowed "to find happiness in living to do good." She said she wanted to "secure the professional advantage of education for my sex equal to that bestowed on men."

Her brother Edward was dean of a boys' school in Hartford, Conn. A school for girls would surely be acceptable, she thought; so, in 1823, with the help of her sister, she opened the Hartford Seminary in a room over a harness shop.

The curriculum went beyond the domestic subjects of so many girls' schools. It included Latin, moral philosophy, logic, chemistry and rhetoric.

Some of the subjects Catherine, herself, needed to learn. With the help of her brother, she managed to stay ahead of the class.

Pupils flocked to the novel school. Soon it was moved to larger quarters and then again to a church. More than 100 pupils jammed the basement, which was partitioned into more than two dozen teaching areas. The noise was deafening, so a larger building was acquired.

A course in calisthenics followed and became a forerunner of today's gym training.

There were eight teachers who had to be trained and supervised. Textbooks had to be slanted to the capabilities of the pupils. Catherine wrote new textbooks and got Harriet to write some. In addition, Catherine took care of the business end of the school.

After eight years, her health broke and she left the seminary.

But her real life's work was just beginning: Her father had become president and professor of theology at Lane Seminary in Cincinnati, and Catherine decided to go there to regain her health.

When she arrived, people begged her to start a girls' school because there was no college for women that far west. Here was her chance to start a women's school equal to a men's college and realize her dream of equal education for women.

Thus, the Western Female Seminary began in a rented building in downtown Cincinnati. Students poured in and it soon became obvious the school needed public financial support.

A committee was organized to raise $20,000. Only about $5,000 was subscribed. The next year, 1857, the building was sold and the school closed.

Heartbroken, Catherine went on a speaking tour. If the West was to prosper, she reasoned, it needed good schools. Everywhere she went she found poor schools, spotty attendance and, worst of all, poorly trained male teachers.

She lectured on the need for teachers for the expanded settlements in the West and organized the Ladies Society for Promoting Education in the West.

She wrote pamphlets with such titles as "Women, Will You Save Your Country?" and "The Evils Suffered by American Women and American Children." When she spoke of a shortage of 5,000 teachers in Midwestern states, 6,000 schools without seats or the proper books, men such as Governor Slade of Vermont volunteered their help.

Catherine often enlisted men to read her excellent speeches for her at public meetings and Slade traveled extensively speaking to concerned citizens about the needs of their community and preparing for the influx of new teachers. Newspapers called the project "Wives for the West."

Meanwhile, Catherine stayed in the East recruiting potential teachers, giving them hasty courses in teaching methods, and telling them of conditions they could expect.

As the new teachers began arriving, some fainted when they saw the conditions they were to work in. Curious Indians peeking from behind thickets were not unusual. One teacher had to share a log cabin with a family of 10. Others found schools unbuilt and many didn't have enough money to last until they were paid. In desperation, some married frontiersmen.

The transporting of women teachers from the East was laced with problems. It became apparent that teachers' colleges must be established in the West.

In 1847, Catherine organized the National Board of Popular Education and in 1852 she set up the American Women's Educational Association. Now, progress came faster. In 1855, schools for women were established in Dubuque, Iowa; Quincy, Ill., and Milwaukee.

Because of lack of public funds, two of the schools went under. But the Milwaukee-Downer College survived as Lawrence University in Appleton, Wis.

In all of the schools, Catherine vigorously promoted domestic training. When other women came to champion women's suffrage, she wrote and spoke against the movement. Eventually, she became a leader of the early antisuffragists.

She wanted equality of education and pay for women, but above all, she felt women must retain their femininity and inspirational graces. She wanted women to be healthy, beautiful, skilled in the domestic arts and good mothers and teachers.

Catherine argued against the lacing of waists, insisting that women exercise, forsake the corset and get physically fit for their duties as wives and mothers.

She wrote a book, "The American Woman's Home," setting forth her idea that a woman needed as much technical education to run her home as did a doctor or an engineer.

Catherine Beecher was one of our great educational pioneers as well as one of the founders of modern teacher training.

Women teachers especially owe much to this inspired crusader. At a time when women could work only as servants or in factories, she led them into the profession of teaching. Without women teachers, America would never had made the rapid progress it did in the 19th and 20th centuries.

Throughout her life the only ornament Catherine Beecher wore was Fisher's engagement ring—except for the distinctive side curls she wore to the day she died in 1878.

Questions for Discussion

1. Trace briefly the history of elementary education in the United States, mentioning only the highlights.

2. What were the basic differences in the early educational programs that developed in the northern colonies, middle colonies, and southern colonies?

3. Briefly describe the function and curriculum of the Latin Grammar School.

4. Trace the historical development of secondary education in the United States.

5. What basic changes have taken place in teacher education in the history of the United States?

Supplementary Learning Activities

1. Develop a creative project centered around some aspect of the history of American education. (Examples: a one-act drama, a history of education game, or a multimedia presentation.)

2. Write a paper on the contributions to education of Horace Mann, Henry Barnard, or Samuel Hall.

3. Seek out and interview an elderly retired teacher about the nature of his or her teacher training, and also about his or her first teaching position. You may wish to tape-record the interview.

4. Attempt to locate some artifact related to the history of education (an old textbook, slate, teaching aid, or school records) and, using library references, write a paper about the artifact.

5. Invite an elderly person to your class to informally discuss "education in the good old days."

Note

1. Frederick Douglass, *Narrative of the Life of Frederick Douglass* (Boston: Published by the Anti-Slavery Office, 1845), p. 43.

Selected References

Cremin, Lawrence A. *The Transformation of the School.* New York: Alfred A. Knopf, Inc., 1961.

Dewey, John. *Democracy and Education.* New York: Macmillan Company, 1916 (chapters 11,12).

Greer, Colin. *The Great School Legend: A Revisionist Interpretation of American Public Education.* New York: Basic Books, 1972.

Historical Highlights in the Education of Black Americans. Washington, D.C.: National Education Association.

Hufstedler, Shirley. "America's Historic Commitment," *American Education.* May 1980, pp. 6–7.

Karier, Clarence. *Shaping the American Education State, 1900 to the Present.* New York: Free Press, 1975.

Matthews, Barbara. "Women, Education and History." *Theory Into Practice* 15, no. 1 (February 1976): 47–53.

Mayer, Frederick. *A History of Educational Thoughts.* 3d ed. Columbus, Ohio: Charles E. Merrill, 1974.

Pendergast, Sister M. Richard. "On Inkwells, Hickory Sticks, and Other Memories," *School and Society* 59 (January 1974): 19–20.

Pulliam, John D. *History of Education in America.* Columbus, Ohio: Charles E. Merrill, 1976.

Ryan, Kevin, and Cooper, James M. *Those Who Can, Teach.* Boston: Houghton Mifflin, 1980.

Spencer, Herbert. *Essays on Education.* New York: E. P. Dutton, 1910 (chapter 1).

Warren, Donald R. *History, Education and Public Policy.* Berkeley: McCutchen, 1980.

Beliefs about Education

11

This Chapter
- Compares the current discord regarding the education of our young to similar historical traces of educational confusion.
- Summarizes public attitude data regarding beliefs about improving the quality of education.
- Identifies central criticisms of American education as cited by public attitude polls.
- Lists characteristics of the traditional view of education from the perspective of the student, the teacher, the curriculum, and the method of teaching.

- Lists characteristics of the progressive view of education from the perspective of the student, the teacher, the curriculum, and the method of teaching.
- Comments on the current adult preference for moral instruction in the public schools.
- Defines the alternative education concept as the most appropriate educational option for students, parents, and teachers.
- Presents a point of view regarding a perspective of America's schools.

The early American immigrants were essentially poor, oppressed people who brought with them different languages, religions, racial backgrounds, and political beliefs. Most of the initial 30 million immigrants were from Europe. Yet, the early American culture was predicated upon white, Anglo-Saxon protestant norms which also became the dominant norms of the colonial school culture. While our early schools helped assimilate millions of immigrants into the Anglo-dominated culture of colonial America, millions of others, including native Americans, black Americans, Hispanics and Asians, have not been assimilated. Nonetheless, the early American thrust toward assimilating the many subcultures into a new, perhaps forced, single larger culture came to be spoken of as the "melting-pot" concept. The growth of the comprehensive American system of education has obviously been aligned with the growth of the American way of life which in turn has been identified with this melting-pot notion. Only within the last twenty-five years have the injustices brought upon those not assimilated served to help us gain a new appreciation of cultural pluralism.

Even though our schools are slow in coming to advocate cultural pluralism as the new ideal which would more readily permit the retention of diverse cultural heritages, selected overall functions will continue to be considered as basic components associated with American mass education.

Regardless of race, color, or creed, the importance of education to freedom, patriotism, and national security will continue to be the theme of writers, orators, and legislators. If we possessed an infallible means of knowing the way of government and the way of our social life for the years ahead we would be able to look to the contents, objectives, and values stressed in our present-day schools for the purpose of meaningful evaluation. Those things which would be deemed worthwhile in the future life of a person, and of a nation, would be taught in the schools. Even though we do not have the infallible means for

The principles of American political freedom embody a
liberal and dynamic educational philosophy.

E. Edgar Fuller

predicting the future, it has been generally approved as a fundamental principle in public education throughout the world that schools should help the student acquire worthwhile knowledge, feelings, and skills deemed important for the student's future life. Lingering questions among legislators, parents, students, and teachers are: what types of knowledge, feelings, and skills are worthwhile to possess? what is the best way to teach those things? what should the school provide? what should other agencies, including home and church, provide? In response to such questions as these, varying beliefs about education surface. Such beliefs vary by race, ethnic character, nationality, economic status, geographical area, and a host of other criteria. It is practically impossible to pinpoint the root cause(s) of one's own educational beliefs. But, each of us as student, parent, or teacher does indeed have convictions about the methods and substance of education. One of the main purposes identified with the study of philosophy of education is to provide prospective teachers with a foundation for isolating and analyzing their individual philosophy of education.

Confusion about Education

Present-day educators are definitely not in accord regarding the education of our young. When one views the magnitude of the business enterprise of compulsory education the confusion regarding the process of teaching (educating) appears distressing. History reminds us, however, that confusion about education is not unusual. In the time of the famous early Greeks, Aristotle (and his contemporaries) could not agree upon the method of educating the young because social conditions were in a state of rapid change. In addition, the political institutions were undergoing change, the economy of Greece was burgeoning, there were international conflicts, problems with foreign trade, and problems resulting from times of war. It was obvious that these several concerns and problems had considerable influence on teaching methods.

Seemingly, the problems regarding education in the twentieth century have similar tones. One of the most noticeable effects of the advance of contemporary science and technology is the constant doubling and redoubling of information and knowledge. The notion that a person may be possessed of almost all knowledge has long been vanquished. Today, the matter of choice boils down to one of deciding in which small area to specialize. Given that specialization decision, subsequent decisions must be made regarding method of study and choice of schools. Through the high school years the choice of schools is limited, but even that dimension is undergoing change. Beyond high school, the school choice is often very much related to methodology and curriculum approaches. It is small wonder that people today, as twenty-five hundred years ago, are raising the age-old questions about how to educate their children to face the dynamic social conditions in which they live. Faced with this

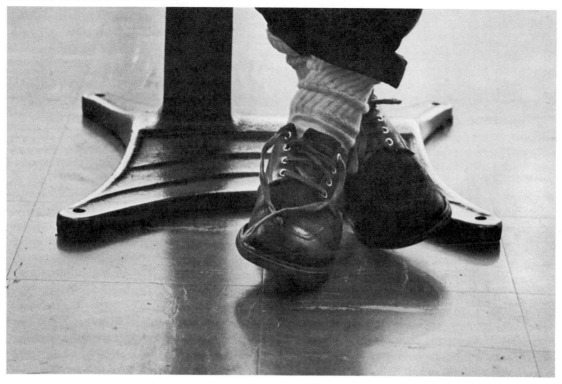

continuing conflict regarding educational practice, beginning teachers are likely to find themselves inconsistent with their classroom tactics and mentally anguished by the lack of direction among their experienced colleagues. Typically, and oftentimes slowly, teachers tend to settle their thinking toward the "traditional" approach, on the one hand, or toward the "progressive" approach, on the other. Beliefs regarding educating from the traditional stance to meet the demands of changing times focus on a program of studies selected for their enduring value. Literature, history, mathematics, sciences, languages, logic, and doctrine provide the basis of subject matter content. The more progressive view stresses content that aims at the reconstruction of experience. Subject matter of social experiences are emphasized through social studies, projects, and problem-solving exercises. The major point of this brief chapter is to call the attention of prospective teachers to this traditional-progressive schism in pedagogical practice. The matter of fashionable advocacy of one approach over the other is of little importance. One often hears that most of our teacher-preparation programs are too progressive-oriented. Whether that be the case or not, beginning teachers, once in the classroom, are just as inclined to traditional as to progressive pedagogy. Since it is almost always difficult to believe one way and practice another way, prospective teachers would do well to begin to think about, to examine, and to pull together their particular beliefs about education. Surely, the pedagogical practice of any one teacher which is consistent with known and verified beliefs about the education of young minds will be the most effective practice that that teacher can provide.

Attitudes toward the Schools

Since education represents a very large public expenditure in most communities, and since education serves the children of those communities, many citizens feel compelled to share their thoughts and criticisms about the schools. Further, lay citizens' views are held in esteem by school teachers and administrators who are responsible for managing the educational program, partly because voter approval is needed to support educational programs, and partly because most teachers and administrators strive to develop programs that are consistent with community views.

Pollster George H. Gallup heads an annual project jointly conducted by the Gallup Poll and the Charles F. Kettering Foundation for assessing the public's attitudes toward the public schools. Each year great care is taken to include new issues of concern to both educators and the public, as well as trend questions that have ongoing impact in the educational world. The Gallup Polls are an established source of reliable information concerning trends in opinions about significant school issues, and they serve as a national benchmark against which local attitudes can be measured. With regard to "beliefs about education," the twelfth annual Gallup Poll[1] sought to determine what could be done to improve the quality of local education. The most popular suggestion identified by 50 percent of the respondents was to hire "well-educated teachers and principals,"

followed by "emphasis on basics such as reading, writing, computation" (49 percent), "teachers and principals personally interested in progress of students" (44 percent), "good parent/teacher relationships" (40 percent), and "careful check on student progress and effort" (32 percent). Note: See Table 6.6 for additional information.

Criticism of American Education

Criticism of American education is as continuously manifested as the previously cited public attitude polls. Professional educators, authors, military and government personnel, and politicians, along with lay citizens, union leaders, workers of all kinds, and cause-oriented group leaders search for the most visible vehicles for expressing their criticisms of education. Honest and responsible criticism is considered essential to the preservation of our free demographic society and, therefore, to the preservation of our schools. At the same time, exaggerated criticism contributes little to educational progress. The gamut of criticisms of education typically span the subject-centered/pupil-centered continuum in a sometimes astonishingly changing thrust.

In some instances, the positions advocated by some critics of education are in harmony with the public mood as reflected by attitude polls. For example, the popularity of the suggestion to "devote more attention to teaching of basic skills" in the Gallup Poll previously cited is consistent with the critics who argued following the Sputnik era of 1957 that schools ought to concentrate on cognitive learning in order to "catch up" with the Russians' space technology. On the other hand, "the romantic critics argued that undue emphasis on subject matter and academic rigor destroys the intrinsic adventure of learning by crippling natural interest and curiosity in learners."[2] In these instances, the critics of education are in contradiction with the public mood as reflected by attitude polls. Practicing teachers can profit from these wide-ranging educational criticisms by using such criticisms to more clearly focus upon the specific teaching problems confronted by the teacher, and then follow with approaches aimed at solving the teaching problems.

Traditional View

Two American educational philosophies form the foundation for what is here considered as the traditional view. William C. Bagley defined Essentialism as a clearly delineated educational philosophy in 1938. Essentialism suggests that emphasis on subject matter provides the essential components of education. The learner is expected to master facts in order to learn through observation and nature. Discipline, required reading, memorization, repetition, and examinations are considered important to learning.

Perennialism, sometimes suggested as the parent philosophy of Essentialism, is a significant part of the traditional view. The early work of Thomas Aquinas is recognized as the cornerstone of Perennialism. Thomism placed much emphasis on the discipline of the mind. In this respect, the

Textbook language and readability is vital to learning.

study of subject matter is considered important for disciplining the mind. Attention to Perennialism in America has been associated with the works of Robert M. Hutchins and Mortimer Adler. Hutchins and Adler advocated study of the great books as a desired means to education. The processes of both Essentialism and Perennialism are strongly subject-centered and authoritarian in that subjects of study are

Table 11.1. Traditional View of Education.

	Traditional View
Student	Reasoning is learned through mental exercise. Student can learn through conditioning. Mind is capable of integrating pieces of learning. Mental calisthenics are important to develop the mind.
Teacher	Model of study, scholarliness, expert stance. Demonstration of content and knowledge. Mental disciplinarian, spiritual leader. Curator of knowledge and tradition.
Curriculum	Literature and history as subjects of symbol. Mathematics and science as physical world subjects. Languages and logic as subjects of the intellect. Great books and doctrine as subject matter of spirit.
Method	Mastering facts and information. Stress on rote and memorization. Assigned reading and homework. Study as a means of intellectual discipline.

prescribed. Advocates argue that the educated person must be firmly drilled in content in order to possess the tools required for rational thinking. This traditional view toward education is probably still the most common approach throughout the international scene.

Table 11.1 outlines a few considerations of the student, the teacher, the curriculum, and the method of education as associated with the traditional view of education. The traditional approach places emphasis on the discipline of the mind as the primary means for gaining knowledge. Also, the rapid development of experimental sciences during the first half of the twentieth century has been a strong factor in the growth of the school testing movement and in the development of educational psychology. The traditional conservatism of the American heritage is strongly present in education as we know it today. The current emphasis on the "return to basics" in American education is suggestive of the popularity of the traditional approach among many parents in the United States.

Progressive View

As previously indicated, Progressivism as an educational view is uniquely American, and was established in the 1920s. The early pragmatism of Charles S. Pierce and William James serves as the origin of Progressivism, while the writings of John Dewey provide the principles of Progressivism as an educational philosophy. Dewey opposed the thesis that schools should be concerned exclusively with the development of the mind. His pragmatic antithesis held that schools should provide for the growth of the whole child. In his view, subject matter of social experience is deemed highly important. This experimental method is held to be one of the best methods of achieving the continuity of unity of subject matter and method. The pragmatic thought of Dewey and his followers has greatly influenced teaching at the elementary level. While teaching at the secondary and college levels has been less affected by the progressive approach, the American teacher-preparation institutions have been greatly influenced toward advocacy of the pragmatic leadership of John Dewey. While the last quarter of the century has unfolded with much

Social experience is very important in the progressive view of education.

criticism of educational Progressivism, the basic tenets of the progressive view still remain as functional alternatives to traditional approaches.

Another dimension of the progressive view concerning education stems from the influence of Existentialism as a newer mode of thought. Existentialism is not considered as a single school of philosophy since it encompasses many variations and opposing views. It is accepted as a movement that touches upon the field of philosophy and human thought with implications for educational practice. With Existentialism most considerations begin with the individual person. The reality of personal existence makes possible freedom and choice. Other significant concepts that can be identified as existentially oriented relate to human personality as a foundation for education and the goals of education expressed in terms of awareness, acceptance, commitment, and affirmation.

Table 11.2 outlines a few considerations of the student, the teacher, the curriculum, and the method of education as associated with the progressive view of education. Most of the polarity regarding views of education in the United States is represented by the concepts outlined in tables 11.1 and 11.2. Obviously, this overly simplistic schism does not allow for the extended degree of differences when examined through educational research and teaching experiences. Many education and philosophy texts further expand on the so-called traditional and progressive strategies for learning (and teaching).

Table 11.2. Progressive View of Education.

	Progressive View
Student	Learner is an experiencing person. Learner has freedom of choice. Student awareness and acceptance highly esteemed. Human experiences important as related to change. Learning through experiences.
Teacher	Research project director. Teacher serves as guide for learner activities. Teacher is never obstrusive, always respecting rights of all. Motivator.
Curriculum	Content should not be compartmentalized. Interest of pupils may demand what is to be studied. Group learning and field trips are valuable. Subject matter of social experience.
Method	Maximum of self-expression and choice. Formal instruction minimized in favor of areas of learning that appeal to the student. Problem solving. Teach how to manage change.

Participation in group activities is an important part of the socialization process and encourages the practice of freedom of choice.

Moral Instruction

The election of President Reagan and the general success of the Republican candidates in the 1980 elections provided new impetus for expressions such as new wave of conservatism, moral majority, swing to the right, demise of liberalism, and other labels all of which have extended implications for the public schools. Generally, the more conservative thinking citizens are strongest in criticizing the schools for betraying the public trust in abdicating the basics in the curriculum, in drifting away from discipline, and in disregarding moral instruction in the schools. It is therefore implied, if not necessarily wholly accurate, that the back to basics movement also includes back to discipline and back to morals concepts. In the early years of public school education, the teaching of morals was regarded as an integral part of the educational program. Early textbooks considered the teaching of morals as important as the teaching of reading. One self-identified educational critic on the Far Right states: "At one time schools supported and promoted traditional values, but today it's a different story. Students are encouraged to adopt only those values that suit them."[3]

As the 1980s begin many adults are strongly in favor of instruction in morals and moral behavior. In a 1975 Gallup Poll, 79 percent of the respondents favored moral instruction in the schools with only 15 percent opposed, and 6 percent with no opinion. Interestingly, in the 1980 Gallup Poll almost identical results were found: 79 percent in favor, 16 percent opposed, and 5 percent with no opinion.[4] The confusion regarding moral instruction resides with methodology rather than favorable preference. Examination of current literature yields a host of approaches such as Values Clarification, Moral Development, Ethics Instruction, Values Analysis, Public Issues Approach, and Cognitive Development Approach. Certainly, there are still objections which suggest that moral education should be provided only in the home and by the church, that teachers are not qualified to teach values, and that moral education is indoctrination. Yet growing numbers of those concerned with education feel that the school should accept responsibility for moral instruction. Whether or not classroom teachers are qualified to teach values, prospective teachers may obtain some guidance from the following suggestion:

In all teaching and learning, the character of teachers and administrators is a critical factor: *who* teachers and administrators are and what they *do* make a decisive difference. Schools cannot develop character and integrity in students unless there are teachers with integrity and character in the classroom with them.

The young will take seriously what they see seriously by others whom they have come to trust. The most important teaching of morality is done by living example. Students learn about how to treat others through the ways in which they themselves are treated. . . .

If education is to serve ideals of morality, teachers and administrators must embody those ideals in their treatment of students and each other. Minimally, this means that teachers and administrators should understand and aspire to be reasonable people of good will, and that they must be willing to tell students what they think and why.[5]

Alternative Education

An outgrowth of the traditional versus progressive approach controversy has been the involvement of the alternative education concept. This concept suggests that the appropriate options for students, parents, and teachers can best be obtained through public schools of choice. In this fashion an entire school district would not be committed to either the traditionally oriented approach or to the progressively oriented approach. Obviously, this does not resolve what has been a generally long-standing schism within education. However, this approach does permit equally good educational programs to exist within the same school system regardless of the divergent beliefs among alternative programs. One of the early advocates of alternative education was Mario Fantini who suggested:

A system of choice maximizes variation in both the substance and personnel of education. For example, consumers who select a school program based on a Montessori model will have important substantive differences from those who select a classical school. Choice does legitimize new programs, each of which carries with it new curriculum and new personnel.

Certainly, professionals who are attracted to a Summerhill-like school are different from those who prefer a classical school environment.

The point is that a public school system that maximizes consumer choice legitimizes new as well as old educational approaches to common objectives. The new educational approach will be made operational by public consent. Moreover, *educators* will also be able to choose from among these educational alternatives, possibly enhancing their sense of professional satisfaction.

This choice model, therefore, tends to minimize conflict among interest groups because *each* individual is making *direct* decisions in educational affairs. Furthermore, as a supply and demand model, the choice system has a self-revitalizing capability. As the options prove successful, they will increase in popularity, thereby increasing the flow of successful programs into the public schools and generating a renewal process for public education.

Under the present system, new programs are introduced into the public schools largely through professional channels, with parents, students, and teachers having little say. However, parents, students, and teachers can actually veto any new program. Some programs, such as sex education, become controversial, especially if they are superimposed by the administration.

School systems are currently structured to present only one model or pattern of education to a student and his parents. If economic factors or religious beliefs preclude nonpublic schools as an alternative, the parent and student have no choice but to submit to the kind and quality of public education in their community. With the exception that one or two schools may be viewed as "better" or "worse" by parents and students (generally because of "better teachers" or because "more" graduates go to college or because the school is in a "good neighborhood"), the way materials are presented and "school work" is done is essentially the same in all schools on the same level. It should be possible to develop within one school or cluster of

The human aspects of education minimizes the current emphasis on technology.

schools within a neighborhood, district, or system several different models that would offer real choices to all those involved in the educative process.[6]

In school districts where alternative education programs have been provided, the primary thrust has dealt with the elementary level. It is administratively and programmatically more feasible to work within the elementary schools when considering the size of the pupil group being served, the clustering of faculty who share common beliefs, and identifying compatible building administrative leadership. Alternative education models at the middle school/junior high school and high school levels are less likely to be found operable to any great degree.

Hopefully, in this chapter some consideration for the importance of identifying and pulling together one's specific view of educational practice has been highlighted. The study of classical philosophy is rigorous and demanding. Our suggestion for prospective teachers is that time and effort invested in philosophical study may be most worthwhile in helping to refine your individual beliefs about education. The most successful classroom practices appear to be those based upon a system of beliefs that is best suited to the particular teacher—whether traditional or progressive in nature.

Point of View

Whatever the means for examining the beliefs about education, whether within the educator segment or within the community segment, lines are usually drawn along the traditional versus progressive views. While there have been all sorts of programs that strive to minimize this polarity within educational philosophy, the traditional–progressive (conservative–liberal) dichotomy appears as vivid as ever.

Over the past two decades several writers have made both pro and con statements regarding education in America. Paul Longo, professor of education at Queens College, developed an extensive article for the January 1980 issue of *Educational Forum* analyzing the substance of the criticisms of American education. Excerpts of Professor Longo's article entitled "America's Schools: A Perspective" are presented here as a point of view for consideration by readers of this text. The major point of emphasis from Longo's statements as a point of view for this chapter is that America's schools have been getting more abuse than guidance from too many of their critics.

America's Schools: A Perspective

Paul Longo

Education in America has been subjected to a heavy barrage of criticism over the past two decades. That criticism of the way we educate our youth should be offered is not only proper, it is necessary. There have been and are many problems, and those engaged in the

Source: Paul Longo, "America's Schools: A Perspective," *Educational Forum,* Vol. 44, No. 2, January 1980, pp. 211–24.

practice of education have not shown themselves any more disposed to facing their difficulties than have professionals in other fields. External prompting is needed in education as elsewhere. Questions must be raised by those affected if educators are to be encouraged to examine deficiencies in the way our schools function.

What is of crucial import is the substance of the criticisms, the manner in which they are put forward, and the rationale that appears to fuel the suggested changes. Offered in a constructive way, such criticisms can lead to reform; offered as an attack, they are far more likely to produce defensiveness and resistance that will only bolster the forces opposing necessary change. If critics are to increase rather than reduce their ability to influence the schools, they must be seen by practitioners as reasoned and reflective in what they propose. Those receiving suggestions for change must feel that the suggestions come from persons who are familiar with and sensitive to the exigencies and hard realities that those in the schools face daily. Such is often not the case.

> A pervasive problem in teaching, and indeed in all the professions, is sometimes couched as a split between theory and practice. Those who conduct the training, usually at universities, typically are associated with "theory" and those who deliver the professional services directly are associated with "practice." It is not difficult to find evidence of the split. Many professors state freely that teachers are undesirably preoccupied with techniques, that they are too craft-oriented. Teachers often accuse professors of being airy, and they lament what they see as insufficient applicability of much university instruction in education to the real problems in the schools.[1]

1. J. Myron Atkin, "Colleges of Education and the Organized Teaching Profession: A Troubled Relationship," New York University Quarterly, Summer 1976, p. 8.

The tension between theoreticians and practitioners is a natural one. The field of education suffers from such a rift between those who actually teach young students and those who would provide them with the appropriate perspective for such instruction. The latter, usually isolated from the reality of the classroom, find all manner of new methods at least possible, often necessary. Their impatience with the inability or the unwillingness of the schools to make the changes that reason and humanity appear to dictate often knows few bounds.

Though invariably presented as flowing from a disinterested, even elevated concern, the career impetus provided by such criticisms has not gone unnoticed by the practitioner. Indeed, it is reasonable to assume that differences in view are not influenced solely by philosophical outlook, but by differences in function as well, for while educational practitioners earn their living by teaching children, theorists or critics more often than not earn theirs by highlighting the deficiencies and inadequacies of that teaching. Kept in perspective, such an arrangement can be mutually beneficial. Too often in the recent past, however, such a perspective has been totally lacking. Criticism has often been offered in a manner that left practitioners feeling angry and alienated. It has been seen as harsh rather than helpful and portraying those in the schools as self-serving in their resistance to changes which would be beneficial to children.

That the schools could and should do better is obvious to the critics. What is less obvious is why they do not. The implication is that teachers do not modify their practices because they are lazy, unconcerned, ignorant, or essentially authoritarian in their outlook. There are cases in which this is so, but to imply that such reasons explain the behavior of an entire class of individuals is neither logically nor scientifically compelling. It meets a need for fixing the blame for failure on a well-defined target and in that sense may be emotionally satisfying. Such a view ignores more than

it explains, however, and it rests on an oversimplification of what is a complex and immensely difficult undertaking. . . .

Our society appears to be suffering the debilitating effects of an atomization of its communal life that is being fueled by an increasing sense of alienation. "Rugged individualism" has been America's blind spot, preached in different form by conservatives and liberals. If children are floundering and finding less guidance from the mature adults in the society, the solution posed by some is to isolate children further by giving them more independence from what few controls remain. If the schools seem fragmented and educators are unable to impose direction or purpose, the solution again is more freedom. In place of the old axiom that knowledge is power, such critics appear to have proposed a new one: freedom is knowledge. It is a view put forward with an assurance that is disarming; for it rests heavily upon a terminology that has attained an easy, uncritical acceptance. . . .

It must be understood that we are dealing with concepts that have heavy ideological overtones, more often political than educational. Because we are entering into a period in which there is mounting resistance to anything labeled permissive, there will be much opposition to such ideas, even in instances where more freedom might prove effective. And there clearly are such instances. The schools, whose purpose is to educate, must become part of this sociopolitical tug of war since beliefs are very much part of one's education. What some critics do not appear to understand is that such differences must be hammered out in the public (i.e., political) arena and will never be resolved exclusively in the schools. Schools do not dictate social views, they are guided by them. In a modern industrial society the function of schools is too complex and critical for people to sit by passively while such institutions are restructured.

Passionate responses have been made by the public to suggested changes in their schools. Such responses have rarely indicated a desire to further liberalize the school structure, and it is this central fact that the critics ignore as they write their books and articles. The practitioner ignores it at the peril of his or her professional future.

We thus encounter a paradox. Visionary suggestions for school organization represent career enhancement for one group and career frustration for the other. Those suggesting a change are not the ones who will have to bear the consequences. This split in who suggests and who implements decisions separates suggested action from responsibility, to the detriment of both groups. One result is that there is a tendency for those suggesting reforms to give too little consideration to their practical difficulties and potential consequences. Insistence upon ignoring the full implication of their suggestions to practitioners has made the views of many critics superfluous to the vast majority of teachers.

Following a decade of steady and unyielding criticism, it is fair to ask why the critics have had so little impact upon the functioning of the schools. Certainly the tack most of this criticism has taken is a major reason. Rarely has it been put forward as an appeal to the broad community of teachers. More often it has appeared as an attack upon teachers, a method of changing behavior that these same critics disparage when used by the classroom teachers they regularly condemn. The result of such persistent criticism has served to force the teaching community even further into a protective posture that isolates them from, and deprives them of, what should be constructive criticism and support. The fact is, schools have been getting more abuse than guidance from too many of their critics.

Questions for Discussion

1. What do teachers mean when they refer to "educating the whole child"? What implications does this have for you as a teacher?

2. Alternative schools are popular notions that offer alternatives to what has been going on in the schools. Why is this notion so popular? How would you defend the education you have received thus far?

3. Some critics say that American education is failing. In what respect? Do you agree? How might a decision to teach or not to teach in the public schools be related to one's philosophy of education? Which educational view seems most satisfactory for you? Why?

4. What differences would exist in the ways in which a traditional teacher and a progressive teacher would direct the classroom? What discipline techniques would be used?

5. At the end of this chapter, Paul Longo's point of view analyzed the criticisms of public schools. To what extent do you agree with his views? Explain how you would work to have helpful criticism affect the functioning of the schools.

Supplementary Learning Activities

1. Arrange a class discussion about the various educational views. Decide which view you prefer and prepare a paper defending your view.

2. List the major current criticisms of the school curriculum and indicate your agreement or disagreement with each. Identify a list of modern critics of education. Research their complaints and share with your peers in a class discussion.

3. Discuss the rationale for the inclusion of athletics, music, drama, and other extracurricular activities

as a part of the school offerings. List the major advantages and disadvantages of such extracurricular activities.

4. Invite a teacher from an elementary school, one from a middle school or junior high school, and one from a high school to your class to discuss their respective philosophies of education as related to their jobs. Summarize the teachers' views in terms of educational philosophy.

5. Invite a superintendent of schools to your class to discuss the meaning of philosophy of education to her or his responsibilities. Make a critical examination of the superintendent's views regarding the schools' course of study.

6. Consider your own schooling and analyze it in relation to the philosophical bases of education explained in this chapter.

Notes

1. George H. Gallup, "Twelfth Annual Gallup Poll of the Public's Attitudes Toward the Public Schools," *Phi Delta Kappan,* September 1980, pp. 35–36.

2. Richard Wynn et al., *American Education,* 8th ed. (New York: McGraw-Hill, 1977), p. 2.

3. Barbara M. Morris, "The Real Issues in Education as Seen by a Journalist on the Far Right," *Phi Delta Kappan,* May 1980, p. 613.

4. George H. Gallup, "Gallup Poll of the Public's Attitudes Toward the Public Schools," *Phi Delta Kappan,* September 1980, p. 39.

5. William J. Bennett and Edwin J. Dellattre, "A Moral Education," *American Educator,* Winter 1979, pp. 6–7.

6. Mario Fantini, "Options for Students, Parents, and Teachers: Public Schools of Choice,"*Phi Delta Kappan,* May 1971, pp. 541–43.

Selected References

Bagley, William C. "An Essentialist's Platform for the Advancement of American Education." *Educational Administration and Supervision* 24, April 1938, pp. 241–56.

Bowles, Samuel, and Gintis, Herbert. *Schooling in Capitalist America.* New York: Basic Books, 1976.

Conklin, Kenneth R. "Theory and Practice as Viewed from the Classroom." *Educational Forum,* vol. 37, no. 3, March 1980, pp. 265–75.

Deal, Terrence. "An Organizational Explanation of the Failure of Alternative Secondary Schools." *Educational Researcher,* April 1975.

Dewey, John. "Challenge of Democracy to Education." *Progressive Education,* February 1937, pp. 79–85.

Dewey, John. *Democracy and Education.* New York: Macmillan Company, 1916.

Grinder, Robert E., and Nelson, Edward A. "Moral Development in Early Adolescence: Perspective on a Perplexing Issue." *The High School Journal,* March 1980, pp. 228–32.

Hutchins, Robert M. "The Schools Must Stay." *The Center Magazine* 6, January–February 1973, pp. 12–23.

Kozol, Jonathan. "Politics, Rage and Motivation in the Free Schools." *Harvard Educational Review,* August 1972, pp. 414–22.

Torrance, E. Paul. "Creativity and Futurism in Education: Retooling." *Education,* Summer 1980, pp. 298–311.

The Learning Process

Section

4

Earlier chapters provided overviews for such aspects of American public education as the career of teaching, the teacher's changing role, selected topics related to the teaching profession, and the role of education including purposes, social problems, historical influences, and philosophical beliefs. Section 4 is concerned with the nature of learners and the learning process, the nature of curriculum including definitions, concepts, and trends, and with the instructional resources available for use in meeting the needs of students.

Since no two persons are exactly alike, it seems reasonable to assume that no two learners learn in exactly the same way. While the general operations of our public schools bring pupils together in groups with one teacher, the obviousness of meeting the individual needs of learners is apparent at the outset. The most effective teachers—those who are capable of assisting their classes (groups of learners), meet the educational expectations for the group while maintaining the individuality of each learner within the group. The study of children and adolescents has been an ongoing activity since our earliest recorded history. Contemporary teachers have vast resources of information about human differences and the learning process, child growth and development, emotional and social development, and motivation for learning, to serve them in helping teach their pupils.

Another dimension of the learning process is the curriculum. In most basic terminology the curriculum consists of "what is taught, or perhaps, what is learned." While experts might disagree on the technical definitions of curriculum,

for purposes of this book it is defined as consisting of three parts: (1) *goals*, or what students should learn, (2) *methodology*, or how they are going to learn it, and (3) *evaluation*, or how well they have learned. The teacher as a front-line person interacting daily with students can be a valuable resource person in developing curriculum.

In the past decade tremendous strides have been made in the area of instructional resources. Chapter fourteen is devoted to this pertinent and important topic. Multimedia resources, while frequently used by one teacher or one learner, are also often used with paraprofessional help. The rapid development of the microcomputer has changed our entire outlook on computer use in education. Future instructional technology will include cost-efficient programs utilizing the telecommunication potential of space satellites. Many of the instructional resources discussed in chapter fourteen are not only helpful in working with classes of learners, but are especially useful in individualizing instruction to meet the unique needs of learners.

The learning process is both fascinating and frustrating. When learning occurs, teaching can be a most gratifying profession. When learning does not occur, teaching can be challenging and frustrating. Teachers exist to facilitate the learning process.

253

The Nature
of Learners

12

This Chapter
- Establishes the need to meet individual differences among learners as a starting point.
- Considers the importance of self-perception and variations in abilities as central to the study of human growth and development.
- Draws attention to differences in maturity levels and differences in rate of maturation among youth.
- Recognizes variations in societal demands as impacting upon the programs of our schools.

- Supplies information from a national study related to differences in educational objectives.
- Devotes attention to the collection of data about and definition of child growth and development terminology.
- Distinguishes motivation as being a complex rather than a simple phenomenon.
- Presents a point of view regarding the effects of discipline on learning.

When children are learning how to speak clearly, or how to add or spell, or how to take part in a group activity, they are doing specific things. Teachers can observe what children do with these kinds of learning activities and help them improve their performances. Likewise, investigators have observed these kinds of specific learning situations in order to find out which are the better ways of learning. From the great number of studies that have been made, it is possible to arrive at certain generalizations that hold true for many different kinds of learning.

The operations of the systems of schools, public and private, that serve the educational needs of youth are geared to bringing groups of learners together with one teacher for all of or part of each of the learner's days in school. This does not mean to imply that teachers and learners shall not have the opportunity to interact on a one-on-one basis. However, the simple economics of the business of education does mandate that the learner/teacher ratio be approximately twenty to one (or higher) for most school systems.

Yet, no matter how the schools group learners, the obviousness of meeting the individual needs of learners is apparent at the outset. So in preparation for becoming a teacher, each person needs the opportunity to learn about ways in which teaching can be facilitated through both group processes and through individualization. Seemingly, the mere learning by teachers about group processes and individualization has the potential for being classified as meaningless unless the teachers first learn about the ways in which learners differ from each other. Further, the more heterogeneous the learner group, i.e., the more representative of the entire learner population, the greater the need for understanding learner differences.

The conventional grade level assignment of pupils tends to obscure the continuing importance of the individual nature of learners, since the upper elementary, middle school, junior high school, high school, and college areas of instruction tend to focus upon subjects of study. Nothing

Allowing students to express their individuality is an important aspect of education.

is intended here to further polarize the concepts of the traditional (subject-centered) view and the contemporary (student-centered) view as related to teaching. Nor is there a suggestion implied for giving priority to a learner-centered approach over a subject-centered approach. The following statement, made as long ago as 1937, does suggest, however, that the approach to teaching may be so subject-centered as to be meaningless or irrelevant for individual learners within the classroom setting.

I Taught Them All
I have taught in high school for ten years. During that time I have given assignments, among others, to a murderer, an evangelist, a pugilist, a thief, and an imbecile.

The murderer was a quiet little boy who sat on the front seat and regarded me with pale blue eyes; the evangelist, easily the most popular boy in the school, had the lead in the junior play; the pugilist lounged by the window and let loose at intervals a raucous laugh that startled even the geraniums; the thief was a gay-hearted Lothario with a song on his lips; and the imbecile, a soft-eyed little animal seeking the shadows.

The murderer awaits death in the state penitentiary; the evangelist has lain a year now in the village churchyard; the pugilist lost an eye in a brawl in Hong Kong; the thief, by standing on tiptoe, can see the windows of my room from the county jail; and the once-gentle-eyed little moron beats his head against a padded wall in the state asylum.

All of these pupils once sat in my room, sat and looked at me gravely across worn brown desks. I must have been a great help to those pupils—I taught them the rhyming scheme of the Elizabethan sonnet and how to diagram a complex sentence.[1]

> Education is the leading of human souls to what is best, and making what is best out of them; and these two objects are always attainable together, and by the same means; the training which makes men happiest in themselves also makes them most serviceable to others.
>
> *John Ruskin*

A counter statement which agrees with the public attitude toward schools as we enter the 1980s suggests that a return to a traditional approach produces positive educational results:

Many educators search for the causes of behavior in the environment, while completely eliminating factors within the individual. They try to psychoanalyze troubled youth, and many times at the expense of the majority. This is harmful to education. The purpose of schools is to teach and teaching cannot take place without discipline. Related to this concept of discipline is our present curriculum structure. Educators have experimented with fads, but now many are returning to a traditional curriculum and the results have been very, very positive.[2]

For most of our educational history, schools have brought students together in groups with a teacher for the purpose of studying (learning) various selected and elected subjects. This so-called traditional arrangement has been the subject of criticism. Some of the complaints about American education have been suggested as:

1. The impersonal nature of it all, the restricted opportunities for teachers and pupils to interact in a personal way.
2. The mass production, assembly line, compartmentalized character of much teaching and learning.
3. The lack of "relevance" of what is taught, meaningless memorization.
4. Extrinsic motivation, over-emphasis on tests and grades.
5. Authoritarian teachers who don't allow for response or individuality.[3]

Stemming from these kinds of criticism has been considerable support for a greater degree of individualization of instruction. Further extension of this thinking suggests that in a freer approach to education the learners will seek what they need to know when they want to do so. Implied is the notion that the student's motives for learning will be intrinsic with a greater degree of persistence associated with what is learned.

While most educators are quick to express the need for greater attention to the individual needs of the learner, most do not sanction undirected chaos in the learning environment. Most students seem to desire direction and consider initiating structure to be important. Likewise, students seem to need some means of knowing that they have accomplished something. The task for the beginning teacher is to experiment with the various techniques available for meeting the needs of individuals within the framework of their school system. More often than not, it takes rare ability to function as a teacher who eliminates such rote dimensions as memorization, all forms of extrinsic motivation, and all tests and grades. It might be noted here that results of the Twelfth Annual Gallup Poll of the public's attitudes toward the public schools indicated that 79 percent of the respondents favored instruction in the school that would deal with morals and moral behavior. Also, 61 percent of public school parents said that not enough attention is given to reading, writing and arithmetic. On the other hand, experienced educators know that strict traditional procedures to the exclusion of the unique needs of each learner is a rather common fault in teaching practice that calls for remediation.

Teachers sometimes tend to minimize the fact that learning is natural. Children do not have to be forced to learn; they have to be forcibly restrained to prevent them from learning something. But this does not mean that they will learn what we want them to learn. Teaching may be generally defined as the process by which one person helps others achieve new skills, knowledge, and attitudes. While teaching involves both the teacher and the learner, learning is an activity of the learner. Guidance for the learner is provided by good teachers who help create conditions that direct learning toward that which the teachers want learned.

Teachers at all levels need mastery of their subject matter specialization. However, mastery of subject matter areas is not enough. In most states, before the teaching certificate is issued, prospective teachers are required to include in their study professional education courses that include educational psychology. A basic intent of educational psychology is to assist teachers in using the principles of psychology (behavior) to help students learn. For example, schools can do a great deal to develop in children desirable attitudes toward their classmates—attitudes of fair play, friendliness, and cooperation—which make their lives and the lives of those around them more agreeable. Schools can also do a great deal

to develop in children desirable attitudes toward their studies, toward their teachers, and toward the whole educational process. In this task, educational psychologists can often help.

Psychology is the science that studies human and animal behavior. Psychologists are interested in understanding the needs and motives of people, their thought processes, their feelings and emotions, and how people learn. Psychology is usually classed with biology, sociology, and anthropology as one of the behavioral sciences. The modern psychologist is concerned with behavior rather than skills, knowledge, and attitudes. Therefore, psychologists generally agree that learning refers to changes in performance (behavior) arising from experience.

Individual Differences

There is a wide range of differences among individuals. At the approximate age of puberty individual differences in physical size among youngsters are particularly evident, including such differences as height, weight, physical fitness, and motor coordination. As children grow and mature, sex differences become pronounced with regard to size and strength, aptitude and motivation. Age differences, socioeconomic differences, and intellectual and academic differences also exist. These many differences among individuals play a great part in the patterns of adjustment pupils make with regard to the typical school setting. Studies of children's behavior

> Teaching might be fun if it weren't for the kids.
> *Anonymous*

as related to school adjustment typically illustrate that approximately 20 percent of students are well adjusted to school, 50 percent have no significant problems, 20 percent are mildly disturbed, and 10 percent are disturbed by school. It would not be surprising to find similar degrees of adjustment for pupils at any level of education, or, for that matter, similar degrees of adjustment for adults in such a setting as their job environment. The point here is that school personnel must constantly be reminded that the school setting in itself does not adequately deal with the wide range of differences among individual pupils.

Schools have responded in one way to individual differences by providing programs centered around ability groups, ranging from gifted children to retarded children to many others. Generally, such attempts by our schools for dealing with individual differences have not been glowingly successful. Classroom teachers are, and have been, somewhat adept at providing for individual differences within our schools. This aspect of the teaching task is becoming increasingly more difficult, since increasing numbers of children of varied abilities and backgrounds are in attendance. The contemporary teacher comes into daily contact with much larger numbers of pupils than ever before. Further, the impact of science and technology on teaching can result in increasing impersonality in the teaching process. Yet teachers are constantly and continually called upon to be skilled at providing for individual differences. In the future, teachers who will

be the most competent at providing for individual differences will be those who continue to learn about learners. This will enable them to know how to better provide for human variability and learning within the group framework of our American public schools.

Human Differences and Learning

Any discussion regarding human differences and learning brings out several theoretical assumptions that are charged with controversy. Hardly a statement can be made regarding human differences and learning that some psychologist or educational psychologist will not take exception to as being oversimplified, incomplete, or irrelevant. Nonetheless, most successful educators agree that the thorough understanding of learners is basic to the task of teaching. When the schools (teachers) are aware of and understand the nature of individual differences among students but fail to serve individual needs, the students' natural zest for learning is dulled. It behooves the classroom teacher, especially, to allow for such human differences as self-perception, intelligence, and rate of maturation. In addition, variations in societal demands are often significant for more thoroughly understanding the nature of learners.

Self-Perception

The most important form of perception is self-perception. Whom does the individual perceive himself or herself to be? Teachers often find that some of their pupils associate prospects of failure with themselves rather than ambitious self-expectations for success. Whether or not such expectations evolved from previous school experiences that involved both their parents and teachers, the self-perception of mediocrity is a major determinant in subsequent behavior of the learner in new classroom settings. If pupils hold low expectations for themselves it is unlikely that they will perform beyond those low expectations.

Another dimension of differences in perception as related to learning, which teachers often overlook, is the fact that people usually behave in accordance with what *they* perceive to be the related conditions rather than what others might wish them to believe the conditions to be. Most of us can quickly recall certain teachers and their "pet" subjects that they taught us to love. For example, one music teacher was sure that each of her pupils would demonstrate appreciation of the musical classics by recognizing various music themes for the rest of their lives, whether the selection was heard in total or as part of a popular tune, or whatever. The outcomes, in terms of the students' feelings, may be far different from the objectives. In the case of at least one pupil, some musical themes have indeed been recalled (from memory). But in this instance there is no pleasure, love, or appreciative feeling associated with such recall. Rather, what is recalled is the painful experience of being hit with a ruler across the knuckles for talking during music appreciation class, or of being shouted at, or of the intense dissatisfaction that accompanied compulsory attendance for that activity. In these instances, the teacher perceives the objectives of the teacher-learning experience differently than the student does. Indeed, in terms of the students' feelings, it could be readily envisioned that some of the learners would come to dislike classical music very much as a result.

With regard to academic self-concept, it has been demonstrated that successful learning experiences enhance positive academic self-concept, whereas unsuccessful school experiences enhance negative academic self-concept. Benjamin S. Bloom, Distinguished Service Professor of Education at the University of Chicago, is a renowned researcher in the field of outcomes of school learning. Citing the relevant research on this topic, Bloom reports that "for the students at the extreme limits of academic achievement (top and bottom fifths), the relation between academic self-concept and school achievement is very strong, with little overlap in academic self-concept between these extreme groups."[4] Bloom also provides figure 12.1 to support his findings.

Figure 12.1. Self-Concept of Ability over Years of Schooling for Successful and Unsuccessful Students.

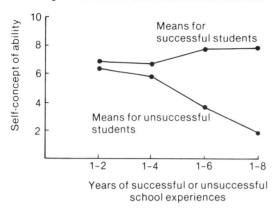

Note: Successful students were in the top fifth on teachers' grades, while unsuccessful students were in the bottom fifth on the same criterion.

Source: Benjamin S. Bloom, "Affective Outcomes of School Learning," *Phi Delta Kappan,* November 1977, p. 197.

Academic self-concept is affected by many variables, of which the teacher-student relationship is the most important.

Many school programs center around individual ability.

Variations in Intelligence (Abilities)

Intelligence and ability have many varying dimensions among children. It should be obvious to educators that the school population represents cross sections of varying levels of ability and intelligence. Some argue over the causes of these differences, while others hold that the schools cannot provide totally adequate learning environments needed to rule out such differences among pupils. Some suggest that the curriculum provisions must be formulated from the premise that "all learners are equal" with equal potential for learning. The adult population provides information which suggests that differences are obvious and continuous. Many adults do not read or compute well, and probably never will read or compute well, and for most of those adults, there may never be a need for improved proficiency in those areas. From this, our conceptions of achievement and success must recognize the fact

that there are many people who are successful in areas unrelated to the utilization of reading and computation skills. If the assumption is valid that each learner has equal potential for learning, then motivational factors are absolutely necessary to overcome certain limited learning rates among pupils for effective learning to occur.

Differences in Maturity Levels

Most educational psychology textbooks devote considerable attention to age level characteristics among pupils. Discussion usually deals with differences such as attention span, muscle coordination, capacity for dealing with self-direction, and many other variations associated with maturation. Consideration is given to characteristics of physical, social, emotional, and mental aspects of development. For example, kindergarteners are extremely active physically; are frequently socially quarrelsome, though quick to forget; tend to express emotions openly; and are skillful with

Children mature at varying levels, depending upon their subjection to physical and social influences.

language—liking to talk. Primary grade children are prone to the common illnesses of childhood; tend to become more selective in choosing friends; are sensitive to criticism and need frequent recognition; and have more facility in speech than in writing. Elementary grades mark the time when a physical growth spurt occurs in most girls; the peer group begins to serve as the standard for behavior; pupils are emotionally torn between the group code and adult rules; and pupils often set unrealistically high standards for themselves. For junior high students, secondary sex characteristics become increasingly apparent; best friends may replace parents as confidants; intolerance and opinionated behavior arise; and comprehension of abstract concepts increases. By the senior high grades, most students reach physical maturity; girls remain more mature socially than boys; anguish and revolt are reflected in changeover from childhood to adulthood; and students have a high degree of intellectual efficiency.[5]

Hopefully, these thumbnail sketches serve to illustrate the strong need for prospective teachers to have considerable knowledge about differences in maturity levels of children in order to best recognize and serve the unique needs of each pupil. Too often, however, teacher preparation programs permit sketchy information to serve in meeting this very strong need. Very much *is* known about the physical, social, emotional, and mental characteristics of children at each age level of development. Likewise, much evidence related to successful teaching illustrates that the best teachers possess such knowledge about their pupils.

Differences in Rate of Maturation

We have just been considering some implications for learning of different maturity levels. It is also important to recognize that among individuals within the same general age group there are wide variations in rate of maturation and development.

Our failure to recognize variations in the rates of development among children, and to recognize the importance of the concept of readiness, can cause us to waste tremendous energy in the

It is more important to know where you are going than to get there quickly. Do not mistake activity for achievement.

Mabel Newcomer

educational enterprise, trying to accomplish objectives that are simply not appropriate to a child at that point. The same goals may be reached quickly and easily when the students have developed the kinds of physical and mental maturity necessary for reaching them. Trying to achieve such objectives too early may leave the children with initial negative experiences.

Successful teachers constantly strive to keep up with the expanding body of knowledge about learners' growth and development. In recent years certain differences in rates of maturation indicate that today's youth do mature early, as indicated, for example, by such dimensions as early biological growth in girls (first appearance of the menses two to five years earlier than in the past), voice changes in boys earlier than in the past (average age just over thirteen years rather than eighteen years), early growth maturity (little if any growth after the age of seventeen or eighteen, rather than twenty-six years), and considerably earlier association with regard to premarital sex, motherhood, and marriage. The greater the extent to which classroom teachers incorporate these deeper understandings of learners with their classroom practices, the greater the probability that classroom teachers will arouse in their learners a profound sense of self-respect and personal integrity.

Variations in Societal Demands

The problems and issues with which the schools are confronted represent kinds of societal expectations associated with the function of the schools. When the public is asked to state opinions about the schools, problem lists are generally formulated (chapter six). Such problem lists reflect those aspects of operations needing remediation as suggested by public opinion. In some cases, segments of society often take up the clamor for solving school problems by bringing direct pressure to bear upon school boards, school administrators, and teachers. The scope of societal demands upon the schools and school personnel is as varied as society itself, and ranges over such dimensions as patterns of school organization, curriculum, facilities, teacher-pupil relationships, race relationships, interscholastic and intrascholastic programs, custodial services, food and health services, and parent involvement in decision-making processes within the schools. While the institutions of society are typically characterized as being slow to adjust to changes in society, societal demands are, nonetheless, ultimately reflected within the total school program.

Much has been said of the rapidly changing nature of the world around us. The pace of change continues to accelerate, bringing with it an increased desire on the part of society for the schools to accelerate the ways in which adjustments to change are being made. Teachers moving into the profession will encounter societal

Societal demands often influence the curriculum of public education.

pressures directly and indirectly. The role teachers play in responding to societal concerns can be of vital importance. It is crucial that the underlying causes and sources of all sorts of school concerns be known by teachers. It is also important that teachers carefully assess the validity of all the demands placed upon them and offer their professional expertise when pressures or criticisms are seemingly unwarranted.

Assorted problems associated with the general welfare of the local, state, and federal community often serve as the basis for new, or renewed, societal demands upon the schools. Governmental crises and criminal activities by local officials in various communities, and by state and national figures prompt suggestions that the nation's schools are educating poorly so far as morality, ethics, and honesty are concerned. Economic slowdowns bring about either unemployment or a tightened job market, or both with the impact upon the schools subsequently represented in demands for more and better retraining opportunities, career and vocational education, and needs assessments to determine new programs to assist students in entering the economic marketplace. Court decisions dealing with religious concerns, individual rights and privileges, segregation matters, academic freedom and academic choice, and sex bias, often alter the processes of school management. Many of these kinds of societal pressures for change in the schools become emotion-laden when transferred to the local community. Much attention is given to localities having difficulty accomplishing local racial integration in the schools, for example, when forces at the local level muster against racial integration. Most of these situations arise when a demand from the national society does not square with the local societal expectation. At the same time, rare attention is given to localities which have little, if any, difficulty accomplishing local racial integration in their schools.

Prospective teachers need to be aware of the emotion-laden views they personally possess as related to the multitude of societal demands upon the schools. How will you serve the school organization as well as the school constituents? What are the principles against which you intend to check your emotions prior to reacting? When, if ever, will the demands of society take precedence over your personal beliefs? It appears relatively simple to assume that modern education must be sensitive to the changing demands today's world places upon our children and their schools. The task is, however, to guarantee that educators actually do more than merely tolerate the fact that changes are necessary to meet the demands of society and the educational needs of children attending school.

Differences in Objectives

One of the most significant statements concerning educational objectives was formulated in 1938 by the Educational Policies Commission of the National Education Association. In that study, a large group of educators collaborated in the development of objectives under the list headings "objectives of self-realization," "objectives of human relationships," "objectives of economic efficiency," and "objectives of civic responsibility." Throughout the years since that report, those lists of educational objectives have served as a basis for much of the curriculum thrust within the schools of America. To be sure, many other study groups, as well as individual educators, have extended, modified, or more definitely specified additional lists of educational objectives. Examinations of various publications reveal objectives by organizational structure to be commonplace. Guidelines, objectives, organizational suggestions, and the like have been detailed from nursery school to kindergarten, to elementary school, to secondary school, to junior college, to higher education, to the realm of continuing or adult education. Considerable attention has also been given to the objectives of career, vocational, and technical education within the school structure.

A vital component in programs for the preparation of future teachers is a comprehensive study of educational objectives with particular emphasis on the level which the student aspires to teach. Further, the study of and work with educational objectives is a continuing dimension of the work of teachers. Classroom teachers must constantly strive to develop and refine appropriate instructional objectives that relate directly to the more general objectives of the total educational program. While it is the professional task of the teacher to formulate instructional objectives, their students sometimes feel that preset objectives are not important for satisfying their learning needs. Some teachers, particularly at the upper grade level, involve their students in the formulation of the most appropriate learning objectives for the particular class activity.

Obviously, there are many variations concerning the specification of meaningful learning objectives. Some of these variations include: (a) the objectives of general education versus specialized education; (b) the objectives linked to the development of a reasonable level of literacy over a broad range of fundamentals, contrasted with the conception of developing considerable depth in one field; and (c) objectives associated with social class or other group factors. Failure to recognize that the purposes of schooling may be quite different for different individuals may cause us to draw many unwarranted conclusions about the appropriateness of certain content or teaching procedures. The sensitive teacher cannot assume that all come to school with the same objectives, or that those with purposes and interests different from those of the teacher must be remade in the teacher's image.

Psychology provides vast additional information that ought to be included in any discussion of human variability and learning. A continuing task of the contemporary educational psychologist is to draw from available information that which has greatest significance for the professional educators. Teacher-preparation institutions are charged with the responsibility of providing relevant and meaningful experiences for prospective teachers enrolled in their programs. Certified teachers are assumed to be knowledgeable regarding the determinants of human behavior, including the concept of needs and satisfaction of needs, motives and theories of motivation, and the effects of child-rearing practices on motivation. Teachers should be competent in understanding learners as persons, with special consideration for their self-concepts.

Child Growth and Development

Growth and development are inclusive terms, each influenced by both heredity and environment. Whether heredity or environment contributes most to one's level of development is open to speculation and disagreement. Of special interest to teachers is knowing the extent to which the behavior of pupils is the result of their inherited potential and/or the result of environmental influences. The influence of inherited factors upon behavior is not under teacher control, but the influence of environmental factors at least partially is. Teachers most effective in bringing out the potential of their pupils are those who are capable of coordinating the maturational processes with the environmental influences of their classrooms.

Our elementary schools have consistently served virtually all youth of school age. Since 1950, marked changes have occurred in the secondary school population of the United States, modifying the nature of that population. In 1950, seventy-six of every one hundred youth aged 14–17 in the general population were enrolled in school. Today ninety-five of every one hundred youth aged 14–17 are enrolled in school. Students with severe basic skill deficiencies now remain enrolled in the upper grades. Likewise, students with mental retardation and physical handicaps are enrolled in secondary schools. Thus, it is increasingly important that all prospective teachers gain considerable knowledge about the growth and development attributes of all learners. In their study of child growth and development, prospective teachers should explore specific aspects such as physical and motor development, emotional development, social development, and individual differences. Adolescence, once expected to begin at age 12 or 13, now may come at age 10 or 11. By their 16th birthday most youth achieve a cognitive and physical capability that approximates full adulthood. The most successful teachers are those who strive to keep abreast of both subject matter content and child growth and development content through continuous study coupled with experience.

Growth and development are inclusive terms.

Physical and Motor Development

Wide variations exist among children of any given age group with regard to physical growth and motor coordination. As a group, girls mature earlier than boys. During the years of approximately eleven through fourteen, girls are superior to boys in height, weight, and motor coordination. One's sense of physical adequacy enhances one's self-concept. Motor proficiency is important in the satisfaction of various needs. Problems associated with physical and motor development, the formation of the self-concept, and the advent of sexual maturity may be relatively serious for both the early-maturing child and the late-maturing child. Schools should provide a variety of motor skill activities to satisfy the needs of children at all levels of development.

Social development involves the ability to get along with others.

Emotional Development

Human behavior encompasses nearly unlimited varieties of emotions. Emotions vary from a state of mild pleasure to intense states of anger and panic. Many body changes occur during intense emotions. Consequently, one's nervous system and endocrine glands work to regulate intense emotions. Emotions are not readily differentiated in a child at birth; emotional differentiation is associated with maturity. Familiarity with the kinds of emotions identified by the age level of the learners, along with knowledge about what constitutes emotional-producing situations, is of great significance for classroom teachers.

Social Development

Social development involves the ability to get along with others. It is important for a person to achieve social adequacy while attaining his or her individuality. Schools can make special contributions to the social development of children. Factors influencing one's social development are peer groups, sex drives, friendships, and sense of security. The importance of group activities upon the social development of group members is great. Manifestations of various kinds of behavior can be viewed as part of the process of attaining social adequacy.

The earlier physical maturing of youth has been accompanied by a number of significant social changes as well. These include diminishing family influence and control, a new interpretation of the constitutional rights of youth, greater mobility and affluence, a media-nourished awareness of the broader world, and a growing separation of the adult world from youth. The impact of these major trends upon youth is of considerable consequence. A discrete youth subculture has formed, one set apart in many ways from adult life. While most youths achieve a cognitive and physical capability that approximates full adulthood by age 16, youths are segregated from adults by adult-created institutions. Youths are relatively powerless to live their lives as adults and see themselves as outsiders to the dominant social institutions. Contemporary youths have diminishing support from persons of other ages and from the family unit. The resultant youth subculture is considered to be a product of the larger social environment rather than an independent youth movement.

As the most significant social institution available to all our youth, the schools, including the teachers, must strive to accommodate the social needs of youth. Schools neglecting the important social development needs of learners also contribute to the alienation of the youth subculture from adult institutions.

Motivation and Learning

Learning takes place best when the learner is motivated. Thus, an important aspect of the teachers' job is to help provide their pupils with motives to learn what is being taught. In addition to a desire to learn all that can be learned about learners, teachers should also desire to learn more and more about motivation and learning.

It may be said that individuals are never without motivation. Each of us continually endeavors to maintain and enhance personal adequacy. We tend to remain motivated toward those activities that provide success rather than failure. It follows that a pupil who does well and likes school will more likely respond to school-related activities than a pupil who does poorly in school. As a consequence of this specific aspect of motivation, considerable speculation and debate exists among educators as to the grading practice in schools, particularly since most grade systems include a failing grade. Some argue that if we wish learners to be continually motivated toward school activities, learning experiences should not permit failure. However, if success consists of reaching a goal, somewhere along the way the determination of whether the goal has been reached must be made by the teacher. Learners must be made aware of their progress toward goals. Hopefully, teachers can provide learning situations in which realistic goals are set for learners at their thresholds of achievement, and motivation encourages each to persist until these goals are successfully reached.

Individuals are never without motivation: good
teachers create it.

Motivation is a complex phenomenon. Factors influencing motivation and learning, in addition to firsthand experiences, include the learner's perception of these experiences, values ascribed to the experiences, and the self-concepts of the learners. Teacher and student variables, such as personality, and teacher and learner styles, are related to motivation and learning.

Self-concept. Increasing evidence indicates a close relationship between self-concept and learning. Inadequate perceptions of the self may bring about misguided motivation and student failures in school subjects. Many students who do poorly in school have learned to consider themselves incapable of being successful in academic work. Students with such low academic self-concepts also perceive others as having little faith in them and in their ability to do well in schoolwork.

Teacher and learner styles. The *best* teacher style or the *best* learner style cannot be generalized. Caution must be taken to avoid the trap of judging a teaching style or a learning style as wrong just because it doesn't match one's own

style or one's own belief about a learning style. There is considerable overlap between the personal characteristics of teachers and teaching styles, and between the personal characteristics of learners and learner styles. Research evidence suggests that when it comes to classroom behavior, interaction patterns, and teaching styles, teachers who are superior in encouraging motivation and learning in students seem to exhibit flexibility, to perceive the students' point of view, to experiment, and to personalize their teaching.

In addition to individual differences in personality factors, assessment of motivation must give consideration to student reactions to praise and blame, student reactions to success and failure, and student differences in learning style. In the interests of effective motivation, it is important to identify each student's learning style as quickly as possible. What is important for one student is not important for another; this is one reason why cookbook formulas for good teaching are of so little value, and why teaching is inevitably something of an art when it comes to motivating students and helping them learn.

What is the process of learning in the classroom setting?

Point of View

For the last few years publishing houses have been searching for new manuscripts that deal with the processes of learning within the classroom setting. Much knowledge has been generated by the research of psychologists as related to learning. The task for the contemporary teacher is relating this kind of knowledge to pedagogy. What goes on in the classroom to deter learning? To motivate learning? What must the teacher know about learning to adequately meet the day-to-day demands placed upon the teacher? Is teaching an art or a science which can be demonstrated? Can teacher effectiveness be enhanced through careful application of the principles of educational psychology? Research continues to strive for better answers to such

questions. At the same time, considerable research in educational psychology is presently available for use by the classroom teacher.

Some of the important elements of the learning process have been reviewed. One of the most important elements recently considered to a significant degree by educators is the simple fact that a wide range of differences among learners must be accommodated by the schools. Teachers have long provided "lip service" to this concern and have practiced their style of pedagogy by plunging along the least common middle ground of the course content being taught. More than that is now expected of teachers. Teachers are expected not only to recognize the individual differences among their students, but to know how to meet those needs through their teaching. Many other considerations must be understood and dealt with by the modern classroom teacher. In addition, human growth and development factors must be studied for knowledge's sake and for incorporation into the teaching style. Differences in perception, variations in intelligence, differences in maturity levels, and differences in rate of maturation are some of the kinds of human variability that teachers must deal with. Other considerations such as various societal demands and differences in objectives are also important considerations for examining the whole of the learning environment.

Many parents, members of the general public, and some teachers share the misconception that everything of importance which takes place in the classroom involves subject matter content exclusively. The current "back to basics" movement suggests that many feel the primary focus of the schools should be subject matter content. The authors concur on the importance of mastery of basic cognitive skills for all learners. At the same time, a too hasty revision of the curriculum for the purpose of responding to the public clamor and/or responding to the ever-tightening school budget could result in the foolhardy denial of sound educational research related to the importance of affective learning.

A very important aspect of teaching—discipline, should be given immediate attention by the schools. Public attitudes concerning our schools call for more discipline. It is consistent with sound educational research that whether the learning (teaching) activity is dealing with subject matter content, values, and/or socialization skills, learners in a group setting must give concerted attention and effort to the task at hand in order for achievement to take place.

In the following point of view article, Professor Gerald L. White of Gardner-Webb College, in commenting on classroom discipline, suggests that "we are so concerned with the rights of the minority that the majority's rights are completely violated. Without discipline this (teaching) is an impossible task." Dr. White's statement also provides a harsh reference which holds that school troublemakers should be given their due process, and then kicked out the front door. While such a stance could not easily be adapted as a universally accepted school policy, prospective teachers should approach teaching with the knowledge that skills in maintaining classroom discipline are very important.

Discipline Is a Basic Requisite for Learning

Gerald L. White

My disillusionment with education was not long in coming. I was a newly minted Ed. D. graduate in the Spring of 1974 and had been hired as a counselor in a junior high school in Meridian, Mississippi. Up to this time my head was filled with all sorts of innovative ideas concerning how to counsel students. I mean, not

Source: Gerald L. White, "Discipline is a Basic Requisite for Learning," *Education,* vol. 101, no. 1, Fall 1980, pp. 85–87.

only did I have a knowledge of the counseling philosophies, I had the expertise in applying them. My favorite was the "Behavior Modification" approach. There wasn't any problem under the sun that I could not handle through the use of behavior modification techniques. That is, until I met Ralph. Now, it will not suffice to say that Ralph was big for his age. He was. Not only was he big, he was huge and about three grades behind his age group in school. Ralph was the terror of the school. All of the kids feared him and not a few of the teachers.

One afternoon, after somehow summoning the courage, a teacher brought Ralph in to talk with me. Now according to Ralph, he had not misbehaved at all. In fact, he was only going through a routine day. Speaking several octaves above normal, the teacher explained that Ralph had completely disrupted her class. Not only had he continued to shout and sing loudly in class, he had started a fight with a couple of smaller boys. When the teacher tried to intervene, Ralph verbally attacked her.

Now, it was my job to try to understand, to empathize with, and to attempt to help Ralph with whatever problem he might have had. It suddenly occurred to me that this was a perfect chance to practice my "token economy" technique. This is a simple technique where students are tangibly rewarded for engaging in socially constructive activities. Payment consists of tokens (such as poker chips) that may be used later to "purchase" such luxuries as more recess time, more gym time, rest period time, etc. One of the keys to the success of this technique is that you have to find something tangible that the student is interested in and wants to obtain. Therefore, I asked Ralph to write on a sheet of paper a list of things that he would like to have and informed him that in exchange for his good behavior in class, he would receive poker chips which could be exchanged for these items. About this time Ralph started listing the things he wanted: "I like blow

pops, yo yo's, M & M, hershey bars, Baby Ruths, hula hoops, etc." he said. All of a sudden I became sick to my stomach. It occurred to me that here I was trying to bribe an overgrown bully into behaving himself in class and what he really needed was a good whacking on the behind and being sent home for awhile.

Now, I cannot tell you what became of Ralph because at the end of that year I left. However, Ralph's problem is not atypical. Many liberals today would say that Ralph had a "deprived childhood" or "he was just misunderstood" or even "perhaps his behavior was caused by his parents not buying him a bicycle until the age of seventeen." Society today seems to search for any reason to explain behavior no matter how ludicrous. It doesn't seem to occur to anyone that perhaps the student is lazy, stupid or just plain mean.

Today, we are so concerned with the rights of the minority that the majority's rights are completely violated. The function of schools today should be to teach, nothing else. Without discipline this is an impossible task. According to Hurletz (1978) you can have 98% good kids in a school, but if you have "two kids that can tell that principal where to head in, that is the end of the ballgame."

Dr. Hurletz goes on to suggest that troublemakers should be given their due process and then kicked out the front door. They do not want an education and in many cases make it impossible for others to obtain one. Jordan (1978) agrees and comments that she has accepted what most educators cannot seem to face. The functions of schools is not to probe tender psyches, not to feed and clothe the homeless, not to be the papa and mama a kid never had. The function is to teach. And the teacher's job is to know his or her subject, and convey it.

It is this author's opinion that the schools are beginning to return some sanity to the classroom, that the days of the "give'away" 60's are past and that we are returning to a more traditional form of education. I sincerely hope so. We have made much progress, but we are not out of the woods yet.

Consider for a moment the problem of "why Johnny cannot read." Since 1963 the national average on the verbal SAT has plummeted 49 points to 429, and 32 points on math, to 470. Many reasons have been presented to explain this. Among them are: schools are too responsive to popular demands, changes in family life, and even turbulence in national affairs.

According to a report (Telegraph, 1978) done by the National Association of Secondary School Principals, which studied 34 high schools whose students have done unusually well recently on the SAT, rigorous academic standards and an avoidance of fads seem to be the secret of success. These schools maintained some specific standards that they considered important to success. The report that the school officials involved relied on tough academic standards showed an unwillingness to subscribe to such educational fads as the open classroom concept.

Pasquale J. Paolantonio, principal of Johnston High School in Rhode Island, one of the high-performance schools, said his school "has maintained a rather traditional curriculum. We have not adopted many of the fads of education."

Larry W. Buchanan, principal of Meadowbrook High School in Richmond, Virginia, said his school's English program has put "a strong emphasis on writing, grammar, spelling, vocabulary, and literature, and moved away from experimenting with mini-courses."

For many people, the educational process in America has been going downhill for the last 10 years. In order to reverse this dangerous trend administrators, faculties, and communities must realize that in order for any learning to occur in the classroom, discipline must be applied. After discipline, the correct type of basic curriculum must be established. This curriculum should be established by local administrators and staff utilizing input from the local community. This would bring back the community school concept which is badly needed in order to return public support to education.

References

Gordon, Suzanne B. "I Wants to go to the Prose." *Reader's Digest,* 1978, Vol. 112, 170–171.
Hurletz, Howard. "Why Johnny Can't Read." C.B.S. Program *60 Minutes.* Aired June 4, 1978.
National Association of Secondary Principals' Report. *Bluefield Daily Telegraph,* 1978, Vol. XXII, 23.
Rose, M. Richard. "Should College Return to Traditional Studies." *Family Weekly,* April 23, 1978.

Questions for Discussion

1. Much recent attention has been directed toward the importance of developing positive self-concepts among learners. Some suggest this is much more important than the content being studied. What should be the relation between self-concept of the learner and what is being studied (taught)?

2. What is your opinion regarding the respective influences of the factors of heredity and the factors of environment upon maturation of children?

3. How important is the knowledge of subject matter to a teacher? In what areas should a teacher be most knowledgeable?

4. Historically, educators have claimed that schools ought to give attention to both sound mind and body. Yet, in setting educational priorities the academic disciplines take precedence. In your opinion, why is it important to stress skill (psychomotor) education as well?

5. What are the various methods that you as a teacher will use to evaluate the progress of your pupils? Do you feel that the various aspects of human differences can be adequately considered in planning for class instruction?

Supplementary Learning Activities

1. Recent attention has been given to the educational needs of our adults. Discuss the role of the public school in the education of adults.

2. Visit a special education class. List the techniques used by the teacher to motivate his/her pupils. Discuss the effects of those techniques.

3. Visit an open classroom and state its advantages and disadvantages. Visit a private school and indicate its strengths and weaknesses.

4. Engage the members of your class in a discussion for the purpose of identifying and listing the competencies for teaching that the content of this chapter suggests.

5. Read and report on the findings of a research study related to self-concept and learning.

Notes

1. N.J.W., "I Taught Them All," *The Clearing House,* November 1937.

2. Gerald L. White, "Discipline is a Basic Requisite for Learning," *Education,* vol. 101, no. 1, Fall 1980, p. 85.

3. Robert F. Biehler, *Psychology Applied to Teaching* (Boston: Houghton Mifflin, 1974), p. 577.

4. Benjamin S. Bloom, "Affective Outcomes of School Learning," *Phi Delta Kappan,* November 1977, p. 197.

5. Biehler, *Psychology Applied to Teaching,* pp. 90–144.

Selected References

Coleman, James. *Youth: Transition to Adulthood.* Chicago: University of Chicago Press, 1974.

Cremin, Lawrence A. *A Public Education.* New York: Basic Books, 1976.

Drayer, Adam M. *Problems in Middle and High School Teaching: A Handbook for Student Teachers and Beginning Teachers.* Boston: Allyn and Bacon, 1979.

Educator's Guide to Free Guidance Materials. 18th Annual Edition 1979. Educators Progress Service, Inc., Randolph, Wisconsin, 1979.

Frazier, Alexander. *Adventuring, Mastering, Associating: New Strategies for Teaching Children.* Washington, D.C.: Association for Supervision and Curriculum Development, 1976.

Hildebrand, Verna. *Introduction to Early Childhood Education.* New York: Macmillan, 1976.

Macht, Joel. *Teaching Our Children.* New York: Wiley-Interscience, 1975.

Margolin, Edythe. *Young Children.* New York: Macmillan, 1976.

Schrag, Peter, and Divoky, Diane. *The Myth of the Hyperactive Child.* New York: Pantheon, 1975.

Woods, Howard. "Education on the Auction Block," *School and Community,* January, 1980, pp. 30–31.

The Nature
of Curriculum

13

This Chapter
- **Identifies the various sources and definitions of curriculum.**
- **Explores the relationship between a curriculum and the pluralistic society in the United States.**
- **Presents the interrelationships of goals and objectives, instructional strategies, and evaluation as they represent the curriculum.**
- **Stresses the important role of teachers in curriculum development.**

- **Explains and appraises innovative techniques in respect to their contribution to improved effectiveness of education.**
- **Points out the difficulties in conducting definitive research on curriculum.**
- **Examines the back-to-basics movement, along with mainstreaming, multicultural education and bilingual-bicultural education.**
- **Provides a point of view on the subject of ethnicity and education.**

Curriculum in its broadest sense represents the purposes of the schools. As such, it has as one of its primary sources the expectations of people at the national, state, and local levels. It has common elements therefore in all schools, yet a uniqueness is present in many schools.

Sources of Curriculum

The primary source of school curriculums is society, with all its expectations. These expectations represent what society desires and values. They also reflect the problems and needs of society. In effect, the expectations of society represent what its members want their society to become for them and their children. Schools, along with families, are major agencies in the transmission of the values of society. Thus, school curriculums emanate from these wishes.

A second source resides within the needs and desires of learners—learners that in our formal

system range from the preelementary school child to the mature adult. Much of the stated curriculum for young children is prescribed for them by adults; however, adolescents and particularly mature learners, as a subgroup (students) of society also have an effect in determining the curriculum.

Expectations are most often translated into course offerings representing a body of knowledge that is referred to as a curriculum. In fact, a standard dictionary definition of curriculum is "all the courses of study offered by an educational institution." School curriculums are more than the courses offered by a particular school. It is a rare school indeed that has formal courses entitled self-worth, self-respect, desire for learning, and respecting others. Yet these characteristics are almost always listed as goals to be attained in school. They are a part of the stated curriculum.

Subject matter is the medium through which the adult mind of the teacher and the immature mind of the learner find communion.

Earl C. Kelley

Definitions of Curriculum

There have been many definitions of curriculum over the years. These various definitions have reflected both the thinking of the times and sources of curriculum as discussed previously. Historically the curriculum was thought of as the list of subjects taught in school. This definition reflects the body of knowledge or subject-centered approach. While more recent definitions tend to be broader, subject matter content is still an important part of curriculum. The subject-centered emphasis dominated the educational philosophy of the 1890–1930s period. Since the 1930s, the idea of experience as proposed by John Dewey has steadily gained impetus.

There are a number of definitions of curriculum that include the concept of experiences.[1] They generally include the premises that the curriculum includes educational experiences that are planned to occur in school and for which the school has responsibility, and that they are developed from expectations that a social group has for the learning outcomes of their children. The concept of "experiences" implies an active involvement of the learner with an educational environment, people and materials, rather than passive receptivity. In addition to reflecting the needs of learners as serving as a source of curriculum, they also relate to the importance of learning theory.

Curriculum in a Changing and Pluralistic Society

It should be noted that society changes, and as it does so do the curriculums of schools. Schools' curriculums in colonial America and through the late 1770s were centered around religion with expectations that they would foster and perpetuate the religious beliefs of the community. From that time until the 1860s the curriculums of our nation's schools were most concerned with producing a literate populace to ensure the preservation of a democratic form of government. The period of the 1860s through the 1920s was a period of economic expansion and growth for the United States. It was during that time that the schools took on a utilitarian approach to provide educated people for filling the large numbers of various jobs that were created. From the 1920s through the present, mass education and equal opportunity for all children have been a central theme. The efforts of the last three decades in the areas of desegregation, rights of women, and the rights of the handicapped are illustrative of the concept of equal educational opportunities. Such equality has not been achieved.

The United States is a pluralistic society consisting of many different subsocieties. This has resulted not only from our multiethnic origin, but also from our emphasis on the protection and enhancement of individual freedoms, as specified in the United States Constitution.

The curriculums resulting during and after the massive immigration to this country

The sciences are an important part of today's curriculum.

(1830–1920) reflected a "Melting Pot" or "Americanization" motive. Elwood Cubberly, a renowned educator and writer, called for the nation's schools to adopt a policy of Americanization through which Anglo-Saxon values would replace the inferior ethnic patterns from countries like Italy, Austria-Hungary, and Russia. He wrote:

These Southern and Eastern Europeans were of a very different type from the North and West Europeans who preceded them. Largely illiterate, docile, often lacking in initiative, and almost wholly without the Anglo-Saxon conceptions of righteousness, liberty, law, order, public decency, and government, their com-

ing has served to dilute tremendously our national stock and to weaken and corrupt our political life. . . . Our national life for the past quarter of a century, has been afflicted with a serious call of racial indigestion.[2]

Further,

To assimilate these people into our national life and citizenship is our problem. We must do this, and, we must, if possible, give them the impression of our peculiar institutions and ideals. National safety and welfare alike demand that we not only teach these peoples to use the English language as our common tongue, but that they be educated also in principles and ideals of our form of government. Even under the best of conditions this will require time, and it calls for a constructive national program if effective work is to be done. Social and political institutions of value are the product of long evolution, and they are safe only so long as they are in the keeping of those who have created them or have come to appreciate them. Our religious, political, and social ideals must be preserved from replacement by less noble ideals if our national character is not to be weakened.[3]

Cubberly's position was reflected in the curriculums of schools by a heavy emphasis on English language instruction, civics, American history, and Anglo-Saxon values. Obviously some "Americanization" took place; ways of speech and ways of dress became largely "Americanized," and an enthusiastic patriotism to the United States developed.[4] Nevertheless, it has become apparent to many scholars "that many individuals and groups will never be able to 'melt' into the American 'pot.' "[5] These groups include Blacks, Spanish Americans, women, and others. These realities, observed by many persons, verify that the United States is a pluralistic society.

A recent thrust in education related to educating people to live in a pluralistic society is multicultural education. There is little agreement on a precise definition of multicultural education; nevertheless the following quotation provides some insights into its meaning.

Multicultural education is preparation for the social, political, and economic realities that individuals experience in culturally diverse and complex human encounters. These realities have both national and international dimensions. This preparation provides a process by which an individual develops competencies for perceiving, believing, evaluating and behaving in different cultural settings. Thus multicultural education is viewed as an intervention and an ongoing assessment to help institutions and individuals become more responsive to the human condition, individual cultural integrity, and cultural pluralism in society. . . .

Further,

Multicultural education could include but not be limited to experiences which: (1) Promote analytical and evaluative abilities to confront such issues as participatory democracy, racism and sexism, and the parity of power; (2) Develop skills for values clarification including the study of manifest and latent transmission of values; (3) Examine the dynamics of diverse cultures and the implications for developing teaching strategies; and (4) Examine linguistic variables and diverse learning styles as a basis for the development of appropriate teaching strategies.[6]

While the previous statements were prepared in respect to teacher education they reflect the spirit and intent of laws recently adopted by many states referring to elementary and secondary education. A recent National Education Association publication states, "Cultural pluralism, multicultural education, and polycultural education all embrace two common ideals: (1) A state of equal mutual supportive coexistence between ethnocultural groups, and (2) one planet of people of diverse physical and cultural characteristics. Basic to the acceptance of these ideals is the belief that every person respects his or her ethnocultural identity and extends the same respect for the cultures of others."[7] The thrust for multicultural education, although somewhat controversial, could perhaps be the primary thrust of the new future in American education.

Goals and Objectives

There are three basic components of any curriculum; goals and objectives, teaching methodology, and evaluation. Goals and objectives, or what it is students are to learn, are fundamental both to teaching methodology and evaluation. Broad goals have been spelled out by a number of national commissions over the years. Broad goals also appear in the philosophy and curricular bulletins of most local school districts.

Illustrative of broad goals prepared by national commissions are those recommended by the White House Conference on Education in 1955. The goals are oriented toward elementary education.

1. The fundamental skills of communication—reading, writing, spelling, as well as other elements of effective oral and written expression; the arithmetical and mathematical skills, including problem solving.
2. Appreciation for our democratic heritage.
3. Civic rights and responsibilities and knowledge of American institutions.
4. Respect and appreciation for human values and for the beliefs of others.
5. Ability to think and evaluate constructively and creatively.
6. Effective work habits and self-discipline.
7. Social competency as a contributing member of his family and community.
8. Ethical behavior based on a sense of moral and spiritual values.
9. Intellectual curiosity and eagerness for lifelong learning.
10. Esthetic appreciation and self-expression in the arts.
11. Physical and mental health.
12. Wise use of time, including constructive leisure pursuits.
13. Understanding of the physical world and man's relation to it as represented through basic knowledge of the sciences.
14. An awareness of our relationships with the world community.[8]

Other commissions over the years that have generated goal statements include: Commission on the Reorganization of Secondary Education, 1918 (Seven Cardinal Principles), and the Educational Policies Commission, 1935–38. Most recently Harold Shane, under the auspices of the National Education Association, convened a conference to review the Seven Cardinal Principles. The results of this conference, which basically confirmed the Seven Cardinal Principles, can be found in a recent publication.[9]

For teaching and evaluation purposes, broad goals must be broken down into specific objectives. For illustrative purposes, let us examine three broad goals and develop specific objectives related to them. The following three goals are taken from the report of the 1955 White House Conference on Education:

1. The fundamental skills of communication—reading, writing, spelling, as well as other elements of effective oral and written expression; the arithmetical and mathematical skills, including problem solving.
3. Civic rights and responsibilities and knowledge of American institutions.
11. Physical and mental health.

The Nature of Curriculum   283

Specific objectives that might be developed from these sample goals for a first grade class might include:

1a. Count aloud from 1 to 100.
2a. Tell other members of the class two ways in which police officers are important.
3a. Wash hands before eating.

At the secondary level, the same broad objectives might yield the following specific behavioral objectives:

1b. Derive the correct algebraic equation to solve a word problem dealing with time, rate, and distance.
2b. List the steps necessary for a bill to become a law in the United States.
3b. After proper medical clearance, run one quarter mile in two minutes.

It should be noted that in this illustration the objectives are written in performance terms; that is, in terms of behavior that can be observed in the learner. The writing of objectives in this fashion facilitates evaluation.

In many states in recent years local school districts have been required by the states to develop overall broad goal statements for their schools. Frequently it was mandated that there be community involvement in goal generation, definition, and development. Such mandates clearly recognize the local community prerogative in determining curricula. The goals so developed must then be translated into general objectives and more specific performance objectives to provide a basis for evaluation. Broad goals and general objectives cannot ordinarily be measured directly. Their attainment is supported by logical inference by the achievement of the performance objectives. The development of general objectives and performance objectives is most often a professional prerogative; that is, the prerogative and responsibility of the teaching, administrative, and supervisory staff. The instructional strategies and teaching methodologies are also considered the prerogative of the professional staff.

The previously identified objectives also illustrate different domains of learning. Bloom has identified three domains of objectives—cognitive, affective, and psychomotor.[10] Cognitive objectives are those that are concerned with remembering, recognizing knowledge, and the development of intellectual abilities and skills. Objectives 1a and 1b are clearly in this category. Affective objectives are those which are concerned with interests, attitudes, opinions, appreciations, values, and emotional sets. Objective 2a, since it may elicit opinions or values, is in the affective domain. Objective 3b is most clearly psychomotor, involving large muscles.

Thus the broad objectives of American education can be specifically transformed into specific objectives for children in classrooms.

Methodology

Objectives are only one part of the curriculum. They represent the desired goals or outcomes. After a teacher has decided upon the objectives, it then becomes necessary to decide upon a

Games are important to academic development; and small muscle motor coordination sometimes provides motivation for learning.

method or means of achieving them. Thus methodology, since it provides the "experiences," is often included in the concept of curriculum.

It is most important at this point in planning that the methodology be appropriate to the attainment of the objective. For example, if an objective for the student is to moderate a small group discussion of four people causing them to arrive at a plan for action on a current social problem, then the teaching method would most certainly include practice discussion sessions. It would probably also include an explanation by

the teacher as to how discussions are led. Using other information from learning theory is also important in determining methodology. For example, in the previous illustration involving discussion leadership, the notion of having the students actually lead and participate in discussions rather than merely listen to an instructor tell them how discussions should be led reflects the principle that active participation results in more learning than passive receptivity. Further, if one were to consider motivation as a factor, the topic for discussion would be very important. Since the objective in this case is not specifically aimed at a precise body of content, the topic of discussion could and should be one in which students are interested. Since methodology, in fact, determines the experiences that students have in achieving objectives, it is an important part of the curriculum.

Evaluation

A third essential part of curriculum is a scheme of evaluation. Teachers, parents, school authorities, and many others need to know what progress students are making. So, in addition to decisions as to what it is students are to learn (objectives), and how they are going to learn (methodology), a curriculum must include a measure of how well students have learned (evaluation). Carefully formulated objectives assist immensely in this task, for it is practically impossible to determine students' achievement if it is not clear what objectives the students are to have achieved. As teachers develop curricula for their students, plans for evaluation which are appropriate for the objective should be included.

The Teacher and Curriculum

While national commissions and community groups write goals, academic specialists analyze content, and other experts theorize about curriculum, it is the teacher on the front line who ac-

tually makes the curriculum. Each day as teachers interact with students they produce and present curriculum. Even without advance planning, as has been advocated, teachers in doing whatever they do with students are in a sense implementing a curriculum.

The role of teachers in formally planning curriculums is becoming increasingly important. Teachers today are asking for greater participation in educational decision making. Perhaps the most important role they can play in decision making is in cooperatively building curricula. Teachers are experts in providing particular information about curriculums from their experiences in working with students. They are also very often academic specialists. They should participate actively in determining objectives, methodology, and evaluation techniques. Once these facets of curriculum have been decided for a school system or a school, the teachers must then put their individual talents into action in implementing the curriculum. Resourceful teachers at this point develop their own style of teaching as they bring their own uniqueness to the task of teaching.

It is not unusual for professional educators or laypersons to debate whether teaching is an art or a science. It is both, and both are essential for superior instruction to occur. Planning—setting objectives, developing instructional strategies, and evaluating performance—is predominately a scientific activity. The act of teaching, however, which involves the orchestration of the plan as teachers interact with students projecting their personalities and using their style, approaches an art.

Teachers are responsible for implementing the
curriculum they have a hand in creating.

Trends

Recent activity in the area of curriculum can be
classified into three areas: (1) efforts that have
to do with reorganizing or restructuring academic
content, (2) efforts that have to do with organizing students to provide for more individualized
learning, and (3) efforts that are designed for
curriculum to be responsive to social demands.

Concepts in Content

It has been mentioned earlier in this text that one
of the problems of selecting the content to be
taught in our schools is that of deciding what
shall be selected out of the tremendous amount

of content available. The knowledge explosion of
the last few years has caused this problem to be
more complex. Scholars in the academic areas
have begun to address themselves to this problem.
At the risk of understating or oversimplifying
their work, it can be said that academic scholars
have attempted to select general concepts from
their disciplines that should be taught, rather
than specific factual materials. Their emphasis
also tends toward process, that is, an emphasis
on the methods of inquiry and discovery, rather
than on the content. In practice one finds that
content, concept, and process are inseparable, but
the relative emphasis can be altered.

For example, the emphasis in mathematics as developed by the School Mathematics Study Group and the University of Illinois Committee of School Mathematics tends more toward problem solving than it does toward basic operations. Other programs developed in mathematics include the University of Maryland Mathematics Project piloted in the school systems of Montgomery County, Maryland, and Arlington, Virginia, designed for the junior high grades and focused upon deductive reasoning, number theory, and logic; and the Greater Cleveland Mathematics Project developed and first implemented in the schools of Cleveland, Ohio and later revised and programmed by Science Research Associates. In programs such as those developed by the Biological Science Curriculum Study Group, Physical Sciences Study Committee, and the Chemical Education Materials Study Group, the emphasis is also placed on basic theoretical concepts rather than on facts, and on discovery through experimentation rather than presentation or perusal of textbooks. Similar activity by scholars has occurred in foreign languages, English, and social studies. Much of the money needed to finance these curriculum efforts have come from private sources such as the Carnegie, Danforth, Ford, Kellogg, Kettering, Rockefeller, and Sloan foundations. The federal government has also participated through grants under the National Defense Education Act, and later under the Elementary and Secondary Education Act of 1965 and its amendments. The National Education Association, through its Project on Instruction, was also active in inspiring and presenting innovative practices.

While many of these projects have been deemed successful, their evaluation has been difficult. As they were implemented they were frequently altered, making a sophisticated research design type of evaluation nearly impossible. Educators have been plagued by inadequate evaluation of their efforts toward improvement. John Goodlad, noted curriculum expert, observed that

Researchers know little about what happens in the classroom: how those carefully developed materials are used if they are used at all; how conflicts between the ideological curriculum of teachers are reconciled; what reaches and attracts the student and what does not, and on and on. . . .[11]

Curriculum evaluation will not be effective until designers clearly specify goals, objectives, and methodologies as baseline data for evaluation. Further, assurances must be made that the program has been implemented as planned.

Organizing Students for Individualized Learning

One problem of instruction that has been mentioned in a number of places in this text is that of finding ways to individualize instuction. We know that students are different—they differ in intellectual capacity, interests, rate of achievement, and many other ways. This knowledge indicates that students should be treated and taught as individuals as much as is possible. At

A signal used for orderly communication in group instruction.

the same time, the United States is committed to universal education, and to accomplish this goal we have tended to group students. Elsewhere in this book it was pointed out that historically the most common grouping pattern has been by chronological age. We have also usually assumed that one teacher can instruct thirty youngsters that are within defined limits of normality. Under these circumstances, try as a teacher may, it is extremely difficult to teach specifically to individuals. In a general way it can be said that teachers tend to teach to what they perceive to be a composite average. Of course, there is no such individual as the "average." The problem of individualizing instruction in mass education within the limits of the public's willingness to pay still plagues our educational system.

Homogeneous Grouping

A number of ways have been attempted to bring about the individualization of instruction. One of the initial methods was that of homogeneous grouping—that is, grouping students by some predetermined criteria such as intelligence, reading achievement, or any number of other criteria. This does reduce the range of differences with which the teacher must work; however, it does not individualize instruction. There are many arguments that can be presented for and against the many ways of homogeneous grouping; yet, the available research on the topic does not indicate that a teacher can consistently achieve better results with homogeneous groups. Grouping is far from the complete answer to individualizing instruction.

> The object of teaching a child is to enable him to get along without his teacher.
>
> *Elbert Hubbard*

Team Teaching and Flexible Scheduling

Teach teaching and flexible scheduling are two closely related organizational schemes designed in part to enhance individualized instruction. Both of these organizational concepts provide opportunities for independent study, an essential for individualization. In team teaching a number of staff members cooperatively plan and carry out instruction for students. Basically, these types of instructional groupings are employed: large group (100–150 students), small group (8–15 students), and independent study. The team usually consists not only of members of the teaching staff with their specialized competencies, but also other staff members such as teacher aides, intern teachers, media specialists, and clerks. The grouping used for instruction is designed to be appropriate for the expected results. Most often special facilities such as resource material centers, learning centers, laboratories, and libraries are made available with capable personnel on hand to guide independent study. It is the independent study phase of the team teaching plan that facilitates individualized instruction.

The time allotted to independent study varies; however, it is generally recommended that independent study consist of 30 percent of the student's time. Flexible scheduling, which is particularly pertinent to departmentalization, is based upon organizing the school day with shorter time periods. Typically school periods are forty-five to sixty minutes; in flexible scheduling the day is composed of twenty- to thirty-minute modules. The shorter modular type of programming permits greater flexibility. Student's programs could consist of some sessions being as short as twenty minutes and other sessions of various additive combinations of twenty minutes, depending upon the learning activity. Flexible scheduling enhances the potential of team teaching. Used together with a combination of special resources available for independent study, team teaching and flexible scheduling have possibilities for individualizing instruction. In and of themselves, however, they do not guarantee individualization. They only create opportunities that staff members need to capitalize on. At the very least, through encouraging independent study, they encourage the development of students toward accepting greater responsibility for their own progress.

Nongraded Programs

An organizational plan that seems to have particular merit for individualizing instruction is that of the nongraded school. Such schools and their programs require a determination of the threshold of achievement of individual learners, and as with most other innovative techniques they require a definite change in the teacher's behavior. Teachers must devote more of their energies to guiding individual learners and acting as resource persons.

The nongraded school operates under the assumption that each child should progress through school at his or her own unique rate of development. The nongraded school, when functioning

as it should, is a form of continuous progress education. The pupils are organized within the school to facilitate their individual development. For example, in an elementary school operating under the nongraded plan, what were originally the kindergarten, grades one, two, three, and four are likely to be called the primary school, while grades five, six, seven, and eight are likely to be called the middle school. In this sense they are open schools. However, this arrangement, in and of itself, does not make a nongraded school. The distinctiveness of the nongraded school lies in the fact that youngsters progress on the basis of achieving specified learning skills, regardless of whether or not those skills are typically thought of as being affixed to a particular grade. In a sense, instead of grouping children by chronological age, they are grouped by their achievement of a specific skill. The skills are arranged sequentially in order of difficulty. Ideally, there is much flexibility among this grouping. For example, the child who learns the elementary skills of reading is moved into another group appropriate to that child's reading development, or perhaps is given more independent study time. It is also possible that a youngster could be placed at an advanced level in attainment of reading skills and at the same time be placed at a lower level in arithmetic reasoning. Nongraded schools, when functioning ideally, permit flexibility. There should be less failure in the traditional sense because grade level standards have been removed. Further, the child who learns rapidly should have greater opportunity to do so because

Opportunities for creative activities are important.

danger that nongraded schools based on developmental achievement grouping can become just as rigid as the traditional graded organization. While most nongraded schools are at the elementary school level, the plan is also used at the high school level.

Open Education

Open education is a concept difficult to define with brevity. Robert H. Anderson has written that schooling may be open in at least five ways: (1) open with respect to the internal environment, (2) open with respect to the surrounding physical environment, (3) open with respect to the organization and administration of the school, (4) open with respect to the curriculum, and (5) open with respect to a humane and child-centered approach.[12] The open internal environment refers to flexibility—or, the ability to create large spaces and small places so that a variety of ways are possible in utilizing human and material resources. Open to the surrounding environment implies that school can be conducted in places other than the conventional classroom. Pupils can be "educated" in other places. These places include the greater community with its many resources, banks, museums, stores, factories, parks, libraries, offices, and many other places. Open organization and administration predicates greater flexibility in the ways in which pupils and teachers interact with one another than is customary in self-contained classrooms or the conventional graded school. An open curriculum implies greater choices and more options. Children can decide what they will study, how long

specific arrangements are made for that child to progress as rapidly as he or she can without being locked into a graded grouping in which it is likely that instruction will be aimed at the "average" child. The nongraded plan attempts through grouping by developmental achievement skills, along with flexibility and the opportunity for movement between groups, to provide greater avenues for individualization. It has potential to accomplish this task. Much of its potential, however, resides in skills of teachers and administrators to assure that it does in fact promote individual development. There is a persistent they will be involved in it, how they will go about it, and what they expect to achieve. Basic skills are not neglected; actually, they are more likely to be learned as a part of a project in which a student is interested. There is structure, but it differs from the structure in traditional classrooms; prime ingredients of open structure are choice and self-direction. Anderson's fifth mode of open education implies that the child's happiness and well-being are central concerns.[13]

Advocates of open education argue that learning—

- is a personal matter that varies for different children, and proceeds at many different rates
- develops best when children are actively engaged in their own learning
- takes place in a variety of settings in and out of school
- gains intensity in an environment where children—and childhood—are taken seriously

Open education has historical roots. The progressive education movement in the early 1900s was similar in conceptualization to today's open education. The writings of scholars such as Rousseau, Pestalozzi, Montessori, Froebel, Dewey, and Piaget are supportive of the concept. In more recent years authors such as Jerome Bruner, John Holt, Herb Kohl, and James Herndon have been supportive.

Open education is consistent with other practices mentioned earlier in this chapter, namely, nongradedness, team teaching, flexible scheduling, and individualization. Elsewhere in this book alternative schools are discussed. Many alternative schools are "open" schools.

Open education has much promise. There is little doubt that it can be accomplished and that it can be effective. Its greatest weakness probably lies in misuse, which could cause it to degenerate into careless permissiveness by teachers who do not understand it or do not have the skills to function in the manner that it requires. Hopefully, open education is being researched in terms of its effectiveness in meeting its purposes.

Responses to Social Demands

Back to Basics

As was pointed out earlier in this chapter, social demands influence the curriculums of schools. Illustrative of this are the back to basics movement, education of the handicapped (PL94–142), multicultural education, and bilingual-bicultural education. The back to basics concept is subject to many interpretations. Generally it could be said that it means instruction in the elementary schools should be devoted to reading, writing, and arithmetic; in the secondary school it should be devoted to English, science, mathematics, and history. Such instruction is to be teacher dominated, with the methodology consisting of drill, recitation, homework, and testing. Promotion is based on mastery only. Frills such as weaving, music, sexism, racism, and sex education are to be eliminated as are electives, innovations, and services such as driver education, guidance, and drug education. Report cards should utilize traditional marks (A, B, C, or 100, 80, 75), and discipline should be strict, including corporal punishment. Patriotism to one's country is to be emphasized.[14]

What are the reasons for the back-to-basics movement? There has been little research and much speculation. The Executive Director of the Council for Basic Education, founded in 1956, has suggested the following causes: Parents are becoming more interested in their children's learning and are insisting on a stronger voice in their children's education; costs are going up, enrollments are going down as is pupil achievement; textbook controversies are growing as is the concept of collective bargaining (loss of parent power); educational innovations proliferated in the late sixties and seventies without major improvements in student achievement; the emphasis in education has been too much on self-image and too little on acquiring basic skills; and, educational outcomes (student achievements) have steadily declined.[15]

A number of states have passed legislation most often referred to as the basics/minimal competency movement. Among them are Florida, New Jersey, Oregon, California, Washington, Virginia, and Missouri. It is predicted that more states will follow suit.

The movement is controversial, particularly between educators and laypersons. Many educators view the movement as a giant step backward ignoring much of what we have learned about teaching and learning; and, maintaining they have always emphasized the basics. Further, they see the movement as shifting more educational policymaking to the states, and a tremendous overemphasis on testing. Perhaps their feelings can best be summarized in the following quotation:

By stressing mechanical skills of communication and computation, by denigrating the arts and creativity, by dehumanizing the learning process and placing it under rote and autocracy, American education, it is charged, will lose the great generating power which has kept the nation free, inventive and productive.[16]

It is pertinent to note that a number of fundamental alternative schools adhering to the essence of the back-to-basics movement have been established.

Public Law 94–142: Least Restrictive Environment

The Education for All Handicapped Children Act, Public Law 94–142, was passed by Congress in 1975 to be implemented in 1978. The legislation is referred to colloquially as mainstreaming. A major thrust of the Act is to provide equal educational opportunities for the handicapped. Important features of the Act, some of which are elaborated upon elsewhere in this book are:

- All handicapped learners between the ages of three and eighteen are to be provided with a free public education.
- Each handicapped child is to have an individualized program, developed jointly by a school official, a teacher, parents or guardian, and if possible by the learner herself or himself.

- Handicapped children are not to be grouped separately—unless severely handicapped, in which case separate facilities and programs would be deemed more appropriate.
- Tests for identification and placement are to be free of racial and cultural biases.
- School districts are to maintain continuous efforts at identifying handicapped children.
- School districts are to establish priorities for providing educational programs.
- Placements of the handicapped require parental approval.
- Private schools are also covered by the Act.
- Retraining and inservice training of all personnel are required.
- Special federal grants are available for school building modification.
- State departments of education are to be designated as the responsible state agency for all programs for handicapped.[17]

The provision for an individualized program is of particular importance to teachers. The complete version of Public Law 94–142 dealing with individualized instruction reads:

For each handicapped child there will be an "individualized educational program"—a written statement jointly developed by a qualified school official, by the child's teacher and parents or guardian, and if possible by the child himself. This written statement will include an analysis of the child's present achievement level, a listing of both short-range and annual goals, an identification of specific services that will be provided toward meeting those goals and an indication of the extent to which the child will be able to participate in regular school programs, a notation of when these services will be provided and how long they will last, and a schedule for checking on the progress being achieved under the plan and for making any revisions in it that may seem called for.[18]

As this legislation is implemented it is anticipated that individualized instruction will increase not only in special education but in all educational settings. Since this legislation also requires parental participation it is also anticipated that more definitive and more specific parental participation will increase in all educational settings.

A second previously mentioned provision of the Act, dealing with the least restrictive environment or "mainstreaming" in its complete version reads:

Handicapped and nonhandicapped children will be educated together to the extent appropriate, and the former will be placed in special classes or separate schools only when the nature of the severity of the handicap is such that education in regular classes, even if they are provided supplementary aids and services cannot be achieved satisfactorily.

It is these two provisions of the Act that have caused some teachers to become thoroughly discouraged. Such teachers feel that the conditions under which they work are so difficult already—for example classes of over thirty students—that to try to give the necessary attention to individualized instruction for handicapped children in their regular classrooms is an added burden which is doomed to failure for both the students and the teacher. Other teachers in more desirable teaching conditions, and who have had some preparation for teaching the handicapped, perceive the Act as reasonable and proper, and find the added tasks challenging and rewarding. It is clear that preservice and inservice training designed to help teachers function effectively in "mainstreamed" classes is needed. It is also clear that unless proper working conditions with support services are available, some teachers will not be effective in "mainstreamed" classes.

There are some indications from the Reagan administration that less federal emphasis will be placed on the implementation of Public Law 94–142 than has been placed in the last few years. Nevertheless, many states have legislation similar to Public Law 94–142, and it is not expected that provisions for the education of the handicapped will be ignored.

Multicultural Education

The concept of multicultural education has been defined and discussed earlier in this textbook, and its relationship to a pluralistic society was explained earlier in this chapter. The task of implementing the concepts of multicultural education into teacher education and into the curricula of elementary, secondary and higher education is beginning to be accomplished. Eleven cognitive and eight affective competencies appropriate for teacher preparation programs

have been developed.[19] The cognitive competencies are:

Knowledge

- Acquire a knowledge of the cultural experience in both contemporary and historical setting of any two ethnic, racial, or cultural groups.
- Demonstrate a basic knowledge of the contributions of minority groups in America to our society.
- Assess relevance and feasibility of existing models that afford groups a way of gaining inclusion into today's society.

Application

- Identify current biases and deficiencies in existing curriculum, and in both commercial and teacher-prepared materials of instruction.
- Recognize potential linguistic and cultural biases of existing assessment instruments and procedures when prescribing a program of testing for the learner.
- Acquire a thorough knowledge of the philosophy and theory concerning bilingual education and its application.
- Critique an educational environment to the extent of the measurable evidence of the environment representing a multicultural approach to education.
- Acquire the skills for effective participation and utilization of the community.
- Design, develop, and implement an instructional module using strategies and materials to produce a module or unit that is multicultural, multiethnic, and multiracial.

Rationale

- Develop a rationale or model for the development and implementation of a curriculum reflective of cultural pluralism within the K–12 school and be able to defend it on a psychological, sociological, and cultural basis.

Each of the competencies in the original source are accompanied by a statement of rationale and instructional objectives.[20] Another volume provides enabling activities.[21] Students seeking more information should refer to original sources. The eight affective competencies are:

- Developing an awareness in the learners of the value of cultural diversity.
- Assisting the learners to maintain and extend identification with and pride in the mother culture.
- Assisting and preparing the learners to interact successfully in a cross-cultural setting.
- Assisting all to respond positively to the diversity of behavior involved in cross-cultural school environments.
- Recognizing both the similarities and differences between Anglo-American and other cultures, and both the potential conflicts and opportunities they may create for students.
- Recognizing and accepting the language variety of the home, and a standard variety as valid systems of communication, each with its own legitimate functions.
- Recognizing and accepting different patterns of child development within and between cultures in order to formulate realistic objectives.
- Recognizing and accepting differences in social structure, including familial organization and patterns of authority and their significance for the educational environment.

As classroom teachers become competent in multicultural education, the goals of multicultural education are likely to become a part of curriculums and therefore be accomplished in the many classrooms throughout the nation. It is pertinent to note that multicultural education is still somewhat controversial; some perceive it as divisive and destructive of American culture, while others perceive it not only as very appropriate, but also as necessary for the survival of society.

Bilingual-Bicultural Education

The Bilingual Education Act, Title VII of the Elementary and Secondary Education Act, was enacted in 1968. The major purpose of the Act was to help with the special educational needs of growing numbers of American children whose first language is not English. Further impetus to the implementation of bilingual education was the *Lau v. Nichols* decision of the U.S. Supreme Court in 1974. That decision mandated that school districts provide all non-English speaking students with special language instruction to equalize their educational opportunities.

Today approximately 25 percent of the United States population speaks a language other than English as a native tongue. Spanish speaking people represent the largest group, followed by Asian immigrants whose numbers are increasing dramatically. Over 30 percent of the American Indians speak a native language as their first language.

Bilingual-bicultural education helps learners to strengthen their identity by including their historical, literary, and cultural traditions in the regular curriculum. An important benefit of bilingual-bicultural education is that it enhances the self-concept of the learner, resulting in better academic achievement.

Bilingual-bicultural education is thought of in two basic ways. One view is that it should be transitional, that is, the student should be converted to the English language as quickly as possible. A second view is referred to as maintenance. The advocates of the maintenance viewpoint feel that students should learn English, but maintain and foster their native tongue at the same time. Teaching English as a second language (ESL) is considered viable from both perspectives. Most persons agree with the concept that instruction in the native tongue is worthwhile and necessary for a period of time while the student learns English. The major disagreement centers around the maintenance approach in the schools—that is providing instruction in both languages throughout the person's formal education. Many of the persons objecting to the maintenance approach, however, do feel that it is a valuable asset to know and speak two languages. Objectors point out that language is the major vehicle of culture, and the fostering of languages other than English can be destructive nationally rather than enhancing or enriching a nation. The debate will undoubtedly continue.

In its first year, the Reagan administration has not indicated strong support for bilingual-bicultural education. Nevertheless, projections of demographic data indicate that the numbers of Asians and Spanish-speaking persons will continue to increase in the future. The schools must be prepared for such students and provide them with an equal opportunity to education, and at the same time provide a mainstream approach so as not to foster what could become a strong ethnic separateness.

Point of View

Two related contemporary curricular issues discussed in this chapter were multicultural education and bilingual-bicultural education, both of which are somewhat controversial. Glazer's essay, "Ethnicity and Education: Some Hard Questions" addresses the basic reasons involved in the controversy. In the essay, Glazer provides an historical perspective of immigration and its effects on the schools, examines the contemporary immigration patterns in the United States, and relates them to the differences in the United States during the early period of the nation and today. He raises a basic question: How can a nation best deal with diversity? In the case of language, should the schools immerse their students in an English language environment? Or, should they be taught in their first language with minimal instruction in English? Glazer discusses both approaches.

Ethnicity and Education: Some Hard Questions

Nathan Glazer

Twenty years ago, had the *Kappan* been celebrating an earlier anniversary, there would have been no need for an article on ethnicity and education. Blacks and education, certainly: Six years after the Supreme Court decision in *Brown,* we still had the resistance of the Deep South. But the rapid acquiescence of the Middle States and the District of Columbia still permitted us to believe, in our innocence, that all that remained was for the states of the old Confederacy to follow the example of Missouri, Kentucky, Maryland, and Delaware in eliminating state requirements for segregation and all would be well.

Immigration was still controlled by quota requirements favoring Northern and Western Europe. The quotas had been instituted in the early 1920s and were only symbolically modified by the McCarran-Walter Act in the 1950s. We could still believe—even if liberals resisted the immigration restrictions—that ours was to be an overwhelmingly European nation, with only one large minority, the blacks, and with scattered communities from Asia and Latin America.

The problems of education, if we could recapture that moment, were problems of academic substance.

Source: Nathan Glazer, "Ethnicity and Education: Some Hard Questions," *Phi Delta Kappan,* January 1981, pp. 386–89.

In the wake of Sputnik, the issue was how we could teach our youngsters mathematics, science, and foreign languages while preventing those from lower socioeconomic groups, black and white, from dropping out prematurely and thus cutting off their access to a higher education we were then rapidly expanding. (We still called it higher, not postsecondary, education.)

The transformation has been startling. The civil rights movement, after its great successes in the middle 1960s, rapidly moved from a demand that blacks should get just what everyone else got in education to a demand—resisted by many black leaders—that blacks needed, and by rights should have, something different: education suited to their needs; education aimed not only at bringing them to the same place in educational achievement as others but education that would seek out, nurture, and develop something distinctive and different.

That this remained essentially an ideology, expressed in action only tangentially, did not reduce the significance of a startling transformation. We have seen scattered examples of a new segregation, now imposed by blacks (with the acquiescence of school authorities) on blacks for purposes of learning more effectively about their distinctive heritage. We now have a principle of uncertain reach put forth by a federal judge in the case of the children of the Martin Luther King, Jr., School against the Ann Arbor (Michigan) School District. The judge declared that "a language barrier existed between the plaintiff children and the teachers . . . because of the failure of the teachers to take into account the home language or dialect of the children in trying to teach them to read standard English," and the Ann Arbor schools were ordered to take "appropriate action." This is the language of a federal statute of 1972, prohibiting the denial of equal opportunity on account of race, color, sex, or national origin, and specifying that one form of this was the failure to take "appropriate action to overcome language barriers." The National Institute of Education has already conducted a conference on the implications of this decision, and we may well see the spread at the elementary and secondary school levels of the teaching of teachers (and if of teachers, can students be far behind?) of "black English."* The impact of the demand for a distinctive education for blacks has probably had its greatest institutional influence at the college and university level, where black studies departments or programs are now regularly established in most leading institutions and in many lesser ones.

European ethnic groups were not far behind in demanding something different, too. Perhaps the most remarkable success has been the establishment and spread of studies of the Holocaust. Since Jews are the merest fragment of American public school children— far fewer than their 3% of the American population, owing to the very low Jewish birthrate and the rising impact of private education for Jewish children—the demand for Holocaust studies at the primary and secondary levels did not rival the demand for black studies. But its impact has been felt, and it has affected the high school curriculum.

Far more significant in bringing ethnic issues in education to the fore than developments among blacks and the descendants of European immigrants has been the great increase in Hispanic populations. The increase is apparent in the Latin American dominance of immigration statistics, and there is substantial undocumented immigration. Europeans have become a small minority of immigrants. They have been replaced by Latin Americans and Asians—Chinese, Filipinos, Koreans, Vietnamese, and Indians—and each group raises separate and different issues for education.**

*See Nathan Glazer, "Black English and Reluctant Judges," *The Public Interest*, forthcoming.

**For 1971–77, only 20% of documented immigrants were from Europe. Some 32% came from Asia and 45% from Latin America. *Statistical Abstract*, 1978, p. 88.

Immigration became an ever more significant issue during the decade of the Seventies, and the easy optimism of the assertion that the U.S. could well absorb 400,000 immigrants a year was shaken by the sharp increase at the end of the decade to perhaps 700,000 a year. Much of that increase was determined not by individual choice and by our own immigration policy but by cynical political actions of hostile countries that pushed out the people they did not want. And the U.S. had to take them in, for it had a political position to maintain in the world as the country of refuge and its own principles to maintain as a country of opportunity.

The new waves of immigration are now principally Hispanic and Asian, but there is no reason to believe that streams from other Third World countries (the Middle East? Africa?) will not follow them. They raise the gravest questions for the American polity and economy. These questions are peculiarly agonizing when it comes to the issue of education. For three other things have happened in this country since the last great waves of immigrant children and children of immigrants were being educated in the Twenties, Thirties, and Forties.

The first has been a general decline of self-confidence in the distinctive virtues of American society, government, and culture. The American economy no longer dominates the world. It has been a strange experience for those of us who went to school in the Thirties and Forties and recall the age of American dominance in the 20 years after World War II to get used to the fact that the U.S. is no longer the richest country in the world, its inhabitants not the most fortunate in the possession of automobiles, telephones, and the other paraphernalia of modern civilization. Or to get used to the fact that we are no longer considered—in the world at large or among a substantial part of our own educated populace—a country of distinctive virtue. It is hard to get used to being called "the Great Satan," and one hears little demurral from this assessment in the developing world, or indeed the free world of those who share with us a common commitment to a democratic polity and an open society.

Must not a change in perception of the role of one's country and culture affect the educational system?

It must, and it has. Laws that once self-confidently insisted—admittedly as a result of a good deal of ignorance and prejudice—that English must be the language of the schools have fallen left and right, to new state legislation, to interpretations of federal legislation, and to judicial orders.

And yet a second important change transforms the discussion of ethnicity and education from what it was during the last great wave of immigration: the growing role of the federal government as a shaper of educational policy for the entire nation. It has always been a matter for wonder and analysis that, despite the paramount role of the states in public education and the weight of the tradition of local control, American education has not been more diverse than it is. But the option of diversity has always existed—and was indeed exercised. There was great variation from district to district in how many immigrant children there were and of what kinds; there was substantial diversity as to how districts responded to the presence of immigrant children. San Francisco tried to segregate Japanese children and created an international crisis. New York had, it would appear, no policy at all except to take them as they came and hope for the best. It was surprising under these circumstances that a permanent class of uneducated, undereducated, and unemployable young people did not develop in the New York City of the 1920s and 1930s, when it was overwhelmingly a city of immigrants and their children. Indeed, those are seen as halcyon years in the history of New York City education by those of us who can still remember them—our memories undoubtedly distorted by the passage of time. Malice or indifference are now featured in accounts of the experience of immigrant children of the Twenties and Thirties. Yet there were many positive experiences; sympathetic teachers and administrators helped children into a new language and a new culture. We are told these were the fortunate and successful few. And yet there must

have been more than a few, for the income and occupations of immigrant Europeans and their children equals or surpasses persons of American parentage.

Undoubtedly this diversity will persist even in the face of federal regulation. Thousands of school districts, and millions of administrators and teachers, are not so easily homogenized. Yet there are consequences of federal regulation that change the relationship between ethnicity and education. In the absence of such regulation, the issue in each school district or school is, What account should be taken of diversity? Black history? Chanukah as well as Christmas programs, or neither? Teaching in Spanish? Or intensive teaching in English? The decisions are endless, and they are the outcome of conflict and argument among administrators, school boards, legislators, the mass media, ethnic representatives, teachers and their organizations, and parents. But federal regulation introduces an interesting shift in the relative power of the disputants: The issue now is who has access to the regulators—indeed, who are the regulators? Clearly they will be different under a President Carter, committed to the appointment of minorities and women (which generally means the appointment of young women lawyers who have come out of an activist tradition) than under a President Reagan.

The federal role in shaping a national policy will not go away, even if President Reagan's appointees are committed to withdrawing the federal government from establishing national standards in bilingual education and other areas. Federal courts, pushed into the fight by skillful advocates educated in the techniques of using constitutional and statutory language to force administrators to undertake the actions the advocates and their constituencies feel desirable, will not let the federal authorities remove themselves from the fray. The federal government must, alas, play a role. Legislation has turned the modest support it gives local school districts into a club to impose national requirements affecting the education of the handicapped, the segregation of the sexes, the employment and distribution of teachers and administrators, the assignment of children by race and ethnic group—and if government refuses to use the club it may well be forced to by successful litigants and powerful judges.

And a final change: In the inner cities, where the impact of the new wave of immigrants is greatest, the public schools have lost much of the prestige they possessed when they dealt with the last great wave of immigrant schoolchildren speaking foreign languages in the 1920s. They are challenged today, far more than they were then, by private schools and by arguments and ideologies supporting them. Catholic parochial school systems, despite some decline in numbers, are still strong competitors to public schools in the inner cities, and they are now joined by Jewish schools, Christian schools, fundamentalist schools, segregationist schools, black schools. Undoubtedly the decline in respect for the public schools is itself the product of a failure—the failure to effectively educate the low-income black populations of the schools, which exploded in the years after blacks replaced European immigrants in great migrations to the Northeast, Midwest, and the West in the Forties, Fifties, and Sixties.

These are the circumstances in which another great wave of immigrant children is coming into American schools, and particularly into inner-city schools, for the central cities are still the main port of entry for immigrants. How will the schools respond? Three quite different models present themselves: positive hostility, official disinterest, and positive reinforcement. The model of positive hostility could be found when laws forbade the use of any language but English in the schools, when children were punished for not speaking English, when their language and background were ridiculed. Officially, this is outlawed. Among the thousands of school districts, tens of thousands of schools, millions of administrators and teachers, some such practices undoubtedly survive. But I doubt that practices of crude Americanization are

widespread; whether or not they are, no one speaks in favor of them.

On the other hand, the model of official disinterest has a great deal of support. (I use "disinterest" both in its original sense and in its common contemporary sense, as meaning "indifference.") Despite the fact that tens of millions of people speaking other tongues emigrated here, the United States remained an English-speaking nation. The establishment of newspapers, schools, churches, and organizations using foreign languages flourished. On the whole, little official notice was taken of this, either to encourage or hamper it. But it turned out that it was hard to maintain this pattern into the second and third generations. The newspapers and schools disappeared; the churches and organizations shifted to English. Was this for the best? Should official policy today try to emulate this earlier policy of disinterest? Children of various backgrounds found that the schools for the most part ignored their backgrounds; whether they came from Russia, Italy, Germany, Ireland, or any of the other countries that made up the American population, the schools taught them that the fathers and heroes of their country were George Washington, Thomas Jefferson, Abraham Lincoln—men very far from these children's own background and roots. It was an odd experience, as anyone who went through these schools can testify, and each of us undoubtedly asked, Should we really take seriously those other fathers and heroes we hear about at home and in ethnic schools, when they seem to be banned from the official and grander American school?

The model of positive reinforcement is probably now the dominant one among educators—not among teachers and administrators and school boards but among those who write and think about the schools and education. How are we to view this new model? As part of a positive development from prejudice to indifference to tolerance to understanding and a true commitment to cultural pluralism? Or should we find in the earlier policies some element of wisdom that we should not abandon? The arguments for the new policy of positive encouragement are clear enough. There are first the simple educational arguments—these children will learn better if they are taught for some period of time in their native tongues, and if the school shows recognition and respect for their heritage. Added to this are political arguments, at least for the large Spanish-speaking groups: This is a demand of at least major segments of the Mexican-American and Puerto Rican communities; they, too, are part of the American polity, and on what basis can this demand *not* be granted? Finally, there are practical arguments: These are ways of bringing teachers and administrators from these communities into the schools, where they are now underrepresented.

The arguments on the other side are at the moment less well formulated. They are in fact scarcely arguments but outbursts, as in the case of the vote in Dade County, Florida, apparently against any use of Spanish that involves expending public funds. Yet the fact that we have a good deal of unthinking resentment and resistance of this kind to bilingual and bicultural education should not blind us to some real problems.

Whatever their other failures, the big-city public schools of the age of immigration taught their charges English. Any child who had spent a few years in these schools could speak English. The circumstances were in many ways similar to those of the Mexican-American and Puerto Rican children for whom we are now told a different approach is necessary. They lived in dense ethnic communities, spoke their mother tongue at home, and played on the street with children of the community who used the same language. If they were to learn English, some forceful intervention from outside was necessary.

By contrast, in one major bilingual and bicultural program currently conducted under court order for Spanish-speaking children in New York, the children get only one double class in English daily and may participate in art, physical education, and shop classes taught in English. They spend almost the entire school day learning in Spanish. Visiting some of the model schools in this program—a high school, a junior high,

and an elementary school—I wondered when they were transferred into English-language classes. It did not seem urgent to the teachers in the elementary school; the children would only be there a maximum of six years, they explained, and it put them under strain to move them away from their playmates: Let the junior high school make the transition. But the change hardly seemed urgent in the junior high school either: They would be there for only three years. Or in the high school—they would be there for only three years.

What troubled me was the fact that these children will nevertheless have to make their way in an English-speaking environment. One could count on television, the streets, the learning experiences of jobs in which they would have to work with others—but the double class in English seemed paltry indeed as an influence. Nor was I impressed by the argument that many middle-class children are sent by their parents to private schools conducted in a foreign language so as to gain the cultural advantage of two languages. These middle-class children, in contrast to the majority of the Spanish-speaking children in the public schools, already speak English at home. The experience of immersion in French or Spanish does them good. But the Puerto Rican and Mexican-American children are already immersed in Spanish. If we are to use the lessons of successful experiments in language teaching to young children, their need is to be immersed in English. Yet a combination of federal requirements, court orders, and local political pressures often prevent them from getting this immersion.

Despite the diversity of present-day immigration, I speak of Mexican-American and Puerto Rican children, for the pressure for bilingualism and biculturalism comes from these communities. I do not see the same pressure from the varied groups of Asian immigrants or from immigrants from other Latin American countries, all of whom seem willing to follow the path of earlier European immigrants. They see the school as an assimilating agency, and on the whole they approve. For Koreans, Filipinos, Vietnamese, Chinese, and Asian Indians, I suspect bilingual and bicultural programs are a matter of indifference; among some one finds a positive hostility.

It is impossible to deal adequately with this issue in a brief article. It will be settled in elections, in fights over legislation, in the courts. I suspect that educational arguments will have precious little to do with what happens. Critics of the new course of positive reinforcement see a departure from the experience of the past, which created a great nation speaking a single language. They see in particular the political dangers of a public polity that maintains language competence and pride in a growing ethnic group stemming from a rapidly growing nation—one with grievances against the U.S.—next door. After one of the studies of immigration that have been completed during the troubled Seventies, a congressman said to me, "We have heard testimony that by the end of the century there will be 140 million Mexicans—and half of them will be living north of the Rio Grande." It is the fate of the polity that will most strongly motivate resistance to the firm establishment of rights to public education in a non-English language.

On the other side, too, I suspect educational arguments are pretexts. A different vision of the United States drives the proponents of the new approach, but it is one whose outlines can scarcely yet be discerned. A key element of course is cultural pluralism. Another is a vision of a future world in which it is no longer necessary for a great nation to worry about its strength and the elements that enhance it. The U.S. in this vision remains the gathering place of the nations, but the nation itself is a cumulative product of the distinctive streams that make it up, each maintaining language and culture. Could such a nation, one wonders, have fought World War II? The new vision insists that war is no longer a relevant test. Perhaps it is not. But the fear that the new responsiveness to ethnicity is undermining what has been on the whole a success will not go away.

Questions for Discussion

1. In what ways will the thrust for multicultural education affect the curriculums of schools?

2. How should national goals or objectives for education be developed? What individuals or groups should be involved? Why?

3. What should be the role of the teacher in curriculum development?

4. Why has it been so difficult to achieve individualization of instruction in American schools?

5. How do you expect that the back-to-basics movement will affect the curriculums of schools?

Supplementary Learning Activities

1. Visit an open school and list its advantages and disadvantages.

2. Visit a school of any level and observe and critique its use of individualized instruction.

3. Interview a practicing teacher about his or her role in curriculum development.

4. Interview lay citizens and teachers to gain their impressions of what a school curriculum should be like. Report your findings to your class.

5. Visit and describe the programs and services of a large comprehensive high school.

Notes

1. Students may wish to read materials by such authors as John Dewey, George Beauchamp, B. Othaniel Smith, Arthur Lewis, Alice Miel, Glen Haas, J. Galen Saylor, William Ragan, J. Minor Gwynn, and William Alexander to gain more knowledge about experiences as related to curriculum.

2. Elwood P. Cubberly, *Public Education in the United States* (Boston: Houghton Mifflin, 1934), pp. 485–86.

3. Elwood P. Cubberly, *An Introduction to Education* (Boston: Houghton Mifflin, 1925), pp. 26–27.

4. See Horace M. Kallen, *Culture and Democracy in the United States* (New York: Boni and Liveright, 1924); and Horace M. Kallen, *Cultural Pluralism and the American Idea* (Philadelphia: University of Pennsylvania Press, 1956).

5. Madelon Stent, William R. Hazard, and Harry N. Rivlin, *Cultural Pluralism in Education*. Copyright 1973 by Fordham University. (Englewood Cliffs, N.J.: Prentice-Hall), p. vii.

6. National Council for the Accreditation of Teacher Education, *Standards for Accreditation of Teacher Education* (Washington, D.C.: National Council for Accreditation of Teacher Education, 1977), p. 4.

7. Robert L. Williams, *Cross-Cultural Education: Teaching Toward a Planetary Perspective* (Washington, D.C.: National Education Association, 1977), p. 10.

8. Committee for the White House Conference on Education, *A Report to the President* (Washington, D.C.: U.S. Government Printing Office, April 1956), pp. 91–92.

9. Harold G. Shane, *Curriculum Change Toward the 21st Century* (Washington, D.C.: National Education Association, 1977).

10. Benjamin S. Bloom, ed., *Taxonomy of Educational Objectives* (New York: Longmans, Green, 1956), pp. 6–8.

11. John Goodlad, "Curriculum: State of the Field," *Review of Educational Research* 39, no. 3 (June 1969): 369.

12. Robert H. Anderson, *Opting for Openness* (Arlington, Va.: National Association of Elementary School Principals, 1973), p. 1012.

13. Ibid.

14. Ben Brodinsky, "Back to Basics: The Movement and Its Meaning," *Phi Delta Kappan* 58, no. 7 (March 1977): 522.

15. A. Graham Down, "Why Basic Education?" *The Education Digest* 43, no. 3 (November 1977): pp. 3–4.

16. Brodinsky, "Back to Basics," p. 527.

17. Leroy V. Goodman, "A Bill of Rights for the Handicapped," *American Education* 12, no. 6, July 1976, pp. 6–7.

18. Ibid., p. 6.

19. H. Prentice Baptiste, Jr., Mira L. Baptiste, and Donna M. Gollnick (eds.), *Multicultural Teacher Education: Preparing Educators to Provide Educational Equity,* vol. 1 (Washington, D.C.: American Association of Colleges for Teacher Education, 1980), pp. 44–72.

20. Ibid.

21. H. P. Baptiste, Jr., and M. Baptiste, *Developing the Multicultural Process in Classroom Instruction: Competencies for Teachers*, vol. 1 (Washington, D.C.: University Press of America, 1979).

Selected References

Baptiste, H. Prentice Jr.; Baptiste, Myra L.; and Gollnick, Donna M. *Multicultural Teacher Education: Preparing Educators to Provide Educational Equity,* vol. 1. Washington, D.C.: American Association of Colleges for Teacher Education, 1980.

Brodinsky, Ben. "Back to Basics: The Movement and
Its Meaning," *Phi Delta Kappan* 58, no. 7,
March 1977, pp. 522–27.

Doll, Ronald C. *Curriculum Improvement: Decision
Making and Process*. Boston: Allyn and Bacon,
1978.

Goodman, LeRoy V. "A Bill of Rights for the
Handicapped," *American Education* 12, no. 6,
July 1976, pp. 6–9.

Hass, Glen. *Curriculum Planning: A New Approach*.
Boston: Allyn and Bacon, 1980.

Kohut, Sylvester. *The Middle School: A Bridge
Between Elementary and Secondary Schools*.
Washington, D.C.: National Education
Association, 1978.

Parker, Franklin. "Ideas That Shaped American
Schools," *Phi Delta Kappan,* vol. 62, no. 5,
January 1981, pp. 314–19.

Reynolds, Maynard C. (ed.). *Futures of Education
for Exceptional Students: Emerging Structures*.
Minneapolis, Minnesota, 1978. (A publication
of the National Support Systems Project under
a grant from the Bureau of Education for the
Handicapped, U.S. Office of Education. Copies
may be ordered from The Council for
Exceptional Children, 1920 Association Drive,
Reston, Virginia 22091.)

Shane, Harold G. *Curriculum Change Toward the
21st Century*. Washington, D.C.: National
Education Association, 1977.

Williams, Robert L. *Cross-Cultural Education:
Teaching Toward a Planetary Perspective*.
Washington, D.C.: National Education
Association, 1977.

Instructional Resources

14

This Chapter
- Describes the use of media available for instructional purposes.
- Explains aspects of the technology involved in producing the final product of many materials used in the classroom.
- Illustrates the various types of media and their utilization by teachers.
- Discusses the learning resource center in relation to instruction and technology.
- Identifies the role of the teacher in utilizing the learning resource center.

- Illustrates media center space relationships in new schools.
- Provides data indicating the influence of corporations as related to educational technology.
- Includes suggestions and opinionnaires for evaluating media programs.
- Presents brief statements regarding the use of community resources and outdoor resources as parts of the total learning environments.
- Presents a point of view about the impact of computers on jobs in computer related fields.

Historically, the teacher's primary role has been that of presenting information to students in a demonstration or lecture discussion manner. Various kinds of devices, including books, have for countless centuries been used by teachers as instructional resources for assisting them in reaching their pupils. During the mid-1400s Johannes Gutenberg invented the type mold, making printing from movable metallic type practical for the first time. Educational historians record this breakthrough in printing as having vast significance, for since that time teachers have had books and other printed materials more readily available as resources. In addition to printed materials, teachers have used such things as wax tablets, slate boards, blackboards and chalk, hornbooks, microscopes, animal cadavers, works of art, architecture, music and musical instruments, and the theatre to facilitate learning. As long ago as 1923 the importance of the general field of instructional resources was formalized by the founding of the Association for Educational Communication and Technology (AECT). At the

half-century mark since the founding of AECT, the idea of instructional technology had solid acceptance.

Schools have undergone a great deal of change since the end of World War II. Extensive building programs and experiments with modular scheduling, team teaching, and educational television were brought about in response to the increasing numbers of students during the 1950s. The suddenly changing world of education was spurred by the launching of the Russian satellite Sputnik in 1957. Following Sputnik, the American public demanded improvements in school curricula. The federal government enacted the National Defense Education Act of 1958, which expanded federal financial aid to education for programs to improve instruction. This act also provided funds to develop audiovisual media services and facilities. Modifications to this act culminated in several federal programs being enacted by the Eighty-ninth Congress. Federal research funds were granted for educational media research and for library research. Big businesses jumped into the competition for this new source of federal money for education and the pace quickened in the development of many kinds of instructional resources.

Title II of the Elementary and Secondary Education Act (ESEA) of 1965 provided federal funds for purchasing prepared materials for the schools. The funding formula of Title II enabled schools to add films, books, journals, learning kits, and other prepared materials which most schools would not otherwise have been able to purchase.

The growth of knowledge and the increase in the financial bases of the schools during the 1960s and 1970s provided not only an additional stimulus to the growth of educational media, but also provided one of the greatest challenges to teaching. Teachers have more and more come to understand that learning is an active rather than a passive process. Information-giving pedagogy and assigning facts to be studied and memorized, is considered out of vogue in many schools today. A contemporary view of the teacher's primary task is that of facilitator, planner, and director of varied active learning experiences. Teachers also serve as diagnosticians who must demonstrate their competencies for organizing instructional material and techniques geared to the achievement of teaching-learning objectives. The

following chart (figure 14.1), called "The Systematic Approach of Instructional Technology," illustrates the elements of instructional planning which all teachers must carefully consider. This chapter emphasizes the materials and equipment (5), physical facilities (6), and evaluation and improvement (7) conditions of instructional technology as presented in the chart.

Use of Media

Educational media are the tools of the professional teacher. Educational media include printed, audio, visual, and real materials. Certainly, texts, graphs, pictures, newspapers, magazines, encyclopedias, and comics are educational media. Other important media include films, filmstrips, film loops, slides, overhead and opaque projectors, commercial and educational television, records, audiotapes, cassette television tapes, and the radio. Other things such as animal pets, insects, models of real things such as skeletons and machinery, simulation devices such as driver trainers and communication kits, as well as computers, desktop calculators, and other electronic devices are also important pieces of ware. The media list is ever-increasing as it must be, to accompany the ever-increasing knowledge growth. Future teachers will be more and more media-minded as they assume their teaching tasks.

Figure 14.1. The Systematic Approach of Instructional Technology.

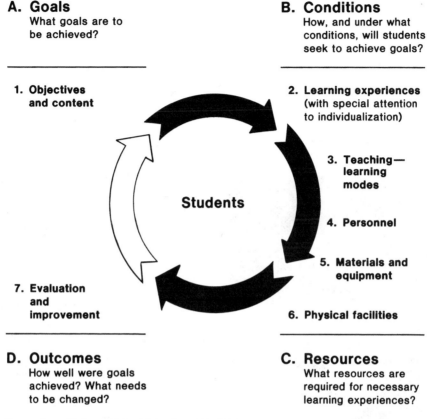

A. Goals
What goals are to be achieved?

B. Conditions
How, and under what conditions, will students seek to achieve goals?

1. Objectives and content

2. Learning experiences (with special attention to individualization)

3. Teaching— learning modes

Students

4. Personnel

5. Materials and equipment

7. Evaluation and improvement

6. Physical facilities

D. Outcomes
How well were goals achieved? What needs to be changed?

C. Resources
What resources are required for necessary learning experiences?

Source: James W. Brown, Richard B. Lewis, and Fred F. Harcleroad, *A-V Instruction: Technology, Media, and Methods* (N.Y.: McGraw-Hill, 1977) p. 13.

Software

Software is the body of content materials that have generally been associated with the teacher. Software includes textbooks, paper and pencil learning materials, workbooks, encyclopedias, newspapers, magazines, graphs, charts, posters, maps, globes, and various kinds of programmed materials. The kinds of materials found in typical school libraries are generally considered as software. Many software products, such as encyclopedias, book-of-the-month publications, and school-oriented papers and magazines, have been manufactured specifically for sale to the home.

Software materials are very important to the teaching-learning process and continue to undergo changes in form and patterns of use. With recent attention being given to the so-called "back-to-basics" movement, printed test and measurement instruments, competency-based materials, and individualized instruction packets are additions to available software.

Title II of the Elementary and Secondary Education Act of 1965 provided millions of dollars to the states to improve educational quality

Federal funds have helped to provide educational
media for our schools.

through grants for the acquisition of school library resources. The three categories of materials eligible for acquisition under Title II included software and hardware of various kinds. The categories were school library resources (includes audiovisual materials), textbooks, and other printed and published instructional materials. Most states allocated all or most of their Title II funds for school library resources, or for a combination of school library resources and other instructional materials. The expenditure of the original Title II appropriations firmed up the trend among schools to capitalize on the availability of new software and hardware in instruction.

Hardware

Only recently have we begun to make applications of technology and the products of technology to improve education. Such hardware products of technology include all kinds of mechanical and electronic devices that aid or supplement the software products. In many schools, movie projectors, filmstrip and slide projectors, record players, tape recorders, opaque projectors, overhead projectors, reading machines, and other devices of an audiovisual nature are stored in a central location so that use of the equipment may be coordinated for the entire faculty. While much equipment usage takes place in learning centers in some schools, the classroom teacher most frequently uses the normal classroom as the laboratory where instructional hardware is used. Many schools employ a director of audiovisual education who is responsible for the maintenance of equipment and for the coordination of teacher use of equipment. The concept of audiovisual (AV) programs to enhance instruction is considered the forerunner for the contemporary thrust in the applications of technology to education.

Availability of federal, state, and local dollars for instructional technology materials and

All kinds of mechanical and electronic devices have proved helpful to learners.

equipment provided impetus for the development of new businesses aimed at the instruction market. Likewise, reputable established businesses also brought into or joined in the production of instructional technology materials and equipment. After-the-fact evaluative efforts have in some instances revealed that not all of the very expensive technologically refined instructional systems have produced results originally hoped for. In some cases large sums of money were invested in equipment now considered obsolete. For example, some of the first videotape equipment was not only unwieldy in size, but was also very expensive. However, the newer electronic equipment is not only much easier to use, but is also less expensive. The application of microcomputers to classroom use is an exciting and cost efficient development. Computer power that was either too expensive or impractical a few years ago is now widely available and easy to use.

From all this rapid activity, there now is apparent a clamor for carefully evaluating the many materials and assorted equipment for the purpose of providing sharper tools for better learning.

Educational software includes books, magazines, and newspapers.

Learning Resource Centers

Existing public school libraries have been criticized severely by various study groups. In 1961, the National Committee for Support of the Public Schools reported that (a) more than 10 million children go to public schools having no libraries, and (b) more than half of all public schools have no library. Such criticism has generated renewed interest in the directions school libraries ought to be taking in order to meet the needs of today's pupils. The development of new instructional technology remains strong, with particular emphasis on software. The traditional concept of the public school library has matured into a concept of a total learning resource center, in which the various mediaware are arranged in a common setting wherein space is provided and specifically allocated for individual and small group usage. Individual study carrels have their own lighting controls and electrical outlets. Small groups can have access to specific resource centers such as math and science centers. Comfortable furniture, small study desks, and carpeting have replaced obsolete furnishings in these modern learning resource centers. The learning resource center concept demands a high level of utilization necessitating flexible schedule arrangements to permit students time to use the center.

Table 14.1. Learning Resource Center Equipment.

Equipment for Learning	Educational Media for Learning
Record Players, Tape Recorders, Radios	Textbooks
Slide and Filmstrip Projectors and Viewers	Supplementary Books
Overhead Projectors	Reference Books, Encyclopedias
Motion-picture Projectors and Viewers	Magazines, Newspapers
Television Receivers	Documents, Clippings
Video-tape Recorders, Players, Viewers	Duplicated Materials
Teaching Machines	Programmed Materials (Self-instruction)
Computer Terminals and Print and	Motion-picture Films
Image Reproducers	Television Programs
Electronic Laboratories: Audio/Video/Access	Radio Programs
and Interaction Devices	Recordings (Tape and Disk)
Telephones with or without Other Media	Flat Pictures
Accessories	Drawings and Paintings
Microimage Systems—Microfilm, Microcard,	Slides and Transparencies
Microfiche	Filmstrips
Copying Equipment and Duplicators	Microfilms, Microcards
Cameras—Still and Motion	Stereographs
	Maps, Globes
	Graphs, Charts, Diagrams
	Posters
	Cartoons
	Puppets
	Models, Mockups
	Collections, Specimens
	Flannel-board Materials
	Magnetic-board Materials
	Chalkboard Materials
	Construction Materials
	Drawing Materials
	Display Materials
	Multi-media Kits

Source: James W. Brown, Richard B. Lewis, and Fred F. Harcleroad, *AV Instruction: Technology, Media, and Methods.* (New York: McGraw-Hill, 1977), p. 11.

The creation of a learning resource center is not an attempt to do away with the school library. Instead, it attempts to utilize the typical verbal materials of the library and supplement them with additional software and hardware instructional media now available to the teacher. As children become involved in the learning process at different rates of growth they have a need to pursue learning on an individual basis and also in small group activities. The teacher may now free the learner to go to a center where materials are provided for individual and small group learning. The center should be equipped with such equipment for learning (hardware), and educational media for learning (software), as shown in table 14.1.

Teacher and the Resource Center

From the preceding general description it appears that the teaching task has been greatly simplified. On the contrary, the teacher must now come face to face with issues in the curriculum that have usually been reserved for administrators, supervisors, and the like. The learning resource center

But whatever they call it, and wherever they put it, public schools everywhere are going to have to find space for reducing, retaining, reproducing and displaying the incredible mountain of information that new technology now makes available. Sooner than we think, a public school without such facilities will be about as educationally effective as a log without Mark Hopkins there on the end.

Aaron Cohodes

Teachers clamor for greater selectivity in the use of prepared materials.

Self-contained systems for computer-assisted instruction have become more popular in our homes as well as in our schools.

is little more than an administratively planned learning area, and as such its purpose is no different than that of the classroom. Although it holds promise in its potential for individualized learning, it must for the greater part be planned and developed by teachers. It should be supplied with materials that teachers have selected and developed through their experiences with children. Many of the hastily developed program series that were sold by commercial publishers anxious to "get on the bandwagon" proved to be too limiting in application. Increasing numbers of teachers clamor for greater selectivity in making more incisive the thrust and use of prepared materials. Similarly, as professional groups and

other agencies increase their dealings with new technology, greater demand is made for specialized materials for the various areas of instruction (driver education, medical programs, technical trades, and the academic disciplines). The production of these materials has added a new dimension to the publishing enterprise.

This type of industrial movement has placed an ever greater responsibility on the teacher working in curriculum. Among the many splendid products on the market today there also may be found hastily developed and poorly researched materials that purport to provide teachers with "the answer" to learning problems. As a result,

Figure 14.2. Proposed Middle School Model.

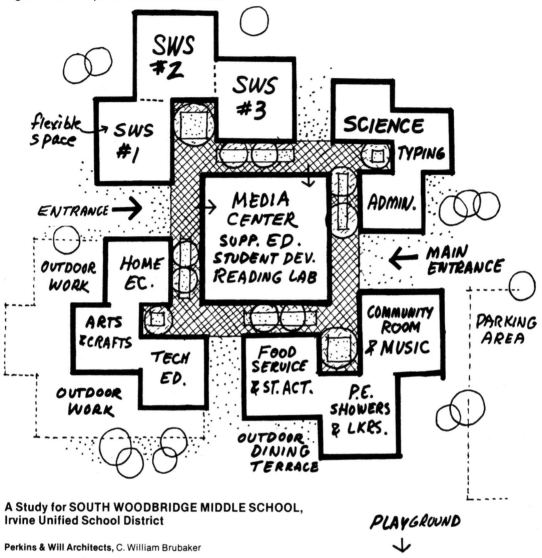

A Study for **SOUTH WOODBRIDGE MIDDLE SCHOOL,**
Irvine Unified School District

Perkins & Will Architects, C. William Brubaker

teachers have the special task of discarding these inferior or worthless programs and adapting those which are useful to the specific situation encountered by each. Of a more highly critical nature, teachers should, in addition to the culling of manufactured materials that may be used for the learning process, continue to develop their own new materials in light of their experience with the learners.

Media Center Space Relationships

The impact that the media center (resource center) concept has had on the planning for a modern school is reflected in figure 14.2. This sketch by Perkins & Will, Chicago (one of the nation's most renowned firms of architects, engineers, planners, and interior designers of school buildings), was from a late 1970s study for a new middle school in California in which the media center is proposed as the hub of the new building.

Around the media center are three schools-within-a-school (SWS #1, #2, #3) clustered in one building unit; a second building unit to house science, typing, and administration; a third building unit to house the community room and music, showers and lockers, and food services; and a fourth building unit to house technical education, arts and crafts, and home economics. The four building units are on one level arranged in the pinwheel cluster around the media center hub. While the climate variable associated with other geographic locations may not be conducive to the open space associated with this multibuilding cluster in California, the media center (resource center) concept as the hub of the educational programs has grown to become generally acceptable for all levels of schooling. Figure 14.3 is a new sketch showing how the South Woodbridge Middle School media center developed. It is physically and visually at the center of the two-story academic building. The media center is at a mid-level with a ramp going up a half level to the "generalized learning areas," and a ramp going down a half level to the "specialized learning areas." The generalized learning areas are clustered in groups of four to encourage the schools-within-a-school concept. It should be noted that considering current attention to microcomputers and other electronic equipment designed for classroom instruction, figures 14.2 and 14.3 appear 1960-ish regarding the primary emphasis on software. The point of presentation here is to illustrate that many school districts which develop programs aimed at reading continue to rely on software (books) as the instructional medium.

Corporations and Educational Technology

Large sums of money have been invested by private business and by federal acts during the past few years for modifying, adapting, and producing hardware for specific classroom use. The effect of this emphasis has been the expanding and upgrading of the audiovisual program concept. The impact of software and hardware development has brought to focus the systems approach to instruction. In effect, the systems approach to instruction brings together the audiovisual program, the school library, and school personnel.

Recently, the nation has witnessed vast mergers of publishing companies, research bureaus, and manufacturers. Seeing a growing need for all kinds of educational software and hardware, it appears that these corporations have struck a bonanza. American businesses operate on the profit motive and market research indicates new profit margins in instructional materials. Capitalizing on a national concern for increased educational output, these corporations now have the capacity to research, develop, produce, and market an endless variety of educational software and hardware which may be used in the learning process. The knowledge explosion, increasing rates of mobility, the quest for more knowledge in a shorter time, the complex pressures of providing individualized educational opportunity for all citizens, and the educational establishment's seeming inability to direct educational change effectively have all contributed to the birth of these corporations.

Figure 14.3. Final Middle School Model (1981).

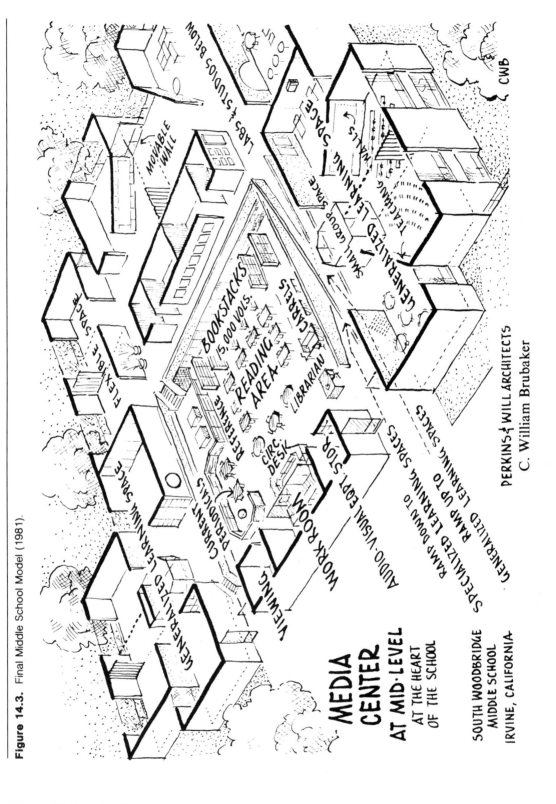

LABS & STUDIOS BELOW

CWB

MOVABLE WALL

GENERALIZED LEARNING SPACE

TEACHING WALLS

SMALL GROUP SPACE

BOOKSTACKS 15,000 VOLS.

CARRELS

FLEXIBLE SPACE

READING AREA

LIBRARIAN

REFERENCE

CIRC. DESK

GENERALIZED LEARNING SPACE

CURRENT PERIODICALS

WORK ROOM

AUDIO-VISUAL EQPT. STOR.

RAMP DOWN TO SPECIALIZED LEARNING SPACES

RAMP UP TO GENERALIZED LEARNING SPACES

PERKINS & WILL ARCHITECTS
C. William Brubaker

VIEWING

GENERALIZED LEARNING SPACE

MEDIA CENTER AT MID-LEVEL
AT THE HEART OF THE SCHOOL

SOUTH WOODBRIDGE MIDDLE SCHOOL IRVINE, CALIFORNIA

An example of a largely industrial company that entered in the field of education is the Westinghouse Learning Corporation, founded in 1967 as a subsidiary of the Westinghouse Electric Company. The primary activity of the Westinghouse Learning Corporation has been in the development of PLAN (Program for Learning in Accordance with Needs), initiated in the fall of 1967 through cooperative efforts of the Westinghouse Learning Corporation, the American Institutes for Research, and several school districts. The system utilizes the computer as an aid to teachers in providing each student with a separate program of study designed to meet the needs, abilities, and interests of that individual. Mathematics, language arts, science, and social studies were the original modules in PLAN. Other subject areas are now being added as modules.

Computer-based Instruction (CBI)

Stuart D. Milner, an education specialist at the National Training Center of the Internal Revenue Service in Arlington, Virginia specifies two application functions of computer-based instruction (CBI).

Direct instructional use is called computer-assisted instruction (CAI). This includes such usage modes as drill and practice, tutorials, simulation/gaming, inquiry/dialogue, information retrieval, and problem solving. Instructional management use is called computer-managed instruction (CMI). This includes such instructional support functions as testing, prescribing, record keeping, scheduling, monitoring, and time and resource management.[1]

The rapid recent development of the microcomputer has changed our entire outlook on computer use in education. Many teacher preparation programs are considering requirements for graduates to be able to apply, use, and manage the microcomputer for instruction. Microcomputers include the same functional components as larger computer systems, but cost less ($400 to $8,000), and are easier to use. Figure 14.4 is an example of a microcomputer which is easy to use both at home and at school. Prospective teachers are urged to examine printed materials about microcomputers available from the many electronic stores. Some of the microcomputer brand names which have educational programs for home and school use are Apple, Radio Shack, PET, Sorcerer, Atari, Texas Instruments, and Terak.

In the future, instructional technology will also include cost-efficient programs utilizing the telecommunications potential of space satellites. When one assesses the speed with which the electronics industries developed microcomputers, it is not farfetched to envision the age of the world as classroom when the space satellite potential is similarly developed.

Another company, Tandberg of America (Armonk, New York), advertises as one of the world's leading producers of learning laboratories. Tandberg has been making learning systems since 1960, and has continued to market their systems successfully while many other manufacturers have gone out of business since the learning systems boom of the 1960s.

Figure 14.4. Microcomputer.

While the listing of each and every company involved in educational technology would be practically endless, the following companies are representative of the entire list: Sperry-Univac (Blue Bell, Pennsylvania); Tektronix, Inc. (Beaverton, Oregon); Time Share (West Hartford, Connecticut); Kodak (Chicago, Illinois); General Electric (Waynesboro, Virginia); Digital Equipment Corporation (Northboro, Massachusetts); Bruning (Schaumburg, Illinois); 3M Company (St. Paul, Minnesota); Apple Computer, Inc. (Cupertino, California); Radio Shack; Altari, Inc.; and Texas Instruments. The very fact that so many reputable business enterprises engage in the manufacture and marketing of educational systems practically assures that technology utilization has become a permanent dimension of educating children. As purchase prices become more reasonable, utilization of educational technology in the public schools should increase. However, since most school budgets most often provide less than 1 percent for media and other instructional materials, government support programs are necessary to greatly increase school expenditures for media.

Evaluating Media Programs

Most school systems have joined the new technology swing in support of instruction for several reasons. In some communities where funds were plentiful, the purchase and utilization of media programs were quickly accomplished as the contemporary thing to do. Federal funds enabled other communities to make expenditures for media programs that were formerly too expensive. The best schools approached the tasks related to the development of media programs on the basis of explicitly stated goals and objectives as related to desired instructional outcomes. Whatever the compelling forces in the development of the various school media programs, media personnel through their professional organization (Association for Educational Communications and Technology) called for the development of instruments that could be used by school personnel in evaluating media programs. Following two years of diligent committee work, the Association for Educational Communications and Technology (AECT) published a draft edition booklet devised especially for field testing.[2] Evaluation instruments are organized into seven sections to provide for the evaluation of those facets of the overall school district related to the media program: School System Profile and Budget, Services, Personnel, Physical Facilities, Collection, Student and Teacher Opinionnaires, and Summary Narrative.

Of particular importance to the prospective teacher are the Student and Teacher Opinionnaires. The rationale for the Student Opinionnaire suggests:

Students are set forth as the chief reason for the existence of media programs in today's schools. The effectiveness of a media program is, therefore, not just indicated by the materials and equipment available, the dollars spent, and the number of persons employed, but also by the reactions of the clientele served. Are the students using the media center? To what extent? How do they rate the services rendered? The student opinionnaire is included in this instrument to gain answers to questions such as these and to other questions.[3]

Figure 14.5 (the student opinionnaire) can be simply completed by placing a check mark in the appropriate box of the five-part scale indicated at the top of the opinionnaire. A composite tabulation of the responses of students would provide invaluable information to the teacher who strives to best utilize the available media materials.

In the evaluation of the media program, the teacher opinionnaire data is central to the total evaluation process. The rationale for the teacher instrument stresses the role of the teacher as the architect and facilitator of learning:

Although the student is always the chief recipient of the media center services, the teacher remains as the architect and facilitator of learning. Are teachers using the media center? What are their opinions concerning

Figure 14.5. Student Opinionnaire.

Subject _____

Grade _____

Always
Frequently
Occasionally
Seldom
Never

1. I can use the media center when I need to as my class schedule permits .... ☐ ☐ ☐ ☐ ☐
2. I do use the media center when I need to as my class schedule permits .... ☐ ☐ ☐ ☐ ☐
3. Our media center is too crowded .... ☐ ☐ ☐ ☐ ☐
4. Our media center is too noisy .... ☐ ☐ ☐ ☐ ☐
5. Learning is improved when a variety of media is used in my classes .... ☐ ☐ ☐ ☐ ☐
6. I can obtain information materials I need from the media center .... ☐ ☐ ☐ ☐ ☐
7. I do obtain informational materials I need from the media center .... ☐ ☐ ☐ ☐ ☐
8. I can get help in finding and using media center materials and equipment .... ☐ ☐ ☐ ☐ ☐
9. I do get help in finding and using media center materials and equipment .... ☐ ☐ ☐ ☐ ☐
10. I can take home materials other than books from the media center .... ☐ ☐ ☐ ☐ ☐
11. I do take home materials other than books from the media center .... ☐ ☐ ☐ ☐ ☐
12. I am asked to help in selecting materials for the media center .... ☐ ☐ ☐ ☐ ☐
13. I do help in selecting materials for the media center .... ☐ ☐ ☐ ☐ ☐
14. My suggestions for purchase of materials are seriously considered .... ☐ ☐ ☐ ☐ ☐
15. I can use school supplies and equipment to make audiovisual materials for my
    school reports .... ☐ ☐ ☐ ☐ ☐
16. I do use school supplies and equipment to make audiovisual materials for my
    school reports .... ☐ ☐ ☐ ☐ ☐
17. I can get help in making audiovisual materials from the media center staff .... ☐ ☐ ☐ ☐ ☐
18. I do get help in making audiovisual materials from the media center staff .... ☐ ☐ ☐ ☐ ☐
19. My teachers expect me to use:
    (a) print materials .... ☐ ☐ ☐ ☐ ☐
    (b) visual materials .... ☐ ☐ ☐ ☐ ☐
    (c) listening materials .... ☐ ☐ ☐ ☐ ☐
20. I am informed when new materials are added to the media center collection .... ☐ ☐ ☐ ☐ ☐
21. Television is used as part of my classroom instruction.
    (a) commercial television .... ☐ ☐ ☐ ☐ ☐
    (b) educational and instructional television .... ☐ ☐ ☐ ☐ ☐
    (c) programs produced by the school .... ☐ ☐ ☐ ☐ ☐
    (d) videotaping for student self-evaluation .... ☐ ☐ ☐ ☐ ☐

Source: *Evaluating Media Programs: District and School.* Publications Department, Association for Educational Communications and Technology, 1201 16th Street, N.W., Washington, D.C. 20036.

the services provided? How do they perceive the administrative support of the program? Teachers' reactions to the types, quantity and quality of media center services are needed to properly assess the contributions of the media center to the total instructional program.[4]

Figure 14.6 (the teacher opinionnaire) is completed in the same fashion as the student opinionnaire by the mere placing of a check mark in the appropriate box following each statement. Whether or not the beginning teacher, or the experienced teacher for that matter, has had explicit preparation in the utilization of media programs in support of classroom practice, each teacher would find considerable direction from the careful analysis of the specific items of the student and teacher opinionnaires.

Community Resources

More than three-fourths of our population now live either in the central city areas or in the suburbs of those areas. Improved transportation facilities have expanded the availability of community resources for school use. Students now have increased opportunities to learn about many things in their own communities. Many school boards, school administrators, and creative teachers are finding different ways to utilize community resources to supplement the learning activities of the schools.

Considerable education planning is a prerequisite to the proper utilization of community resources. Educators ought to carefully develop community resource guides for the purpose of identifying and describing available educational resources, including community resource persons. Proper utilization of community resources for educational field trips requires preliminary planning that considers certain educational criteria for field trips. Finding and using resource persons, either at their place of work or in the classroom, also requires careful planning for coordinating the contributions of the resource person with the sequence of work students are doing in the classroom.

Obviously, the scope of available community resources is prescribed to a large measure by the nature of the community. However, every school community, large or small, has community resources at its disposal.

Outdoor Education

The concept of outdoor education has gained considerable acceptance during the last few years. Programs of outdoor education are increasing in popularity at all levels of the school organization. The simple essence of the outdoor education concept deals with activity and study in an outdoor setting. In some areas the community resources of agencies such as Boy Scouts and Girl Scouts, YMCA and YWCA, churches, private clubs, and service organizations are utilized in providing outdoor facilities for educational programs sponsored by the local schools. With continued acceptance of the concept, the trend has been

Figure 14.6. Teacher Opinionnaire.

Subject _____

Grade _____

Always
Frequently
Occasionally
Seldom
Never

1. I can easily find relevant materials in the media center .... ☐ ☐ ☐ ☐ ☐

2. I use instructional materials in my classes .... ☐ ☐ ☐ ☐ ☐

3. My requests for assistance from the media center staff are promptly, adequately, and conveniently filled .... ☐ ☐ ☐ ☐ ☐

4. Lack of resources affects my use of the media center .... ☐ ☐ ☐ ☐ ☐

5. Indifference to my requests affects my use of the media center .... ☐ ☐ ☐ ☐ ☐

6. Inadequate staffing prevents my fullest use of the media center .... ☐ ☐ ☐ ☐ ☐

7. The professional materials collection is up-to-date and relevant .... ☐ ☐ ☐ ☐ ☐

8. I use the professional materials collection .... ☐ ☐ ☐ ☐ ☐

9. I am asked to participate in the selection of new materials .... ☐ ☐ ☐ ☐ ☐

10. I do participate in the selection of new materials .... ☐ ☐ ☐ ☐ ☐

11. My requests for new materials are honored equally with other requests as budgetary limitations permit .... ☐ ☐ ☐ ☐ ☐

12. My requests for new equipment are honored equally with other requests as budgetary limitations permit .... ☐ ☐ ☐ ☐ ☐

13. I participate actively in media in-service workshops as offered .... ☐ ☐ ☐ ☐ ☐

14. The media center staff offers a wide variety of media in-service workshops during the school year .... ☐ ☐ ☐ ☐ ☐

15. I make media items for instructing my classes .... ☐ ☐ ☐ ☐ ☐

16. I have the media center produce materials for my teaching .... ☐ ☐ ☐ ☐ ☐

17. My students produce original media materials .... ☐ ☐ ☐ ☐ ☐

18. I utilize types of television as follows:
    (a) commercial television .... ☐ ☐ ☐ ☐ ☐
    (b) educational and instructional television .... ☐ ☐ ☐ ☐ ☐
    (c) programs produced by the school .... ☐ ☐ ☐ ☐ ☐
    (d) videotaping of teacher and student self-evaluation .... ☐ ☐ ☐ ☐ ☐

19. My students make independent use of media .... ☐ ☐ ☐ ☐ ☐

20. My students successfully locate materials in the media center collection .... ☐ ☐ ☐ ☐ ☐

21. Time is available to preview instructional media .... ☐ ☐ ☐ ☐ ☐

22. The principal supports the media center staff in providing a full array of media services .... ☐ ☐ ☐ ☐ ☐

23. The superintendent recognizes the need for and supports quality and variety of media services needed for an effective instructional program .... ☐ ☐ ☐ ☐ ☐

24. The Board of Education recognizes the need for and supports the quality and variety of media services needed for an effective instructional program .... ☐ ☐ ☐ ☐ ☐

Source: *Evaluating Media Programs: District and School.* Publications Department, Association for Educational Communications and Technology, 1201 16th Street, N.W., Washington, D.C. 20036.

Community resources may be used to supplement the learning activities of schools.

toward the development of especially designed and planned outdoor education facilities that are maintained as cooperative ventures among several school districts. In this fashion, the cooperating districts would have at their disposal the services of professionally trained outdoor education personnel hired on a full-time basis. Classroom teachers involved in outdoor education programs would then typically accompany their students on the overnight expeditions to the outdoor education facility.

Many teacher-preparation programs have built into their programs professional laboratory experiences with children in an outdoor setting. For example, the Lorado Taft Campus in Oregon, Illinois, is the outdoor education extension of Northern Illinois University, which is located in DeKalb, Illinois, approximately forty miles away. The elementary teacher-preparation program of the university requires periods of several days to be spent at the outdoor education facility by both junior and senior students. Other teacher education programs that require senior year experiences at the outdoor education facility are in special education, women's physical education, and industry and technology. The university also offers a master's degree program in Outdoor Education, which leads to the supervision and administration endorsements required by Illinois state law for directors of outdoor education facilities.

Another reason for the growing acceptance rate for outdoor education is its successful implementation in other nations. The international influence of outdoor education is apparent in the field study centers of Great Britain, the country schools in Germany, and the schools of the snow in the French Alps. Australia and Japan are leaders in the outdoor education movement in their part of the world. One of the noticeable program trends, especially on the international scene, is the rapid development of so-called outward bound schools. Such schools usually pit the physical prowess of the participants against the elements of nature. Thus, emphasis on physical survival and adventure experiences are basic to these programs.

The laboratory concept as associated with today's schools requires the availability of many kinds of materials, equipment, and facilities to assist the teacher in his or her work with students.

The range of such needs includes the software and hardware; library resource centers or learning centers where multimedia systems may be assembled and operated; and utilization of available community resources, including the use of outdoor education facilities. All of these things add to the excitement of teaching and greatly assist teachers in meeting their daily tasks.

Point of View

The small personal computer is quietly acquiring massive capabilities in our day. This generation of more information and records than ever before in our history fosters increasing reliance on the storage and retrieval capacity of easy-to-use computers. Computers are even being developed that can not only speak, but also recognize voice patterns. Once the computer is able to understand human speech, it could retrieve data by being orally requested to do so. This awesome computer capacity often surfaces in conversations about machines replacing teachers in the classroom. While the authors do not believe that computers and other electronic media will actually replace classroom teachers, it is acknowledged that perhaps their total impact on teaching will certainly change the type of teachers needed in the classrooms.

When extended consideration is given to the many ways in which information is communicated outside school classrooms, it becomes apparent that present-day computers must surely dictate the number and types of employees in the television industry, the newspaper and magazine fields, advertising, and many other communication-related businesses. Whether or not it is a sanguine view to believe that computers will never replace people might be considered when reading the following point of view statement. The authors of the article entitled "Your Job Is On the Line" are Harvey B. Black, professor of instructional science at Brigham Young University in Provo, Utah and Richard Evans, journalist with the Fairfield Daily Republic in Fairfield, California. The point of this presentation is to illustrate the major transitional role remaining for media professionals (teachers of tomorrow).

Your Job Is on the Line

Harvey B. Black and R. Richard Evans

Present-day computers pose no immediate employment threat to anyone in the instructional community. They are still far too limited or costly. In fact, computers presently provide more jobs in instruction than they replace.

Many of us assume that computers will continue to fall into that large category of adjunct media, which support education but will never replace an educator. This sanguine view is not consonant with events that are already occurring.

Within five years, education will probably catch up with other fields in making heavy automation economically practical. Costs will continue to drop until

Source: Harvey B. Black and R. Richard Evans, "Your Job Is on the Line," *Instructional Innovator*, November 1980, vol. 25, no. 8, pp. 6–7.

powerful computers with multimedia capability will cost no more than a single book. And they will be as portable and easily used as a book.

The bottom-line question is, Will this massive intrusion of the low-cost computer into education deprive you of your job? Some evidence suggests that computerization probably will take over many functions now performed by instructional media professionals, but may provide other roles for those willing to adapt.

All the News That's Fit to Input
For convincing evidence of impending change, look at the effects of computerized automation on our close cousins, the newspapers. Because journalism is more centralized in product and general operation than most education institutions, it has more easily entered the computer age. While the average school has done little more than computerize a few administrative functions, the computer is at the very center of the modern newspaper system.

One of the most dramatic effects of computerizing newspapers has been upon the employment of printers. In many respects, this is analogous to the instructional media function. Automated typesetting led to an immediate reduction in jobs and a dramatic shrinking of the International Typographical Union. The preparation of graphics for advertising copy is automated to the point that a nonprofessional can produce art that professionals previously could not achieve within their budgets. Automation has also reduced considerably the number of persons involved in the packaging and delivery of newspapers.

One future development will eliminate entirely the newspaper delivery staff and substantially change the functions of editors. Viewdata systems, now operational in England and being tested in the United States, permit one to sit in front of a television set and select from a menu of thousands of information items. Using a small keyboard wired into a cable television system, the househunter can request listings on homes in a desired price range and neighborhood, the sports enthusiast can ask for scores and standings, the investor can see how various stocks are doing, and the homemaker can ask the price of bacon at local supermarkets. Each individual reader will determine which elements constitute his or her "personal" newspaper.

What Will Happen to Us?
The implications of viewdata systems for many of us are obvious. Why should packaged films or videotapes be mailed, or delivered via closed-circuit television, when they can be received on request on one's home monitor or pocket computer? Who needs the local editorial function of selecting a film library when the student can bypass it and deal directly with any remote depository?

There are other obvious parallels. Automation will allow film producers to accelerate their initial filming, editing, and processing. The electronic camera, for example, takes hundreds of still or motion pictures that are instantly available for inspection and editing. The emergence of large and inexpensive memories on videodisc will make it possible for viewers to compose and see several versions of filmed sequences, and program these to suit their personal needs.

The most important effect, however, is that technology encourages and makes inevitable the sharing of the authoring functions. As the creation and distribution of film, tape, or text become easier and cheaper, students will produce much of their own films, texts, and other instructional materials. Just as the news consumer will one day play an increased role in the production of news, so may the student soon become the primary producer of educational materials.

Emergence of the Student
The fact that the center of control is shifting to the consumer is momentous. No longer a mere object to be manipulated by the media, the consumer may soon

virtually create the media. Those who survive and prosper in the emerging news arena will be those who are best able to help the news consumers help themselves. Similarly, the emerging role of the instructor and media specialist will be to help students exercise both message and media control over incoming and student-produced messages.

In addition, the media specialist can serve an important function by generating new information in direct response to student request. This means becoming a kind of educational reporter, creating through various media the "feature articles" that are not already part of the student's massive and accessible database resources.

A major remaining role for media professionals is transitional. We must find ways to help students prepare themselves to take increasing responsibility for the preparation of their own instructional packages. This new role may also include working with students so that their input into personal and public databases meets existing standards. Both functions will be facilitated each time students are allowed to be more directly involved in creating, packaging, storing, distributing, and implementing instructional information.

The Future

Will the 1985 pocket computer replace you or me as an instructional media specialist? The answer is yes if we ignore the signals indicating that the consumer-student will become our immediate client rather than the instructor. Those of us who can't change should have time to slip quietly out of the profession during the next decade. Those of us who can will discover new dimensions in the instructional media profession.

Questions for Discussion

1. How could uses of new educational media aid in solving some of the school problems arising from the great range of abilities and varied backgrounds among students?

2. Discuss the following statement: Modern technology is on the threshold of producing a revolution in education.

3. Do you believe that school districts should spend additional money to send students outside the school building for outdoor education experiences? If outdoor education trips require overnight lodging, is it reasonable to require classroom teachers to accompany their classes?

4. How would you use educational television and commercial television as teaching resources? overhead projectors?

5. List the changes in school building construction that have been prompted by new instructional technology. How do you plan to use the learning resource center in your teaching?

Supplementary Learning Activities

1. Using the lists of learning center software and hardware given in this chapter, visit an elementary school and a high school for the purpose of evaluating the kinds of software and hardware available to the students. Determine the reasons for inadequacies you discover.

2. Interview the personnel of the instructional technology staff of a school system. Obtain information about the kinds of services offered and the extent of their use in the classes.

3. Select a desirable field trip for your teaching field in your community. Visit the location selected and develop the plans needed for the class visit.

4. After reading several articles on the topic, prepare a paper that discusses the use of commercially prepared technological instructional systems (reading programs, computer assisted instruction, Westinghouse PLAN, etc.).

5. Visit a local travel agency to obtain various materials advertising foreign countries. Arrange these materials in a display for use in elementary and high school classroom instruction situations.

Notes

1. Stuart D. Milner, "How to Make the Right Decisions about Microcomputers," *Instructional Innovator,* September 1980, p. 13.

2. *Evaluating Media Programs: District and School.* Publications Department, Association for Educational Communications and Technology, 1201 16th Street, N.W., Washington, D.C. 20036, 80 pp.

3. Ibid., p. 69.

4. Ibid., p. 71.

Selected References

Cawelti, Gordon F. "The Competency Based Movement and Curricular Changes." *North Central Association Quarterly,* Fall 1977, pp. 310–15.

Dwyer, Francis. *Strategies for Improving Learning.* Learning Services, State College, Pennsylvania, 1979.

Educational Technology: A Glossary of Terms. Association for Educational Communication and Technology, 1979.

Heinich, Robert (editor). *AV Communication Review.* Association for Educational Communication and Technology. Washington, D.C., Winter 1977.

Humphrey, Darrell. "Computers in the Media Center of Tomorrow." *Audiovisual Instruction.* November 1977, pp. 24–26.

Kapfer, Phillip G., and Kapfer, Miriam B. *Learning Packages in American Education.* Englewood Cliffs, N.J.: Educational Technology Publications, 1974.

Kemp, Jerrold E. *Planning and Producing Audiovisual Material* (4th edition). New York: Harper and Row, 1980.

Milner, Stuart. "How to Make the Right Decisions about Microcomputers." *Instructional Innovator.* September 1980, pp. 12–19.

Schramm, William. *Big Media—Little Media.* Beverly Hills, Calif.: Sage Publications, 1977.

Van Hoose, John J. "The Impact of Television Usage on Emerging Adolescents." *The High School Journal.* March 1980, pp. 239–43.

The Organization and Administration of Public Education in the United States

This section of the book is devoted to the ways in which schools in the United States are organized, controlled, and financed. Each of these functions of the educational enterprise has evolved as the nation has developed. Patterns of organization, control, and finance reflect rather directly the needs and expectations of society.

The patterns of organization for public education in the early days of the nation were not complicated. Our society was basically an agrarian one with a widely scattered population. Men and women as pioneers were concerned with conquering the frontier. One-room schools for grades one through eight were built in the rural areas, while the multigraded common school developed in towns and cities. Private universities were also established in the very early days. As the frontier was developed, and as the nation began to change to an industrial and urban way of life, the needs of the nation changed and so did its patterns for the organization of education. Today we have public education from nursery school level through the university, along with many other forms of adult education. Each of these levels has purposes and programs rooted in the needs of society and the expectations of people.

The control of education in the United States is both unique and complicated. It is unique because of its decentralization. Local people in the United States have more of a say about education than do local people in most other nations of the world. It is complicated because it involves at least three and sometimes four levels of government. The legal responsibility for education in the United States rests with state government, while the actual operation of schools is delegated to local government; at the same time the federal government shows an interest in the enterprise. Again, as our society has changed from agrarian to industrial, and as our population has become increasingly mobile, the patterns of control of education have changed. The trend has been toward greater direct control of education at the state and federal levels, particularly in the areas of human and civil rights, and state and national problems. New patterns of control continue to emerge.

The financing of education has changed from an almost completely local effort to a point where, in most states, the local contribution is currently down to about 50 percent. The state and federal government make up the remainder of the costs. The property tax provides most of the revenue at the local level; sales and income taxes at the state level; and federal income tax at the federal level. State contributions to school financing have tended to equalize the amount of money spent per pupil in a state. Federal monies have been directed toward specific projects at specific times in our history.

As society changes, the methods of organizing, controlling, and financing education are also likely to change. Frequently the institutions of society lag in making the necessary accommodations to society. It should be remembered that institutions are created to serve society, and therefore should be changed by society when necessary and desirable. Institutions also have the responsibility of looking to the future and providing information to their constituencies as to the probable, possible, and preferable directions society may face and/or create for the future.

sing sang
go went
jump jumped
eat ate eaten
look looked
take took
am was
set sat sat
set set

Organization for Learning

15

This Chapter
- Relates the purposes and goals of the various levels of education to the structure provided at each level.
- Presents the rationales for the growing emphasis on early childhood and adult education.
- Appraises the success of secondary schools in meeting their expressed purposes.
- Explains the current thrust in providing education for all handicapped children.
- Analyzes the alternative school movement.
- Recognizes the role of private education in the United States.
- Provides a point of view which examines the proliferation of protestant fundamentalist schools.

As indicated earlier in this textbook, formal programs of education evolve from the needs and expectations of societies and individuals. As our colonial settlements grew and developed, the colonists recognized that some of their desires for the education of their children could be better met by organizing children in groups and assigning specific adults from the communities to serve as teachers. Thus began the formal organizational patterns for education in the United States. They began with a basic idea of efficiency; it was felt that one adult could teach a group of children, and in so doing permit other adults to pursue other important duties. As the population began to grow and people began to cluster in communities, other principles of organization emerged—for example, the grouping of children by age so that one teacher could concentrate his or her efforts in teaching specific content in the most appropriate way to a particular age group. Later the principalship and superintendency emerged as specialties needed to effectively conduct the educational program in an organized fashion. While there is still disagreement regarding the *best* organization for learning, particularly for the individual child, it is nevertheless quite clear that American education was organized on at least two basic principles: (1) division of labor—that is, let some adults teach while others engage in other productive work; and (2) classification of students by age or common developmental levels. Organization for learning in the United States, while it has become increasingly refined, still reflects these two basic principles.

Purposes and Programs

Today four general divisions of vertical progression in educational organization are clearly recognized: preelementary, elementary, secondary, and higher education. Within these levels many subdivisions exist. Figure 15.1 illustrates the overall status of educational organization as it exists today.

At each of the levels certain goals and purposes are expected to be accomplished. A sequential program is envisioned based primarily on developing maturity and content complexity. One pertinent general observation that can be

Figure 15.1. The Structure of Education in the United States.

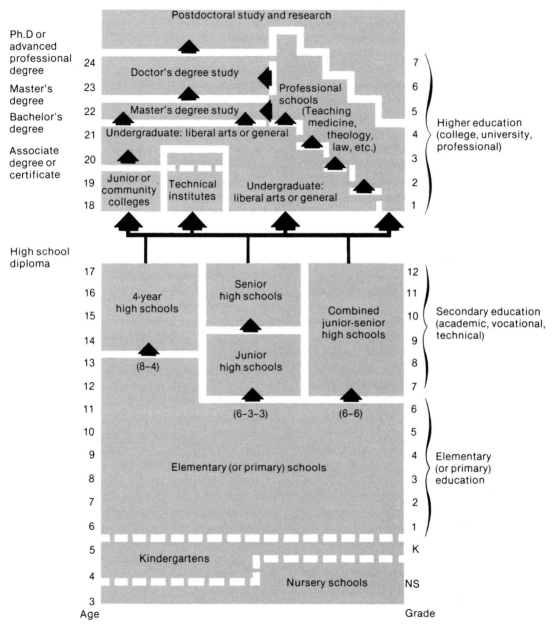

Source: W. Vance Grant and Leo J. Eiden, *Digest of Educational Statistics, 1980 edition.* Washington, D.C.: National Center for Educational Statistics, 1980. (Available from U.S. Government Printing Office, Washington, D.C. 20402).

Figure 15.2. The Decrease in Time Allotted to General Education as Related to Vertical Progression.

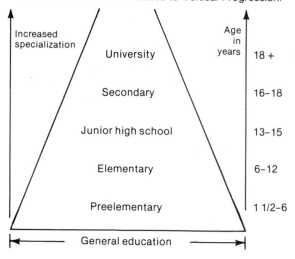

3. Social and group living: history, geography, government, community living, human relations, citizenship, value building, character building and sensitivity to problems of group living.
4. Science: understanding of scientific phenomena and natural law, the use of methods of science in problem solving, understanding the world.
5. Aesthetic development: music, art and handicrafts.
6. Health: knowledge of the body, nutrition and health habits.
7. Recreation: play, physical education and handicrafts.[1]

Specialized education represents that part of the program, generally elective, wherein an individual student pursues a specialty. For example, Johnny Jones and his parents may decide at the end of the eighth grade that the only general education that Johnny will take in the future is that which is required by law, and that his program in secondary education will be vocational with his eventual goal that of becoming an automotive mechanic. At the same time, Ray Noble and his parents may decide that Ray will continue on to higher education and therefore take a specific college preparatory curriculum in high school. Ray may eventually decide to become a lawyer and then will specialize further at the university level. Ann Smith may decide to pursue the college preparatory curriculum in secondary school and, if she so desires and is financially able, could pursue liberal arts in higher education, and in so doing specialize almost completely

made about content is that as the vertical progression proceeds from preelementary to higher education the overall educational programs contain less general education and become increasingly specialized. Figure 15.2 illustrates this idea. General education is that portion which concerns itself with the development of basic skills and common understandings. These include:

1. Communication arts: speech, language usage, reading, writing, listening, discussing, and spelling.
2. Computational skills and quantitative thinking: arithmetic, reasoning, and problem solving.

Early childhood education helps prepare children for
future social and academic demands.

in general education. It is significant to note that
the choice of specialization in the United States
is with that of the individual student and her or
his parents, and not that of the government or
society. To be sure, various state laws do pre-
scribe general education requirements, and societal and economic conditions do often limit the
available occupational choices, but basically the
choice is the individual's, limited only by her or
his particular talents, ambitions, and financial
circumstances. In general, today, elementary and
secondary education is assured for all regardless
of their individual financial resources. Higher education in the form of tax-supported community

colleges has increased its availability to all. The
trend in the United States today is toward making more and more education available for academically able students.

The remainder of this chapter presents brief
descriptions of the organization and purposes of
each of the major levels of education.

Preprimary—Early Childhood
Basically, early childhood education consists of
two divisions: nursery school and kindergarten.
Nursery schools generally include children from
the ages of eighteen months to four years,
whereas kindergartens generally accept children
between the ages of four to six years.

The number of children enrolled in early childhood programs is increasing rapidly.

The first nursery school in the United States was opened in 1826, in the model community established by Robert Owen in New Harmony, Indiana; however it was not until 1919 that the first public nursery school was established. The concept of nursery school education has gained acceptance slowly. Public nursery schools seem to have achieved their greatest impetus in the depression era. More recently, in the 1960s and 1970s through the war on poverty, nursery school education was again stimulated. Operation Head Start, operating under the Office of Economic Opportunity, was illustrative of this trend. The number of day-care centers is also increasing, resulting in part from the increased numbers of working mothers. While many day-care centers admittedly do not represent the epitome of nursery schools, they do in fact represent a form of early childhood education that is carried on outside of the home and family.

The latest data available indicate that the proportion of three- to five-year old children enrolled in preprimary education rose from 25 percent in 1964 to 50.3 percent in 1978. In 1974, approximately 20 percent of the three-year-olds were enrolled in schools, as were 38 percent of the four-year-olds, and 79 percent of the five-year-olds. In 1978, approximately 25 percent of the three-year-olds were enrolled in school, as were 43 percent of the four-year-olds, and 82 percent of the five-year-olds. Twice as many of the prekindergarten three-through five-year-olds are enrolled in nonpublic schools as are enrolled in public schools. At the kindergarten level six times as many children are enrolled in public schools as are enrolled in nonpublic schools. The trend toward increased enrollments of preprimary children in school is expected to continue in the future.

There are a number of reasons why there is an increased emphasis on early childhood education, which correspond with why there are more children enrolled in early childhood programs. Evidence strongly suggests that it is during the first four or five years of life that many personal behaviors, that is, language, attitudes, and values, begin to take on the form they will retain for a lifetime. Further, rich and wholesome learning environments tend to help children not only socially but academically in the future. It seems only reasonable therefore that investments made in early childhood education should reduce the need for remedial and compensatory programs later in life. It could also help foster a less divisive society in the future, yet one where cultural differences would be appreciated and respected. Life-styles, politics, and economics also have affected the increase in early childhood education. As more and more women enter the world of work outside the home, the preprimary schools benefit because they provide a desirable service for child care. Elementary school enrollments have dropped in recent years because of a shortage of elementary-age children, so facilities and staff formerly engaged in elementary education can now be utilized in early childhood programs.

Nursery schools can be categorized by their form of financial support: public or governmental, private, and parochial. Nursery schools that serve as a downward extension of the local public elementary schools and are supported by local district tax monies are very rare. However, the impetus being provided by the federal government to develop preschool programs for children of poverty, accompanied by research findings that indicate the significance of early childhood experiences to later intellectual development, may very well cause more local school systems to extend their public school education to include the nursery school group. While Head Start did not have the dramatic effect that was anticipated, it did have an effect, and perhaps the experience served to point out that greater effectiveness could have been achieved with children younger than four years of age. While public schools hesitate for a variety of reasons—primarily financial, coupled with public reluctance—to embrace the nursery school children into their system, private and parochial nursery schools will continue to function, fulfilling the needs of those who want this service and can afford to pay for it, or who happen to be fortunate enough to have philanthropic facilities available.

Kindergartens have received greater public acceptance than nursery schools. The first permanent public school kindergarten in the United States was established as a part of the St. Louis, Missouri, public school system in 1873. Since then public school kindergartens have grown slowly but steadily. In 1940 approximately 661,000 pupils were enrolled in kindergarten. Currently there are approximately 2.4 million five-year-olds enrolled in kindergarten. Kindergarten enrollees are largely, by a wide margin, in public schools.

Kindergartens and nursery schools have similar goals. Major efforts are made to: (1) develop physical skills, (2) develop skills in interpersonal relationships, (3) enhance the development of a positive self-concept, (4) develop both oral and written language skills, and (5) enhance intellectual concept development. In addition to these developmental tasks, which incidentally are applicable at all levels of education, the preelementary curriculum content includes mathematics, science, social science, humanities, health, and physical education. The uniqueness of preelementary education resides in the selection of appropriate content and materials, and the use of appropriate methodology for very young children. Preelementary programs are extremely flexible; the key principle is in learning by

Reading is a basic skill heavily emphasized in elementary education.

doing—that is, in gaining enriching experiences without the encumbrance of performing specific tasks and in so doing, learning to work and play effectively with others.

Elementary

The elementary schools have been the backbone of American education. Historically they are referred to as common schools, and traditionally, under the graded organization system, they contained grades one through eight. As was indicated earlier in this text, elementary schools were organized in the colonies. The "Old Deluder Act," passed in Massachusetts, required towns to establish and maintain schools. While Massachusetts had the first compulsory school attendance law in 1852, Pennsylvania, in 1834, became the first state to provide a program of free public schools. The phrase "public schools" as used in the early days of the nation is practically synonymous with the term "elementary schools" today. Horace Mann, known as the "father of the common schools," was most influential in spreading the concept of the importance of a common school education for all citizens of a democracy. An elementary school education was at one time considered to be the terminus in formal education in America. Now it is more truly only the end of one of our most basic steps.

The traditional elementary school organization contained grades one through eight. This traditional organizational structure consisted of three levels: (1) *primary*, containing grades one through three, (2) *intermediate,* containing grades four through six, and (3) *upper*, containing grades seven and eight. After the completion of the traditional eight grades in the elementary school the student entered a four-year high school. This traditional plan (8–4) dominated the organizational scene up to and through the early twentieth century. In fact, 94 percent of the public secondary schools were four-year high schools in 1920.

Modifications have been made in this plan. In 1910, the first junior high schools were established. They included the upper grades of the elementary schools, and, in some instances, if legal district organization permitted, they included the first year of the four-year high school. This was the beginning of the 6–3–3 plan. By 1958 only 25 percent of the public secondary schools were of the traditional four-year high school variety. Twenty percent of the schools were two- or three-year junior high schools. By 1966, 31 percent of the schools were traditional four-year schools, while 30 percent were of the two- or three-year junior high school variety. The trend seems to be returning to a four-year high school, with a two- or three-year feeder school.

There is a decided decline in the high schools made up of five or six years. Under the 6–3–3 plan elementary education is thought of as including only the first six grades.

Another modification of a more recent vintage is the grouping of grades five through eight and referring to that grouping as a middle school. With this arrangement the ninth grade is considered as a part of a four-year senior high school. A school system using the middle school organization is referred to as having the 4–4–4 plan. In addition to the 8–4, 6–3–3, and 4–4–4, other plans are used including 6–6, 7–2–3, and 8–2–2. There are a number of reasons for these various plans, some directly related to the goals of instruction, others being only tangential. Let us briefly examine the goals of elementary education as they relate to the organizational patterns.

The goals of the elementary schools, particularly through grade six, are the goals of general education stated earlier in this chapter. Many of these goals are related to coursework and can be sequentially developed. In arithmetic, for example, children count before they add, and add before they multiply. This reasoning is sound and the graded organization is in part based on this rationale. However, other goals of general education such as those dealing with interpersonal relationships, group living, and socialization are more closely related to the personal-social needs of learners. It is from these personal-social needs, resulting from learners' developing maturity, that different organizational patterns have emerged. It reflects an effort again to group students, again

Home economics programs are offered in most junior high schools.

by age, but based on developmental personal-social needs of the members of an age group rather than the purely academic content-oriented function of the school.

Junior High School

The junior high school student is a young adolescent. Thirteen-year-old seventh or eighth graders in terms of personal and social development have significantly different needs than preadolescent ten- or eleven-year-olds. This fact suggests a separate organization for these youngsters with somewhat different goals and procedures. Most junior high schools recognizing these differences provide exploratory education. The student is introduced to a variety of specialized educational areas. He or she may be given the opportunity to explore course work in business, agriculture, home economics, and various trades, plus being

given counseling regarding his interests and abilities for further academic pursuits. The junior high school is looked upon organizationally as including the group of youngsters between childhood or preadolescence and the recognized adolescent of the senior high school. Tangentially, many junior high schools came into existence to facilitate school building housing problems. In very practical terms, many junior high schools are converted senior high school buildings. As such, new high schools could be constructed, the old high school put to good use, and pupil housing pressures reduced at the elementary school level. Unfortunately, this type of growth has admittedly produced at times a distinct junior high building and a distinct organizational structure, but *not* a distinct or unique educational program for young adolescents.

Middle Schools

The middle school represents a recent effort to bridge the gap between childhood and adolescence. The junior high school, while designed for this purpose, has tended to become high school oriented. Perhaps the knowledge explosion and the concomitant increased knowledge expectations for younger children, along with increasing social maturity at a lower chronological age, have in part precipitated this development. Nevertheless, many educators feel that today a fifth or sixth through eighth grade grouping can more suitably meet the needs of the ten- to fourteen-year-old population than can either the elementary or junior high school grouping.

The number of middle schools in the United States has increased dramatically. In 1967 there were only 599 middle schools identified in the United States. By 1969 there were 2,298. It has been estimated that in 1980 there were over 5,000 middle schools throughout the nation, based on grade organization and stated program philosophy.[2]

Table 15.1 points out what educators expect the middle school to do as well as what many educators perceive that the junior high school is doing.

It should be noted that the differences pointed out in table 15.1 are matters of emphasis. Further, they are presented as ends of a continuum. In reality, probably very few schools could be clearly designated as functionary at either end.

It is possible that a middle school in operation could emphasize the characteristics attributed to a junior high school and a junior high school could emphasize the characteristics of a middle school. It seems true, however, that many junior high schools have drifted away from the unique rationale that brought about their creation. The middle school represents yet another effort to create educational experiences most appropriate for the preadolescent age groupings. Educationally, if it functions as it should, the middle school provides a gradual transition from teacher-directed study to responsible independence, and greater flexibility and opportunity for various instructional methodologies. It also encourages the development of programs designed specifically for preadolescents. Socially and physically it groups youngsters of similar levels of maturity together. Administratively it permits a four-year sequence in high schools, may fit into an overall building pattern, and many facilitate plans for social and academic integration. A combination of these factors brought about the middle school. The middle school has potential, yet it may not be a panacea for the education of preadolescents.

It is important to point out again that organizational patterns are related to goals, but they are also related to physical facilities, and to social problems in the case of the middle school. It is further pertinent to note that in order to achieve efficiency in educating the masses, the American education system has attempted to group pupils by age and by developmental characteristics. While these efforts have resulted in

Table 15.1. Differences Between Middle Schools and Junior High Schools

A middle school program is designed to recognize the uniqueness of the growth stage spanning the transition from childhood to adolescence.

The junior high has evolved into exactly what the name implies—*junior* high school.

MIDDLE SCHOOL EMPHASIZES—	JUNIOR HIGH SCHOOL EMPHASIZES—
. .a child-centered program	. .a subject-centered program
. .learning how to learn	. .learning a body of information
. .creative exploration	. .mastery of concepts and skills
. .belief in oneself	. .competition with others
. .student self-direction, under expert guidance	. .adherence to the teacher-made lesson plan
. .student responsibility for learning	. .teacher responsibility for student learning
. .student independence	. .teacher control
. .flexible scheduling	. .the six-period day
. .student planning in scheduling	. .the principal-made schedule
. .variable group sizes	. .standard classrooms
. .team teaching	. .one teacher for a class
. .a self-pacing approach, with students learning at different rates	. .a textbook approach, with all students on the same page at the same time.

A middle school program is designed to foster the intellectual, social, and emotional growth of children without snatching their childhood from them.

Source Educational Research Service Circular, *Middle Schools in Action*, Washington, D.C.: American Association of School Administrators, 1969, p. 17. Used with permission.

admirable accomplishments, the public schools still have not resolved organizationally the nagging persistent problem of individualizing instruction. Each student is a unique individual who develops and learns at his or her own rate. Can a plan of universal education designed to serve the masses of elementary school children be organized to suit each and every individual? Can each student be made to feel important? Can the individual expectations of each student be met? These are some of the challenges facing educators today, not only at the elementary school level, but at all levels.

Secondary

Secondary education began in the early colonies with the establishment of the first Latin Grammar School in Boston in 1635. Its purposes reflected the expectations of the people. It was to prepare students for college—colleges in those days were predominantly concerned with preparing clergymen, and clergymen could in turn help the people achieve their goal of salvation. The Latin Grammar School was eventually replaced by the tuition academy, the first of which was established by Ben Franklin in Philadelphia. Franklin is credited with broadening the base of secondary education. His academy included students who did not intend to go on to college as well as those who did. He recognized that our developing nation needed men trained in commerce and surveying, for example, as well as in theology and the classics. The concept of the academy grew and flourished, reaching its greatest heights in the middle of the nineteenth century. It met in part the societal needs of a developing nation. It was semipublic in nature, and was supported chiefly by tuition and donations. The academies were gradually replaced by the free public high school, the first of which was

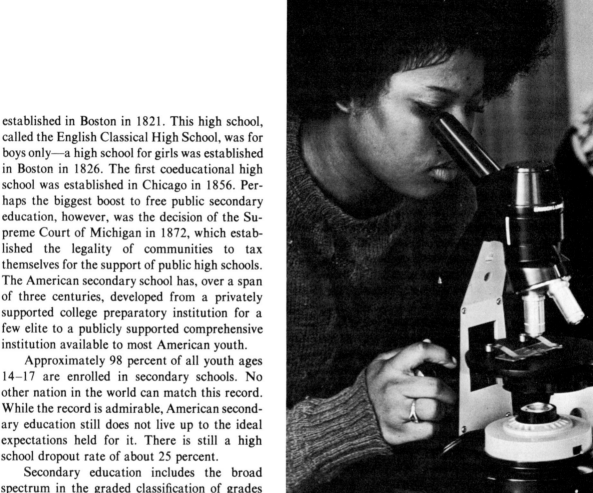

Modern equipment facilitates science education.

established in Boston in 1821. This high school, called the English Classical High School, was for boys only—a high school for girls was established in Boston in 1826. The first coeducational high school was established in Chicago in 1856. Perhaps the biggest boost to free public secondary education, however, was the decision of the Supreme Court of Michigan in 1872, which established the legality of communities to tax themselves for the support of public high schools. The American secondary school has, over a span of three centuries, developed from a privately supported college preparatory institution for a few elite to a publicly supported comprehensive institution available to most American youth.

Approximately 98 percent of all youth ages 14–17 are enrolled in secondary schools. No other nation in the world can match this record. While the record is admirable, American secondary education still does not live up to the ideal expectations held for it. There is still a high school dropout rate of about 25 percent.

Secondary education includes the broad spectrum in the graded classification of grades 7–14. The lower portion of the spectrum includes the junior high while the higher portion is represented by community colleges. The middle portion, including either grades 9–12 or grades 10–12 describes the senior high school. Let us consider briefly the senior high school.

The ideal senior high school is a comprehensive school. Comprehensive means that (1) its curricular offerings present a balance of general and specialized education along with sufficient guidance services and elective courses as to enable a student to pursue a program of his or her choice, and (2) its pupil population is diverse, representing different cultures and socioeconomic groups. If its program is functioning effectively, students should become increasingly different in their achievement levels; that is, the attainments of higher ability students should become increasingly superior by comparison to the attainments of the less able students. This principle should be equally applicable in the college preparatory, vocational, and general curricula students. The comprehensive high school should also permit one to elect courses of one's choice in any of the curricula. In other words, a college preparatory student would not be prohibited from taking a beginning course in typewriting. While students should ideally become increasingly different in their pursuits of specialized education, the comprehensive high school also should cause them to become increasingly alike in such things as their social insight, their attitudinal commitments toward democratic principles, and their empathy for others. Further, students should be prepared to live in a culturally pluralistic society, respecting the differences of cultural groups. Are our high schools accomplishing these goals? Can we have effective comprehensive high schools in this country when demographically, for example, the poor live with the poor, the rich with the rich, and the black with the black? Can students learn to live with others when they only interact with their own kind in schools? Is the comprehensive high school a realistically attainable organizational goal? Can a high school in a rural area with a total pupil population of less than four hundred pupils be comprehensive? The answers to these questions are being sought—they constitute part of the task of secondary education in America.

Special Education

Handicapped children and adults are present at all age and grade levels. It has been estimated by the Council for Exceptional Children (CEC) that there are approximately 8 million handicapped preschool-age and school-age children in the United States. HEW's National Center for Health Statistics estimated that in 1977 2.7 percent of the population under 17 had at least some limitation of activity due to "chronic conditions."[3] About 40 percent of all handicapped children receive special schooling either in segregated facilities or in regular public schools.[4] The remainder either attend regular schools that do not have special services, or are excluded from the educational world.

There are a number of kinds of handicaps: speech impaired, learning disabled, mentally retarded, emotionally disturbed, hard-of-hearing, deaf, crippled, partially sighted, and blind; also those persons suffering from cerebral palsy, epilepsy, muscular dystrophy, multiple sclerosis, drug addiction, heart disease, diabetes, and alcoholism. It is estimated that nearly one out of six Americans is handicapped.[5]

As was mentioned earlier in this text, Public Law 94–142, the All Handicapped Children Act could dramatically improve the educational opportunities for the handicapped. The Act specifies that a free public education will be made available to all handicapped children between the ages of 3 and 18 by no later than September

Under federal legislation handicapped persons shall be educated with nonhandicapped persons whenever possible.

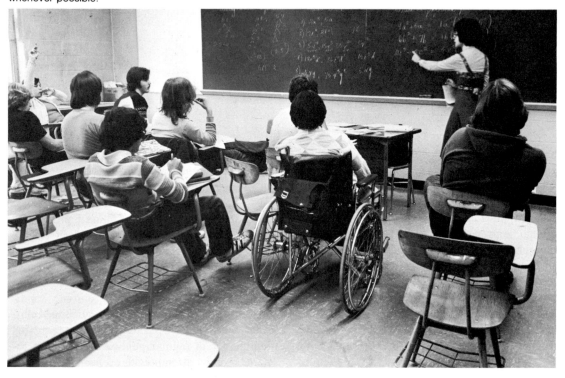

1978, and all those between 3 and 21 by September 1980. They will be provided with an "individualized educational program" as mentioned earlier, and will be educated with nonhandicapped children to the maximum extent appropriate. In other words they will be "mainstreamed." Advocates of mainstreaming offer the following reasons for its support: handicapped children do a better job of achieving, both academically and socially, when their isolation ends; a regular school setting does a better job of helping handicapped children adjust to and cope with the real world when they grow up than that of a segregated setting, and exposure to handicapped children will help normal children understand individual differences in people and help diminish the stereotyping of the handicapped.[6]

The physical facilities of many institutions are being modified to accommodate the handicapped. It is most appropriate that the United States enhance the opportunities and benefits for the handicapped and also gain the benefits that they can provide to our society and economy.

Community Colleges
The junior college or community college has emerged on the American scene in the last seventy years. The Joliet Junior College, established in Joliet, Illinois, in 1901, has the distinction of being the oldest extant public junior college; that is, of the public junior colleges founded in the late 1800s and early 1900s, the Joliet Junior College survived and continues to operate as a junior college today. It is interesting to note that it was originally conceived as an extension of the high

Community colleges provide for "at home" post-high-school education.

school and therefore considered a part of second- ary education and not higher education. The organizational chart presented earlier in this chapter illustrates the junior college as being a part of higher education. Therein lies part of the dilemma of this sector of the American educa- tional organization.

Perhaps it is most accurate to state that for some students the community college is truly an extension of secondary school; for others it is truly higher education, for they often transfer to four-year colleges or universities and graduate; for others it is terminal in specialized education and not an extension of high school, for they pur- sue goals not related to their previous secondary school experience. The confusion of classification in the educational hierarchy is normal for emerg- ing institutions such as the community college.

The community colleges as they are now orga- nized and operated do have characteristics in common with both high schools and universities. This is as it should be, particularly if community colleges are truly going to become unique edu- cational organizations dedicated to their pur- poses.

These purposes are, in a general way, to pro- vide:
- Occupational education of post-high-school level
- General education for all categories of its stu- dents
- Transfer or preprofessional education
- Part-time education
- Community service

In the light of these avowed purposes, it is easy
to understand why it is difficult to classify the
community college unequivocally as either secondary or higher education.

The community college, in meeting its purposes that reflect both individual and societal
needs, has emerged as a unique and growing segment of American education. From meager beginnings in the early twentieth century the
number of junior colleges has grown currently to
1,190 institutions which enroll nearly four million
students.[7]

The community college provides for "at
home" post-high-school education. Students who
cannot financially afford to pursue higher education elsewhere can start in the community college. Others, not seeking higher education, as
such, can acquire necessary occupational skills.
If an institution is truly a community college, it
is responsive to the needs of the members of the
community, and provides services for the people
of the community. As such it fulfills the expectations of the people for education, expectations
that either cannot or may not be met by other
institutions. Therein may reside the reason for its
uniqueness and success.

Higher Education

Higher education, the capstone of American education, began in the early colonies with the establishment of Harvard College in 1636. It is
significant to note that higher education began
as a private endeavor. Today, approximately 63
percent of the 3,000 institutions of higher education are still under private control. Nevertheless, almost two-thirds of the students in higher
education are enrolled in public institutions. The
Morrill Act signed into law by President Lincoln
was a tremendous boost to public higher education. This Act provided 30,000 acres to each state
for each representative and senator then in Congress, or when a state was admitted, for the "en-
dowment, maintenance and support of at least
one college where the leading object shall be,
without excluding other scientific and classical
studies and including military tactics, to teach
such branches of learning as are related to agriculture and mechanic arts."

The organization of higher education is such
that it facilitates the accomplishment of its purposes. Great responsibilities are placed upon the
independent judgment of the students as they
pursue their elected course of study; freedoms are
provided for professors as they conduct their research; and both philanthropic and public monies
are provided to sponsor research in the public
interest.

The diversity of institutions both in kind and
control contributes to meeting the purposes of
higher education. The kinds of institutions include community colleges, technical colleges,
liberal arts colleges, municipal colleges and
universities, land grant colleges and universities,
and graduate and professional schools. Control
differences include local, state, federal, sectarian,
and nonsectarian private. This diversity permits
a wide offering of specialized courses befitting the
needs of individuals and society, and at the same

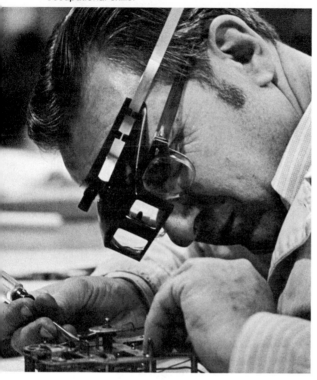

Students in adult education update or learn new occupational skills.

time assures academic freedom and responsibility through an almost automatic system of checks and balances.

There are slightly over three thousand higher education institutions in the United States enrolling approximately 11 million students. One major change in the past thirty years has been the dramatic reduction of men's and women's colleges as such. In 1945 schools enrolling only one sex constituted 30 percent of almost all the institutions; today they constitute only 9 percent.

Adult Education

Adult education in its broadest sense includes any learning activity engaged in by adults to provide them with better living opportunities. In a more restricted sense it refers to programs of education formally organized for people beyond the compulsory school age. These programs are offered by colleges and universities, employers and unions, private specialty schools, armed forces and other governmental agencies, and public elementary and secondary schools. They may be oriented toward a degree or a certificate, or toward specific occupational or life skills. A report by the Carnegie Commission on Higher Education has proposed the following definitions that clarify adult education beyond high school.

Postsecondary education as all education beyond high school.

Higher education as oriented toward academic degrees or broad educational certificates. It takes place on college or university campuses or through campus-substitute institutions such as the "open university" with its "external degrees."

Further education as oriented toward more specific occupational or life skills rather than academic degrees. It takes place in many noncampus environments—industry, trade unions, the military, proprietary vocational schools, among others.[8]

Adult education, of course, does include persons who have not completed high school. There are many purposes for adult education. Among them are the attaining of literacy and basic education skills by adults whose schooling for one reason or another was incomplete, and for non-English-speaking U.S. citizens; updating occupational and vocational skills in order to keep pace with industrial and technological changes; to gain a better understanding of increasingly complex social, economic, and political institutions; finding ways of utilizing increased leisure time; and adjusting to problems of aging and retirement. One need only read the advertisements in newspapers and magazines, or examine the offerings of the many community colleges, to recognize some of the specific purposes of adult education.

The number of participants in adult education between 1969 and 1975 rose by 30.8 percent. *Adults* for this purpose are defined as those age 17 and older who are not full-time students in high school or college, and those persons over 35 regardless of their enrollment status. There were approximately 17 million participants in adult education in 1975 as opposed to 13 million in 1969.[9] This trend is expected to continue in the future. The largest number of participants are in programs sponsored by union or professional organizations, followed by those of two-year colleges. These two types of programs also recorded the largest percentages of change between 1969 and 1975; they had increases of 116 percent and 95 percent respectively. Occupational training represents the study area in which most participants enroll, yet the fastest growing area percentagewise is the study area of social life and recreation, followed by personal and family living.[10]

While a number of both general and specific recommendations were made in the Carnegie report *Toward a Learning Society,* the central messages of the report were:

- That postsecondary education should be concerned comparatively less with the welfare of a minority of the young and more with that of a majority of all ages.

- That more and better channels for all of youth should be created into life and work and service; for the one-half that do not now go to college, as well as for the one-half that do go.
- That age should be welcomed along with youth into the facilities for education; that continuing education, like libraries and museums, should be open to all ages; that the educational barriers separating the age groups should be removed.
- That education should help create an easier flow of life for all persons from one endeavor to another; that it be a more universal tool of leverage on the processes of life; that, in particular, the walls between work and education and leisure be torn down.
- That postsecondary education take more forms; but that academic programs remain at the center of attention with the highest prestige and the greatest support.
- That higher education concentrate on academic programs, leaving the quasiacademic and the nonacademic programs largely to others; that it continue as the great source of scholarship and the preeminent leader in terms of high standards of effort.
- That new policies reflecting these goals be developed on financing, accreditation, and coordination.
- That the "learning society" can be a better society.[11]

The recommendations are powerful ones. They reflect the concept of continuing education, that is, learning throughout life. The adult education now under way is only a beginning toward continuing education. Continuing education has been defined as "a way of life—namely that of a single, vital, genetic, developmental continuity."[12] It embraces the notion that education is qualitative as well as quantitative—that it can lead to a quality life for all, that education is more than increasing one's storehouse of knowledge.

The declining birth rate combined with the trend for increased longevity has resulted in increases in the percentages of older adults (sixty-five and older) and middle aged adults (fifty to sixty-four). In the next decade, those persons born during the baby boom following World War II will be moving into the young-middle age adult category (thirty-five to forty-nine) increasing the percentage of our population in that category. The percentage increases in children and teen-agers will continue to be smaller than those in the under thirty-five category. These population tendencies, along with the economic and social factors previously mentioned, point up the compelling need for adult education programs. Societal conditions seem right for the implementation of the concept of continuous education—developmental in nature, for all who desire more education with freedom and easy access. "Drop-ins" should be welcome.

While adult education took on many forms early in our history, the beginning of the modern era of the organized movement occurred in 1926 with the formation of the American Association for Adult Education. This organization later merged with the Department of Adult Education of the National Education Association to form the Adult Education Association of the U.S.A. Much of the inspiration and support to organize adult education came from the Carnegie Corporation and its president, Frederick P. Keppel.

Alternative Education

Alternative education has been available for many years in this nation through the vehicle of private or parochial education. Parents who were dissatisfied in one way or another with public schools organized private schools. Frequently private schools were formed because of religious reasons. In the late sixties and early seventies there was renewed pressure for alternative education, a pressure also inspired to some extent by dissatisfaction with public schools. As such, many alternative schools were started with a negative ideology, that is, the initiators "know what they did not like about traditional schools—bigness, regimentation, tracking, passive learning and student powerlessness."[13] At the same time, since the dissatisfaction is multifaceted, private schools were started with either too many goals, unclear goals, or in some cases no goals. Their founders frequently ". . . emphasize process, believing that things will work out naturally when everybody 'gets it together,' believing that, in the absence of the restrictions of traditional schooling, students and staff alike will immediately embrace or create new patterns of interaction and become the new man, the new woman.[14]

Gross has conceptualized alternative education as the third step in the movement of change in American education. Prior to alternative education, the change movement went through the innovative period of the mid-fifties, followed by the radical reform efforts of the late sixties and early seventies.[15] Writers such as John Holt, Paul Goodman, George Leonard, Peter Marin, and Edgar Friedenberg have all castigated the existing public school system in a variety of ways.

Alternative schools have been organized both within the outside of the public school system. The trend today seems to be toward alternative schools within the existing school structure. In some alternative schools within the system the human and physical resources of the cities are the environment for education. Students "study" in businesses, museums, universities, social agencies, and with a number of community groups and individuals. They may even have some classes at "headquarters." Counseling is an integral part of these programs. These programs and others like them are described in detail in educational periodicals and popular magazines.

The alternative school movement has resulted in providing options within and outside the public school system for those who want different programs. Successful developments regarding alternative learning programs are sure to find their way into the mainstream of American education within the near future.

Private Education

As was mentioned earlier, private education has been available for many years as an alternative to the public schools. Most frequently private schools have been founded and sponsored by religious groups, with Roman Catholic schools having far greater enrollments than other religious schools. Total enrollment in nonpublic or private schools decreased by about 28 percent between 1965 and 1975.[16] Much of this decline was due to a decrease in enrollments in Roman Catholic schools, from approximately 5.6 million in 1965–75 to 3.3 million in 1977–78.[17] During this same period of time non-Catholic nonpublic school enrollment increased from about 615,000 to 1.4 million or approximately 134.7 percent.[18] Enrollments in fundamentalist schools increased from approximately 160,000 to 347,000.

The reasons for this dramatic surge of growth in fundamentalist schools was partially explained by parents in a recent study asking why they withdrew their children from public schools: poor academic quality, lack of discipline, and the fact that public schools were seen as promoting a philosophy of secular humanism that these parents found inimical to their religious beliefs.[19] Many evangelical Protestants have come to believe that the public schools espouse a philosophy that is completely secular, perhaps even antireligious.[20] It is likely that the overall back to basics movement has also spawned much of this growth along with the efforts of the so-called "moral majority," an active fundamentalist-religious group in the late 1970s and early 1980s.

While some people may disagree with the fundamentalist school movement, it is clearly within the rights of parents to establish private schools (*Pierce* v. *Society of the Sisters, 1925)*. The same legal precedent also made it clear that a state may regulate all schools, public and private, and require the teaching of specific subjects. It is also pertinent to note that some people also disagreed with the concepts of the more "liberal" alternative schools referred to earlier in this chapter. The public schools, as successful as they have been over the years, cannot meet the expectations of all people. Private schools are an alternative.

A study was conducted in 1980 to help determine the role that private schools should play in American education.[21] Readers should recognize that the information provided herein is from a draft report summarizing major findings. The draft report provoked debate on both the analyses and conclusions of the study. Two conclusions that the authors of the report made with relatively strong convictions were that (1) private schools produce better cognitive outcomes than public schools, with the caveat that "despite extensive statistical controls on parental backgrounds, there may very well be other unmeasured factors in the self selection into the private sector that are associated with higher achievement,"[22] and (2) private schools provide a safer, more disciplined, and more ordered environment than do public schools.[23]

The role of private education in America was and still is an important one. We had private nursery schools, kindergartens, elementary schools, secondary schools, and colleges before any of them were accepted in the public domain. In a sense the expectations of a few people were met through private means, before they became the expectations of many and gained public acceptance. In this sense, private schools provide a seed bed for innovative activity.

Summary
As the organizational patterns of the past evolved from the needs and expectations of individuals and society, we can expect that the patterns of the future will arise from these same sources. Educators and citizens must be perceptive in order to recognize and delineate their goals, and then effective in designing patterns of organization to meet those goals. Teachers should not only expect change; they should be agents of change.

Point of View

This chapter concluded with a brief discussion of private education. As was mentioned elsewhere in this book, private education has always been an important part of American education. The percentage of students attending nonpublic elementary and secondary schools, however, has dropped from 13.6 percent in 1961 to 10.1 percent in 1971; in 1979 it rose to approximately 12.3 percent. During this entire period of time the Roman Catholic schools, the largest enrollment segment of private schools, decreased in enrollment, while the enrollment in nonpublic, non-Catholic schools was increasing. A large portion of the growth in nonpublic, non-Catholic schools has been in protestant fundamentalist schools. The article by Nordin and Turner, in addition to supplying enrollment data, provides research information on the growth and the reasons for the growth of protestant fundamentalist schools.

More than Segregation Academies: The Growing Protestant Fundamentalist Schools

Virginia Davis Nordin and William Lloyd Turner

The most rapidly growing segment of American elementary and secondary education is that of private Protestant fundamentalist schools. The percentage of students attending nonpublic elementary and secondary schools in the U.S. declined from 13.6% in 1961 to 10.1% in 1971 (the most recent year for which figures are available).[1] This decline was due almost entirely to a decrease in the enrollment of Roman Catholic schools. Roman Catholic enrollment reached a peak of 5,600,519 in the 1964–65 academic year; it had declined to 3,364,000 by 1976–77, or 40%.[2]

During the same period, the enrollment in non-Catholic, nonpublic schools was increasing. Between 1965 and 1975 the number of students enrolled in such schools increased from 615,548 to 1,433,000, or 134.4%, according to an estimate by the Bureau of the Census.[3] Total enrollment of all nonpublic schools has declined 22.7% during the years 1965–1975, according to these estimates.[4] This increase has been unevenly distributed among non-Catholic populations. While Lutheran school enrollment remained relatively stable

during the decade and Adventist and Christian Reformed schools experienced slight declines,[5] the so-called "Christian" or fundamentalist schools grew rapidly. Exact figures for these schools are difficult to obtain, as they do not all belong to one central organization as is the case with Catholic schools. The majority of such schools, however, belong to one of four major organizations: the National Association of Christian Schools, the American Association of Christian Schools, the Association of Christian Schools International, and Christian Schools International. Enrollment in the schools holding membership in these four organizations has increased from 159,916 in 1971 to 349,679 in 1977, or 118%.[6]

Although both the number of fundamentalist schools and the number of students enrolled in them appear to be increasing rapidly in virtually all sections of the U.S., few reliable figures are available, nor do we know much about their methods of operation or the quality of education they provide.[7] In several states fundamentalist schools have filed suit to prevent the collection of these data; in most states regulation of nonpublic schools is not attempted.

Many authors have charged that these "Christian" schools are only a new type of segregation academy, similar to those that sprang up in the South after passage of the 1965 Civil Rights Act. These "new segregation academies" are said to be adopting a religious guise in order to claim First Amendment guarantees of religious protection and thus escape federal

Source: Virginia Davis Nordin and William Lloyd Turner, "More Than Segregation Academies: The Growing Protestant Fundamentalist Schools," *Phi Delta Kappan,* vol. 61, no. 6, February, 1980, pp. 391–93.

1. National Center for Education Statistics, *Statistics of Non-Public Elementary and Secondary Schools,* 1971–1972 (Washington, D.C.: NCES, 1973), pp. 5,6.
2. Department of Health, Education, and Welfare, *Statistics of Public Elementary and Secondary Day Schools* (Washington, D.C.: National Center for Education Statistics, 1976), p. 47.
3. Ibid., p. 6.
4. Ibid.

5. National Union of Christian Schools, *1977–1978 Directory* (Grand Rapids, Mich.: NUCS, 1978), p. 21.
6. Based on a telephone interview with Herman Van Schuyver, executive director of the National Association of Christian Schools, 25 September 1978.
7. While total enrollment figures for fundamentalist schools are not available, enrollment in those schools belonging to the four largest fundamentalist school organizations (American Association of Christian Schools, Association of Christian Schools International, National Association of Christian Schools, and Christian Schools International) increased by 118.7% from 1971 to 1977 (the most recent year for which figures are available). The number of member schools in these organizations has increased by 144.8% during the same period.

desegregation regulations.[8] But research conducted in early 1979 on fundamentalist schools in Kentucky and Wisconsin disputes this claim and suggests that the factors producing this new wave of fundamentalist schools are more complex than previously supposed.[9]

This research shows that fundamentalist schools are growing rapidly in both states at present. The number of fundamentalist schools in Kentucky had increased from eight in 1969 to 33 in 1978, or 313%. In Wisconsin the number increased from five to 26 during the same period—420%. Enrollment in Kentucky fundamentalist schools increased from 787 in 1969 to 4,090 in 1978, or 420%. In Wisconsin fundamentalist enrollments increased from 426 in 1969 to 1,592 in 1978, or 274%.[10] This study also found that 72% of Kentucky and 50% of Wisconsin fundamentalist schools did not belong to any national "Christian" school organization, suggesting that the total number of students enrolled in fundamentalist schools in the U.S. is substantially larger than the totals reported by the four national organizations.

While some of the Kentucky schools appear to have profited by widespread public opposition to racial integration, the growth of fundamentalist schools in rural Wisconsin, where integration is not a factor, indicates that "Christian" education is a national, not a regional, phenomenon. Unlike the "segregation academies" that appeared in the South, these schools do not appear to attract students from a cross section of the community. Parents who enroll their children in these schools tend to come from churches of the sponsoring denomination or from churches holding similar doctrinal positions. The parents and students who patronize them are regular in church attendance and participate actively in the life of their congregations.

As part of the above research, William Turner analyzed two fundamentalist schools in Louisville, Kentucky, and one such school in Madison, Wisconsin. Approximately 20 of these schools have been founded in Louisville during the past decade, and it is frequently asserted that they are being used as one-year "havens" by parents wishing to avoid forced busing. This research does not support that assertion, as the percentage of students in the two fundamentalist schools who were subject to busing during the current school term was smaller than the percentage of such students in the general population. Furthermore, the average student in the survey was found to have been enrolled in his or her present school for a period of four years. Only one of the 68 families surveyed in the Louisville fundamentalist schools was using the nonpublic schools as a "haven" to avoid busing for one year.

While there is no question that nonpublic enrollments in Louisville have increased substantially since the implementation of forced busing in the fall of 1975, families who are entering the nonpublic sector are not doing so on a one-year basis. This research found that once parents had decided to leave the public sector of education, they usually withdrew all of their school-age children simultaneously; and once they had entered the nonpublic sector they tended to remain there for the duration of their children's school careers. There was also little tendency to move from one nonpublic school to another. The majority of persons surveyed also indicated their willingness and ability to continue bearing the cost of nonpublic tuitions for the foreseeable future.

8. "In the past year, die-hard segregationists who are the parents of school-age children have financed the opening of almost 50 new 'Christian Academies' (in North Carolina). . . ." Harry Golden, *The Nation,* 22 December 1969, p. 697. See also David Nevin and Robert E. Bills, *The Schools That Fear Built* (Washington, D.C.: Acropolis Books, 1976).
9. William Lloyd Turner, "Reasons for Enrollment in Religious Schools: A Case Study of Three Recently Established Fundamentalist Schools in Kentucky and Wisconsin" (Doctoral dissertation, University of Wisconsin, Madison, 1979).
10. It should be noted that these data are based on a response rate of 50% from Kentucky schools and 35% from Wisconsin schools. This underscores the difficulty of collecting such data, and the reluctance of these schools to reveal any information about their educational programs.

Although the two cities surveyed are geographically distant and have differing cultural backgrounds, fundamentalist parents in both gave the same reasons for withdrawing their children from public schools. Most frequently they alleged poor academic quality of public education, a perceived lack of discipline in public schools, and the fact that public schools were believed to be promulgating a philosophy of secular humanism that these parents found inimical to their religious beliefs.

While both parents and administrators of "Christian" schools in both states insisted that they were not opposed to integrated education, it was found that more than 95% of the students enrolled in fundamentalist schools in these states are white; fewer than 2% are black. No black teachers were employed by fundamentalist schools in either state.

The segregated nature of these schools might merely reflect the segregated nature of the sponsoring churches, or it could be a reflection of divergent values in the black and white communities, since respondents indicated that the only blacks who would be permitted to enroll were "those who are willing to abide by our standards." A more basic issue than integrated schools, it appears, is integrated marriage. All respondents from both states strongly opposed interracial marriage, although their reasons for doing so remain unclear.

The majority of students enrolled in these schools also seem to come from relatively stable home backgrounds. Most of the families surveyed could be characterized as middle income (the average family income was $25,000); 89 of the 91 families surveyed owned their own homes. Only two of the 91 families surveyed had experienced divorce and remarriage, while the divorce rate in the general population is one in two.

While there are relatively few of these schools at present, their potential for growth is considerable, both in number and in enrollment. Baptist schools comprised the largest group of schools in both states. Baptist churches in the U.S. had a total membership in excess of 25 million in 1975, and are the largest Protestant body in this country.[11] When other fundamentalist groups that operate schools are added to the Roman Catholics, Lutherans, Adventists, and various Jewish groups engaged in nonpublic education, it is apparent that the impact on public education would be considerable should they withdraw even a slightly larger percentage of their children from the public schools. Any significant trend in this direction could make it far more difficult for public school districts to pass tax referenda and approve bond issues.[12] Furthermore, this trend would be accelerated should any of the tuition tax credit plans now before Congress be enacted.

There is little or no regulation of nonpublic schools in most states, and fundamentalist groups are resisting attempts to impose any.[13] While this resistance has been successful to date, the issue has not been finally resolved, and it seems likely to be a source of continued controversy. For related reasons, these schools will continue to resist data collection concerning their growth.

The motivation for founding and maintaining nonpublic schools appears to be more than racial prejudice. In recent decades religious influences in American public education have eroded rapidly. Many evangelical Protestants have come to believe that the public schools now espouse a philosophy that is completely secular, perhaps even antireligious. Hence

11. Frank S. Mead, *Handbook of Denominations in the United States*, 6th ed. (Nashville, Tenn.: Abingdon Press, 1975), p. 32.
12. Albert Shanker, president of the American Federation of Teachers, stated his belief that a loss of as little as 5%–7% of students of these schools would severely "cripple" public schools by depriving them of their best-motivated students and parents. *Education Daily*, 17 January 1979, p. 1.
13. Fundamentalists successfully challenged the right of the state to regulate their schools in Ohio (*Ohio v. Whisner*, 351 N.E. 2d 750, Ohio, 1976) and Vermont [*Vermont v. Lebarge*, 134 Vt. 276 (1976)]. Similar challenges are under way in Kentucky (*Kentucky State Board of Education v. Hinton*, Franklin Circuit Court, Division 1, Civil Action No. 88314, 1978) and North Carolina (*State of North Carolina v. Columbus Christian Academy et al.*, 78—OVS—1678).

many conservative Protestants have withdrawn their children from public schools and have established sectarian schools with quite different standards and curricula.

Fundamentalist educators perceive a basic philosophical difference between themselves and the leaders of public education. Like the seventeenth-century Puritans, they believe in the "innate depravity of man." Because they believe that the corrupt nature of humanity can be changed only through a supernatural infusion of Divine grace, religious "conversion" becomes the basis of all education. Furthermore, since human nature is utterly depraved, children require strict supervision and authoritarian guidance if they are not to be overcome by Satan and the evil within their own nature.

Fundamentalists see public education, by contrast, as proceeding on John Dewey's conviction that human nature is basically good, that students will naturally seek the highest and best if left to themselves, and that the adversary is therefore not Satan or an evil nature but poverty, ignorance, and prejudice. Fundamentalists try to approach the educational task from a different philosophical perspective, using different methodology and pursuing different goals.

Because they perceive that the Protestant ethic has disappeared from public education philosophy, fundamentalists have voiced an increasing nostalgia and a desire to return to the practices of former days. One hears frequent references to the "old-time religion," "old-fashioned" virtues, and the "faith of our fathers." This has produced schools that attempt to recreate the environment of past generations. "Rock" music, movies, and most television programs are forbidden; hair and clothing styles resemble those of a bygone era; textbooks stress "traditional" concepts in math, while education gets "back to the basics." Sex roles are sharply defined, and school policies are enforced through the administration of corporal punishment by an authoritarian teacher or principal.

Like the Amish, with whom they share a common origin, fundamentalists seek the security of the past and have rejected the values of modern society in favor of an earlier and simpler mode of life. This similarity was acknowledged by courts in Kentucky and Ohio, which have granted fundamentalist schools an exemption from state regulation similar to that earlier accorded the Amish.[14]

While the Amish are readily identified as a distinct cultural group by the fact that they live in separate communities, reject modern technology, and dress in a distinctive manner, the fundamentalist subculture is less readily apparent. Fundamentalists are dispersed through the larger community, accept most modern technology, and dress in a more conventional (though distinctive) manner. However, like the Amish, they comprise a distinctive cultural group based on religious beliefs. Also, like the Amish, their practice of religion extends to virtually all areas of life. The Kentucky District Court took note of this fact in a recent case involving regulation of private schools, saying:

> In the face of truancy charges leveled by the state, what is shown by these plaintiffs . . . is a sober and devout belief that their religious faith should and does pervade every aspect of their lives, their churches, and their schools.[15]

Earlier research has failed to grasp this point. Focusing only on the issue of race, researchers have confused fundamentalist religious schools with segregationist academies and have failed to discover the true nature of fundamentalist education. While fundamentalist schools deny that they discriminate on the basis of race, they admit that they discriminate on the

14. *Kentucky State Board of Education v. Hinton, supra; Ohio v. Whisner, supra.*
15. *Kentucky State Board of Education v. Hinton, supra.*

basis of religion, and they feel that they have a constitutional right to do so. They cannot recruit mathematical quotas of students randomly from the larger community, as advocated by the Internal Revenue Service, when their institutions are based on religious adherence. In view of the predominantly religious nature of their schools, fundamentalists feel that they are entitled to the same exemption from federal regulations accorded the Amish and other religious groups.

In their 1953 study, *The Small Town in Mass Society,* Arthur Vidich and Joseph Bensman found that the only ties fundamentalists had to the larger community were political and educational.[16] In this context, the development of religious schools by fundamentalist churches may be viewed as representing a severing of the educational tie and as another step in their withdrawal from the community and from modern society. This withdrawal seems likely to continue and even accelerate, as fundamentalists remain locked into rigid, theologically based positions on many issues while American society moves forward. As this occurs, it seems likely that increasing numbers of fundamentalist parents will withdraw their children from public schools.

As this process accelerates, and we believe it will, American education must assess the impact on society of the withdrawal of large numbers of students from public education. The courts must weigh the parents' right to direct the religious upbringing of their children against the rights of the children as citizens to know, to be exposed to a wide diversity of viewpoints, and to join the mainstream of American society. As is true with all cultural minorities, the relationship of fundamentalists to the larger society presents both a problem and a challenge. At issue is the right to maintain cultural diversity in an increasingly complex and interdependent society.

In the early days of our republic, Henry David Thoreau wrote, "If a man does not keep pace with his companions, perhaps it is because he hears a different drummer. Let him step to the music which he hears, however measured or far away."[17]

Fundamentalists are listening to a different drummer, and they are marching resolutely toward the values of their past. While their right to do so is beyond dispute, one may question whether they should take a growing percentage of America's youth there with them.

Questions for Discussion

1. Do you anticipate that the numbers of children enrolling in nursery schools will continue to grow rapidly? Why?

2. How are the developmental tasks specified as kindergarten goals applicable to other levels in the organizational hierarchy?

3. Is individualized instruction possible in mass education as it exists in the United States today? Why?

4. What is the rationale for teaching the educable mentally handicapped child in a regular classroom rather than in a special education classroom?

5. What purposes do alternative schools serve?

Supplemental Learning Activities

1. Visit a middle school looking specifically for evidence pertaining to its purpose.

2. Visit a nursery school to observe the specifics as to how the developmental goals are being accomplished.

16. Arthur J. Vidich and Joseph Bensman, *The Small Town in Mass Society* (Princeton, N.J.: Princeton University Press, 1968), p. 255.

17. Henry David Thoreau, *Walden,* XVIII (1854).

3. Interview a nursery school teacher to determine why the children are in attendance, and in so doing look for a relationship to social forces.

4. Invite a community college official to your class to discuss the relationship of the community college to the community.

5. Visit an alternative school, seeking to determine how its purposes differ from those of traditional schools.

Notes

1. Galen J. Saylor and William M. Alexander, *Curriculum Planning* (New York: Holt, Rinehart and Winston, Inc., 1954), p. 356. Used by permission.

2. Sylvester Kohut, Jr., *The Middle School: A Bridge Between Elementary and Secondary Schools* (Washington, D.C.: National Education Association, 1980), p. 7.

3. Marjorie Watson, *Mainstreaming with Special Emphasis on the Mentally Retarded* (Washington, D.C.: National Education Association, 1977), p. 7.

4. Ibid.

5. Ibid., p. 16.

6. Ibid., pp. 10–11.

7. W. Vance Grant and Leo J. Eiden, *Digest of Educational Statistics,* 1980. National Center for Educational Statistics. (Available from U.S. Government Printing Office, Washington, D.C. 20402.)

8. Carnegie Commission on Higher Education, *Toward a Learning Society,* p. 15. Copyright McGraw-Hill Book Co., 1973. Used by permission.

9. Grant and Eiden, *Digest of Educational Statistics,* 1980, p. 167.

10. Ibid.

11. Carnegie Commission, *Toward a Learning Society,* p. 15.

12. Maxwell H. Goldberg, Continuous Education as a Way of Life," *Adult Education* 16 (Autumn 1965): 6.

13. Robert C. Riordan, *Alternative Schools in Action* (Bloomington, Ind.: Phi Delta Kappa Foundation, 1972), p. 39.

14. Ibid.

15. Ronald Gross, "From Innovations to Alternatives: A Decade of Change in Education," *Phi Delta Kappan,* September 1971, pp. 22–24.

16. Virginia Davis Nordin and William Lloyd Turner, "More than Segregation Academies: The Growing Protestant Fundamentalist Schools," *Phi Delta Kappan,* vol. 61, no. 6, February 1980, p. 391.

17. Ibid.

18. Ibid.

19. Ibid., p. 392.

20. Ibid., p. 392.

21. Coleman, James, Thomas Hoffer, and Sally Kilgore. *Public and Private Schools* (a draft report to the National Center for Educational Statistics under Contract No. 300–78–0208 by the National Opinion Research Center). March, 1981. Available from Educational Research Service, Inc., 1800 North Kent Street, Arlington, Virginia 22209.

22. Ibid. p. xx

23. Ibid. p. xxii

Selected References

Cross, Patricia K. "Our Changing Students and Their Impact on Colleges: Prospects for a True Learning Society," *Phi Delta Kappan.* Vol. 61, no. 9, May 1980, pp. 627–30.

Fantini, Mario D. *Alternative Education: A Source Book for Parents, Teachers, Students, and Administrators.* New York: Anchor Press, Doubleday, 1976.

Goodlad, John I. *What Schools are For.* Bloomington, Indiana: Phi Delta Kappa Foundation, 1979.

Harrington, Fred Harvey. *The Future of Adult Education.* San Francisco: Jossey-Bass, 1977.

Hass, Glen. *Curriculum Planning: A New Approach.* Boston: Allyn and Bacon, 1980.

Kohut, Sylvester, Jr. *The Middle School: A Bridge Between Elementary and Secondary Schools.* Washington, D.C.: National Education Association, 1980.

Nordin, Virginia Davis, and Turner, William Lloyd. "More Than Segregation Academies: The Growing Protestant Fundamentalist Schools," *Phi Delta Kappan.* Vol. 61, no. 6, February 1980, pp. 391–94.

Sandberg, Lucille, and Swedlow, Rita. *Early Childhood Education: A Guide for Observation and Participation.* Boston: Allyn and Bacon, 1980.

Sergiovanni, Thomas; Burlingame, Martin; Coombs, Fred; and Thurston, Paul. *Educational Governance and Administration.* Englewood Cliffs, New Jersey: Prentice-Hall, Inc., 1980.

Watson, Marjorie. *Mainstreaming with Special Emphasis on the Educable Mentally Retarded.* Washington, D.C.: National Education Association, 1977.

The Control of American Education

16

This Chapter

- Presents the roles and interrelationships of federal, state and local governments in American education.
- Explains the federal role in education particularly as it relates to the protection of individual rights under the Constitution of the United States, and in using federal aid under the general welfare clause to utilize education as a vehicle in resolving domestic and foreign issues.
- Points out the role of Congress in the area of civil and human rights, particularly in respect to the privacy of educational records and the rights of women.

- Describes education as a function of the state, and discusses the roles of the various state controlling bodies.
- Evaluates the operation of education by local school districts in terms of both strengths and weaknesses.
- Identifies the impact of the increased role of the federal judiciary, federal and state legislation, teacher power, and parent power in the operation of local school districts.
- Provides a point of view describing the loss of control by local school boards.

The educational system of the United States is unique among the nations of the world. In terms of control, its most distinctive feature is decentralization. In other words, local governments have decision-making powers in terms of operating local school systems. Education in the United States is a legal function of state government; however, much of the authority of the separate states has been delegated to local government—more specifically, to local boards of education. The federal government also plays a role which can perhaps best be described as one of an interested party. As the educational system in the United States has developed, the roles of the different levels of government have changed. While education still basically remains a local operation, the participation of state and federal governments has increased. The remainder of this chapter examines the current roles of the various levels of government as they relate to the control and operation of education today in the United States.

Federal Government

The federal government has become involved in education in four different, yet related, ways: (1) the application of the United States Constitution, (2) the function and operation of the Department of Education and the National Institute of Education, (3) the direct operation of educational programs by various agencies of the federal government, and (4) the provision of federal aid in its various forms.

United States Constitution

The United States Constitution is the basic law of the land, and as such has had its effects on education. While no specific mention of education is made in the Constitution, the Tenth Amendment has been interpreted as implying that education is a function of the respective states. This interpretation resulted in the development of fifty

> "The powers not delegated to the United States by the Constitution, nor prohibited by it to the States, are reserved to the States respectively, or to the people.
> *Tenth Amendment United States Constitution.*

> "Congress shall make no law respecting an establishment of religion or prohibiting the free exercises thereof; or abridge the freedom of speech or of the press; or the right of the people peaceably to assemble and to petition the government for redress of grievances."
> *First Amendment United States Constitution*

different state systems of education. Further, it reinforced the type of educational decentralization that had begun to develop in colonial America. While the fifty states are markedly similar in their patterns of education, differences do exist. Examples of differences that exist include: (1) requirements for teacher certification, (2) provisions for financial aid, (3) regulations for compulsory attendance, and (4) provisions for teacher pension plans.

The First and Fourteenth Amendments have also had a definite impact on the administration of education in the United States. The First Amendment insures freedom of speech, religion, the press, and the right of petition. The Fourteenth Amendment provides for the protection of specified privileges of citizens. Based upon these amendments, the Supreme Court of the United States has made many decisions that have influenced the course of education in the United States.

Court Decisions: First and Fourteenth Amendments

Court decisions based upon the First Amendment have been particularly influential in clarifying the relationship between religion and education. There have been a number of these decisions, and basically they can be classified into three groups: (1) those having to do with the rights of parents to educate their children in private schools, (2) those having to do with the use of public funds to support private education, and (3) those

having to do with the teaching or practice of religion in the public schools.

An important case influential in determining the rights of parents to provide education for their children was the Oregon case. Briefly, in 1922 the legislature of Oregon passed a law requiring all children to attend public schools. The United States Supreme Court ruled that the law was unconstitutional (*Pierce* v. *Society of Sisters,* 1925). The reasoning of the Court was that such a law denied to parents the rights to control the education of their children. This decision of the Supreme Court in addition to establishing that private schools have a right to exist, and that pupils may meet the requirements of compulsory education by attending private schools, also established that a state may regulate all schools, public and private, and require the teaching of specific subjects. The Oregon decision reinforced a historical tradition of private and sectarian education in the United States and gave further impetus to the development of private schools. Thus, two systems of education, public and private, developed in the United States.

Cases having to do with the use of public funds to support private education are numerous. Prominent among them are the *Cochran* and the *Everson* cases. In *Cochran* v. *Louisiana State Board of Education,* 1930, the United States Supreme Court held that a Louisiana textbook statute that provided for furnishing textbooks purchased with tax-raised fund to private school pupils was valid. The ruling was technically based on the Fourteenth Amendment.

Public education is a function of the states under
the Tenth Amendment of the United States
Constitution.

Many students in rural areas are provided
transportation to their schools.

More recently the United States Supreme Court supported a New York law providing for the free loan of public school books to students in private schools (*Board of Education of Central School District No. 1, Towns of Greenbush et al. v. Allen*, 1968).

The majority opinion stated "The law merely makes available to all children the benefits of a general program to lend school books free of charge. Books are furnished at the request of the pupil and ownership remains, at least technically, in the state. Thus no funds or books are furnished to parochial schools, and the financial benefit is to parents and children, not to schools."

In *Everson* v. *Board of Education,* 1947, the United States Supreme Court held that tax-raised funds in a New Jersey school district could be used to reimburse parents for bus fares expended to transport their children to church schools. The decision of the Court in the *Everson* case was based on a five-to-four vote. These decisions permitting the use of public funds to provide transportation and textbooks for students attending private schools were based in the main on *child benefit theory,* the rationale being that the aid benefited the children and not the school or religion. Child benefit theory, while seemingly becoming an established phenomenon at the federal level, has not been unanimously accepted by the states.

Since the *Everson* v. *Board of Education* decision, the highest courts in a number of states, under provisions in their own constitutions, have struck down enactments authorizing free busing of children attending denominational schools. Other state supreme courts have upheld enactments providing for the use of public funds for the transportation of students to denominational schools.

Two recent cases both originating in Missouri tend to further define the use of public funds for free transportation of parochial school students, and the loaning of textbooks free of charge to parochial school students. In 1975 the United States Supreme Court affirmed a federal district court decision in Missouri (*Luetkemeyer* v. *Kaufman*), noting that although a state may provide free transportation to parochial school students, principles of equal protection do not require a state to do so merely because such services are provided to public school pupils. In 1974 the Missouri Supreme Court held that it was a violation of the state constitution for the state to loan textbooks free of charge to parochial school students. The U.S. Supreme Court denied review of the case, thereby preserving the state court decision. "Thus, although a state *may* lend textbooks to parochial school students, the Court declined to *compel* a state to do so if it is supplying free books to public school pupils."[1]

The matter of the use of public funds for private education is far from settled. Rising costs have made it increasingly difficult for nonpublic schools to survive. As nonpublic schools close, and their pupils enroll in public schools, the financial effort for public schools must be increased.

Equal educational opportunity is an important goal in American education.

Since 1968 many states have introduced legislation providing for a variety of forms of direct aid to nonpublic schools. Legislation originating in Pennsylvania and Rhode Island eventually was ruled upon by the United States Supreme Court. The Court ruled in both the Pennsylvania case (*Lemon* v. *Kurtzman,* 1971) and the Rhode Island case (*DiCenso* v. *Robinson,* 1971) that the respective laws were unconstitutional. The majority opinion stated: "We conclude that the cumulative impact of the entire relationships arising under the statutes in each State involves excessive entanglements between government and religion." Entanglements were anticipated in accomplishing the necessary state supervision to ensure that state aid would support only secular education in nonpublic schools.

After denying other proposals to aid nonpublic school pupils in Pennsylvania and New York, the United States Supreme Court in 1975

(*Wolman* v. *Walter*) did approve parts of a legislative proposal originating in Ohio. The parts approved as being constitutional included providing nonpublic school pupils with books, standardizing testing and scoring, diagnostic services, and therapeutic and remedial services. Proposals for instructional materials and field trip services were ruled unconstitutional. Perhaps the very carefully drafted Ohio legislation will serve as a model for other states. In general, the Ohio law in the opinion of the Supreme Court avoided excessive entanglements between government and education.

The matter of the practice of sectarian religion in public schools has been treated by the United States Supreme Court as recently as 1963. In that instance they ruled that the reading of the Bible and the recitation of the Lord's Prayer are religious ceremonies, and if done in public schools are in violation of the First and Fourteenth Amendments to the Constitution. The decision resulted from the appeals of two lower court decisions, one from Pennsylvania, *Schempp* v. *School District of Abington Township,* and the other from Maryland, *Murray* v. *Curlett.* These earlier decisions had held that reading the Bible and saying the Lord's Prayer were not illegal. In *People of the State of Illinois ex rel. McCollum* v. *Board of Education of School District No. 71, Champaign, Illinois,* 1948, the Supreme Court ruled that release time for religious instruction, with voluntary pupil participation, but conducted on public school property, was a violation of the separation of church and state. In 1952 in *Zorach* v. *Clausen,* the Court upheld a New York statute which provided for release time for religious instruction off the school premises.

The rights assured under the First Amendment have been tested in their relationships to education in areas other than religion. A landmark decision in the area of student rights was made by the United States Supreme Court in 1969 (*Tinker* v. *Des Moines Independent Community School District*). The *Tinker* case centered around a school board's prevention of the wearing of black armbands by students protesting the hostilities in Vietnam. The Court in its majority opinion stated:

. . . the wearing of armbands in the circumstances of this case was entirely divorced from actually or potentially disruptive conduct by those participating in it. It was closely akin to "pure speech" which, we have repeatedly held, is entitled to comprehensive protection under the First Amendment. . . .

It can hardly be argued that either students or teachers shed their constitutional rights to freedom at the schoolhouse gate.

The *Tinker* case has and will undoubtedly affect the age-old doctrine of *in loco parentis*. The in loco parentis doctrine functioned under the traditional notion that schools and teachers could exercise total control over students because they acted as parent substitutes and out of concern for student welfare. Undoubtedly the Court's opinion in the *Tinker* case will have an effect on the operation of schools in the United States.

A most pertinent illustration of the use of the Fourteenth Amendment was the United States Supreme Court decision in *Brown* v. *Board of Education of Topeka,* 1954. The impact of this landmark decision repudiating the separate but equal doctrine is still being felt and reacted to. The judicial pronouncement in this case had legislative power added to it by the Civil Rights Act of 1964.

A number of cases directly related to the *Brown* decision have arisen. Most notable in recent years are those dealing with metropolitan desegregation (Richmond, Virginia; Wilmington, Delaware; Louisville, Kentucky; and Detroit, Michigan). The metropolitan desegregation case arising in Richmond was heard by the United States Supreme Court in 1973. With a 4–4 tie vote, with Justice Powell disqualifying himself, the Court upheld a U.S. Court of Appeals for the Fourth Circuit reversal of the metropolitan plan. In general, the metropolitan plan would have called for the consolidation of the Richmond, Virginia, schools with the suburban Henries and Chesterfield County school systems. Richmond schools were approximately 70 percent black, while the suburban schools were approximately 90 percent white.

In 1974, the United States Supreme Court in *Milliken* v. *Bradley,* in a 5–4 vote overturned lower court orders requiring the cross-busing of children between the Detroit city school system and fifty-three suburban school districts. In effect the Supreme Court said: "Before the boundaries of separate and autonomous school districts may be set aside . . . it must first be shown that there

Busing is one means to achieve desegregation, but most often it is controversial.

has been a constitutional violation within one district that produces a significant segregative effect in another district. . . ." In 1975, metro desegregation orders were upheld in both Wilmington, Delaware, and Louisville, Kentucky. In both instances it was determined, in effect, that school reorganization or interdistrict actions had the effect of maintaining segregation.

In addition to the First, Tenth, and Fourteenth Amendments to the United States Constitution, the Preamble to the Constitution has also had its effect on the development of education in the United States. The phrase "promote the general welfare," known as the *general welfare clause,* has been the basis for much of the federal support of education. The general welfare clause permits the infusion of federal monies into education as seen fit by the Congress.

In summary, the United States Constitution, while it has been interpreted as delegating the function of education to the states, does contain within it protection for the rights of individuals, which must not be violated in the operation of education by states and local districts.

Federal Legislation

In addition to court decisions, federal legislation has decided effects on local school districts. In the last five years, the Buckley Amendment, Title IX, and Public Law 94–142 have had significant impacts. Public Law 94–142, Education for All Handicapped Children Act, has been discussed elsewhere.

The First Amendment to the United States
Constitution guarantees freedom of speech.

Buckley Amendment—Privacy of Educational Records

The Buckley Amendment has been federal law since 1974. In essence, it precisely defines who may or may not see individual student records. The Act sets forth the following requirements: (1) allow all parents, even those not having custody of their children, access to each educational record that a school district keeps on their child, (2) establish a district policy on how parents can go about seeing specific records, (3) inform all parents what rights they have under the Amendment, how they can act on these rights according to school policy, and where they can see a copy of the policy, and (4) seek parental permission in writing before disclosing any personally identifiable record on a child to individuals other than professional personnel employed in the district.[2] The Amendment has caused school districts and their teachers and administrators to recognize and implement appropriate procedures in the disclosure of pupil records.

Title IX

The Education Amendments of 1972 make sex discrimination, once a philosophical or moral issue, a legal issue as well. The key provision in Title IX reads: "No person in the United States shall, on the basis of sex, be excluded from participation in, be denied benefits of, or be subjected to discrimination under any educational program or activity receiving federal financial assistance."[3] Any educational institution, public or private, that receives federal monies by way of grant, loan, or contract (other than a contract of insurance of guaranty) is required to comply with Title IX. Schools at all levels are covered, from preschools to graduate schools. Most public schools at all levels, and many private schools receive federal assistance. Title IX covers virtually all areas of student life: admissions, financial aid, health services, sports, testing, differential rules, and the like.[4] The implementation of Title IX, while still evolving, is having decided impacts on education.

Federal Agency Involvement in Education

The United States Office of Education represents a formalized federal effort in education. It was originally established in 1867 as the Federal Department of Education. In 1953, after several changes of names, its title officially became the United States Office of Education, and it became part of the Department of Health, Education, and Welfare with a secretary in the President's cabinet.

In October 1979, the Department of Education was created. The Department will take on the functions of the U.S. Office of Education. The Office collects and publishes information about all phases of education in the United States, engages in conducting and disseminating educational research, provides leadership, and administers much of the federal funding for education. From a meager and mild beginning, the Office of Education, particularly in the last few years, has grown to become a powerful and influential agency.

The new Department of Education was created in a context of political controversy and is still somewhat shaky. Those who favored the creation of the new department felt that education was too important to be lost in the gigantic Department of Health, Education and Welfare.

Opponents took the position that a national Department of Education would result in more federal control and standardization. Most educational groups, however, supported the creation of the department. In addition to the U.S. Office of Education, the new department will have the National Institute of Education, National Center for Educational Statistics, Civil Rights Office (education activities), and the National Science Foundation within its jurisdiction. Shirley Hufstedler, a judge, was named as the first secretary of the department, within a year of her appointment but she was replaced by Terry Bell. The Reagan administration has pledged to eliminate the Department of Education.

Federally Operated Schools

The federal government has accepted responsibility for and directly operates some educational institutions. The Congress provides funds for the operation of the school system of the District of Columbia. The Department of the Interior is responsible for the education of children of National Park Employees, and for outlying possessions (Samoa), and trust territories (Caroline and Marshall Islands). The Bureau of Indian Affairs finances and manages schools on Indian reservations. The Department of Defense is responsible for the four military academies, and also operates a school system for children of military personnel wherever they may be located.

Federal funds have been allocated to science education.

Further, the education given in the various training programs of the military services has made a tremendous contribution to the overall educational effort in our nation.

Federal Financial Support

Federal funding represents a fourth way in which the federal government has become involved in education. Table 16.1 lists some selected illustrative federal acts that have, either directly or indirectly, provided support for education.

The list of federal acts presented in table 16.1, while by no means exhaustive, is illustrative. Some general observations can be made from an examination of the list. It is apparent

that federal funding for education is not a new phenomenon. The 1785 and 1787 Northwest Ordinance Acts encouraged the establishment of education in the Northwest Territory. The Ordinance of 1785 required the reservation of the sixteenth section of each township for the maintenance of schools. Federal funding since this early beginning has increased steadily. It is also apparent that the funding has been categorical—that is, for a specific purpose. Each of the acts listed had or has a purpose. Let it suffice for purposes of illustration to point out that (1) the Morrill Acts and the Hatch Act encouraged expanded agricultural, mechanical, and scientific education in institutions of higher education; (2) the Smith-Lever and Smith-Hughes Acts encouraged vocational education in secondary schools; (3) the CCC, PWA, NYA, and WPA,

Table 16.1 Selected Federal Acts That Have Provided Funds for Education.

1785	Ordinance of 1785
1787	Northwest Ordinance
1862	Morrill Land Grant Act
1887	Hatch Act
1914	Smith-Lever Agriculture Extension Act
1917	Smith-Hughes Vocational Act
1930	Civilian Conservation Corps
1933	Public Works Administration
1935	National Youth Administration
1935	Works Program Administration
1940	Vocational Education for National Defense Act
1941	Lanham Act
1944	G.I. Bill of Rights
1946	National School Lunch Act
1950	National Science Foundation
1954	Cooperative Research Program
1958	National Defense Education Act
1963	Manpower Development and Training Act
1964	Economic Opportunity Act
1965	Elementary and Secondary Education Act
—	Amendments of ESEA
1981	Omnibus Budget Reconciliation Act (Block Grants)

Federal funds have been provided to aid schools in securing sophisticated equipment.

"Religion, morality, and knowledge being necessary to good government and happiness of mankind, schools and the means of education shall forever be encouraged."

Northwest Ordinance, 1787

while in the main designed to alleviate the economic depression of the 1930s, provided incidental aid to education and youth; (4) the NDEA Act specifically affirmed the feelings of Congress toward the importance of education for national defense; and (5) the ESEA provided many thrusts, including efforts to meet the needs of children of poverty and to encourage research. The ESEA was somewhat unique in federal funding legislation in that it came as close to general aid as any federal legislation ever has, and it further provided the means whereby federal tax funds could be made available to private and church-related schools. In a sense it represented an infusion of the judicial child benefit theory attitudes into legislation. ESEA has been regularly extended with amendments since 1965.

A fourth observation that can be made is that federal funding originates and is administered through a number of federal agencies. For example, in addition to the former Department of Health, Education, and Welfare, funds are administered through the new Department of Education, and the Departments of Agriculture, Defense, Housing and Urban Development, Labor, and Interior; and through agencies such as the Office of Economic Opportunity, Veteran's Administration, and the Peace Corps.

Federal Influence: Direct and Subtle

In summary, the federal government is an influential agent in American education. Its influence has been felt directly in terms of protecting individual rights as provided in the Constitution, attaining equality of opportunity for all, promoting general welfare in terms of domestic social and economic problems and national defense, and operating specific educational agencies. Its subtle effect is most strongly exerted through the financial incentives offered to stimulate specific programs. The Reagan administration has pledged to reduce the influence of the federal government in education, and to restore more power to state and local governments.

State Government

Public education in the United States is a state function. States have recognized this function in their respective constitutions and have established laws directing the way in which it shall be conducted. Most states, the exception being Wisconsin, have established state boards of education. The executive duties of administering education at the state level are primarily the responsibility of a state department or office of public instruction. These departments in the various states are headed by a chief executive officer, frequently called the state superintendent of public instruction or the chief state school officer. Let us briefly examine how each of these segments of control and operation at the state level influence education.

State Constitutions

The constitutional provisions of the states for education, while differing slightly in their precise wording, are markedly similar in their intent. An illustrative example is a statement in Section 2, Article VIII, of the Constitution of the State of Michigan. It reads, "The Legislature shall maintain and support a system of free public elementary and secondary schools as defined by law. Each school district shall provide for the education of its pupils without discrimination as to religion, creed, race, color, or national origin." The various state constitutions are interpreted by state courts and legal counsel as conflicts arise. The decisions of state courts may be appealed to the United States Supreme Court. The United States Supreme Court will usually hear the case if in their judgment it is in the domain of the United States Constitution or federal law.

State Legislatures

The enabling legislation to conduct the educational enterprise is prepared by state legislatures. This legislation is usually classified and bound in a volume referred to as the *school code*. Legislation is both mandatory and permissive, and therefore directs and guides local school boards in their task of operating schools. The greater the tendency to enact permissive legislation, the greater the amount of control delegated to the local boards of education. State legislation is concerned with many aspects of education—for example, district organizational patterns, teacher certification and tenure regulations, financing of schools, and attendance laws.

State legislatures, because of their important position in education, are the subject of much lobbying. In the realm of education the laws that they formulate deal with children and money,

Lunch programs are provided in many schools.

both of which are precious to most citizens. Influential lobbying groups may include: taxpayers' federations; patriotic groups; labor, business, and professional organizations; humane societies; and the various organizations concerned directly with education, such as state teachers' associations, school administrator associations, and school board associations.

State Boards of Education

State boards of education concerned with elementary and secondary education are now in operation in forty-nine of the fifty states, with Wisconsin as the exception: however, Wisconsin does have a state board for vocational education, since this is a federal requirement in order to be eligible to receive funds for these activities.

Historically, the prototype of the modernday style of state boards of education was the board established in Massachusetts in 1837. It was the first state board with an appointed secretary—in the person of Horace Mann. Henry Barnard, another pioneer educator, became the first secretary of the Connecticut State Board of Education, and later, after serving in the same capacity in Rhode Island, became the first United States Commissioner of Education.

The duties of state boards of education vary; however, in general, they serve in a policymaking capacity. Policies are formulated and rules and regulations are adopted as are necessary to carry out the responsibilities assigned to state boards by the respective state constitutions and statutes. They submit annual reports, hear appeals resulting from their own rules and regulations, and determine the extent of their own power in accordance with the law. State boards are also regulatory, that is, they establish and enforce standards in such areas as certification of teachers and accreditation of schools. Other duties may be considered as advisory. Such duties may include considering the educational needs of the state, and making recommendations to the governor and the legislature.

Membership on state boards is attained in three ways: election by the people or their representatives, appointment by the governor, or ex officio by virtue of other office held. Table 16.2 provides this information for each state.

It is interesting to note the differences among states as to their preference in methods of selection. Iowa, New York, and Washington are somewhat unique in their elective procedures. In Iowa, conventions of delegates from areas within the state send nominations to the governor, on the basis of which the governor makes the appointment; in New York the Board of Regents is elected by the legislature; and in Washington the state board is elected by members of boards of directors of local school districts. Needless to say, there are advantages and disadvantages to both the elective and the appointive procedures in selecting state school board members. The appointive procedure is considered by its proponents to be more efficient in that it is more likely to establish a harmonious relationship with the governor, and that it facilitates the placement of highly qualified persons who would not for various reasons seek election. The proponents of the elective procedures cite the "grass-roots" control feature, and the lesser likelihood of political manipulation. In either case, once members are selected, they usually have staggered terms to avoid a complete change in membership at any one time; they also usually serve without pay, but with reimbursement for their expenses. Both of these provisions serve as safeguards against political patronage.

Chief State School Officers

The chief state school officer occupies an important position in the administration of education within each respective state. Usually this individual is the executive head of the state department of education, and as such, through the administrative staff of the office, provides leadership and supervisory service in addition to the customary clerical and regulatory functions of state departments of education. The chief state school officer presents interpretations of educational needs to the governor, state board of education, and legislature, and frequently influences legislation, both directly and indirectly. While the provision for the state school officer's duties vary from state to state, the duties are specifically delineated by a combination of the respective state constitution and school code. Chief state school officers are likely to receive direction from the state board of education.

Information as to how chief state school officers are selected is also presented in table 16.2. Currently, nineteen state officers are elected by the people or their representatives, twenty-seven are appointed by state boards of education, and

Table 16.2 Methods of Selection of State School Board Members and Chief State School Officers

State	Members of state boards of education			Chief State School Officers		
	Elected by people or represent. of people	Appointed by governor	Ex officio	Elected by popular vote	Appointed by state board of education	Appointed by governor
Alabama	x				x	
Alaska		x			x	
Arizona		x		x		
Arkansas		x			x	
California		x		x		
Colorado	x				x	
Connecticut		x			x	
Delaware		x			x	
Florida			x	x		
Georgia		x		x		
Hawaii	x				x	
Idaho		x		x		
Illinois		x			x	
Indiana		x		x		
Iowa	x				x	
Kansas	x				x	
Kentucky		x		x		
Louisiana	x			x		
Maine		x			x	
Maryland		x			x	
Massachusetts		x			x	
Michigan	x				x	
Minnesota		x			x	
Mississippi			x	x		
Missouri		x			x	
Montana		x		x		
Nebraska	x				x	
Nevada	x				x	
New Hampshire		x			x	
New Jersey		x				x
New Mexico	x				x	
New York	x				x	
North Carolina		x		x		
North Dakota		x		x		
Ohio	x				x	
Oklahoma		x		x		
Oregon		x		x		
Pennsylvania		x				x
Rhode Island		x			x	
South Carolina	x			x		
South Dakota		x		x		
Tennessee		x				x
Texas	x				x	
Utah	x				x	
Vermont		x			x	
Virginia		x				x
Washington	x			x		
West Virginia		x			x	
Wisconsin	(No state board)			x		
Wyoming		x		x		
Total	16	31	2	19	27	4

four are appointed by the governor. The trend has been away from election and toward appointment, specifically appointment by the state board of education. Arguments advanced in favor of appointment include the notion that policymaking should be clearly differentiated from policy execution; that educational leadership should not depend so heavily on one elected official; and that a greater likelihood exists of recruiting and retaining qualified career personnel. Opponents to the appointment procedure claim that, in the main, the official selected under this system would not be responsible to the people. A major objection raised to gubernatorial appointment is the danger of involvement in partisan politics. It is important to note that an elected state school officer is legally a state "official," while an appointed officer is an "employee." As a result of this difference, the working relationship of an elected official with the state board of education is not likely to be as clear and cleanly defined as it is in instances where the chief state school officer is appointed by the state board of education and therefore clearly an employee.

State Departments of Education
The state departments of education, under the direction of the chief state school officer, carry out the activities of state government in education. Their activities have been classified into five categories: operational, regulatory, service, developmental, and public support and cooperation.[5] Until recent years, their activities have been largely operational and regulatory. Operational activities are those that have to do with the direct operation of schools such as those for the deaf or blind; regulatory activities center around the enforcement of state regulations for schools, such as making certain that only properly certified teachers are employed, and that buildings are safe. The service function has to do with helping local school districts. It includes the sharing of the knowledge and expertise of the state by providing consultant service, research information, or legal advice. Most states have improved their service activities in the past few years. Developmental activities have to do with planning in order to improve the state departments themselves so that they may further develop their capabilities. Public support and cooperation activities involve communicating effectively with the people of the state, the legislature and governor, and other governmental bodies.

While the traditional roles of state departments have emphasized the operational and regulatory functions, the problems of education today indicate that the state departments of education should play a stronger leadership role.

Intermediate Units
The intermediate unit of school organization is that unit between the state department of education and local school districts. Historically, the intermediate unit served a liaison function. In rural areas, with a preponderance of small schools, it also served a direct educational function such as providing guidance or special education services.

Educational issues frequently are discussed in large forums.

The basic purpose of the intermediate unit today is to provide two or more local districts with educational services that they cannot efficiently and economically provide individually. Recently, great strides have been made in this regard, particularly in the providing of special education and vocational-technical education. Area "vo-tech" schools have been aided by relatively high infusions of federal monies. Other examples of services that intermediate units can provide include audiovisual libraries, centralized purchasing, in-service training for teachers and other personnel, health services, instructional materials, laboratories, legal services, and consultant services.

Local School Districts

The agency of control in education most visible to both citizens and teachers is the local school district. The school district is controlled by a governing board made up of citizens residing in the geographical area that makes up the district.

Local school districts, while similar in their major purpose—the education of children—are widely different in their characteristics. There are currently about 16,000 school districts in the United States enrolling approximately 43 million students in elementary and secondary schools.[6] These districts differ in many ways: geographical size; enrollment; geographical location (urban, suburban, rural); socioeconomic composition; heterogeneity and homogeneity; wealth; type of organization (K–8, 9–12, K–12); and in many other ways. Most of the school districts in the United States are small in terms of enrollment. It has been estimated that 27 percent of the districts enroll less than 300 pupils, and that this total enrollment makes up only about 1.2 percent of the total national enrollment. Yet, only about 1.2 percent of the districts have enrollment greater than 25,000, but these districts enroll about 28 percent of the total national enrollment.[7] The trend in school district organization has been to reduce the number of districts to obtain a more effective and efficient organization. The number of districts has been reduced from over 100,000 in 1945 to the current 16,000. Such school reorganization is a slow but inevitable process. Along with consolidation the trend has also been to establish more districts that include both elementary and secondary education (K–12).

While the "putting together" or consolidation of smaller districts is being encouraged, problems have become apparent in very large city systems such as New York, Chicago, and Los Angeles that can be partly attributed to their immense enrollments. Communications in such districts can become distant and distorted. Patrons in such systems often express strong feelings that their districts are not responsive. They are calling for decentralization to enable them to gain some control over their neighborhood schools. Experimental efforts toward decentralization are being made in large urban areas such as New York, Chicago, and Pittsburgh to meet these desires.

Local Control

Local control becomes a reality through the governing boards of local districts. They may make decisions within the power delegated to them by the state. Some of their powers include those to raise monies; obtain sites; build buildings; provide curricula; employ teachers and other personnel; and admit and assign pupils to schools. Local school boards must conform to mandatory statutes, and operate within powers delegated to them. It is within their power to enact local policies for education providing those policies do not violate existing state laws. Board members are local people. Ninety-five percent of them throughout the United States are elected by popular vote, most frequently in special elections on a nonpartisan basis; the remaining 5 percent are appointed. Appointed boards occur most often in school districts enrolling over 25,000 pupils.

Local control is a characteristic that can be either advantageous or disadvantageous. The local school district, represented in person by board members, often provides the closest relationship that many citizens have with a local form of government. The administration of local schools concerns people deeply, dealing directly as it does with their children. Schools also frequently represent the agency that collects the largest amount of local tax monies. Further, education is viewed by more and more citizens as the most practical way to resolve social problems, particularly at the grass root level. There is little doubt that local control permits citizens to have their say in providing school programs that will be responsive to their local desires and needs. Conversely, local control also permits wide variances in educational opportunity. Local control historically has been conservative and provincial, each district's concern being for their own welfare without a strong regard for state or national problems. It can be argued, for example, that one

Local citizens may exhibit strong feelings about their schools and educational issues.

factor, the mobility of our population, is sufficient reason to support greater centralization. Further, national domestic problems and our national defense require national policies and programs to be implemented in local schools. Social and economic trends in the last few years have resulted in a gradual erosion of local control of schools.

Local Schools

Local schools can be the subject of much controversy. Controversy can originate over a program such as sex education, a change in attendance center boundaries, textbooks, methods of discipline, or losing too many athletic contests. It may be stirred up because more emphasis is put on athletics than on music or art, or not enough emphasis on basic subjects. Sometimes the dismissal or transfer of a principal or teacher brings out very strong feelings. Controversy may even result from the enforcement of a federal or state mandate that the local citizens don't agree with. The focus of the controversy is usually the members of the board of education—the elected representatives of the people.

Members of boards of education cannot avoid politics as many of them would wish to do. Their election or reelection depends on how well the people feel they are representing them, and how successful the schools are in educating their children. Board membership is frequently a thankless task at best. Yet, many board members enjoy their service, and many of them do a great job in providing direction for local schools—the essence of local control.

Erosion of Local Control It is obvious that local boards of education do not have the control they once had. Court decisions and federal legislation cited earlier have been a significant factor in this loss of local control. Another major factor has been the increasing power of teachers and their associations. A third thrust, parent power, has just recently been exerted. Parents want a much stronger voice in education, particularly in relation to school programs and high taxes. Their apparent immediate target is the local district board of education. Parents feel that they are being locked out of collective bargaining sessions that are determining a widening range of education policies.[8]

Teacher Power

There was a time in our history when teachers for all practical purposes had little or no influence in determining the conditions of their employment, let alone enough power to influence educational policies. In recent years, however, teachers have begun to exert their power through their professional organizations. Local teacher groups are affiliated with national organizations, namely the the National Education Association or the American Federation of Teachers. The topic of professional organizations and their roles in teacher power was considered in an earlier chapter. Let it suffice to say at this point that today teachers do have power.

Teacher power is manifested at the local district level by the use of a local organization to press for collective bargaining. While the term *collective bargaining* has been defined in many ways, in terms of power it means a formalization of access procedures to the legally defined school power structure. Physically it results in a written document, called an *agreement,* which most frequently spells out conditions of employment. The question of what is and what is not negotiable has not yet been clearly defined. It ranges from the broad definition of everything that affects a teacher, including curriculum, textbooks, in-service training, student teaching programs and many other items, to a narrow limitation considering just salaries. In some states the legislature has clearly defined the subject matter for negotiation while in other states the issue is still wide open. Teacher groups have been extremely powerful in lobbying for and against various negotiation bills at the state level.

The power that teachers have gained they have gained through organization. Their ultimate weapon has been a work stoppage or strike, which incidentally is not considered under the traditional judicial view as being legal. Nevertheless, the number of teacher strikes has steadily increased.

Teachers have asked for, and in some cases demanded, a share in educational decision making. In some cases these requests have been formalized, and in a sense legitimatized as a part of a negotiations agreement. In general, teachers have expressed disagreement and resistance to the traditional flow of authority for decision making from the top down. They have been asking to be heard as citizens and as responsible, trained professionals. Their voices are being heard today. As they collectively speak, they should be constantly aware of their responsibilities—responsibilities that they have as citizens and educators for the destinies of children and our society. If their actions and their use of power are perceived by many citizens as being irresponsible, which they are in some instances, it is likely that the power of the general public will be exerted as a counterthrust, as it has been in some instances. The ultimate power for education in a democratic nation resides in the people.

Federal-State-Local Interrelationships
The federal-state-local relationships of the past evolved as our country grew and developed. As our nation changed from basically a sparsely populated and agrarian society to an urban industrialized society, the nature of the federal-state-local relationship changed. While the states have been and still are the major source of legal control, the federal government has increased its influential and legal roles, particularly in efforts to assure constitutional rights and to respond to both foreign and domestic issues. The federal government's response to domestic problems that relate to education, such as poverty and segregation, and its tendency to attack such problems quite directly, rather than channel its efforts through state agencies, has at least in part caused state school officials to organize to have their views heard. The Education Commission of the State was formed and currently has many states as members. The defined purpose of the organization is to further a working relationship among state governors, legislators, and educators for the improvement of education. It is interesting to note that ECS is now playing a major role in national assessment, a project designed to assess educational achievement on a nationwide basis.

New federal-state-local relationships are emerging. Each level of government tends to look at the purposes of education from its own perspective: local school districts see their immediate local needs; states, the welfare of the state and its overall constituency; the federal government, its concern with equality, national security, and national domestic problems. While it is difficult to predict what the future relationships will be, it is clear that educational purposes and problems that are not resolved at the local level are likely to be taken on by another level of government. The problems that we face seem to be of a magnitude that make state and federal involvement necessary to resolve them. A new federal-state-local educational partnership is necessary and is emerging to forge solutions to problems of and related to education.

Point of View

Over the years the relationships of the federal, state, and local governments in respect to the control of education have changed. One result of the change has been a reduction of the decision-making options or power of local boards of education. Court decisions, along with legislation in the areas of civil and human rights as provided for in the United States Constitution, have caused local school boards to adopt policies and implement procedures in harmony with the Constitution and the constitutions of the respective states. Teachers' organizations, by their power, have also succeeded in gaining more control in the educational arena. As more funds have become available at the state level, more control over local education has followed. What should the role of local boards of education be in the governance of education?

Lee Davies, in the article "The School Board's Struggle to Survive," has addressed the issue of the role of local boards of education in the governance of education. Davies provides a contemporary analysis of the issue and suggests that the price of local control is high.

The School Board's Struggle to Survive

Lee K. Davies

> The School Board . . . is elected by the people of the county to represent them in determining policy and rules and regulations covering the entire school system. The School Board is held responsible under . . . law and by

the citizens . . . to see that an effective educational program is conducted. Its prime function is to represent the people by establishing policy. The School Board shall operate, control, and supervise all free public schools within the School District and determine the rate of District taxes within the limits prescribed by law.[1]

This is the *stated* role of Florida's Orange County School Board, on which I have served since January 1969. But, is the sanctioned, authoritative role of the Orange County Board and others like it truth or fiction?

Month after month, one finds the educational magazine rack full of articles that would appear to point to the fictional side of the issue. In one newsletter, for example, Paul B. Salmon, Executive Director of the American Association of School Administrators, has stated that:

> Even now the sides are clearly drawn. The teachers unions [the American Federation of Teachers and the National Education Association] have . . . agreed to support a national collective bargaining bill. . . . Fighting to retain control are the public, the boards of education which represent them, and the school administrators who serve those boards.[2]

Add to these contending groups student activists, parent groups, state legislators, and courts, and the picture begins to take on all the aspects of a major battle for control of public education in the United States. When and where did it begin: How is it to end?

Source: Lee K. Davies, "The School Board's Struggle to Survive," *Educational Leadership* 34, no. 2 (November 1976): 95–99. Reprinted by permission.

1. "Official Policies, Rules, and Bylaws of the School Board of Orange County, Florida." Adopted in official session, August 26, 1974 and September 9, 1974. Section 9000 (a): Powers, Purposes, and Duties.
2. Paul B. Salmon. Guest editorial. American Association of School Administrators' *Newsletter* 32(6): 19; June 1975.

Amplified Conflict

Conflict and struggle have always been the road for education, but it would appear that, in today's society, the struggle is amplified. No longer are we a nation of small communities and slow change, nor do our citizens continue to enjoy the closeness and unity of purpose which once characterized America. Instead, we have become a metropolitan nation with instant access to influential news reports and a growing impatience with the *status quo.*

Orange County, Florida, is a case in point. The board which was elected in 1968 campaigned under the shadow of the statewide teacher walkout. Within less than a month of taking office in January 1969, board members were in Federal District Court, as defendants in the case of *Ellis vs. Board of Public Instruction,* a continuation of the litigation resulting from *Brown vs. Board of Education*[3] and subsequent desegregation cases. This litigation spawned a system-wide boycott by black students, protesting a tentative agreement between the board, as defendant, and the NAACP Legal Defense Fund, as plaintiff.[4] Virtually every experience of the Orange County School District, the thirty-second largest in the United States,[5] can be seen to closely parallel similar experiences in the nation as a whole.

The controversy over sex education in Orange County resulted in a thirteen and a half hour public hearing in September 1969.[6] Between then and now we have witnessed ever increasing levels of state funding, and thus, control. New courses and programs have been legislatively mandated, though not necessarily funded. Federal guidelines affected employment practices, class grouping procedures, personnel allocations, lunch policies, and even student assignment to physical education classes. During 1975, the board found it necessary due to inadequate funds from the state, to adopt a new method of secondary scheduling, reducing teaching personnel accordingly, and the citizens of the county turned to the board and asked, "Why?"

Why, indeed? Is the idea of local control of schools now relegated to the position of myth? The above brief recitation of history would make it appear so. Given that all this has occurred in just eight short years, it would appear that the draining of control from a local school district is accelerating as inevitably and as swiftly as the proverbial snowball melts. But, what are the forces involved? Is local control truly a thing of the past?

Lay Groups are Active

Parents and citizens alike have always been vitally interested in education. Parent-Teacher Associations date back to their founding in 1897, and currently boast a membership in excess of 37,000 local chapters, and 8,000,000 individual members.[7] Findings of a recent survey,[8] seem to indicate that in the minds of the population as a whole, some type of cooperative effort, legal or otherwise, exists between school boards and PTA's in the operation of the public school system. Other parent and citizen groups continue to be in the picture, both organized and not so organized. Their members' voices can be heard on virtually every side of any emotional issue. Many communities have experienced good working relationships with citizen committees and recent trends point to legislatures' mandating citizen advisory committees to work with

---

3. Brown *vs.* Board of Education of Topeka, 347 U.S. 483, 1954.
4. *Orlando Sentinel Star,* March 6, 1969.
5. According to a 1974 publication of Educational Research Service, Arlington, Virginia.
6. Official Minutes, School Board of Orange County, Florida, September 29, 1969.
7. *World Book Encyclopedia.* Volume 14. Chicago, Illinois: Field Enterprises Educational Corporation, 1974.
8. National School Boards Association. *The People Look at Their School Boards.* NSBA Report No. 1975–1. Washington, D.C.: the Association, 1975.

elected boards. More recently the membership of citizen committees has expanded to include representative groups of students, adding a new dimension to citizen participation.

The problem of control presented by parent and student activism is not insurmountable. Quite the contrary, citizen interest is an indispensable aid to the board in the decision-making process. The problem is rather the apathy of those who do not become involved. The involved citizen is the informed citizen for whom there is no such thing as a "community attitude." Those who are actively involved are aware of pluralism and are willing to make their opinions known within the present governing structure for public schools.

Judicial Decisions

Major players in the current struggle have been the courts. Admittedly, the reason for much court action in education is the inaction of local school boards, and, thus, the people who elect them. Boards, traditionally, have been reluctant to change. Few boards, have had the foresight to forge ahead in areas of civil rights and due process, largely due to the certainty of public censure and reprisal during future elections. As a result, individual cases have been filed, the results of which have caused boards to act, as a matter of policy, to implement the decisions of the more progressive courts.

The first of these actions to gain any widespread attention was the Supreme Court's Brown decision. Today, the rightness of this decision is hardly questioned. What local board, in 1954, however, could have withstood the political pressures resulting from its own initiative to end segregation? Desegregation, however, is only one of the more dramatic areas in which the courts have occasionally assumed the role of educational policy makers. The courts have heard cases on everything from hair length to student suspension, from maternity leave to due process. Supreme Court

Justice Powell has stated about a recent decision involving education that it:

> . . . unnecessarily opens avenues for judicial intervention in the operation of our public schools that may affect adversely the quality of education . . . of course, we don't want to keep on being the Black Robed School Board running things from Washington, D.C.[9]

Yet, on many issues, over many years, this appears to be exactly what has been happening. Early in the 1960's the Supreme court struck down Bible reading[10] and prayer.[11] More recently, the Tinker[12] decision placed due process in the classroom, causing observers to wonder what effect this would have on school discipline. Even the process of maintaining competence in the teaching ranks has come under a cloud.[13]

The legal puzzle has become so complex that, during the summer of 1974, when the Orange County School Board spent many long hours upgrading and recodifying its policies, it was necessary to keep the board attorney in constant attendance. Page after page of the resulting two-volume document carries, of necessity, abundant lists of legal references.

It has been charged that the "secretive way" in which boards adopt policy is the main reason the "public" has felt it necessary to find access to decision making through the courts. Perhaps there are communities where this is so, but not in Florida. Florida boards operate constantly within the requirements of Florida's Sunshine Law.[14] The previously mentioned policy

9. Goss *vs.* Lopez. U.S. Supreme Court: 43 L.W. 4181, 1975.
10. School District of Abington Township, Pennsylvania *vs.* Schempp, 374 U.S. 203, 1963.
11. Engel *vs.* Vitale, 370 U.S. 421, 1962.
12. Tinker *vs.* Des Moines Independent Community School District, 393 U.S. 503, 1971.
13. Roth *vs.* Board of Regents, 408 U.S. 564, 1972 and Perry *vs.* Sindermann, 407 U.S. 593, 1972.
14. Florida Statutes. The Florida Sunshine Law requires all public bodies to refrain from excluding any member of the public from consideration of said bodies.

meetings were well advertised and open to any citizens who wished to avail themselves of the opportunity to attend. Any and all comments were welcome, and the board sought the advice of any group known to be affected by the policy under consideration.

Was the input from the community vital and abundant? Unfortunately not. From a community of over 400,000 people,[15] the board was fortunate to draw as many as ten people; too few citizens were willing to take the time. Members of one group, "deeply concerned" about a particular policy under consideration, did not even bother to attend the meetings to make their feelings known to the board. They were reported to be willing, instead, to go to court, if the resulting policies were not to their satisfaction.

Legislative Actions

Still other combatants are the legislatures of the various states, whose major area of conflict with school boards is the problem of school funding. Originally, the major share of all funding fell to local property taxes. Even into the 1940's property taxes were almost the only source of school revenue. Increased enrollments, higher salaries, and inflation have helped cause a sharp rise in educational costs. Between 1960 and 1970, public education costs in the United States for kindergarten through twelfth grade alone, have increased by 261 percent.[16] As a result, local property taxes are no longer adequate to provide for the total funding of education.

School boards—in need—have turned to state legislatures to take up the slack, Boards have gained funds; they have sacrificed control.

In Florida, what was once a Minimum Foundation Program (allowing counties to surpass state goals in order to meet the needs of the county) has become a maximum foundation concept in which no county can levy a tax in excess of eight mills, with approximately 80 percent of this locally collected money becoming part of the state funding formulas[17] and thus, unavailable for local option programs. Local programs are thus reduced to levels specifically funded by the state.

Nor is funding the only area of conflict. Often legislatures view themselves as a court of last resort for the citizen who is in opposition to the local school board. Often the citizen whose view was not predominant at the local level will turn to the legislature for relief. In the case of sex education in Florida and in a controversy over the contract of an appointed superintendent, this approach resulted in the introduction of legislative bills in opposition to the action of the local board. The Florida Legislature has now adopted a far-reaching Administrative Procedures Act, establishing the method for policy revision and requiring eight days' notice before any item of business can come before the board, except under emergency circumstances. In addition to tightly controlled financial resources, the implementation of a statewide collective bargaining bill for public employees has introduced still another adversary to the battle for control of education.

The question naturally arises as to whether state control of dollars is compatible with local collective bargaining. Unlike the private sector, where it is possible to raise the cost of a product in order to fund a new employee contract, the public sector is totally dependent upon the existence of public funds to support bargaining agreements.

How can a local school system, required by law to adopt a balanced budget, provide to the employee organization in the bargaining process, funds in excess of those provided by the legislature? To approve such benefits is not possible without seriously and adversely

15. East Central Florida Regional Planning Council, First Quarter, 1975.

16. *World Book Encyclopedia*. Volume 6. Chicago, Illinois: Field Enterprises Educational Corporation, 1974.

17. A. J. Nolle, Associate Superintendent for Business Affairs, Orange County Public Schools, Florida.

affecting the program in the classroom, the very program for which the board is responsible by law and by the expectations of citizens. As a result, the initial goal of both the National Education Association (NEA) and the American Federation of Teachers (AFT) has shifted. Once dedicated to the improvement of the financial welfare of the classroom teacher, both organizations now believe that the name of the game is "power."

Organized teachers no longer operate only at the bargaining table, discussing salaries and conditions of employment; they want to run the system.[18] Under the leadership of Al Shanker, President of the AFT, members of the organized teaching profession have begun functioning in the political arena, choosing as adversaries—with frightening efficiency—the very school boards responsible for their employment.[19]

Political Realities

The final, most powerful, and yet most elusive player in this drama is politics itself. Even the word is almost undefinable. And yet, all that is done or dreamed of in education must have the active support or, at least, the apathetic ignorance of the political structure. Because politics is "of people," the final credit, or blame for any change in the control of education must lie in the laps of the citizens themselves.

School boards, throughout history, are not themselves innocent of the erosion of their power. Long ago, boards should have sought to be more aware of the conflicting forces within the communities they serve. Perhaps the inclusion, at the suggestion of the board, of: (a) both citizen and student advisory committees, (b) structured communication procedures between the

18. Thomas E. Williams. "Governance Is the Real Issue: A Management Manifesto." *Phi Delta Kappan* 56(8):561–62; April 1975.
19. Bernard Bard. "Albert Shanker: A Portrait in Power." *Phi Delta Kappan* 56(7):466–72; March 1975.

boards and its employees, and (c) a general lack of abuses in the areas of civil rights and due process would have set aside, or at least delayed, this erosion of power. But board members, like the communities which elect them, have all the strengths and weaknesses that can be attributed to any human being alive today. The cause of the power struggle must be deeper than this.

We have become a people of apathy. We have become a people who run to the courts at the least provocation, finding it easier to spend our dollars there than our efforts in the political process. As voters, we have been taken in by labels, cliches, and platitudes, not caring enough to ask penetrating questions of those candidates who present themselves for election.

We have allowed ourselves to fall victim to the department store syndrome, always moving higher and higher in the organizational structure until we hopefully receive satisfaction. In politics, this concept has disastrous consequences. Too often when we say, "They never listen to us," what we really mean is, "They didn't do what we wanted them to do."

Representative government is a badly misunderstood concept. The idea that an individual office holder is charged with the responsibility of finding out all that is possible to know on an issue and then voting his or her conscience, subject to the constituents' approval or disapproval at the conclusion of his or her term, is a concept to which many people pay only lip service. Too often we become impatient. Victims of the department store syndrome are dissatisfied citizens who contact successively higher levels of government seeking satisfaction, until what is at heart a local issue falls into the hands of some federal agency.

Do such actions cause erosion of local control? Inevitably, for even if a decision at the local level is a wrong one that disregards local attitudes, the recourse in a constitutional republic is to vote the offender out of office. Instead, impatience and unwillingness to make representative government work have moved the center of power from the local level to a higher level of government, one that is less responsive to the needs of the community, if only by reason of its size and distance.

Perhaps local control of schools should be a thing of the past. Perhaps, in an age of rapid transportation and easy communication when the average citizens do not live out their lives in the community of birth, the idea of local control is not functional. It may be necessary that, in such a society, we must have a national curriculum and national policies made available on an equal basis for all citizens, regardless of domicile.

On the other hand, however, perhaps we, as a people, do not wish to relinquish that much control over the destiny of our children. Perhaps we still believe that freedom indeed implies the freedom to be different, and to maintain control over the schools at a local level.

The two positions are irreconcilable. I would argue for local control, believing that local people know better what they want for their children than do any higher levels of government. Hopefully, the citizenry of this country will recover from its apathy and again become actively involved in the education of young people. If local control continues to erode, power will continue to move first to the state and then to the federal government; if the electorate loses its voice to organized labor—then let it be because that is the decision of the people, not the result of their apathy and impatience.

We must become aware that, as citizens, we have responsibilities as well as rights. We must learn that our rights end when they interfere with the rights of our neighbor. And, above all, we must exercise our major right and our prime responsibility, that of diligently selecting those who are to represent us and our views. The price of local control is high. Are we willing to accept the challenge?

Questions for Discussion

1. What factors have caused the federal government to increase its participation in the educational enterprise?

2. Can education in the United States continue to be effective by continuing its longtime tradition of local control? Provide a rationale for your answer.

3. Should members of local boards of education be typically representative of the social composition of their respective communities? Why?

4. How have local boards of education had their traditional powers reduced?

5. How can teachers' organizations best use their power in fostering local education improvements?

Supplementary Learning Activities

1. Visit local school board meetings and report your observations to the class.

2. Examine copies of the school code for your state.

3. Interview persons from nonpublic schools to seek out their opinions as to the concept of separation of church and state.

4. Interview a superintendent of schools to discover the major responsibilities and problems of his office.

5. Interview officers from a local teachers' association to seek out their opinions on teacher power.

Notes

1. Thomas J. Flygare, "State Aid to Public Schools: Diminished Alternative," *Phi Delta Kappan* 57, no. 3 (November 1975): 204.

2. Lucy Knight, "Facts About Mr. Buckley's Amendment," *American Education* 13, no. 5 (June 1977): 6

3. Bernice Sandler, "Title IX: Antisexism's Big Legal Stick," *American Education* 13, no. 4 (May 1977): 6.

4. Ibid.

5. Roald F. Campbell, Gerald E. Stroufe, and Donald H. Layton, *Strengthening State Departments of Education* (Chicago: University of Chicago Press, 1967), p. 10.

6. W. Vance Grant and Leo J. Eiden, *Digest of Educational Statistics, 1980.* National Center for Educational Statistics, p. 60. (Available from the U.S. Government Printing Office, Washington, D.C. 20402.)

7. Ibid.

8. *Education USA* 19, no. 14 (December 6, 1976).

Selected References

Campbell, Roald F., et al. *Introduction to Educational Administration.* Boston: Allyn and Bacon, 1977.

Doyle, Denis P. "Public Policy and Private Education," *Phi Delta Kappan.* Vol. 62, no. 1, September 1980, pp. 16–19.

Hansen, E. Mark. *Educational Administration and Organizational Behavior.* Boston: Allyn and Bacon, 1979.

Hudgins, H. C. Jr., and Vacca, Richard S. *Law and Education: Contemporary Issues and Court Decisions.* Charlottesville, Virginia: The Michie Company, 1979.

Knight, Lucy. "Facts About Mr. Buckley's Amendment." *American Education* 13, no. 5, June 1977, pp. 6–9.

Ornstein, Allan C. "Decentralization and Community Participation Policy of Big School Systems," *Phi Delta Kappan.* Vol. 62, no. 4, December 1980, pp. 255–57.

Sandler, Bernice. "Title IX: Antisexism's Big Legal Stick," *American Education* 13, no. 4, May 1977, pp. 6–9.

Sergiovanni, Thomas; Burlingame, Martin; Coombs, Fred D.; and Thurston, Paul. *Educational Governance and Administration.* Englewood Cliffs, New Jersey: Prentice-Hall, Inc., 1980.

Stephens, E. Robert. *Regionalism: Past, Present and Future.* Arlington, Va.: American Association of School Administrators, 1977.

Valente, William D. *Law in the Schools.* Columbus, Ohio: Charles E. Merrill Publishing Company, 1980.

Financing the Educational Enterprise

17

This Chapter
- **Identifies the magnitude of the educational enterprise in terms of monies expended and people involved.**
- **Analyzes the concept of education as an investment in individuals, government, social development, and the economy.**
- **Explains the separate sources of public school revenue, their advantages and disadvantages, and their systematic relationship to one another.**

- **Presents the basic relationship between school finance and the concept of equality of opportunity.**
- **Identifies the reasons for the current call for accountability and suggests proposals for responsive action.**
- **Provides a point of view on the concept of accountability in local schools.**

Education in the United States is big business. Currently, there are over 50 million pupils enrolled in public and private elementary and secondary schools, over 2 million teachers employed to provide instruction for those students, and approximately $98 billion spent for current operating expenditures to conduct this enterprise. It has been estimated that in 1985 there will be approximately 46 million pupils, 2 million teachers, and the current operating expenditures will exceed $125 billion based on 1975–76 dollars. Another way to look at the magnitude of the enterprise is to recognize that education today is the major occupation of 62 million people in the United States. Included in the 62 million are 58.4 million students enrolled in schools and colleges, 3.3 million teachers, and 300,000 administrators and supporting instructional staff. In a nation with more than 220 million people, about three out of every ten persons are directly involved in the educational process.[1] It is also pertinent to note that in many communities education is the biggest business in the community.

Education as an Investment

As a nation our investment in education has been a sizable amount. Figure 17.1 illustrates the nation's effort to support education by comparing educational expenditures with gross national product (GNP). Gross national product, calculated by the Bureau of Economic Analysis, U.S. Department of Commerce, represents the total national output of goods and services at market prices. It measures this output in terms of the expenditures by which the goods and services are acquired. The expenditures comprise purchases of goods and services by consumers and government, gross private domestic investment, and net exports of goods and services. GNP provides one measuring stick of our national investment in education. With some fluctuation educational expenditures as a percentage of GNP have steadily risen from about 4.0 percent in 1939 to 8.0 percent in 1975. The lowest percentages, all below 3.0 percent, occurred during World War II in the period between 1941 and 1945.

Figure 17.1. Total Expenditures for Education as a Percentage of the Gross National Product: United States, 1939–40 to 1979–80.

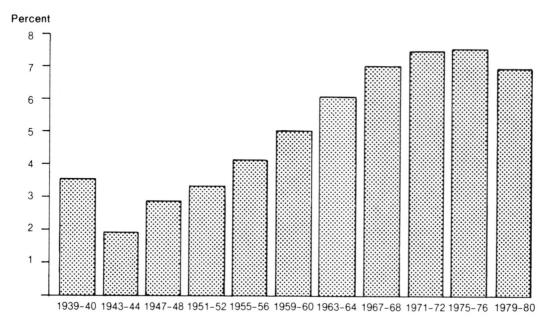

Source: W. Vance Grant and Leo J. Eiden. *Digest of Educational Statistics, 1980.* (Washington, D.C.: National Center for Educational Statistics, U.S. Government Printing Office), p. 24.

Education competes with other governmental needs for the tax dollar. An indication of its priority is demonstrated by the fact that approximately forty cents out of every dollar spent by local and state governments is spent for education, as compared to thirteen cents for highways, and eleven cents for welfare, health and hospitals.[2] Many citizens are calling for greater cost-effectiveness. Still others decry the lack of a solid research base that clearly demonstrates the relationship between the dollars expended for education and the resultant benefits to individuals and society. How much should a nation spend for education?

While it approaches the impossible to estimate what proportion of the wealth of a nation *should* be allocated for education, it does seem clear that we in the United States are limited more by our willingness to pay than by our ability to pay. In other words, our task as a nation seems to be to delineate a hierarchy of values—that is, to clearly spell out and place in rank order what we desire or what "ought to be." Once this is done we must commit monies to convert our words into action.

Social development, closely intertwined with economic development, is also related to education. A basic premise undergirding our form of government is that informed citizens are necessary to our national survival. The skills (such as literacy) necessary to be an informed citizen and the skills necessary for problem solving are enhanced through education. The values of society, or the ways of life that we cherish, are transmitted in part through our educational system.

Investment in education is an investment in society, both economically and socially. Education in a sense is the servant of society. Americans must continue to use education to foster the achievement of their ideals.

Education is an investment, not a cost. It is an investment in free men, it is an investment in social welfare, in better living standards, in better health, in less crime. It is an investment in higher production, increased income, and greater efficiency in agriculture, industry, and government. It is an investment in a bulwark against garbled information, half-truths, and untruths, against ignorance and intolerance. It is an investment in human talent, human relations, democracy, and peace.

President's Commission on Higher Education

There are obviously two educations. One should teach us how to make a living, and the other how to live.

James Truslow Adams

Expenditures for school libraries are investments in America's future.

Sources of School Revenue

The monies used to finance the public educational enterprise today come largely from taxation, but this has not always been the case. In colonial America monies for schools were often obtained from lotteries and charitable contributions. Churches of the various denominations financed education for some. It was not unusual in the very early days of our nation for the patrons of the schools to provide services such as supplying wood, making building repairs, or boarding teachers in lieu of money.

Public support for education in this nation in terms of taxes was secured only after a long, hard battle. However, the concept that education should be a public responsibility dates back to our early heritage. The Massachusetts laws of 1642, 1647, and 1648 referred to earlier in this text illustrate the New England attitude that at least common school education should be a public rather than a private responsibility. In the early 1800s, the movement for free public schools gained impetus. Pennsylvania in 1834 became the first state to adopt free elementary education. In 1872, the village of Kalamazoo, Michigan, voted to establish a public high school to be supported by taxation. A lawsuit was filed to test the legality of using taxation to provide a high school. The opinion of the State Supreme Court of Michigan was that the action was legal and constitutional. By the end of the nineteenth century, public schools were financed almost completely by local funds derived from local taxation.

Effective science teaching is enhanced with appropriate equipment and materials.

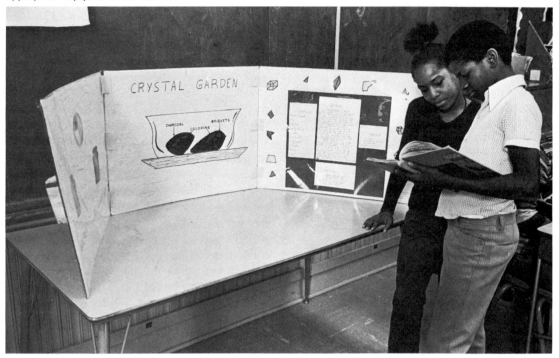

Important to the rise of public financial support for education (taxes) was the belief that education benefited the public as well as the individual or the family. Today money to support education comes from a variety of taxes collected by local, state, and federal governments. These governments in turn distribute taxes to local school districts to operate their schools. The three major kinds of taxes used to provide revenue for schools are property taxes, sales or use taxes, and income taxes. In general, local governments use the property tax, state governments rely upon the sales tax—though they are increasingly using the income tax—and the federal government relies heavily upon the income tax.

It is important to note the percentage of support for public elementary and secondary schools contributed by each level of government. In 1919–20, about 83.0 percent of school revenues came from local governmental sources, 16.5 percent from state sources, and about .3 percent from federal sources. Over the years this has changed, with a marked increase in state support up to 1978, and most recently in 1978, a definite increase in federal support. Table 17.1 illustrates the percentage of revenue received from the three sources since 1919.

While table 17.1 provides data from an overall national viewpoint, an examination of the data from selected individual states reveals wide variations from the national statistics. It should be remembered that education is a function of the state and therefore variability is to be expected. Table 17.2 illustrates the estimated percentages of revenue by governmental source for public elementary and secondary schools for selected states. The states are arranged in the table in a descending order in terms of local support. The average percentages in the United States for the

Table 17.1. Percentages of Revenue Received from Federal, State, and Local Sources for Public Elementary and Secondary Schools.

| School Year | Percent of Revenue | | |
	Federal	State	Local
1919–20	.3	16.5	83.2
1929–30	.4	16.9	82.7
1939–40	1.8	30.3	68.0
1949–50	2.9	39.8	57.3
1955–56	4.6	39.5	55.9
1957–58	4.0	39.4	56.6
1959–60	4.4	39.1	56.5
1961–62	4.3	38.7	56.9
1963–64	4.4	39.3	56.3
1965–66	7.9	39.1	53.0
1967–68	8.8	38.5	52.7
1969–70	8.0	39.9	52.1
1975–76	8.9	41.6	46.5
1977–78	9.5	43.0	47.6

Source: W. Vance Grant and Leo J. Eiden. *Digest of Educational Statistics, 1980.* (Washington, D.C.: National Center for Educational Statistics, U.S. Government Printing Office), p. 77.

Table 17.2. Estimated Percentage of Revenue by Governmental Source for Public Elementary and Secondary Schools, for Selected States.

| State | Percent of Revenue | | |
	Local	State	Federal
New Hampshire	86.6	6.3	7.1
Nebraska	76.7	16.1	7.2
Illinois	53.7	37.7	8.6
Pennsylvania	46.8	44.5	8.7
Florida	37.9	50.6	11.4
North Carolina	22.8	63.2	14.0
Alabama	21.9	61.5	16.6
Alaska	18.6	67.3	14.1
New Mexico	16.7	65.0	18.3
Hawaii	1.0	82.8	16.2

Source: W. Vance Grant and Leo J. Eiden. *Digest of Educational Statistics, 1980.* (Washington, D.C.: National Center for Educational Statistics, U.S. Government Printing Office), p. 71.

same period are estimated to be: local 47.6, state 43.0, and federal 9.5.

The variation in state financial support illustrated in table 17.2 represents primarily a variation in general state aid. That is, state monies are provided to supplement the local education effort, and for the most part are not "earmarked" or "tagged" for special purposes or programs. The variation in federal support in the main is a reflection of *categorical aid*—that is, specific aid

for a specific purpose or to resolve a unique problem. For example, the Smith-Hughes Act provided a stimulus for vocational education; the National Defense Education Act of 1958 emphasized the enhancement of science, mathematics, foreign languages, and counseling services; the Elementary and Secondary Act of 1965 had as one important feature the provision of monies to assist school districts in providing programs for

Financing the Educational Enterprise   399

children of poverty. Other federal aid programs
are designed to aid school districts that are affected by federally induced population impaction
such as may occur near a military installation or
major federal research installation. Both state
and federal aid are aimed at enhancing equality
of opportunity, which is to be considered later in
this chapter. The Reagan administration has indicated its desire to reduce federal aid. Furthermore, the various categorical grants will be
consolidated into block grants, providing greater
freedom to the states in deciding how they wish
to spend the money (Omnibus Budget Reconcil-
iation Act of 1981).

As was mentioned earlier, local support for
schools comes predominantly from the property
tax. The property tax is one of the oldest forms
of taxation, based on the premise that a measure
of a man's property was a measure of his wealth.
Property is most often considered in two categories, real estate and personal. Personal property
may include such things as automobiles, furniture, machinery, livestock, jewelry, and less tangible items as stocks and bonds. The property tax
was particularly appropriate for an agrarian
economy.

The property tax, as with most forms of taxation, has both distinct advantages and disadvantages. Its major advantage is that it provides a
regular and stable form of income. While it is
perhaps not as sensitive to economic changes as
the sales and income taxes, neither is it absolutely
rigid. The stability of the property tax will likely
cause it to continue to be the mainstay of local
public school support.

A major disadvantage of the property tax
has to do with establishing equality of assessment. In other words, parcels of property of equal
value should be assessed at the same value. This
is extremely difficult to accomplish. Wide variations exist within school districts, states, and the
nation. Studies have indicated variation in assessment of residential property from 5.9 percent
of sale value in one state to 66.2 percent in another. Inequality of assessment causes the property tax to be an unfair tax.

The property tax is most generally thought
of as a proportionate tax, that is, one that taxes
according to ability to pay. However, inequality
of assessment and the trend in an urban economy
for wealth to be less related to real estate than
it was in an agrarian economy have caused the
tax to become somewhat regressive. Regressive
taxes are those such as sales and use taxes that
have a relatively greater impact on lower income
groups.

State support for schools comes mainly from
the sales tax and income tax. Sales and income
taxes are lucrative sources of state revenue, and
both taxes are relatively easy to administer. The
sales tax is collected bit by bit by the vendor, who
is responsible for record keeping and remitting
the tax to the state. The state income tax can be
withheld from wages, hence facilitating collec-
tions. The sales tax is considered a *regressive tax*
because all persons pay the sales tax at the same
rate; therefore, persons in low income groups pay
nearly as much tax for essentials as do those in
high income groups. Income taxes are referred to
as *progressive taxes* because they are frequently
scaled to the ability of the taxpayer to pay. Both

School financing directly affects the quality of educational opportunity.

state sales and income taxes are direct and certain, they are responsive to changes in the economy, and they can be regulated by the state legislature, which is responsible for raising the money. It is interesting to note that on a nationwide basis approximately 55 percent of all state revenue came from sales taxes, and 29 percent from income taxes. The remainder came from licenses and miscellaneous taxes.

Federal support for schools comes from monies raised primarily from personal and corporate income taxes.

School Finance and Equality of Opportunity

The opportunity for equal education is related to the financial ability of specific areas to pay for education. While wealth is not the only factor related to equality of opportunity, as was pointed out by the *Brown* decision, it certainly is an important one.

Children are educated in local school districts, which by and large still produce nationwide about 48 percent of the monies used for education. These monies are raised primarily with the property tax, and therefore are dependent upon the real estate wealth of the district. Wealthy districts, therefore, can provide more monies for education than poor districts with the same tax effort. Suppose, for example, that the

While some school districts have vacant buildings because of declining enrollment, other districts and their schools remain overcrowded.

total assessed valuation, that is, the value of all the property as determined by a tax assessor of a district, is $100,000,000, and that the district has 2,000 pupils. This hypothetical district would have then an assessed valuation of $50,000 per pupil. A tax rate of $2 per $100 of assessed valuation would produce $1,000 per pupil. By the same token if a neighboring district had an assessed evaluation of only $10,000 per pupil the same $2 per $100 rate would produce only $200 per pupil. With the same rate, or the same effort, one of these districts could spend $1,000 per pupil while the other could spend only $200. In general,

this results in children in wealthy districts being provided greater opportunities for education than children in poor districts.

Great differences can exist in wealth per pupil from school district to school district. Industrial developments can increase valuations in some districts, while at the same time neighboring districts may be largely residential with little valuation and large numbers of pupils.

A number of court cases have arisen in respect to inequality of education as a function of the wealth of school districts. The *Serrano* case is illustrative. In *Serrano* v. *Priest* the California Supreme Court was called upon to determine whether or not the California public school financing system, with its substantial dependence on local property taxes, violated the Fourteenth Amendment. In a 6–1 decision on August 30, 1971, the Court held that heavy reliance on unequal local property taxes "makes the quality of a child's education a function of the wealth of his parents and neighbors." Furthermore, the Court declared, "Districts with small tax bases simply cannot levy taxes at a rate sufficient to produce the revenue that more affluent districts produce with a minimum effort." The data presented in the *Serrano* case revealed that the Baldwin Park school district spent $577 per pupil, while the Beverly Hills school district spent $1,232. Yet, the tax rate of $5.48 in Baldwin Park was more than double the rate of $2.38 in Beverly Hills. The discrepancies are a result of the difference in wealth between the two districts. Beverly Hills had $50,885 of assessed valuation per child, while Baldwin Park had only $3,706 valuation per child—a ratio of thirteen to one. Suits similar to *Serrano* have been filed in at least twenty-two states.

The United States Supreme Court consented to hear an appeal of the *Rodriguez* case, which originated in Texas and was similar to *Serrano*. In *Rodriguez* the U.S. Supreme Court, in 1973 in a 5–4 decision, reversed the lower court and thus reaffirmed the local property tax as a basis for school financing. Justice Potter Stewart voting with the majority admitted that "the method of financing public schools . . . can be fairly described as chaotic and unjust." He did not, though, find it unconstitutional. The majority

opinion written by Justice Lewis F. Powell stated "we cannot say that such disparities are the product of a system that is so irrational as to be invidiously discriminatory." The opinion also noted that: the poor are not necessarily concentrated in the poorest districts; states must initiate fundamental reform in taxation and education; and the extent to which quality of education varies with expenditures is inconclusive. Justice Thurgood Marshall in the dissenting opinion charged that the ruling "is a retreat from our historic commitment to equality of educational opportunity." A number of commissions have made recommendations to improve the financing of schools. States have also attempted to alter their methods of financing schools. A brief description of state aid prior to *Rodriguez* provides a basis for understanding the problem today.

State Aid—Historically

States have recognized the disparaging differences in wealth among local districts, and through state aid programs, have attempted to provide financial equalization for educational purposes. This makes good sense, particularly since the state has the primary responsibility for education.

State aid can be classified by its use as being either general or categorical. General aid may be used by the recipient school district as it desires. Categorical aid is "earmarked" for specific purposes. Examples of categorical aid include monies for special education, driver education, vocational education, or transportation. Categorical aid is sometimes used as an incentive to encourage programs that are perceived as being needed.

General aid usually represents the states' efforts to equalize opportunity. The underlying premise is that each child, regardless of his or her place of residence or the wealth of the particular school district in which he or she lives, is entitled to receive essential basic educational opportunities. General aid is usually administered through some type of foundation program. The foundation concept involves the establishment of a per pupil dollar value, which represents the desired foundation education in a state. The usual connotation of the word *foundation* is basic or minimum. Therefore, the foundation level is usually less than the actual per pupil expenditures. A state, in establishing a foundation level, is in effect assuring that the amount of the per pupil foundation level will be expended for education for each pupil in the state. Foundation programs do encourage equality of opportunity from a financial viewpoint; however, *it is important to observe that they assure equalization only to a prescribed level*. Districts can and do vary greatly in their expenditure per pupil.

The actual monies used to achieve the foundation level expenditures come from both state and local sources. Most often a minimum local tax rate is established, and the money this tax rate produces is subtracted from the foundation level with the remainder being paid by the state.

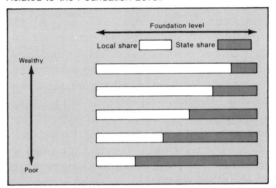

Figure 17.2. The Principle of Equalization as Related to the Foundation Level.

The local tax rate will produce more money in a wealthy district than it will in a poor district. This concept is also a part of the equalization principle. Figure 17.2 presents a graphic representation of equalization and the foundation principle. *It is important to note, however, that local districts can, and frequently do, spend more than the foundation level.*

Wealth Differences among States

Differences in wealth exist among states just as they do among school districts within states. Since assessment practices differ from state to state, it is difficult to use assessed valuation per pupil as an index to compare the wealth of states. A more accurate index is personal income per

Monies available for schools affect class size.

"Come now, Miss Twist,
your class isn't *that* large!"

capita. States with per capita income greater than $8,000 include Alaska, California, Connecticut, Illinois, along with the Federal District of Columbia, while Alabama, Arkansas, Maine, Mississippi and South Carolina all have per capita personal incomes lower than $5,700. Average per capita income in the United States is $7,042.[3]

Expenditures per pupil vary widely, partly because of the differences in wealth among dis-

tricts and states. The average current annual expenditure per pupil in the United States is $1,823. Alaska, New Jersey, and New York, along with the Federal District of Columbia, all spend in excess of $2,400 per pupil while Arkansas, Georgia, Kentucky, Mississippi, South Carolina, Tennessee, and Utah all spend less than $1,350 per pupil.[4]

As indicated previously in this chapter, federal aid has increased. However, as discussed earlier in this book, the aid has been categorical. The Elementary and Secondary Act of 1965 with its subsequent amendments and with its emphasis toward improving educational opportunities for children of poverty, while categorical, comes as close to general aid as any federal aid ever has. Greater federal support is necessary to bolster equality among states.

Recommendations for Establishing Equality in Financing Education

It is clear that differences in wealth among school districts can and often do result in vastly different expenditures per pupil. It is also clear that wealthy school districts, using the same effort (tax rate) as that of poor districts, can provide more monies for education. Two of the overall goals of a variety of proposals to improve school financing therefore are: to achieve equal or nearly equal expenditures per pupil, and at the same time to equalize the effort that school districts

Education is an investment in society.

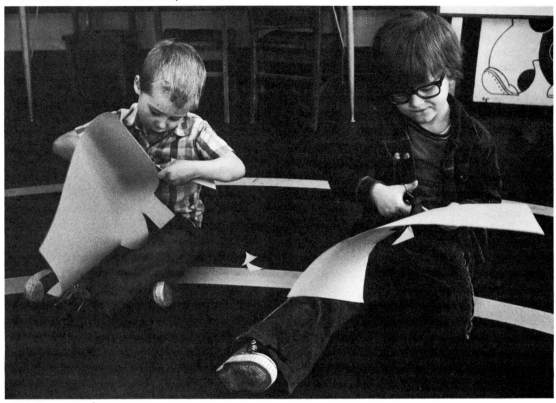

must expend to equalize expenditures. These goals cannot be accomplished without states providing a larger portion of the support of education at the local level.

As indicated earlier, the foundation-equalization approach was an initial effort in this respect. The major difficulties with the foundation-equalization approach were and still are (1) foundation levels established were not sufficient to overcome gross inequities, and (2) local school districts were given "local leeway" (freedom) to exceed the foundation-equalization level. Attempts made in the past few years (post *Serrano*) to establish equality have emanated from the basic foundation-equalization model. The crucial elements of this model are (1) the foundation-equalization level established, (2) the degree of local tax effort required, and (3) the amount of local leeway permitted. One approach suggested is to limit the amount of local leeway. Basically, this approach reduces the discrepancy in per pupil expenditures. A second approach provides no local leeway, thereby producing equalized per pupil expenditures with state monies supplementing the local tax yield to the equalization level. The same end result could be realized with full state funding, a position some authorities have taken.

A third approach gaining in popularity involves equalized percentage grants, and is referred to as *power equalization*. It is designed to satisfy fiscal equality, and at the same time permit local school districts to use higher than state-established tax rates. School districts are permitted, usually within limits, to establish their own level of expenditure beyond the required state minimum. The level of expenditure selected results in a state-designated local tax rate. In this approach the state guarantees equal levels of expenditure for equal tax effort, and in that respect may meet the equal-protection clause of the Constitution. The plan does, however, result in unequal expenditures per pupil brought about by variations in effort and not wealth. The problem of equal educational opportunity based on equal per pupil expenditures will not easily be solved.

Other issues that are likely to make the financing of schools more difficult in the years ahead include inflation, taxpayer revolt, decreasing enrollments, and mandatory programs. In the case of inflation, public school revenue has simply not kept up with expenses, and with continuing inflation it is not likely to do so. It is difficult for taxpayers to understand why it costs more to educate fewer pupils; the reason is inflation. Inflation may also be part of the reason for taxpayer revolt. Efforts to legislatively limit taxing power have been underway as a result of this revolt. A second possible reason for taxpayer revolt is the growing dissatisfaction with the results of public education; an example has been the general decline in student achievement over the past few years. Inflation is not the only factor that will be eating away at public school revenues. Since state aid in most instances is tied to enrollments, declining enrollments result in less state aid. Finally, state and federal mandates, which have increased in the last few years, frequently are not accompanied by providing funds to carry out the mandate.

Accountability

Earlier in this book reference was made to the expressed dissatisfaction with the educational accomplishments of public school pupils. In a sense the educational expectations of individuals and society were not being met. Questions were being raised about the notion that increased spending brings about better education. The term *cost-effectiveness* was being used in respect to education. The roots of accountability rest in unmet expectations and increased costs as they relate to education. The call for research and data to determine the relationship between dollars expended for education and benefits accrued to individuals and society represents the thrust of accountability.

To be accountable means to be responsible. In schools this requires (1) explicit results that represent achievements, and (2) the dollar costs of these achievements. The end product should be a report of the costs of programs in terms of the accomplishments of the programs.

A danger that lurks in the implementation of an accountability system is the chance that goals that do not lend themselves to objective measurement will be dropped. This must be avoided. A great effort must be made to measure *all* goals as best they can be measured.

Can the effects of excellent libraries on student learning be measured?

Expectations and Expenses

Early in this chapter it was said that our expenditures for education were limited more by our willingness to pay than our ability to pay. They also seem to be limited by our inability to demonstrate definitively the value of education. Do we have the willingness to support our expectations for education? What are our national priorities? As a nation compared to other nations in the world we are wealthy. We do have pockets of poverty, and parts of our nation are more able than others to support education. If, as a *nation*, we believe that education is important, and that education can help us achieve our national goals and professed ideals, then we must effectively muster and utilize our financial resources accordingly.

Point of View

Accountability, in a sense, means responsibility. In education it means being responsible for student learning and the costs associated with that learning. Emphasis is placed on results—that is, on the knowledge, skills, attitudes and behaviors that students exhibit after having learning experiences in school. Accountability calls for direct measures of results, and the cost of the results.

Frequently, the question of who is accountable for what in education is raised, and rightfully so. In the article by Allen S. Norris that follows, "The Accountability Concept in Local Education," the accountability concept is analyzed. Norris provides specific suggestions for the potential of accountability to improve the local educational effort. Conversely, he points out ways in which accountability can be applied and effectively impair the local educational effort. Accountability has been and is a controversial topic when applied to education. Nevertheless, the notion of high expectations of attainment at the lowest cost is going to continue to be applied to education. Teachers, as those who interact directly with students, are those most likely to bear the responsibility for student achievements.

The Accountability Concept in Local Education

Allen S. Norris

The accountability concept can be constructive if it is based on a realistic understanding of the local educational process. The potential of accountability as a constructive force is its emphasis on explicitness. When accountability becomes an "ism," it ignores the interdependency and distorts the humanism of the educational effort. It then becomes a destructive force in education.

Source: Allen S. Norris, "The Accountability Concept in Local Education," *The School Administrator* 34, no. 10 (November 1977): 18–19. Reprinted by permission.

Local public education is a pluralistic, interdependent effort. Who influences local public education? Federal, state and local elected and appointed officials and their staffs; employees of the local school system; students, parents, and citizens at large, and special interest groups, to name a few. Each affects the others in this interactive and interdependent network of relationships. This interdependence makes it difficult to effect change; yet, at the same time, it provides stability.

Although the structure and process of local education has changed little over the years, public education has become more complex in its attempt to meet increasing diversity among the needs and desires of its clients. Concurrently, with the exception of union-management relationships, institutional control relationships among the participants have changed little. Likewise, the network of accountability has changed little. Citizens have held elected officials accountable through the ballot. Elected officials have held the appointed officials accountable through re-appointment. The appointed officials have held staff accountable through performance evaluations, rewards, and negative incentives. Teachers have held students accountable for their performance through marking and rewards, and/or disciplinary actions. Likewise, students and their parents have very real spheres of influence.

Another characteristic of the local education effort is that it directly involves a very large number of people in face to face encounters. It is labor intensive—over 80 percent of the annual budget is accounted for in terms of salaries and salary related costs. Teaching and learning involve the interactions of people, and the product of this interaction—student performance—is behavioral in nature.

What does the term accountability mean when applied to the local educational effort? Often its meaning is "in the eyes of the beholder." To all of the participants, it generally implies judgment on their performance. Whether the term "accountability" evokes a positive, neutral, or negative reaction from individuals depends on their perception of the understanding and fairness with which their performance is being judged.

Why the recent emphasis on accountability in public education? Have we really become more capable and sophisticated in our identification of accountability relationships and in the techniques of measuring performance? Have we become more enlightened in understanding the nature and capacity for control of the learning process? Probably not. But, the competition for local tax dollars has increased. Also, there is growing citizen pressure to "prove" that appropriate educational services are being provided.

As steward of the public's resources, the school system is being urged to define and defend its general and particular plans of action, and to measure the degree to which *desired* achievements have become *actual* achievements. Too often, when the desired objectives involve student performance, only a few participants are held accountable. That is a nice, tidy, but oversimplified perception of the dynamics of the local educational process. Should only the teacher be held accountable for student achievement? Should not other professionals, students, parents, school boards, local funding authorities, and taxpayers share in the accountability? This question does not necessarily argue for an elaborate network that defines the accountability of each of these and other special interest groups. It does, however, ask for a recognition that a student's achievement is only partially a by-product of the teaching/learning processes managed by the teacher. Moreover, it calls for a response that does not over-elaborate the measurement of student performance. Much of the time and effort spent on measurement of student performance for purposes of

accountability could be better spent in understanding the relationship between plans of action and the students' actual achievements. Pragmatically, a few good measurements with a lot of understanding of the relationship of action to student achievement are more useful than a lot of measures with a little understanding of why the student achieved at the measured level.

Current questions about accountability in public education include:
- Who should hold whom accountable for what?
- How can accountability be measured?
- What measure of difference is significant?
- If the measure of difference is significant, what action should be taken?
- Would the action taken make a difference in subsequent performance, especially student performance?

The answer to the first question, "Who should hold whom accountable for what?" becomes difficult when considering the network of relationships among the participants involved in local public education. Given the difficulty of resolving this issue for the "other guy" (which is the all too prevalent approach), a constructive approach would be for each participant to define their own realm of jurisdictional accountability. The perimeters for each realm would be the extent of the local public education situation that the particular participant can control and/or influence.

"How can the accountability be measured?" The answer to this question has proved to be elusive. Students, teachers, and parents, however, seem to find grades useful in reporting individual student performance. Most system-wide measures cluster around standardized test scores of students' academic performance. Most participants have not yet reached a consensus regarding the significance and usefulness of these test scores, except that they do provide a benchmark for comparing the next standardized test scores. At best, they are general measurements weakened by qualifying variables such as ability levels, socio-economic factors, teaching to the test, poor administration of the test, and others.

A pragmatic approach would be for the measurements used by any participant to be those which concern a performance (action) they can control and/or influence. In this way, linking staff plans of action to student achievement does make sense because the staff receives the necessary information to understand why certain actions work with certain students.

Question number three: "What measure of difference is significant?" Again, we are brought back to "the eyes of the beholder." For example, participants often view a given amount of change in standardized test scores as having varying degrees of significance. Measurements in education are controversial—they are soft. Too often, participants want to "prove" something, and they attempt to convince other participants that the difference is significant. The irony is that the linkage of staff actions to student achievement is often unknown and/or assumed, or somehow inferred. At the individual student level, the determination of a significant difference in performance is possible and useful. At this level, the relationship of staff actions to student achievement can be identified and can serve as a basis for corrective and constructive action.

What criteria could be used to determine whether a difference in student achievement is significant? Before the achievement data is collected, this question should be addressed to—and satisfactorily answered by—the participants who will be involved in determining what actions should be changed. All too often achievement data is collected, and then we try to determine whether it shows something significant. This is a drain on the organization's resources and energy.

"If the measure of difference is significant what action should be taken?" By now the need to understand the relationship between staff actions and student achievement should be clear. Those who need to take action will recognize their responsibilities if they have applied the concept of jurisdictional accountability to their own sphere of influence.

This brings us to the fifth question: "Would the action taken make a difference in subsequent performance—especially student performance?" The answer to this question obviously depends on the responses to the previous questions. The probability of making a difference declines in proportion to the degree that various participants are holding "the other guy" accountable.

The concept of accountability has the greatest potential for improving the local educational effort when it is:

a. applied by each participant to his/her particular realm of action and responsibility.
b. focused on the relationship of particular plans of action with particular students' achievement;
c. intended to provide information to facilitate improved performance—particularly at the individual student level.

The concept of accountability has the greatest potential for impairing the local educational effort when it is:

a. applied by one participant for another participant;
b. focused on performance measures which are not linked to a casual relationship of actions to student achievement;
c. intended to provide a justification for some preconceived change or for maintaining the status quo.

Local education is a highly interdependent human effort. It needs mutually supportive relationships to work successfully, not increases in adversarial relationships.

Education is a very complex and significant human enterprise. It is essential to understand what works in this effort. Only then will the participants have a sound basis for seeking out and developing more effective actions, and for evolving toward a more mutually supportive local educational enterprise.

Questions for Discussion

1. What are the three main kinds of taxes used to produce revenue for schools? Discuss each of these in terms of their productivity and fairness.

2. How would you defend the support of education through taxation?

3. What essentially is the meaning of a "foundation" plan?

4. What factors in our society have caused the change in the educational support level provided by the three levels of government?

5. What have been some of the noticeable effects of both state and federal categorical aid in the public schools of your area?

Supplemental Learning Activities

1. Obtain a copy of a local school district budget and examine it. Explain your observations to your class.

2. Discuss the problem of financing the schools with property taxes with local school officials in the light of recent court decisions and actions by your state legislature.

3. Invite a county or township tax assessment official to your class to discuss the assessing process in your area.

4. Study and evaluate the plan for state support of education in your state.

5. Collect and examine data related to the wealth of school districts in your immediate area or state.

Notes

1. W. Vance Grant and Leo J. Eiden, *Digest of Educational Statistics, 1980.* Washington, D.C.: National Center for Educational Statistics, U.S. Government Printing Office, p. 1.

2. U.S. Department of Commerce, Bureau of the Census.

3. Grant and Eiden, *Digest of Educational Statistics,* 1980, p. 77.

4. Ibid., p. 78.

Selected References

Benson, Charles S. *The Economics of Public Education* (3rd ed.). New York: Houghton Mifflin, 1978.

Campbell, Roald F., et al. *Introduction to Educational Administration.* Boston: Allyn and Bacon, 1977.

Garms, Walter L.; Guthrie, James W.; and Pierce, Lawrence C. *School Finance: The Economics and Politics of Public Education.* Englewood Cliffs, N.J.: Prentice-Hall Inc., 1978.

Hansen, Mark E. *Educational Administration and Organizational Behavior.* Boston: Allyn and Bacon, 1979.

Harrison, Russel S. *Equality in Public School Finance.* Lexington, Mass.: Lexington Books, D.C. Heath, 1976.

Kern, Alexander, and Forbis, Jordan K. *Educational Need in the Public Economy.* Gainesville, Fla.: University Presses of Florida, 1976.

Mann, Leo L. "School Finance Reform in Connecticut," *Phi Delta Kappan.* Vol. 62, no. 4, December 1980, pp. 250–51.

Miller, Irving. "Tax Referendum Strategies: A Perspective for the Eighties," *Phi Delta Kappan.* Vol. 62, no. 1, September 1980, pp. 22–23.

Persell, Caroline H. *Education and Inequality.* New York: The Free Press, 1977.

Sergiovanni, Thomas; Burlingame, Martin; Coombs, Fred D.; and Thurston, Paul. *Educational Governance and Administration.* Englewood Cliffs, N.J.: Prentice-Hall Inc., 1980.

Glossary

ability grouping Organizing pupils into homogeneous groups according to intellectual ability for instruction

academic freedom The opportunity for a teacher to teach without coercion, censorship, or other restrictive interferences

academy An early American secondary school which stressed practical subjects

accountability Holding schools and teachers responsible for what students learn

accreditation Recognition given to an educational institution that has met accepted standards applied to it by an outside agency

aesthetics Refers to the nature of beauty and judgments about it

affective domain Attitudinal and emotional areas of learning, such as values and feelings

alternative education Unconventional educational experiences for students not adequately served through regular classes; such alternatives include schools without walls, street academies, free schools, and second-chance schools

alternative school A school—private or public, innovative or fundamental—that provides alternatives to the regular public school

American Federation of Teachers (AFT) A national organization of teachers primarily concerned with improving educational conditions and protecting teachers' rights

anecdotal record A brief, written report of an individual's exceptional behavior

aptitude The ability to profit from training or instruction of a specified kind

articulation The relationship existing between the different elements of the educational program—the different curricular offerings, the school's program and out-of-school educational activities, and the successive levels of the educational system

attendance area An administrative unit consisting of the territory from which children may legally attend a given school building

audiovisual material Any device by means of which the learning process may be encouraged or carried on through the sense of hearing and/or the sense of sight

back to basics A broad, largely grass roots movement evolving out of a concern for declining test scores and student incompetence in math and reading

behavioral objective Precise statement of what the learner must do to demonstrate mastery at the end of a prescribed learning task

bilingual education Educational programs in which both English-speaking and non-English-speaking students participate in a bicultural curriculum using both languages

board of education Constituted at the state and local levels, these agencies are responsible for formulating educational policy. The members are sometimes appointed, but more frequently they are elected at the local level.

busing A method for remedying segregation by transporting students to schools that have been racially or ethnically unbalanced

career education The totality of educational experience through which one learns about occupational opportunities and about work

categorical aid Financial aid to local school districts from state or federal agencies for specific, limited purposes only

certification The act, on the part of a state department of education, of granting official authorization to a person to accept employment in keeping with the provisions of the credential

Chief State School Officer Usually the executive head of a state department of education

child advocacy movement A movement dedicated to defining, protecting, and ensuring the rights of children

child-centered instruction Instruction that is designed for the interests, abilities, and needs of individual students

classroom environment The physical structure, emotional climate, aesthetic characteristics, and learning resources of a school classroom

collective bargaining A procedure, usually specified by written agreement, for resolving disagreements on salaries, hours, and conditions of employment between employers and employees through negotiations

common school A school open to the general public and providing similar education to all classes

competency The demonstrated ability to perform specified acts at a particular level of skill or accuracy

competency-based education Learning based upon highly specialized concepts, skills, and attitudes related directly to some endeavor

comprehensive high school A secondary school which attempts to cater to the needs of all students by offering more than one course of specialization in its program

compulsory education School attendance which is required by law on the theory that it is for the benefit of the commonwealth to educate all the people

computer-assisted instruction (CAI) Direct two-way teaching/learning communication between a student and programmed instructional material stored in a computer.

consolidation The act of forming an enlarged school by uniting smaller schools in order to provide better school facilities and increased educational opportunities

content Subject matter

continuing education An extension of opportunities for study and training following completion or withdrawal from full-time high school and/or college programs

cultural bias Accepting one's own cultural values as valid for all

cultural pluralism A way of describing a society made up of many different cultural groups coming together to form a unified whole

curriculum All educational experiences under supervision of the school

dame school A low-level primary school in the colonial and early national periods usually conducted by an untrained woman in her own home

day-care center A place or institution charged with caring for children

decentralization A process whereby some higher central source of responsibility and authority assigns certain responsibilities and authority to subordinate positions

de facto segregation The segregation of students resulting from circumstances such as housing patterns rather than from school policy or law

de jure segregation The segregation of students on the basis of law, school policy, or a practice designed to accomplish such separation

desegregation The process of correcting past practices of racial or any other form of illegal segregation

differentiated staffing Education personnel, selected, educated, and deployed so as to make optimum use of their abilities, interests, preparation, and commitments; it gives them greater opportunity and autonomy in guiding their own professional growth

due process The procedural requirements that must be followed in such areas as student and teacher discipline and placement in special education programs. It exists to safeguard individuals from arbitrary, capricious, or unreasonable policies, practices, or actions.

early childhood education Any systematic effort to teach a child before the normal period of schooling begins

eclecticism Drawing elements from several educational philosophies or methods

educable child A child of borderline or moderately severe mental retardation who is capable of achieving only a limited degree of proficiency in basic learnings, and who usually must be instructed in a special class

educational technology Scientific application of knowledge of educational institutions for purposes of instruction or institutional management

educational television (ETV) Educational programs in the broadest sense—cultural, informative, and instructive—that are usually telecast by stations outside the school system and received on standard television sets by the general public

elementary school   Grades 1–6 inclusive; grades 1–8 inclusive in some school systems

equal educational opportunity   Giving every student the educational opportunity to fully develop whatever talents, interests, and abilities she or he may have without regard to race, color, national origin, sex, handicap, or economic status

essentialism   The doctrine that there is an indispensable, common core of culture (knowledge, skills, attitudes, ideals, etc.) that should be taught systematically to all, with rigorous standards of achievement

evaluation   Testing and measurement to determine the effectiveness, quality, and progress of learning and instruction

exceptional learner   One who deviates from the normal intellectually, physically, socially, or emotionally in growth and development so markedly that she or he cannot receive maximum educational benefits without modifications in the regular school program.

existentialism   A philosophy that emphasizes the ability of an individual to determine the course and nature of her or his own life

expulsion   Permanent withdrawal of a student's privilege to attend a certain school or class

flexible scheduling   A technique for organizing time more effectively in schools to meet the needs of instruction by dividing the day into uniform time modules which can be combined to fit the task at hand

full potential   The talents, skills, and abilities an individual can acquire and/or develop if provided with the proper learning experiences and environments

general education   Those learnings which should be the common possession of all educated persons

gifted learner   The term most frequently applied to those with exceptional intellectual ability, but may also refer to learners with outstanding ability in athletics, leadership, music, creativity, and so forth

graded school system   A division of schools into groups of students according to the curriculum or the ages of pupils as in the six elementary grades

handicapped learner   One who is mentally retarded, hard of hearing, deaf, speech-impaired, visually handicapped, seriously disturbed emotionally, crippled, or otherwise health-impaired

hardware   Mechanical and electronic devices that aid in classroom instruction

Head Start programs   Federally funded programs at the preelementary school level designed to provide learning opportunities for those children who have not had access to environments and experiences conducive to academic achievement

heterogeneous grouping   A group or class consisting of students who show normal variation in ability or performance

homogeneous grouping   The classification of pupils for the purpose of forming instructional groups having a relatively high degree of similarity in regard to certain factors that affect learning

hornbook   A single printed page containing the alphabet, syllables, a prayer, and other simple words, and which was used in colonial times as the beginner's first book or pre-primer. Hornbooks were attached to a wooden paddle for ease in carrying, and were covered with a thin sheet of transparent horn for protection.

independent school   A nonpublic school unaffiliated with any church or other agency

individualized education program (IEP)   The mechanism through which a handicapped child's special needs are identified; goals, objectives, and services are outlined; and methods for evaluating progress are delineated

Individualized instruction   Instruction that focuses on the interests, needs and achievements of individual learners

in-service education   Continuing education for teachers who are actually teaching, or who are in service

instructional materials center (IMC)   An area where students can withdraw books, newspapers, pamphlets, and magazines, and have access to sound tapes, slides, and films; spaces are usually provided for the learner to use these materials

instructional technology The application of scientific method and knowledge to teaching and learning either with or without machines, and which is commonly responsive to the learning needs of individual students

instructional television (ITV) Lessons telecast specifically for educational institutions and received usually only by special arrangements and on special equipment

integration The process of mixing students of different races in schools to overcome de facto segregation

interest centers Usually associated with an open classroom, such centers provide for independent student activities related to a specific subject

international education The study of educational, social, political, and economic forces in international relations with special emphasis on the role and potentialities of educational forces; also includes programs to further the development of nations

kindergarten A term coined by Froebel who began the first schools for children aged four, five, and six years

land-grant college A college maintained to carry out the purposes of the first Morrill Act of 1862, and supplementary legislation granting public lands to states for the establishment of colleges that provide practical education, such as agriculture and mechanic arts

Latin Grammar School A classical secondary school with a curriculum consisting largely of Latin and Greek, the purpose of which was preparation for college

learning A change of behavior as a result of experience

learning resources center A specially designed space containing a wide range of supplies and equipment for the use of individual students and small groups pursuing independent study

least restrictive environment The program best suited to meet a handicapped child's special needs while remaining as close as possible to the regular educational program

mainstreaming A plan by which exceptional children receive special education in the regular classroom as much of the time as possible

mentally handicapped student A student whose mental powers lack maturity or are deficient in such measure as to be a hindrance to normal achievement

mental retardation Below average intellectual functioning

methodology Procedure used to teach the content or discipline

microteaching A clinical approach to teacher training in which the teacher candidate teaches a small group of students for a brief time while concentrating on a specific teaching skill

middle school A type of two-to-four year school organization containing various combinations of the middle grades (commonly grades 5 to 8), and serving as an intermediate unit between the elementary school and the high school

minicourse A short, self-contained instructional sequence

minimum competency testing Exit level tests designed to ascertain whether students have achieved basic levels of performance in such areas as reading, writing, and computation

motivation Impetus that causes one to act

multicultural education Education for cultural understanding and acceptance

multi-purpose high school Features comprehensive, diversified offerings to meet the needs of all the students regardless of their special interests, aptitudes, and capacities

national assessment A massive national testing program which helps ascertain the effectiveness of American education and how well it is retained

National Council for the Accreditation of Teacher Education (NCATE) An organization that evaluates teacher education programs in many colleges and universities

National Education Association (NEA) The largest organization of educators, the NEA is concerned with the overall improvement of education, and of the conditions of educators

nongraded school A type of school organization in which grade lines are eliminated for a sequence of two or more years

nonverbal communication The act of transmitting and/or receiving messages through any means not having to do with oral or written language, such as eye contact, facial expressions, or body language

normal school Historically, the first American institution devoted exclusively to teacher training

nursery school A school that offers valuable supervised educational experiences for prekindergarten children, giving them opportunities to express themselves and develop relationships within their peer group

objective Purpose or goal

open classroom A modern educational innovation in which self-contained classrooms are replaced with an open plan with individualized instruction and freedom for the child to move about the school

open enrollment The practice of permitting students to attend the school of their choice within their school system

open space school A school building without interior walls

outdoor education Activity and study in an outdoor setting

overachievement Performing above the level normally expected on the basis of ability measures

paraprofessional One who serves as an aide, assisting the teacher in the classroom

parochial school An institution operated and controlled by a religious denomination

pedagogy The scientific study of education

perennialism Educational philosophy emphasizing constancy and unchanging truths

performance-based education Learning designed to produce actual accomplishment as distinguished from knowing

philosophy of education Principles that guide professional educators in decision making

pragmatism A philosophy that maintains that the value and truth of ideas are tested by their practical consequences

progressive education An educational philosophy emphasizing democracy, the importance of creative and meaningful activity, the real needs of students, and the relationship between school and community

progressivism Educational philosophy in which learning focuses on the experiences of the child while she or he is acquiring the content of the curriculum

psychomotor domain Motor skill area of learning

psychomotor learning The acquisition of muscular development directly related to mental processes

PTA Parent Teacher Association; officially the National Congress of Parents and Teachers

Public Law 94–142 A federal law mandating equal educational opportunity for handicapped persons

racial bias The degree to which an individual's beliefs and behavior are prejudiced on the basis of race

racial discrimination Any action that limits or denies a person or group of persons opportunities, privileges, roles, or rewards on the basis of race

racism The collection of attitudes, beliefs, and behavior that results from the assumption that one race is superior to other races

reorganization The act of legally changing the designation of a school district; changing the geographical areas of a school district or incorporating a part or all of a school district with an adjoining district

school finance Ways in which monies are raised and allocated to schools

school superintendent The chief administrator of a school system, responsible for implementing and enforcing the school board's policies, rules, and regulations, as well as the state and federal requirements

secondary school Junior and senior high school; usually grades 7–12 inclusive

self-contained classroom A form of classroom organization in which the same teacher conducts all or nearly all the instruction in all or most subjects in the same classroom for all or most of the school day

self-instructional device A term used to include instructional materials that can be used by the student to induce learning without necessarily requiring additional human instructional assistance, including computers, programmed textbooks, and other devices

separate but equal A legal doctrine that holds that equality of treatment is accorded when the races are provided substantially equal facilities, even though those facilities are separate

sexism The collection of attitudes, beliefs, and behavior that results from the assumption that one sex is superior to the other

softwear Textbooks, paper and pencil materials, workbooks, maps and other like materials that aid in classroom instruction

special education A school program designed for the child who is exceptional, that is, either gifted or below normal in ability

subject-centered school or curriculum A curriculum organization in which learning activities and content are planned around subject fields of knowledge, such as history and science

teacher aide A lay person who assists teachers with clerical work, library duties, housekeeping duties, noninstructional supervision, and other nonprofessional tasks

Teacher Corps A federally funded program that gives teachers and student teachers opportunities to work with disadvantaged children in their homes and communities while attending courses and seminars on the special problems they encounter

teaching center Combination library, workshop, and laboratory with rich resources to help teachers solve problems and grow professionally

team teaching A plan by which several teachers, organized into a team with a leader, provide the instruction for a larger group of children than would usually be found in a self-contained classroom

tenure A system of school employment in which educators, after having served a probationary period, retain their positions indefinitely unless dismissed for legally specified reasons through clearly established procedures

tracking The method of placing students according to their ability level in homogeneous classes or learning experiences

ungraded school Synonymous with nongraded school

values Principles that guide an individual in terms of personal decision making

values clarification A model, comprised of various strategies, that encourages students to express and clarify their values on different topics

vocational education Training which is intended to prepare the student for a particular job, or to give a basic skill needed in several vocations

voucher plan A means of financing schooling whereby funds are allocated to students' parents who then purchase education for their children in any public or private school

work-study program Program that combines part-time classroom study with gainful employment in industry or in the community

Photo Credits

Index